THE HAMLYN
GREEK AND ROMAN MYTHOLOGY

THE HAMLYN
CONCISE DICTIONARY OF

GREEK AND ROMAN
MYTHOLOGY

MICHAEL STAPLETON

Introduction by
Stewart Perowne

HAMLYN

LONDON · NEW YORK · SYDNEY · TORONTO

THIS BOOK IS FOR
MY NIECE, KIM AND
MY NEPHEW, IAN

*A Dictionary of Greek and
Roman Mythology*

First published 1978
Concise edition 1982

Published by
The Hamlyn Publishing Group Limited
London · New York · Sydney · Toronto
Astronaut House, Feltham, Middlesex, England

ISBN 0 6000 33237 3

Filmset in 8 on 9 pt Linotron 202 Bembo by
Input Typesetting Limited, London
Printed in Great Britain by
Hazell Watson & Viney Ltd,
Aylesbury, Bucks

CONTENTS

★

INTRODUCTION

To our degenerate ears a myth is just a story, fiction, not fact. To those who invented the myths, a myth was both, because they made no moral distinction between fiction and fact. They were, those old Greeks, just as liable to disaster as we are; and so they, like us, did their best to encompass two things: to ward off disasters which might occur, and to account for those that did.

An earthquake – was it about to happen? It nearly always was, as it nearly always is. We have seismological stations; the Greeks had gods and heroes. The result was exactly the same – the earthquake happened. With us, it is a disaster to be explained, and so it was for them. But instead of a table, with digits and squares and cubes, the Greeks had an enthralling story – a myth, in fact. Zeus was angry, or Hera was jealous. So Poseidon, the Earthshaker, got to work, and there you were – if you had survived, that is. Myth or bluebook? They preferred the myth, and so do most of us. That is the enduring charm and solace of mythology.

Greek mythology, by its very nature, is extremely old, because once philosophy had got to work, which it did in Ionia in the sixth century, rational explanations began to replace poetic fantasies. The mythologies survived, were occasionally even augmented, simply because they were, and are, so attractive. Where did they come from? The answer is that, alone of Greek creations, they came from all over Hellas, from Thrace, from Boeotia, from Attica, from the Peloponnese, Argos and Mycenae, and from many of the islands. One favourite story, that of Pyramus and Thisbe, familiar to us from Shakespeare's *A Midsummer Night's Dream*, came from as far afield as Babylon.

There were, nevertheless, three major sources of mythologies, which are of prime importance not only because they are so abundant in themselves, but because more than any others they provided the great dramatists with most of their plots (the Greek word for plot is *mythos*). These three sources have been epitomised by our own great classic mythologist John Milton:

> *Sometime let gorgeous Tragedy*
> *In sceptered pall come sweeping by,*
> *Presenting Thebes, or Pelops' line,*
> *Or the tale of Troy divine.*

Troy, Thebes and Mycenae were the triple fountain. Readers of this book will at once realise how surely its author has grasped the essential affinity of myth and drama, because he gives us, for the first time, not only details of all the characters involved in the original myths, but also synopses of the plots of the *Iliad* and *Odyssey*, of the *Argonautica* and *Aeneid*, and of all the major plays of the great Athenian dramatists. Homer is the supreme source. Matthew Arnold sums up Homer's 'four qualities' as follows: 'That he is eminently rapid; that he is eminently plain and direct both in the evolution of his thought and in the expression of it, that is both in his syntax and in his words; that he is eminently plain and direct in the substance of his thought, that is in his matter and ideas; and finally that he is eminently noble . . . Homer invariably composes "with his eye on the object", whether the object be a moral or a material one.'

In fact, morals seldom came into the argument. Matthew Arnold was a moralist, as was his father, the famous headmaster of Rugby. 'Conduct is three-fourths of life' he proclaimed. His morality was drawn from the Christian scriptures (rather freely interpreted) plus a tincture of Stoicism, itself of un-Hellenic origin – its founder, Zeno, was a Semite from Kitium in Cyprus. Primitive Greeks did not think in terms of right and wrong as we understand these words. They thought in terms of destiny. Gods were like men, only more so. They committed all the pleasant sins and the unpleasant ones, too: murder, rape, adultery, incest, treachery, even cannibalism – it is remarkable how often this last turns up in Greek mythology, when men were but imitating 'those above'. The goddesses were hardly any better: but how could you expect a junior goddess to behave herself when the chief goddess of all, Hera, sister-wife of Zeus, had every reason to be jealous and vindictive?

Which brings us to one of the fundamental reasons for the creation and perpetuation of myths. We read them with pleasure, because we are in no way involved in them. If, for instance, Marsyas is flayed, Sysiphus, Prometheus, Ixion condemned to everlasting torment, our withers are unwrung – a vital point which Shakespeare used to high effect in one of his greatest scenes: 'What's Hecuba to him or he to Hecuba, that he [a mere actor] should weep for her?'

But to a primitive Hellene it was everything. For this reason: the life of a primitive Greek was dominated, not by the gods, but by what dominated the gods themselves, and that was Fate. Fate was onmipotent. Fate bent gods and men to Fate's will. Any breach of obligation to Fate, even if it were involuntary and unavoidable by man's will or contrivance, brought the inevitable penalty, Guilt.

That is why so many myths are what we would call *apotropaic* – designed to turn aside from us the blows of fate – by showing how often Fate had won in the past over the most elaborate schemes to thwart it. Was not Achilles invulnerable? No. His heel, the part of him held by his mother when she dipped him in the Styx to make him invulnerable, would be the death of him. Would not that son or grandson – a very common theme of which Oedipus is the best known example – destined by an oracle to commit patricide, would he not be saved from committing the crime by being hidden away, or left to perish on a mountainside? No, he would not. Fate is part of the order of the universe, and that not even the gods can gainsay. This triumph of Fate is one of the commonest of all mythological themes. Inevitable Guilt follows, and Guilt must be purged. The *Furies* (Eumenides) of Aeschylus is one of the most explicit expositions of this postulate. The great playwright does not simply examine it, however: he challenges it, too.

Not all of mythology treats of these sinister and dolorous histories, because although mortals are obsessed with impending disaster, they do enjoy intervals of felicity, though tales of pure happiness are very rare indeed. 'Philemon and Baucis' is unique: but this delightful story is not Greek in origin. The happy couple lived in Phrygia, the country in Asia of Midas, and Gordius of the famous knot.

Besides the Fate-Guilt source of so much mythology – this combination being by far the most prolific manifestation of human desires, deserts, defeats and triumphs – there are two others, which have given us some of our most loved sagas, if so alien a word may be used of them. They are, firstly, the fertility stories, and secondly the Hero tales. Of the former the tale of Persephone is by far the best known, and the most endearing. It is, too, so easy to understand. Persephone wins where Orpheus lost, and we are left in no doubt why: Demeter, Mother Earth, can make even Zeus do her will. Orpheus had no such ally.

In the second category we find Theseus, Perseus, Asclepius, Heracles, Odysseus: heroes, all of them. And, in origin no doubt, real men, men who performed great deeds of valour and so were honoured with a mythology of their own, robes of honour, as it were, to be worn for all time. Just as in our own annals, the doings of Arthur or Alfred are similarly magnified.

And why not? One of the many virtues of this excellent book, is, in my view, that it makes us enjoy the Greeks, makes us love them, for what they were and are, for what they did and suffered, for the childlike belief in themselves and in their wisdom; for the way, above all, in which they lead us into that realm of which they will for ever be the masters, where reality and fantasy dissolve, and come together again as immortal poetry.

Stewart Perowne
London 1977

★

DICTIONARY OF GREEK AND ROMAN MYTHOLOGY

★

A

Absyrtus The son of Aeëtes, King of Colchis, and the young brother of Medea. There are differing accounts of the part played by this hapless prince in the escape of Jason and Medea after the theft of the Golden Fleece. One version says that he was sent in pursuit of the *Argo* by King Aeëtes, and managed to trap the ship near an island at the mouth of the Ister (Danube). Medea persuaded her brother to meet her on the island, sending him a message saying that Jason had abducted her. But it was Jason who went to the island, and there he murdered Absyrtus. Another version tells how Medea persuaded her brother to accompany her on board the *Argo* when she fled with Jason. Their father Aeëtes nearly caught up with the fugitives near the mouth of the Ister, whereupon Medea murdered Absyrtus and cut his body into pieces. She scattered the fragments on the waves, knowing that her father would stop to collect them to make sure they were given decent burial. Thus Jason and Medea made good their escape.

See also *Argonautica*.

Achaeans The name by which the invaders of Troy are known in the *Iliad* – Homer never calls them Greeks, though he sometimes uses the description 'Argive' or 'Danaan'. According to modern scholars the first Hellenic people to move into Greece from the north settled in two territories which were called Achaea, hence the name. They gradually spread into all of Greece, and their supremacy is marked by their leadership during the war against Troy. They lost their power soon after the Trojan War to another wave of migrants, the Dorians, who occupied Argos and destroyed Mycenae and Tiryns, the principal Achaean cities. Agamemnon, the leader of the army that invaded Troy, was King of Mycenae.

See also Migrations.

Acheron In mythology one of the rivers of the nether world. The actual river has its source in the southern part of Epirus. It is joined by a tributary, the Cocytus, and flows into the sea at the Thesprotian Gulf.

Achilles The principal warrior among the Greeks who took part in the Trojan War. He was the son of Peleus and Thetis, a Nereid, who was fated to bear a child who would be stronger than his father. Zeus himself loved Thetis, and he knew that he could be in danger if he had a child by one of his loves. But he only knew a part of the danger – he did not know which of them it would be. The secret of her identity lay with Prometheus, whom Zeus had punished by chaining him to a rock in the Caucasus mountains. Prometheus yielded the knowledge to Zeus when he was released, and so it was by Zeus' command that Thetis was married to Peleus, since no mortal's son could ever be a threat to the king of the gods.

When Achilles was born his mother, daughter of the sea god Nereus, tried to bathe him in fire to burn away his mortality. Peleus interfered, and the angry mother left him, taking her son with her. She knew what his future as a mortal would be and she did everything she could to protect him. She bathed him in the river Styx to make him invulnerable, holding him by the heel, and then entrusted him to the care of the wise and gentle centaur, Chiron, who taught him and raised him to manhood. But when the Greek leaders began to prepare for the Trojan War Thetis took her son away from Chiron: she knew that Achilles would meet his death at Troy, so she took him to the court of Lycomedes, King of Scyros, and disguised him as girl. However, Calchas, the seer who advised the Greek leaders, told them that Troy would never be taken without Achilles, so Odysseus was sent to search for him. Odysseus traced him to Scyros, and tricked him into revealing himself by taking lavish presents to the King and his court. Among them were a fine suit of armour and some weapons – which a certain 'girl' unhesitatingly chose.

Lycomedes gave Achilles his daughter, Deidamia, in marriage and she bore him one son, Neoptolemus, who joined the Greeks at Troy after his father's death.

Achilles is the central figure of Homer's *Iliad,* if not of the whole story of the Trojan War, and it is on the wrath of Achilles that the action of the poem turns. He goes to Troy knowing that he will die there, having learned from his mother that the choice is between a short and glorious life and a long life of obscurity. His contingent numbers fifty ships and he commands his own army, unlike the other Greeks who acknowledge the nominal leadership of Agamemnon.

Achilles captures a number of towns both on the coast of Troy and inland, and at one of these, Lyrnessos, his prizes include a beautiful slave girl, Briseis. Another captive, the maiden Chryseis, falls to Agamemnon: but she is the daughter of a priest of Apollo and the angry god inflicts a plague on the Greek camp. Calchas warns Agamemnon that he must return the girl to her father – only then will the plague cease. The Greek leader does so, with bad grace, and to make good his loss takes Briseis away from Achilles.

Achilles, furious, withdraws from the fighting, and for a time it seems certain that the Trojans will gain the upper hand. This is the quarrel from which the events of the *Iliad* follow.

Achilles is a vivid figure, perhaps the most believable – if hardly the most attractive – of the characters depicted by Homer. He is barbarous, with his liking for cruel (even in terms of the period) practices such as human sacrifices at funerals, his despoliation of Hector's body and his violent rages during which he spares no one. He is the fighting man of all ages, whose only fulfilment is on the battlefield. He is likeable in the facets of his character which, paradoxically, might seem like weaknesses to Achilles himself. He knows that his savage anger at the death of his cousin, Patroclus, may blind him to the need for chivalry when King Priam begs him to return Hector's body for burial; his love for Patroclus, who dies in combat with Hector, is the very stuff of which legends are made. Achilles is also truthful, a rare quality among the Greeks of the *Iliad*.

Neither the story of Achilles among the women of Scyros, nor that of his being made invulnerable by being bathed in the Styx by his mother, appear in Homer. The detail was added to the story by Statius, a Latin Poet of the first century AD.

See also Aeacus, *Iliad*, Myrmidons, Peleus, Thetis.

Actaeon The son of Aristaeus and Autonoë, he was the young man who aroused the wrath of the goddess Artemis when he chanced on her bathing at Orchomenus. Enraged that any man should have seen her naked, the virgin goddess changed Actaeon into a stag, so that his own dogs tore him to pieces.

Admetus The King of Pherae whom Apollo had to serve for a year as a punishment for killing the Cyclopes. He proved to be a kind master and earned Apollo's gratitude. Admetus was destined to die young, and when Apollo learned this from the Fates he tried to get the pattern changed on behalf of Admetus. He plied the Fates with wine and did his best to persuade them: but the most they would promise was that Admetus could live longer – if someone else could be found to die in his place at the appointed time. When the time came Admetus went to his parents; but they declined to take his place, saying that they were still enjoying life, and that all men should accept their appointed lot. It was the King's wife, Alcestis, who came forward to die in his place. One version of the story says that when Alcestis arrived in the nether world she was refused admittance by Persephone, who promptly returned her to her husband.

See also *Alcestis* (Euripides), Cyclopes.

Adonis The beloved of Aphrodite, whose name has become synonymous with masculine beauty. Cinyras, King of Cyprus, had a beautiful daughter, Myrrha, whom he rashly proclaimed outshone Aphrodite herself. The goddess, in revenge, made Myrrha fall in love with her own father, and seduce him when he was rather the worse for wine. The result of this incestuous union was a son, and Cinyras, horrified, would have killed the child had not Aphrodite stolen him and hidden him in a box. She entrusted the box to Persephone, who was understandably curious about its contents. One day Persephone opened it, and found inside a little boy so beautiful that she decided to keep him for herself. Aphrodite, when she heard of this, inevitably wanted Adonis – now a young man – returned to her. Persephone refused: Aphrodite appealed to Zeus, who decided that neither goddess had a stronger claim than the other. So each was allowed to keep him for half of the year.

Another version of the myth of Adonis relates that he was killed by a boar while he was hunting, and it was then that Persephone determined to keep him for her own – immediately falling in love with him when he arrived in the nether world. A further variation makes the boar the weapon of the god Ares, who loved Aphrodite and killed Adonis out of jealousy.

Adonis personifies the spirit of the fruitful year, and the character originates in the Near East, where he he was known as Tammuz. Tammuz was also killed by a boar, as were the Egyptian god Osiris and the Celtic hero Diarmuid, and the reason for the frequency with which the boar occurs in myths connected with fertility is simply that he is the oldest of mankind's sacrificial animals, much older than the bull or the horse.

The name of Adonis also belongs to the Near East. It is a version of *Adon*, the Phoenician word for Lord.

See also Aphrodite, Persephone.

Adrastus The son of Talaus, King of Argos, Adrastus was the victim of dynastic rivalries and to save his life fled to Corinth (another version says he fled to Sicyon) where his maternal grandfather ruled. Adrastus married the royal heiress and eventually gained the throne. Secure in the possession of one kingdom he was able to gain another when his father died and his brother-in-law, Amphiaraus, held the kingdom for his return as the rightful ruler. Amphiaraus had the gift of foreseeing the future.

Adrastus had two daughters, Argeia and Deipyle – and so many suitors for them that he was driven to consult the oracle at Delphi to have the choice of husbands settled for him. The answer told him to marry them to 'the lion and the boar that fight in your house'.

To Argos came two exiles: Polynices of Thebes, dispossessed by his brother Eteocles with whom he should have shared the throne, and Tydeus of Calydon who was driven out by the people who believed him guilty of the murder of his brother. One night in the palace Adrastus came upon his guests in the middle of a quarrel so violent that a murderous fight was certain to follow. Adrastus watched them for a moment, and then realised that the oracle's condition was being fulfilled. He stopped the quarrel, and offered each prince one of his daughters in marriage. The emblem of Thebes was a lion: the emblem of Calydon a boar. Adrastus promised them help in regaining their kingdoms.

At this point in the story, Adrastus and his ambitions become part of the great cycle of Theban epic which includes the story of Oedipus; Polynices was his son. It was Polynices whom Adrastus decided to help first: he would invade Thebes and dethrone the other son of Oedipus, Eteocles. The army was led by Adrastus, Polynices, Tydeus and three other champions. Another was needed, because the city of Thebes had seven gates, and the obvious choice was Adrastus' brother-in-law, Amphiaraus. But his gift of seeing the future made Amphiaraus decline, though this obvious warning about the outcome was not perceived by the others. To persuade him, Polynices went to Eriphyle, the wife of Amphiaraus, and reminded her that in the past she had kept peace between husband and brother by making them swear to abide by her decisions. If she would persuade Amphiaraus to go with the army, Polynices would give her the most precious jewels of Thebes, the necklace Aphrodite gave to Harmonia which bestowed unfading beauty on its wearer. Greedy for the necklace, Eriphyle agreed, so her brother Adrastus and her husband Amphiaraus joined the other five. These were The Seven Against Thebes.

As Amphiaraus had foreseen, the expedition was dogged by misfortune. On the road to Thebes the army halted for water in Nemea, where they asked a woman carrying a child to show them to a spring. The woman, Hypsipyle, put down the child and took them to a pool of fresh water: when she returned to the child she found it dead, bitten by a snake. The child was the King of Nemea's son, and Amphiaraus warned his companions to pay heed to this omen. But they managed to save Hypsipyle from the King's wrath, and as an offering instituted the Nemean Games in memory of the child.

The attack on Thebes was a disastrous failure. Of the Seven only Adrastus survived, escaping from defeat on his winged horse, Arion. Amphiaraus, because he was a seer, was taken down to the nether world alive at the behest of Zeus. The rest all perished, including Tydeus. Adrastus made another attempt to gain Thebes when the children of the Seven, called the Epigoni, were old enough to take arms. He succeeded in his second attempt but it was a hollow victory because it cost him his only son, Aegialeus. Adrastus died of grief when he heard the news.

See also Amphiaraus, Epigoni, Eteocles, Harmonia, Oedipus, The Seven Against Thebes, Tydeus.

Aeacus The son of Zeus and the nymph Aegina. The jealous Hera, when she learned that Zeus had sired another son during one of his amorous adventures, was determined that someone should suffer for it. She was furious to find Aegina, the island where the son was born, prosperous and contented, with Aeacus ruling over it. She poisoned the streams and then called up the south wind to blow over the island without cease. The crops died and famine ensued: the islanders, in the scorching heat, died from the water in the poisoned streams. In desperation Aeacus appealed to his father Zeus, who sent down a shower of rain and a shower of ants. The ants turned into men and women, and then the rain fell steadily, counteracting the south wind and cleaning the foul water from the streams. The dying island revived and the

Myrmidons (ant people) worked hard to restore its prosperity. Aeacus divided the land among his new subjects and Aegina was once more at peace.

Aeacus was the father of Telamon and also of Peleus, who became the father of Achilles, who took an army of Myrmidons to the siege of Troy.

See also Aegina, Peleus.

Aedon The daughter of Pandareos and wife of Zethus, King of Thebes. The King's brother, Amphion, was married to Niobe, the over-proud mother of seven sons and seven daughters. Aedon, with only two children, Itylus and Neis, felt a murderous jealousy and planned to kill Niobe's firstborn. She made her way at night to the room where all the children slept – but went to the wrong bed. The child she killed was her own son, Itylus. Zeus changed her into a nightingale, and her mourning can be heard in its nightly song.

Aegeus In mythology, the King of Athens who sired a son, Theseus, at Troezen when he visited his friend King Pittheus after a journey to Delphi to consult the oracle. Aegeus was childless: but the answer he was given was the usual enigmatic one and he could not understand it. He was told to keep his wine-skin sealed until he reached the topmost height of Athens – if he did not he would one day die of grief there.

On the way to Troezen he stopped at Corinth, where he met the sorceress wife of Jason, Medea. She extracted a promise from him to give her refuge in his kingdom if she ever needed it: in return, she promised that her magic powers would help him get a son.

When he arrived in Troezen, Aegeus told King Pittheus what the oracle had said. Pittheus said nothing – but he understood the oracle and knew that a son conceived on Aegeus' travels was destined for greatness. He presented his daughter, Aethra, to his guest, and made him thoroughly drunk at dinner – knowing that enough wine could be the means of unsealing another wine-skin.

Aegeus and Aethra shared a bed that night, and a child was conceived. But there was another sire, of whom Aegeus knew nothing: the god Poseidon.

When he left to resume his journey to Athens, Aegeus told Aethra that if a son were born to her she must rear him quietly in Troezen with Pittheus as his guardian. Then he took her out of the city to a rock that stood by the road. He lifted the rock and under it placed his sandals and his sword – a weapon of particular value, which had belonged to the first King of Athens, Cecrops. When the boy was old enough, Aethra was to bring him to the rock: if he could lift it and recover the tokens, she was to send him to Athens, where he would be acknowledged as the King's son.

Pittheus saw the oracle fulfilled – a son was born to Aethra, and because she was unmarried Pittheus let it be understood that the boy's father was Poseidon. The story, from this point on, belongs to the heroic myth of Theseus.

See also Cecrops, Medea, *Medea* (Euripides), Theseus.

Aegina One of the beautiful daughters of the river god Asopus and the nymph Merope, daughter of the river Ladon. The sisters excited the lust of the gods and Zeus was determined to have Aegina. He carried her off, her angry father in pursuit. Zeus discouraged Asopus with some well-aimed thunderbolts, and took his prize to an island in the Saronic Gulf. He made love to her in the form of an eagle and she bore him a son who was named Aeacus. Her son gave the island the name of Aegina in memory of his mother.

See also Aeacus.

Aegisthus One of the descendants of Pelops, and a victim of the curse laid on the family of Pelops by Myrtilus as he died. Aegisthus was the son of Pelopia, who was raped by her father Thyestes while she was serving as a priestess of Athene. Pelopia did not know that her attacker was her own father but when a son was born to her she had him exposed on the mountainside to die because of the horror of his begetting. The baby survived – suckled by a she-goat – to play his part in the events that sealed the doom of his house.

See also *Electra* (Sophocles and Euripides), the *Oresteia* (Aeschylus), Pelops, Tantalus.

Aegyptus The brother of Danaus, and the father of fifty sons. Danaus was the father of fifty daughters. Aegyptus gave his name to Egypt, which he won as a kingdom, while his brother ruled Libya for their father, King Belus. After the death of Belus the brothers quarrelled over the inheritance, and Danaus fled to Argos with his fifty daughters and founded a new kingdom.

See also Amymone, Danaus, Io.

Aeneas The son of the goddess Aphrodite and Anchises, of the Trojan Royal house, and nephew of King Priam. In the *Iliad* he takes part in the action and fights, at various times, Diomedes, Achilles and Idomeneus. For all that his stature in the epic is something less than heroic, since his piety gains him divine protection more than once, notably in the combat with Achilles when Poseidon saves his life. At this point in the narrative (Book XX) Homer makes Poseidon utter the words which became a pointer for later writers, who raised the stature of Aeneas to that of a true hero.

Poseidon declares that Priam's line is doomed, and that Aeneas will one day rule over the Trojans. But the *Iliad* ends with the funeral of Hector, and though there were stories enough about the fall and destruction of the city a persistent strain suggested that Aeneas had survived. Hellanicus, a Greek writer of the early fourth century BC, took the hero's wanderings as far west as Latium, where the great civilisation of Rome had its modest beginnings. A large number of disconnected stories were in existence when Virgil, 400 years later, wrote his *Aeneid* and made them into an epic poem on the founding of Rome.

Aeneid, The Virgil's poem was composed during the last eleven years of his life (30–19 BC), after the Battle of Actium had established Augustus as sole ruler and Rome as the supreme power of the western civilised world.

Virgil's debt to his Greek predecessors is plain, and he followed them in his use of mythology. But he was a man of later age and this is clearly seen in his treatment of the visit to the nether world by Aeneas: it is a remarkable poetic synthesis of the beliefs about the afterlife which were current in his day.

BOOK I Aeneas has been making his way to the west. It is seven years since he and his followers escaped from the burning city of Troy and they are about to leave Sicily on the next stage of their journey. Juno, the goddess who favoured the Greeks in the Trojan wars, calls on Aeolus, the god of the winds, to loose a storm. Aeneas' fleet of twenty ships is scattered and some ships sunk: but Neptune, who recognises the quality of Aeneas, calms the seas and enables Aeneas and the rest of his men to reach the coast of Libya. There Aeneas is visited by his mother, the goddess Venus, who tells him that he is in the land of the Phoenicans and that the great city of Carthage, nearby, is ruled by

Queen Dido, who fled from Tyre when her husband was murdered. Venus, to safeguard her son from the spite of Juno and the wiles of the Phoenicians, ensures that Dido will fall in love with him.

Book II Dido, captivated by the handsome Trojan, makes him her guest, and after a feast in her palace asks him to relate his adventures. He tells her how the Greeks built a huge wooden horse, which they left outside the gates of Troy. The Trojans found the plain outside the city deserted, the Greek ships gone. They argued about the wooden horse – but ignored the warnings of Laocoön, the priest of Neptune, who said he feared the Greeks even when they brought gifts, and hurled a spear at the wooden monster. The Trojans also disregarded the warnings of the prophetess Cassandra, daughter of King Priam. Then a band of Trojans arrived with a Greek captive, who said his name was Sinon. He confirmed that the siege was ended and he told the Trojans that the wooden horse was an offering to Minerva, whose temple the Greeks had dishonoured and whose wrath they feared. Once installed in Troy, the wooden horse would seal the fate of the Greeks. While the Trojans were considering this two great serpents emerged from the sea and made for the altar of Neptune, where Laocoön and his two sons were offering a sacrifice. The serpents killed both father and sons, and the horrified bystanders were convinced that Laocoön was punished for profaning the offering to Minerva. They opened the gates of Troy and took the wooden horse into their city. That night, the Trojans gave themselves up to feasting to celebrate the end of the war; Sinon slipped away and opened a trapdoor in the horse's belly, and out crept Ulysses and a carefully chosen band of Greeks. They murdered the sentries and threw open the city gates – to admit the Greek army which had been lying in wait off the island of Tenedos. It was the end of Troy.

Aeneas, in his sleep, was warned of the disaster by the ghost of Hector. He awoke to find the city in flames and the Greeks breaking into the palace. He saw the aged Priam and his sons salughtered and the women of the royal house dragged away as slaves. He saw the beautiful Helen, and would have killed her as the cause of the war had not Venus prevented him, saying the gods were to blame: Aeneas must save himself and his family. So Aeneas hurried to his home where he found his father Anchises, his wife Creusa, and their son Ascanius still alive. He hoisted his father on to his shoulder and took his son by the hand. Creusa followed them through the burning city, and Aeneas did not dare rest until he reached the shrine of Ceres on a hill outside the city – then he found that his wife was no longer with them. He raced back into the city to find her but his frantic search yielded nothing: he was sick with despair when her ghost appeared to him and told him not to grieve – he had a great destiny to fulfil and must not look back.

BOOK III Aeneas, with his father and son and a group of Trojans who had managed to escape from the city, built a fleet of ships and sailed across to Thrace. There they built an altar, and looked for some fresh leaves to cover it. Aeneas and his men tried to pull up some shrubs from a clump growing near the shore but found to their horror that the plants oozed drops of blood. Then they heard a voice warning them that Thrace was not a friendly land, though Priam had believed the King to be his ally. Priam had sent a hoard of gold to Thrace for safe keeping, entrusting it to Polydorus. But the Thracian King had murdered Polydorus, whose voice now gave Aeneas the warning. The King had simply changed sides when the Greeks looked like winning.

So the Trojans left the dangerous land of Thrace and, in need of counsel, sailed to Delos to visit the shrine of Apollo. Praying there for guidance, Aeneas and his father felt the ground shake and heard the voice of the god tell them that they must return to their motherland, where Aeneas and his descendants would be the founders of an empire. Anchises believed the motherland to be Crete, since the first King of Troy, Teucer, had come from there. But when they tried to settle in Crete disaster overtook them: the crops died and pestilence killed some of the group. Sick at heart, Aeneas was saved from complete despair by the appearance of the gods of Troy in a dream. They told him that his true homeland was Italy.

The Trojans set out again, and called at an island in the Strophades where they saw fat cattle grazing in rich pasture. They prepared a rich feast but suddenly they were attacked by the Harpies, ravenous birds with the faces of hideous women, who proved immune to the Trojans' spears. They attacked the men and fouled the food and their leader, Celaeno, addressed Aeneas from a high rock. She told him that the Trojans' intrusion would be punished, and that Aeneas must continue his journey to Italy. The Trojans would never, she proclaimed, found a city until hunger compelled them to eat the very tables that held their food.

Aeneas sailed north, and came to Chaonia which was part of Epirus. He found the ruler to be another Trojan – none other than Helenus, his kinsman and the twin brother of Cassandra. Like his sister, he possessed the gift of prophecy. He was married to Hector's widow, Andromache, and they lived in peace after the terrible years of the siege of Troy. Helenus and Andromache welcomed their Trojan kin, and Helenus prophesied the future: Aeneas must found his city on a river bank on the far coast of Italy, on a spot where he would find a white sow with a litter of thirty young. He gave Aeneas further advice about his route: he must avoid the dangerous rocks of Scylla and Charybdis, and he must consult the Sibyl of Cumae, the priestess of Apollo.

Taking the advice of Helenus, the Trojans managed to avoid the dangers of Scylla and Charybdis, but their ships were driven into the shelter of a gloomy bay under the lee of the sinister volcano, Etna. On the beach they found a starving Greek, who warned them that they were in the land of the Cyclops, gigantic monsters with a single eye. He had somehow been left behind when Ulysses and the rest escaped from the cave of Polyphemus after blinding him, and now he expected no mercy from a band of Trojans. But Aeneas and Anchises calmed him and promised him fair treatment: then they were all forced to flee when Polyphemus, his blind eye glaring bloodily from the centre of his forehead, heard them and called the rest of the Cyclops to help him destroy the intruders. They got away safely, and were thankful to rest on the gentle shore of Drepanum on the north of Sicily. Aeneas, however, had to face another grief: his beloved father died, worn out by their harrowing journeys. It was when they resumed their journey from Sicily that the Trojans met the storm that drove their ships into Libya and brought about the meeting with the Queen of Carthage.

BOOK IV Dido listens to the story of Aeneas' adventures with growing interest. By the time he concludes, the will of Venus has done its work and she is in love with him. She confesses this to her sister Anna, and confides her unease because she made a vow, when her first husband was killed, never to marry again. For this reason she has turned away many suitors, including Iarbas, of a neighbouring kingdom. Anna tells her to let love take its course, and points out that the valiant Aeneas would give great strength to her kingdom. One day, during a hunt, Dido and Aeneas are caught in a storm. They shelter in a cave, and in its privacy surrender to the passion which Venus has aroused.

Iarbas, jealous of the handsome Trojan, now hears that Dido is besotted with him. He appeals to Jupiter, who sends his messenger, Mercury, to Carthage to remind Aeneas that his destiny is already decided: he must leave Carthage at once and continue his journey. Unhappily, Aeneas bows to the will of the gods – but he cannot bring himself to tell Dido that he is going to desert her. But she discovers that the Trojans are preparing to go and she implores Aeneas not to leave her. His reasons for going sound hollow, even to him, and Dido replies to them with contempt: faith and love, she says, are easily put aside when a man decides that the gods are commanding his destiny. Unable to face life alone she orders a funeral pyre to be built, and spends that night tormented by rage and grief. Aeneas, at another word from Mercury, sets sail before daybreak and the dawn shows Dido an empty seashore, the Trojans and Aeneas gone for ever. She takes up Aeneas' sword and kills herself.

BOOK V The Trojans return to Sicily, and are welcomed to the country of Acestes, himself the son of a Trojan mother. A year has passed since the death of Anchises, so funeral games are held in his honour. While they are in progress the women of the Trojan band remember the past and mourn the end of their homes – their life is now an apparently compulsive wandering from place to place. The goddess Juno, observing this, sends down Iris in disguise to mingle with the women and fan their grief into anger. The way to put an end to these wanderings, she tells them, is to burn the ships and make a home in hospitable Sicily. To set an example she hurls a blazing torch into the fleet lying at anchor. The other women, roused, follow her example and the whole fleet is threatened: but Aeneas and Ascanius see the flames and Aeneas implores Jupiter's help. The god sends a rainstorm and most of the ships are saved: but four are destroyed and Aeneas decides to leave their companies to make homes in Sicily. Many of the women remain also.

The remainder of the Trojans embark, and Venus secures them a peaceful passage to Italy from Neptune. One man is lost, Aeneas' friend Palinurus, the helmsman, who falls asleep at the tiller and tumbles into the sea. Aeneas mourns for him, and takes the tiller himself for the rest of the voyage.

BOOK VI At long last Aeneas and his Trojans arrive in Italy, at Cumae on the western coast. Aeneas remembers the instructions given him by Helenus, and seeks out the Sibyl, the priestess of Apollo who lives in a deep cavern. She warns him that despite his prayers to Apollo his struggles are not yet over. He will arrive in Latium unopposed but he will not be able to found his new domain without bloody wars. The goddess Juno remains his enemy and he, the foremost Trojan, will have to face another warrior as powerful as Achilles.

Aeneas asks to be allowed to visit the nether world. The Sibyl tells him he must first find the tree that bears the Golden Bough. Without it he would never return from a journey so fraught with danger. At her direction Aeneas plunges into a gloomy forest, and two doves show him the way to the tree. He breaks off the bough and takes it back to the Sibyl, and after making sacrifices to the gods they descend to the nether world by way of a cave near the gloomy, mist-shrouded lake of Avernus. They reach the river Styx, and on the bank are surrounded by the shades of those unburied, who must wait for a hundred years before being taken across. One of these is Palinurus, to whom the Sibyl promises a tomb.

Charon, the ferryman of souls, refuses to take Aeneas and the Sibyl across – they are not dead. Living men, such as Theseus and Hercules, have always brought him trouble – Hercules even stole his dog, Cerberus, who now menaces the visitors, snarling and showing the awesome teeth in his three heads. But Charon bows to the authority of the Golden Bough and ferries them across the Styx, and the Sibyl quietens Cerberus with a drugged honey cake.

In the kingdom of Pluto they meet many groups of dead: the souls of infants who died too soon; those who fell in war; those unjustly condemned; and those who died for love. One of these is Dido, and Aeneas foolishly protests his innocence again. Dido offers no comfort, and utters no word.

Aeneas and the Sibyl now come to where the path divides – one road leads to Tartarus, where the wicked suffer. The Sibyl guides Aeneas to the other road, which leads to Elysium, the abode of the blest. Among them is Orpheus and his fellow poet Musaeus, once his pupil. Musaeus shows Aeneas where Anchises rests in peace in that beautiful world, and Aeneas hurries to embrace his father. But he cannot embrace a shade, and Anchises comforts his son by explaining the meaning of what he sees. He explains that the river where souls without number come to drink is Lethe, the river of forgetfulness. Those souls will be reincarnated; they drink from Lethe to find release from all memory of their former lives. Anchises shows his son the line of his descendants as yet unborn – the son who will be born after his death; Romulus, the founder of a great new city; Numa, Tullius and early rulers of that city; great men who will adorn its history such as Regulus, Fabricius, and the Gracchi, and the great house of Caesar. He shows him Augustus, who will be emperor of a mighty nation. Then Aeneas and the Sibyl return to the upper world, and Aeneas and the Trojans resume their journey.

Book VII The Trojans disembark in Latium at the mouth of the Tiber. Their food is nearly exhausted and they even devour the dry cakes of bread on which they arrange such food as they have. Aeneas realises that prophecies are about to be fulfilled (Book III). He sends an emissary to Latinus, the King.

Latinus has been told of strangers in his dreams, and how the mingling of their blood with that of Latium will beget a great race. He has also been told that his daughter Lavinia must marry one of the strangers, and for this reason he has avoided concluding the sought-for marriage for her with the noble young Turnus, King of the Rutulians. When Aeneas' emissary arrives Latinus welcomes him, offers Aeneas an alliance and his daughter's hand in marriage, and sends him a chariot as a gift. Juno sees the opportunity to make more trouble for the Trojans.

She sends one of the Furies to sow jealousy in the heart of Turnus, and hatred in the heart of Lavinia's mother, Amata. Amata rouses the city against the strangers and hides her daughter – just at the time when Ascanius wounds a stag from the royal herd of Latium. In the affray that follows two of Latinus' men are killed. Latinus' hopes for a peaceful alliance are destroyed; the tribes of Italy prepare for war with Turnus as their leader.

Book VIII Aeneas watches the Italian armies massing on the far bank of the Tiber. He tries to remember all the words of hope he has heard on his journey and particularly the words of the Sibyl. He falls asleep on the river bank, and is visited in his dreams by the river god Tiberinus, who tells him that the very spot where he lies asleep will be the

site of a city, Alba, which his son Ascanius will build. He also tells
him he will find an ally in Evander the Arcadian, who rules not far
away with a city on the Palatine Hill. The next morning Aeneas takes
two boats up the Tiber to find Evander, and one of the first things he
sees on the bank is a white sow with a litter of thirty young. He
remembers Helenus's prophecy, and, full of renewed hope, approaches
Evander's city. He carries an olive branch to show that he comes in
peace. He is received by Pallas, Evander's son, and is taken to where
a ritual sacrifice is being offered to Hercules, who had defeated the
giant, Cacus, on that spot. Aeneas recalls that Trojans and Arcadians
have a common ancestor in Atlas, and secures an alliance. Evander tells
him that the Etruscans, in revolt against Mezentius, the tyrant King of
Caere, will also fight with him. Suddenly there is a violent thunderstorm, and the clash of arms echoes across the sky: Venus appears, and
gives Aeneas his weapons and a suit of armour, and a wonderful shield
forged by her husband, the god Vulcan. On the shield is engraved the
future events of the history of Rome, down to the Battle of Actium,
which will make the empire secure.

BOOK IX Turnus, meanwhile, at a hint from Juno, takes advantage of
Aeneas' absence and moves to attack the Trojan camp. The Trojans,
obeying the orders of their absent leader, withdraw behind their defences and resist every effort by the Rutulians to force them out and
into battle. Frustrated, Turnus orders the destruction of the Trojan
ships, and is alarmed when the burning vessels break their hawsers and
seem, of their own accord, to plunge beneath the waves. A host of sea
nymphs rise in their place, indicating to Turnus that there is divine
power arrayed against him.

Meanwhile two Trojans, the inseparable friends Nisus and Euryalus,
devise a plan for slipping through the enemy lines and recalling Aeneas.
In the Rutulian camp they see soldiers sprawled out asleep by their
watch fires: they fall on them and slaughter as many of the defenceless
men as they can before they in turn are cut down by a column of Latin
soldiers. Turnus is roused and when he sees the havoc wrought by the
two Trojans, he orders an attack. In a fierce engagement Ascanius has
his first taste of war, and Turnus manages to lead an assault right into
the Trojan camp. The Trojans rally and manage to close the breach,
leaving Turnus trapped inside. He escapes by plunging into the Tiber
in full armour and swimming back to his own lines.

BOOK X Meanwhile the gods, on Olympus, engage in a heated argument. Jupiter is angry that hostilities have broken out, while Juno accuses the Trojans of unprovoked aggression. Venus pleads with Jupiter not to desert the Trojans, who at that very moment are surrounded by stronger forces. However, Aeneas has succeeded not only in securing the help of Evander but also an alliance with the Etruscans. He sails down the Tiber with a fleet of thirty ships, accompanied by Pallas and Tarchon, King of the Etruscans. On the journey they meet the sea nymphs, who tell them of the Trojans' plight and urge them to make haste.

The Trojans are overjoyed to see their leader return with a large force at his back, and Turnus tries to keep the two forces from joining. He lines the far bank with picked troops but the Trojans swarm ashore and Aeneas, with the shield of Vulcan, god of fire, is practically invulnerable. He also has the protection of Venus. The Trojans and their allies regain the camp and the whole force is united. The battle continues.

Turnus kills Pallas in single combat, and takes his sword belt as a trophy. Aeneas seeks Turnus to kill him in revenge for Pallas – but Juno interferes once again. She conjures a phantom of Aeneas and Turnus, in pursuit, is drawn away from the field. He pursues the phantom Aeneas to a ship, which immediately breaks loose from its moorings. Juno then spirits Turnus back to his own city. Aeneas, in the meantime, is challenged by Mezentius, who has killed a number of Trojans. Aeneas wounds him, and Mezentius' young son tries to help his father. Aeneas kills him and then finishes off Mezentius.

BOOK XI The Trojans celebrate a victory, and Aeneas sends the body of Pallas home with full battle honours. Evander sends a message to Aeneas, begging him to avenge his son's death. King Latinus sends envoys to Aeneas, requesting a truce for the burial of the fallen: Aeneas agrees, and fighting ceases for twelve days. Aeneas has no quarrel with Latinus, who had offered him both friendship and marriage with Lavinia, so he offers to conclude the war by fighting Turnus in single combat. Turnus is prepared to accept the challenge – but he tells the Latins that those who would come to terms with the invaders, and who want him to abandon his plans to marry Lavinia, are losing sight of the victory which is within their grasp. Then comes news that

Trojan and Etruscan cavalry are approaching the city. The war is resumed.

Turnus calls on a new force, the Volscian cavalry led by the warrior maid Camilla. The two armies clash within sight of the city walls and the fighting, though fierce, is indecisive. Camilla, with her band of chosen warrior maidens, is in the thick of the fight, and many Trojans die. Then a lucky javelin cast by Arruns, the Etruscan, kills Camilla. Arruns is killed in turn by an arrow from Opis, the messenger of the goddess Diana – but the death of Camilla demoralises the Rutulian cavalry and they flee back to the city in disorder.

BOOK XII Defeat for the Latins now seems inevitable, and Turnus is prepared to stake everything on his pledge to single combat with Aeneas. Latinus and his Queen, Amata, try in vain to dissuade him. The two champions prepare but Juno is loath to give Aeneas even the chance of victory. She persuades Juturna, sister of Turnus, to try and prevent the combat. Juturna, wearing the uniform of a Latin soldier, is sucessful in rallying her brother's armies and the two champions are forced to return to full-scale battle. Inside the city, Amata sees the battle resumed and believes Turnus to be dead: she hangs herself in grief.

The news of her death is taken to Turnus, who now recognises his sister as the breaker of the truce. He stops the fighting: the armies fall back as he and Aeneas stride out to meet each other. On Olympus the gods agree to interfere no more in the fortunes of Aeneas. Juno is ordered to abide by the decision.

Aeneas, protected by the arms and shield of Vulcan, wins an easy victory over Turnus. When Turnus falls from a wound in the thigh Aeneas is prepared to spare his life: but he sees that Turnus is wearing the sword-belt of Pallas whom Aeneas is sworn to avenge. He kills Turnus, and the Trojans are victorious.

Aeolus The ruler of the winds who appears in the *Odyssey,* Book X. He gives Odysseus a great leather bag in which the winds are confined – all except that which blows from the west. Aeolus was attempting to ensure Odysseus a calm passage home – the west wind would blow his ship back to Ithaca.

Aeolus, son of Hippotas, lived on a floating island with his six sons and six daughters – married to each other, and later to found kingdoms in Italy and Sicily. The winds were confined in a cliff in the Tyrrehenian Sea by Zeus, who found they required too much attention for safe control. Hera, in her original character as mother goddess, was responsible for bestowing the care of them on Aeolus – the winds were her messengers.

Aeolus also appears in the *Aeneid,* Book I, where he is a minor god of Aeolia, keeping the winds imprisoned in a cave.

See also *Aeneid, Odyssey.*

Aesculapius In Roman mythology the god of healing – but he is in fact the Greek god Asclepius. His cult was taken to Rome when, after a plague in 239 BC, messengers were sent to consult the oracle at Delphi. Upon the oracle's advice, one of the snakes was taken to Rome from Epidaurus, and legend says that the creature itself chose an island in the Tiber, south-west of Rome, for the sanctuary. A temple was built, and dedicated on the first day of 291 BC.

See also *Asclepius.*

Aeschylus One of the great tragic poets of ancient Greece. He was born at Eleusis in 525 BC, the son of Euphorion of the noble Eupatrid family. He fought in the wars against Persia: certainly at Marathon (the statement is in his epitaph) and probably at Salamis, a battle he describes vividly in one of his plays, *The Persians.*

Aeschylus wrote something like ninety plays, of which only seven have come down to us: *The Suppliants, The Persians, The Seven Against Thebes, Prometheus Bound,* and the great trilogy, *The Oresteia,* which contains *Agamemnon, Choephoroe* (The Libation Bearers), and *Eumenides* (The Kindly Ones).

Aeschylus is credited with the apparently simple but nevertheless epoch-making innovation of a second actor: before him drama had only one actor appearing at a time. In his plays the drama took a gigantic step forward – dialogue brought a vivid immediacy never known before. He also developed the use of costumes and of special effects (essential in a play like *Prometheus Bound).* His themes were of the grandest and it is a measure of his greatness that his language always proved equal to them. Pericles himself undertook the financial responsibility for the assembling, costuming and training of the chorus for one of Aeschylus' plays.

The poet died at Gela in Sicily in 456 BC, when he was the guest for the second time at the court of Hieron, the brilliant and cultured ruler of Syracuse.

See also *The Oresteia*, Prometheus.

Aesop The fable (typically an anecdote with a moralising application) was a familiar feature of ancient Greek story-telling. Toward the end of the fifth century BC the greater part of fable in Greece was ascribed to Aesop, though the first known written collection did not appear until one was prepared by Valerius Babrius, a Roman writing in Greek in the second century AD. Aesop's name was familiar to Aristophanes, and to Plato: Socrates, while imprisoned, put some of Aesop's fables into verse.

All that is known about Aesop comes from Herodotus (Book III), where he is described as the slave of Iadmon, a Thracian who lived in Samos in the sixth century BC.

Agamemnon The son of Atreus and brother of Menelaus, Agamemnon was High King in Argos and led the Achaean armies to Troy. The Achaean fleet assembled at Aulis but was halted there by the lack of a favourable wind. Calchas, the renegade Trojan seer, declared that Agamemnon had once offended Artemis, the divine huntress, by declaring himself a better hunter than she: now the goddess demanded the sacrifice of Agamemnon's daughter, Iphigenia. Agamemnon refused: he offered as a reason the certain refusal of Clytemnestra, his Queen, to let their daughter go. The other Achaean leaders then threatened to shift their allegiance to Palamedes, son of Nauplius, and Odysseus suggested the trick (that Iphigenia was sought in marriage by Achilles) that forced Agamemnon's hand. Odysseus went to Argos and returned with Iphigenia, who was sacrificed so that the Achaeans could proceed with their war.

Clytemnestra, when she learned that she had been tricked into allowing her daughter to go to her death, nursed the hope of being able to make Agamemnon pay for his crime.

After the long siege of Troy Agamemnon returned, victorious, with the Trojan princess Cassandra as part of his share of the spoils. Meanwhile, Clytemnestra had taken a lover, Agamemnon's cousin Aegisthus, and her resolve that Iphigenia's murder should be avenged had strengthened. She provided the returning King with an appropriate welcome, and then murdered him and Cassandra with the help of Aegisthus.

One of the principal characters in the *Iliad*, Agamemnon is as unsympathetic as the rest of the Achaean leaders. It is Homer's genius that makes him a completely believable man: his position as a warrior king being no mitigation of his selfish and mean-spirited nature. He is brave enough in combat, but that is all – indeed his small-mindedness nearly leads to disaster for his own side, for it touches off the quarrel with Achilles that sets the scene for the events at Troy.

The number of appearances of Agamemnon in Greek mythology, apart from those in the *Iliad,* suggest that there was a king of that name in Argos or Mycenae, and L. R. Farnell notes that much later – in historical times – there were cults of Agamemnon, as hero, in various places in ancient Greece.

See also Achilles, Aegisthus, Clytemnestra, *Iliad,* Pelops, *Oresteia* (Aeschylus), Iphigenia.

Agave   The sister of Semele and the mother of Pentheus, she was also aunt of the god Dionysus, whose worship she at first rejected when he came to Thebes. She is the unwitting instrument of Dionysus when he brings about the destruction of Pentheus.

See also *The Bacchae* (Euripides), Dionysus.

Agenor   In Greek mythology the name of a character who appears on the fringe of a number of stories, principally the one that tells of Europa and her rape by Zeus in the form of a bull. Agenor, King of Tyre, was her father, and his sons were sent in search of their sister. They were told not to come back to Agenor's kingdom without her and inevitably they became the founders of nations elsewhere. Phoenix was the ancestor of the Phoenicians, Cilix the Cilicians: most celebrated of all was Cadmus, who settled in Boeotia at the direction of the Delphic oracle and built the Cadmea, which became the citadel of the city of Thebes.

See also Cadmus, Europa, Thebes.

Ajax   1.   The son of Telamon, King of Salamis, and called great Ajax or Telamonian Ajax to distinguish him from his Locrian namesake at the siege of Troy. Homer describes him as a man of great size and strength – one who is always ready to lead an attack. He is never described as merely stupid but he is stolid and unimaginative and the events in the narrative convey a portrait of a man who carries more muscle than brain. His strength gives him the better of a duel with Hector: it is no help against the wily Odysseus, a smaller man, who holds him to a draw in a wrestling match. With Odysseus and Phoenix he tries to persuade Achilles to bring back his forces on the Achaean side after the quarrel with Agamemnon.

Great Ajax appears in other stories apart from the *Iliad*. One concerns his birth, when Heracles visits Telamon. Heracles stands on his lion's skin and prays that his host's expected child will be a son and as strong as the skin. Zeus sends an eagle to show that the prayer has been heard. The familiar theme of the invulnerable hero is present in another story: the infant Ajax was wrapped in the lion's skin to make him strong and the skin covers him – almost. The circumstances of his death are not told in Homer though he makes an appearance in the *Odyssey* (Book XI) as a bitter and resentful shade who refuses to speak with Odysseus in the nether world. Ajax and Odysseus had contested for the prized arms of the fallen Achilles, and Odysseus had won. The narrative simply says it was this that sent Ajax to his grave. Other stories say he went insane with anger at losing, and killed himself.

Ajax 2. The son of Oileus, and chief of the Locrians at the siege of Troy. Sometimes called the lesser Ajax because he was a small man, he was noted as being the finest spearsman among the Achaeans and the fastest runner. He was also vulgar and rude – and justly served by Athene, when she makes him slip in cattle dung and lose the foot race to Odysseus in the funeral games for Patroclus. Ajax is aware that the goddess made him fall and says so while spitting out dung (*Iliad*, Book XXIII). He also earns the wrath of Poseidon and this costs him his life. In the *Odyssey*, Book IV, Menalaus relates how Ajax's homeward bound ship was wrecked: but Ajax was helped by Poseidon and managed to scramble ashore on the Gyraean rocks. However, he boasted loudly that he had saved his own life – in spite of the gods. Whereupon the furious Poseidon split the rock with his trident: Ajax was thrown into the sea and this time he drowned.

One of the stories of the sack of Troy relates that Ajax dragged Cassandra away from the altar of Athene, where she had sought refuge; another that he also raped her. That either – or both – of these stories is true is as arguable as the truth of the *Iliad*; but it has been established beyond doubt that a custom persisted for a thousand years among the Locrians (the people of Ajax) of sending two virgins every year to serve in the temple of Athene in Ilium (Troy). The classical explanation is of a penance by the Locrians for the crime of Ajax and this, together with the fact that there should have been two heroes of the same name, strongly suggest their historical existence.

See also *Iliad, Odyssey*.

Alcestis The daughter of Pelias, her father refused her in marriage to any suitor who could not yoke two wild beasts to a chariot and then drive them. Admetus, King of Pherae, was able to call on the help of Apollo, who brought him a lion and a boar already yoked; Admetus drove away with his bride beside him.

See also *Alcestis* (Euripides), Admetus.

Alcestis A play by Euripides which takes as its theme the sacrifice of her life – to save her husband's – by Alcestis. It opens with a dialogue between Apollo and Thanatos (death). Thanatos has come to the palace at Pherae, where all mourn the coming death of Alcestis. He finds Apollo there: Apollo asks for the life of Alcestis but Thanatos says that nothing will deny him what he came for. Apollo warns him that one is coming who will wrest Alcestis from death. Thanatos scorns Apollo's words, and enters the palace. Alcestis dies.

Later in the day Heracles arrives: he is on his way to Thrace to capture the horses of Diomedes, and seeks hospitality. But when he learns of the grief that hangs over the palace he declares he will respect it and find another roof. But Admetus insists: his grief will not make him deny a wayfarer. From a servant Heracles learns the whole story, and out of friendship to the courteous Admetus goes to Alcestis' tomb and wrestles with Thanatos for her life. He wins the struggle, and restores Alcestis to her husband.

A notable feature of the play is the character of Heracles. Rough, warmhearted and generous, he provides a quality of lightness in what would otherwise be – in spite of the happy ending – a very sober drama.

See also Admetus.

Alcmaeon The son of Amphiaraus, one of the Seven Against Thebes, and so one of the Epigoni who took part in the later expedition against that city. On his return to Argos he takes revenge on his mother Eriphyle who, coveting the necklace of Harmonia, had persuaded Amphiaraus to join the first fatal expedition. The necklace was her payment. Alcmaeon kills her, and Eriphyle's dying curse is that no land shall ever shelter him. Alcmaeon becomes the prey of the Furies, who hunt him from place to place, denying him rest. Eventually he reaches the court of Phegeus, King of Psophis in Arcadia, who at the request of Apollo does his best to purify him. He also offers Alcmaeon the hand of his daughter, Arsinoë, and Alcamaeon gives his bride the necklace of Harmonia. But the Furies return, and famine threatens the land, and Alcmaeon, remembering his mother's curse, goes in search of new land where he might settle. He finds it at the mouth of the river Achelous, where silt has formed a new island – land which did not exist at the time he killed his mother.

Trying to begin a new life, Alcmaeon marries Callirhoë, the daughter of Oeneus, King of Calydon. But Callirhoë learns about the necklace of Harmonia and demands it for herself, and Alcmaeon is driven to try and retrieve it from the King of Psophis. He tells the King that he wants to place the necklace in the shrine of Apollo at Delphi. Phegeus gives it to him – but then learns the truth from one of Alcmaeon's servants. Furious, he has Alcmaeon ambushed and murdered as he leaves the palace.

Arsinoë had only supposed that the necklace was to be taken to Delphi. She knows nothing of Callirhoë, witnesses the murder of her husband and wishes death on her father, who meanwhile, sends the fatal necklace to Delphi in the hope that no further harm will come of it. But the curse has begun to work, and eventually Alcmaeon's sons by Callirhoë avenge their father by killing King Phegeus and all his family.

Alcmene The wife of Amphitryon and the mother, by Zeus, of Heracles. While her husband was at war Zeus visited her in Amphitryon's guise, and made one night last the length of three. She bore two sons together – Heracles to Zeus, and Iphicles to Amphitryon.

Alcmene was, according to Hesiod, incorruptible and chosen by Zeus because he wished to sire a champion for both gods and men. That was why he wooed her disguised as her husband. When she died Alcmene was taken, at Zeus' instructions, to the Islands of the Blest.

See also Amphitryon, Heracles.

Alcyone The daughter of Aeolus, guardian of the winds. She married Ceyx of Trachis, and their life together was so happy that she called her husband 'Zeus'. This angered the god, and when Ceyx was on a sea voyage Zeus let loose a thunderstorm over his ship. Ceyx was drowned, and his ghost appeared to Alcyone in Trachis to tell her the news. Alcyone, in her grief, threw herself into the sea to join her husband, and the gods in pity turned them both into kingfishers.

The origin of the word halcyon (Alcyone) for kingfisher, is ascribed to this ancient tale, and so is the term Halcyon Days – the seven days before and after the winter solstice, when Aeolus forbids his winds to blow across the seas.

Alpheus A river in Greece. It rises in the mountains of Arcadia and flows north and west into Elis with many small tributaries on the way, waters the plain of Olympia, and enters the Ionian Sea near Pyrgos. The river god Alpheus is famous in myth and poetry as the lover of the nymph Arethusa.

See also Arethusa.

Althaea The mother of Meleager, and wife of Oeneus, King of Calydon. When Meleager was seven days old the Fates visited Althaea. They pointed to a stick burning in the hearth, and told her that the child's life would last as long as the stick would in the fire. Then they departed, and at once Althaea snatched the stick from the hearth, and put out the flame. She hid the stick away and was able to see her son grow to manhood. But the events of the Calydonian boar hunt turned her against him, and she killed him by burning the stick which controlled his life.

See also Meleager.

Althamaenes The son of Catreus, who was the son of Minos, King of Crete. An oracle predicted that Catreus would be killed by one of his children, and to escape the possibility of being guilty of such a deed Althamaenes and his sister Apemosyne sailed away from Crete and settled on the island of Rhodes.

Catreus, in his old age and without an heir to his kingdom, decided to go in search of his son. Eventually his ships reached Rhodes: but it was night and his landing party woke all the watch dogs. The islanders believed they were being attacked by pirates and raised the alarm, and Althamaenes rushed down to the shore with his men to repel the supposed raiders. He killed his father with a spear thrust before he discovered who the strangers were. The oracle was fulfilled, and Althamaenes prayed for death. The gods granted his wish – a chasm opened in the earth and swallowed him up.

Amalthea The she-goat that suckled the infant Zeus on Mount Ida in Crete. In some versions Amalthea was a nymph who brought goat's milk to nourish the baby, and Zeus gave her the goat's horn when he attained his power, endowing it with the property of producing whatever its owner desired. This is the origin of the horn of plenty, the *Cornucopiae*.

Amazons The warrior maidens of mythology. Their name is derived from the Greek word meaning 'breastless', and they were believed to destroy their right breasts for the purpose of using arms – bows, spears etc. – to better effect. To provide offspring they coupled at certain intervals with men: the male children became slaves, or were otherwise disposed of, and the females were trained for war and fighting. They usually fought on horseback.

They make numerous appearances in myth and are twice mentioned in the *Iliad* (Books III and VI). However, the story of their Queen, Penthesilea, fighting on the Trojan side and being killed by Achilles, is a later addition and not in Homer.

Perhaps the best known myth concerning them is the Ninth Labour of Heracles, when he captures the girdle of the Amazon Queen, Hippolyta. Heracles' companion, Theseus, bears the brunt of their wrath: an Amazon army invades Attica and lays siege to Athens. Theseus wins the battle, and Hippolyta becomes his prisoner and his first wife. The warrior maid of the *Aeneid*, Camilla, is an invention of Virgil's and has no connection with Greek mythology.

The Amazons are a curious fancy, and the origins of the myths concerning them are not known. Robert Graves advances the explanation that they were probably derived from the priestesses of the Moon goddess, who bore arms, and would certainly have resisted the coming of the new gods with the arrival of the peoples who migrated into Greece.

See also Heracles, Hippolyta, Penthesilea, Theseus.

Amphiaraus The seer of Argos, who married Eriphyle, the sister of King Adrastus. His gift of foreseeing the future made him advise against the attack on Thebes mounted by Adrastus to restore Polynices to the Theban throne. It also explains his reluctance to become the seventh champion in the Argive forces. Eriphyle, greedy for the necklace of Harmonia, invoked a vow which bound Amphiaraus to her decision when there were differences between husband and brother: the necklace bought her decision that Amphiaraus should go with the army. But he was not deceived and made his son Alcmaeon swear to avenge him on his wife if he should not return.

His point of attack, when the army reached Thebes, was the Homoloian Gate; but the Argive army was routed and Amphiaraus fled from the field pursued by Theban soldiers, who would have killed him but for the intervention of Zeus. He vanished into a cleft in the earth opened by the god's thunderbolt, and the spot became famous as an oracular shrine.

The shrine was known in historical times, and it is likely that Amphiaraus was originally a hero, credited with supernatural powers by those who came after him.

See also Adrastus, Alcmaeon, Epigoni, Harmonia, The Seven Against Thebes.

Amphion and Zethus The sons of Zeus and Antiope, and descendants of Cadmus. Antiope's father, Nycteus, persecuted her when he found her pregnant and she fled to Sicyon: but her brother Lycus attacked Sicyon and took her prisoner. She was his captive when her twin sons, Amphion and Zethus, were born. Lycus ordered that the babies were to be left to die on Mount Kithaeron but they were found by a shepherd, who brought them up. Antiope, meanwhile, was taken back to Cadmeia by Lycus, who had succeeded to the kingdom. Dirce, his Queen, was a cruel woman who tormented Antiope and threatened to murder her.

When the twin boys grew up they attacked Lycus in his city and rescued their mother. They killed Lycus and his evil Queen and built a new city just below Cadmeia. Zethus brought the stones for the walls and Amphion played on a magic lyre given him by Hermes: the music moved the stones into whichever place they were needed. The twins ruled jointly in their new city, and it received its name, Thebes, when Zethus married Thebe. Amphion married Niobe, who incurred the displeasure of the gods by declaring her children to be superior to those of Leto (Apollo and Artemis).

See also Antiope, Cadmus, Dirce, Niobe.

Amphitrite A Nereid, she became the wife of Poseidon. The sea god's first choice was Thetis, her sister: but it was prophesied that any child born to Thetis by one of the gods would be strong enough to overthrow them, so Poseidon turned his attention to Amphitrite. But she was not pleased with his advances and hid herself in the Atlas Mountains. Poseidon sent an ambassador, Delphinus, to seek her out and to plead his cause, and Delphinus was successful. Amphitrite became Poseidon's consort, and in gratitude to Delphinus the god set his image in the stars as the sign of the Dolphin.

Amphitrite soon found that Poseidon was as faithless as his brother Zeus, and the objects of his love were always in grave danger of her wrath.

See also Poseidon, Scylla, Thetis.

Amphitryon The grandson of Perseus, and King of Troezen. His brother Electryon was High King of Mycenae and father of Alcmene. Electryon's kingdom was raided by an army commanded by Pterelaus, who claimed the throne of Mycenae. The raid was devasting for Electryon: his cattle were driven off and eight of his sons were killed. Electryon assembled an army and set off to avenge his sons and regain his cattle, and commanded Amphitryon to act as regent during his absence. He promised Amphitryon his daughter Alcmene if all went well.

During Electryon's absence the King of Elis sent a message to Mycenae saying that the cattle were now in his possession, and demanded the customary ransom. Amphitryon immediately paid him and the cattle were returned. But when Electryon arrived on the scene he was angry that a large ransom had been handed over for what was rightfully his – and to the man who had killed his sons. In the squabble that followed Amphitryon accidentally killed Electryon, and a sentence of banishment was pronounced on him.

The kingdom was seized by Amphitryon's uncle, Sthenelus, and Amphitryon fled to Thebes with Alcmene. They were given refuge by King Creon, who also purified him of the blood guilt for the accidental death of Electryon. Alcmene, however, would not marry Amphitryon until he fulfilled the quest of Electryon, which was vengeance upon those who had murdered her brothers. Creon was sympathetic to Amphitryon's cause, and offered to provide him with a Theban army if Amphitryon would first help *him* – for the land was terrorised by the Teumessian vixen.

This creature was partly divine and part of the fear it aroused was the belief that it could never be caught. Wherever it preyed it had to be appeased by the sacrifice of a child every month. Amphitryon appealed to Cephalus, the Athenian who owned a marvellous hound, Laelaps; it was the gift of Artemis, and could catch anything it pursued. Cephalus lent him the hound – and at once an impossible situation arose, since the vixen could never be caught. Zeus, consulted about the dilemma created by these semi-divine creatures, solved it by simply turning them both to stone.

So Amphitryon got his army, and went off to reclaim his kingdom, and while he was gone Zeus visited Alcmene, and that led to the birth of the great Heracles.

Amphitryon was successful, partly because of the treachery of Comaetho, Pterelaus' daughter. Comaetho fell in love with Amphitryon and hoped to gain his favour, and she knew that her father was the grandson of Poseidon. There was a single strand of gold in Pterelaus' hair, put there by Poseidon to make him immortal. One night Comaetho plucked out the golden hair and her father died. After Amphitryon's victory she went to him and told him how much of it was owed to her. Amphitryon was so horrified that lust had driven Comaetho to kill her father that he ordered her to be put to death.

See also Alcmene, Cephalus, Heracles.

Amycus The mythical King of the Bebryces, a savage people of Bithynia. He possessed enormous strength and liked to challenge newcomers to a fist fight, the loser's life and freedom to be at the disposal of the victor. The Argonauts land in his country during their voyage, and Amycus issues his challenge. It is accepted by Polydeuces, whose skill enables him to defeat the greater strength of Amycus. In one version Amycus is killed during the fight, in another he is enslaved as the loser.

See also *Argonautica*.

Amymone One of the fifty daughters of King Danaus and one of the two known by name (the other is Hypermnestra). She was sent to look for water by her father when they arrived in Argos, and disturbed a sleeping satyr who tried to rape her. She called on Poseidon, who appeared and hurled his trident at the satyr, the trident missed and stuck in a rock, and the satyr escaped. Poseidon found the girl irresistible and took her himself, and created the spring, Amymone, at her request. The spring is the source of the river Lerna.

See also Danaus.

Ancaeus 1. One of the brothers of Althaea, the mother of Meleager. He takes part in the Calydonian boar hunt and objects to the presence there of Atalanta, who is plainly favoured by Meleager and who will, Ancaeus believes, be the cause of trouble. He is killed during the hunt.

Ancaeus 2. The son of Poseidon, from Tegea. He sailed with the Argonauts, and became their navigator after the death of Tiphys. After the voyage he returned to his home in Tegea where, despite the warnings of a seer that he would not live to enjoy its fruit, he had planted a vineyard in his garden. Ancaeus arrived back to find the vineyard fruitful and wine from it ready for him to drink. He called for the seer, and showed him that he had been wrong – here he was, about to drink a cup of wine from the vineyard. The seer gave him another warning: 'There's many a slip twixt cup and lip!' At that moment a servant rushed in to tell Ancaeus that a wild boar was in his vineyard: Ancaeus put down the cup and, grasping a spear, rushed out of his house. But the boar was hidden by some bushes and saw Ancaeus first. The boar killed him before he had a chance to use his spear.

Anchises The prince of Troy who became the father of Aeneas by the goddess Aphrodite, whom he met and loved while pasturing his herds on Mount Ida. He was forbidden to reveal the identity of Aeneas' mother but one day he boasted of it among his friends. He was punished by a blast of lighting which lamed him permanently – hence the story of his being carried out of burning Troy on the shoulders of Aeneas.

See also Aeneas, *Aeneid*.

Androgeus One of the sons of Minos, King of Crete, and in some versions of the Theseus story the direct cause of Minos' demand for annual tribute. On a visit to Athens, Androgeus took part in the games and was a successful and popular contestant. King Aegeus (Theseus' father) at that time feared a plot by Pallas to usurp his throne, and noted that the sons of both Pallas and Minos were close friends. When Androgeus continued his travels and was on the road to Thebes, Aegeus had him waylaid and murdered. The annual tribute of seven youths and seven maidens was the price exacted by Minos as payment for the crime.

See also Minos, Theseus.

Andromache The wife of the great Hector and a touching and tragic figure in all the myths in which she appears. The daughter of the King of Thebe in Cilicia, she lost her father and her brothers when Achilles destroyed the city after arriving at Troy. When first encountered in the *Iliad* (Book VI) she is fearful of Hector's safety but obeys his injunction to care first for her part as a wife and a mother and leave the business of fighting to the men.

After the fall of the city, when the women of the royal house are shared out as spoils among the Achaean leaders, Andromache is given to Neoptolemus: her son Astyanax, the heir of Hector, is taken from her and murdered by Odysseus, who insists on the slaughter of every male of Priam's line. In Thessaly, as Neoptolemus' slave, she is cruelly treated by his wife, Hermione, but later finds peace with Helenus, her kinsman.

See also *Andromache* (Euripides), Hector, *The Trojan Women* (Euripides).

Andromache A play by Euripides, dealing with the events in the life of the Trojan princess after she was taken back to Thessaly by Neoptolemus. She bears him a son, Molossus; but after ten years Neoptolemus tires of his royal concubine and marries Hermione, daughter of Menelaus, King of Sparta. Hermione is childless, and hates Andromache, whom she decides is responsible for her barrenness through the exercise of magic arts. When Neoptolemus goes to visit Delphi, Andromache seeks sanctuary from Hermione's hatred in the shrine of Thetis (Neoptolemus is the son of Achilles, the son of Thetis), but Hermione and Menelaus get possession of her son. They threaten to murder Molossus to make Andromache leave the safety of the shrine: but they really intend the death of both of them. Their scheme is denounced by Peleus, the aged father of Achilles, and frustrated by the arrival of Orestes, to whom Hermione was originally betrothed. He has encountered Neoptolemus at Delphi, and killed him.

The play concludes with the appearance of Thetis herself, who orders matters so that the hapless Andromache will at least find peace as the wife of her fellow-captive, the Trojan prince Helenus.

Antaeus The son of Poseidon and Gaia (Mother Earth), and King of Libya, he appears in some versions of the Eleventh Labour of Heracles. Of gigantic stature, he was always on the watch for strangers passing through his kingdom. These he would force to wrestle with him – and he never lost because his strength was continually renewed by contact with the earth. He always killed his exhausted opponents. After delivering the Apples of the Hesperides to Eurystheus, Heracles went to Libya and challenged Antaeus. When they fought, Heracles noted that each time he threw Antaeus, his opponent seemed to grow stronger. He seized Antaeus and held him in the air, crushing him until he died.

See also Heracles, Labours of.

Antenor An elder of the city of Troy. In the *Iliad* (Book VII) he advises the Trojans to return Helen to her husband, Menelaus. Later stories make him a traitor to his city, for which the Achaeans spare his life and the lives of his family.

Anticlea The mother of Odysseus. In the *Odyssey* (Book XI), she is the daughter of Autolycus and wife of Laertes: Odysseus is their son, and his cunning nature is attributed to his grandfather Autolycus, a notoriously clever rogue. Later writers, notably Sophocles in *Philoctetes,* make Anticlea the mother of Odysseus by one even cleverer, Sisyphus, the King of Corinth.

See also Autolycus, Odysseus, Sisyphus.

Antigone The daughter of Oedipus and his mother-wife, Jocasta. A striking figure and the central character in one of Sophocles' greatest plays, she may well be a purely poetic creation. The story of her incestuous parents is mentioned by Homer in the *Odyssey* (Book XI), but he says nothing of any children of that fatal marriage. The text of Aeschylus' *Seven Against Thebes,* as we have it, closes with Antigone determined, in the face of authority, to see her brother's body properly buried. Scholars agree that this is an addition by another hand – yet it is remarkable that it should also be the whole point of the *Antigone* of Sophocles.

In its familiar form the story of Antigone begins with the closing scene of Sophocles' *Oedipus,* when the blinded King bids farewell to his daughter before going into exile. He commends them to the care of their uncle, Creon. In a later play, *Oedipus at Colonus,* Sophocles presents Antigone as attendant on her blind father, now a wandering beggar at the mercy of everyone. She and her father have arrived at Colonus, near Athens, and she does her best to protect him from the animosity of the people.

She comes into her own in the third of Sophocles' Theban plays, *Antigone*. Her father has died and she has returned to Thebes, where the struggle between her brothers for possession of the city has taken place. Both are dead, and Creon has forbidden the burial of Polynices, the brother who led the invading army and thus made himself the enemy of Thebes. Antigone, though she knows it will cost her her life, is determined to give him at least formal burial. (Ill-treatment of the dead was regarded with horror by the ancient Greeks: but it was the Theban practice to leave fallen enemies where they lay.) She succeds in her design, and pays with her life.

A later play than either *Antigone* (the date is uncertain, but Gilbert Murray places it about 441 BC) or the *Seven Against Thebes* (467 BC) is *The Phoenician Women* of Euripides, which might be said to fill the gap between *Oedipus* and *Oedipus at Colonus*. Antigone, in this play, is outraged when Creon invokes the words of Tiresias, who has said that Thebes will have no peace while Oedipus dwells there. Oedipus is driven out, and Antigone goes with him. (She is betrothed to Creon's son, Haemon, but the hatred she feels for Creon drives her to say that she would murder his son on her wedding night if the betrothal were enforced. Creon turns her out of the city with her father.) The use of the Theban cycle of myths is different in Euripides – but Antigone is recognisably the same girl as presented by Sophocles.

See also *Antigone*, *Oedipus* and *Oedipus at Colonus* (Sophocles), The Seven Against Thebes.

Antigone The celebrated tragedy by Sophocles. The two sons of Oedipus have warred over the succession to the throne of Thebes. Eteocles has held the city, while Polynices has gathered an army with the help of Adrastus, King of Argos, and tried to take it from his brother by force. The attack has failed – and both brothers have been killed. Eteocles, defender of the city, has been buried as a hero, while Polynices, the attacker, has been named a traitor. Creon, uncle of the two princes and now the King of Thebes, orders that the body of Polynices must lie unburied, food for carrion eaters. Antigone and Ismene are the sisters of Eteocles and Polynices.

The play opens with Antigone imploring her sister's help; she wants to defy Creon's edict and perform the proper funeral rites over their brother's body. Ismene is afraid, so Antigone dismisses her and goes off to perform the rites alone. The Theban elders are told by Creon that his order is to reinforce the authority of the state – Thebes has been shaken, first by the affair of the doomed Oedipus, then by the attack on the city by one of its own sons. Polynices' body will be guarded night and day to stop anyone giving it even formal burial. A guard enters, one of those sent to watch the body of Polynices. He tells Creon that they found the body covered with dust and dry earth – the funeral rites have been performed. The King, furious, orders that the body be exposed again: this is done, but the wind rises and Antigone hurries back to cover the corpse again, believing that the wind itself had exposed it. She is caught and taken before Creon, and sentenced to be buried alive.

Haemon arrives, and a violent scene with his father follows. Creon, enraged by his son's turning against him, orders the death sentence to be carried out. Going to her death, Antigone tells him that she obeys the laws of humanity, not of the state. Creon feels the loyalty of the Elders slipping away; but he is trapped by the laws of his own making. The arrival of Tiresias, the blind seer of Thebes, brings him no comfort: indeed, the old man tells him it is wrong to try and wound those already fallen – the wrath of the gods is aroused. The seer's words break Creon's resolve. He orders the burial of Polynices and the release of Antigone. But he is too late; Antigone has hanged herself in the tomb where she was immured. Haemon has found her, and he kills himself after an ineffectual attack on his father. His mother, Queen Eurydice, takes her life when she hears the news, and Creon is alone with his grief when the play closes.

Antinous One of the suitors of Penelope in the *Odyssey* (Book I). He is the one whom Odysseus kills first when he returns home to Ithaca.

Antiope 1. Daughter of Nycteus, one of the Spartoi, and one of the loves of Zeus. She was imprisoned by her brother Lycus after giving birth to twin sons, Amphion and Zethus. Lycus ordered that the babies be left to die. During her captivity Antiope was cruelly treated by Lycus' wife, Dirce, but she was avenged by her sons who escaped death and grew to manhood.

See also Amphion and Zethus, Cadmus, Dirce.

Antiope 2. One of the names of the Amazon Queen who appears in the myths of Heracles and Theseus. She is sometimes called Hippolyta, and sometimes Melanippe. Robert Graves points out that these two are definitely connected: both names point to an association with horses. Scholars believe that the confusion of these with Antiope – as well as with each other – arises from the story of Theseus, which was roughly modelled on that of Heracles, who was a hero figure of greater antiquity.

See also Amazons, Heracles, Hippolyta, Theseus.

Aphrodite The Greek goddess of beauty, fertility and love; probably in origin a very ancient deity. Some authorities trace her description as the 'Cyprian' or 'Paphian', i.e. as coming from Cyprus, to the island where the Greeks would have first encountered her cult. But she would have been, in any case, a familiar goddess to the Greeks of the Aegean since she personified aspects of the female deity common to all the settled communities of the Mediterranean and the Near East. The story of her love for Adonis (Tammuz) is not Greek and is a strong indication of her Near Eastern origins where she is clearly recognisable as Astarte, or Ishtar.

Her name is connected with the myth of her beginnings as told by Hesiod. When Cronus overthrew his father, Uranus, he castrated him and threw the genitals into the sea. Around these gathered white foam, *aphros,* and from this the goddess arose. She stepped ashore at Paphos in Cyprus, and where she trod flowers and grasses grew: her most famous centre of worship in antiquity was at Paphos.

Homer makes her the child of Zeus and Dione, the god's consort at Dodona. Modern scholars point out that Dione's name is a feminine form of Zeus: Dione was probably, therefore, an ancient sky-goddess whose cult was absorbed by Zeus during the ascendancy of the male gods in Greece. She is mother to Aphrodite in Homer, nonetheless, and appears as such in the *Iliad* (Book V).

Homer also describes Aphrodite as the husband of Hephaestus, the son of Hera and the divine artificer. But Hephaestus was both lame and ugly and Aphrodite soon found an exciting lover in Ares, the war god. She bore Ares three children: Phobus (fear), Deimos (terror), and Harmonia (concord). But her adultery with Ares was seen by Helios, the sun, when he rose in the heavens, and he told Hephaestus what his wife was up to.

Hephaestus retired to his forge to work out a plan that would not only expose Aphrodite but would also revenge him on the handsome, quarrelsome Ares. He constructed a magnificent bronze hunting net, of great strength but of workmanship so fine that the strands were invisible. This he arranged with great care above his bed, and then he told his wife that he was off to visit Lemnos, an island he loved.

Hephaestus was hardly out of sight before Aphrodite sent a message to Ares. As soon as he arrived they leaped into bed, concerned only with enjoying eath other and unaware that Hephaestus had returned. When he marched into his bedroom they tried to spring up and cover their nakedness – and found themselves held fast by his wonderful net. Hephaestus, to their horror, flung open the doors and called the rest of the gods. The Olympians crowded into the room and surrounded the bed, and soon the house of the divine artificer was rocking with laughter, though Hermes admitted to Apollo that he would be glad to change places with Ares even if there were three times as many nets. When Hephaestus removed the net Ares fled, humilated, to his palace in Thrace, while Aphrodite hurried off to Paphos to be bathed and soothed by her sympathetic attendants, the Graces.

The story of Ares and Aphrodite is told in the *Odyssey* (Book VIII) and in the *Iliad* Homer shows her as being firmly on the side of the Trojans. In fact she loved a Trojan, the prince Anchises, whom she saw pasturing his herds on Mount Ida. She bore him a son, Aeneas, and made him promise never to reveal the identity of the boy's mother. But he forgot his promise, and one day boasted to his friends that he had loved Aphrodite herself. This infuriated Zeus, who blasted him with lightning. Aphrodite mananged to lessen the force of the blow but Anchises was lamed for life.

She had many other loves, of whom the most famous was Adonis. She made love with Hermes, and presented him with a son, Hermaphroditus, who enjoyed the benefit of being both male and female. Her nights with Poseidon resulted in two more sons, Rhodius and Herophilus, and those with Dionysus in a son also. This time Hera was irritated both by Aphrodite's bouncing pleasure and her fruitfulness, and caused the boy to be born with a penis of great size, and his name, Priapus, became an adjective to describe the rampant male.

There were many aspects of Aphrodite, and some of them point to her origins as the ancient three-fold Earth mother: *Melaina* (the black one), *Androphonos* (killer of men), *Epitymbidia* (she upon the graves). More familiarly she is *Anadyomene* (emerging from the sea), *Urania* (sky borne), *Pandemos* (goddess of all people). She was an odd woman out, so to speak, among the Olympians, related to them in a tenuous way – but so essential to the scheme of things that she would have to be invented if she had not, like her sisters, existed already in another form. Aphrodite had no important festivals, though she was much honoured at Corinth, where there were sacred prostitutes to represent her cult. She was often worshipped by sailors and seafaring people and this, again, suggest Near Eastern (possibly Phoenician) origins. As a force of nature, it could be dangerous to deny her, as Euripides pointed out in *Hippolytus*.

See also Adonis, Anchises, Ares, Hephaestus, Hermaphroditus, *Hippolytus* (Euripides), Priapus, Uranus.

Apollo 1. The Greek god of medicine, music and prophecy. He was also the divine archer, associated with the care of herds and flocks *(Nomios),* and with light *(Phoebus,* the bright) though not as sometimes believed, with the sun. He was the ever-youthful god, just and wise, and his counterpart can be found in the mythologies of Egypt and India in the figures of Horus and Rama. But he is for many the essentially *Greek* god, though in fact he was a late arrival among the Olympians.

His character as a pastoral god suggests that his true origins lay with the people who moved down into Greece during the Indo-European migrations: certainly his function as the god of the oracular shrine at Delphi was acknowledged by the Greeks as the result of a series of events and not as something which had always existed.

Apollo himself represented a level of moral excellence and his cult at Delphi had enormous influence; it became the most venerated shrine in Greece and the Delphic oracle the supreme authority on matters of religion and statecraft. From its influence there arose an extension of tolerance: the discouraging of vengeance and blood feud, and the recognition that crime must be expiated, no matter what the power or stature of the guilty person.

That is the character of the later Apollo; the myths surrounding him show that the original god may well have been one to fear, as Marsyas and Midas were to discover.

The story of his birth, in Hesiod, makes him the son of Zeus and Leto, daughter of the Titans Phoebe and Coeus. Leto became, inevitably, the victim of Hera's spite, and no country would give Leto sanctuary to bear her children in case they incurred the wrath of the jealous goddess. Leto's wanderings took her to the floating islands of Ortygia and Delos, which only became firmly fixed after her children were born. Artemis was the first, on Ortygia, and soon after she was born she was able to help her mother across to Delos where Apollo was born, on the northern slopes of the hill of Cynthus.

A favoured child from the moment of his birth, Apollo was fed on nectar and ambrosia by Themis, and this divine food brought him to manhood in the short time of four days. Then Hephaestus made arms for him, and Apollo was ready to assume his godhead.

First he went in search of the serpent, Python, whom Hera had created and sent to torment Leto during her wanderings. He found him on Mount Parnassus on the mainland of Greece, but Python evaded Apollo's arrows and fled for sanctuary to the oracular shrine of Mother Earth at Delphi. Apollo tracked him down and killed him by the cleft in the earth from where the oracle spoke.

In his haste Apollo had defiled a sacred place, and for this Earth demanded atonement. Zeus sent his son to the Vale of Tempe in Thessaly to undergo ritual purification (in some versions Apollo's servitude to King Admetus is part of his penance), and instituted the Pythian Games to commemorate Python – or Apollo's victory over him (the myth is ambiguous). After his purification Apollo returned to Delphi, and took the shrine for himself. The priestess through whom the oracle spole became his servant.

Apollo's role as a god of prophecy is very ancient and it is not known when the oracle actually became his. The persistent indications that he came into Greece with the migratory peoples are reinforced, in addition to the names already mentioned, by the epithet *Lykeios,* and by his connection with the Hyperboreans. Lykeios (wolfish) might be explained as an aspect of him that herdsmen feared and ritually placated – the god who protected them from wolves could, if offended, deny them his protection or even, in anger, give tangible form to what they feared.

The Hyperboreans were a people of the far north, beyond the borders of Greece, who worshipped Apollo and sent ears of wheat as an offering to him at Delos each year. Max Cary suggests that these were the 'first fruits' from a Greek colony somewhere on the lower Danube. Herodotus places them *beyond* the Issedones, 'whose land was north-east of the Scythians'; he says also that the land of the Hyperboreans reached the sea (Book IV). In modern geographical terms, this would place them in the centre of the Eurasian plain – plausible enough, in terms of the migrations. Herodotus does not, and probably could not, identify the sea in question, so we are left with a field of speculation which, if enough facts were found, would give way to some fascinating knowledge about the true origin of this most 'Greek' of Greek gods.

Apollo had many lovers, the most important of them Coronis, the princess who bore him Asclepius, the god of healing. His loves are described at greater length in further references.

See also Aristaeus, Asclepius, Cassandra, Daphne, Delos, Delphi, Hyacinthus, Idas, Marsyas, Midas, Migrations, Themis, Tityus.

Apollo 2. In Roman mythology, he was first a god of healing. He reached Rome from the Greek settlements in Italy and by way of the Etruscans; Roman dealings with Greece quickened his acceptance and he was soon acknowledged by the Romans as some god of prophecy also, and the Sibyl of Cumae became his priestess *(Aeneid, Book VI)*. A temple to him was built in Rome after the plague of 433 BC, and he was especially honoured by the Emperor Augustus, who built a magnificent temple to him on the Palatine Hill after the Battle of Actium.

Apollo was the only god common to Greece and Rome. The Romans had no deity as attractive and inspiring, and therefore none to relate him to, so they also kept his name.

See also Sibyl.

Apollonius Rhodius The author of The *Argonautica,* the Greek epic based on the stories of Jason and the voyage of the Argo. He was a native of Alexandria and lived from 295–215 BC. He was called 'Rhodius' because he spent his retirement on the island of Rhodes.

Arachne A story told by Ovid in his *Metamorphoses* which seems to stem from a Greek original. Arachne, the daughter of Idmon of Colophon in Lydia, has no equal as a weaver. People say that she must have been taught by Pallas (Athene) herself, but Arachne denies this, and declares that Pallas can come and compete with her, if she wants. If the goddess should prove the better, Arachne declares, she is prepared to suffer any penalty.

An old woman visits her, and advises her to reconsider her words – there is still time to avert the goddess's wrath. Arachne rudely tells her that she has lived too long, and that she should go and advise her daughters – if she has any. For that matter, the goddess is plainly avoiding her challenge; where is Pallas? The old woman stands up, her guise of decrepit old age vanishes, and she is revealed as Pallas herself.

The contest follows, and Arachne's work is flawless, but she has chosen as her theme the amours of the gods, and the squalid tricks they resorted to when they wanted their way. Pallas is furious at Arachne's mockery: she tears the work to pieces and destroys the loom. Arachne, in despair, tries to hang herself but Pallas' revenge is not quite complete; she turns Arachne into a spider, so that she will spin and weave for ever.

Ares The son of Zeus and Hera. Though numbered among the Olympians he was a god for whom the Greeks seem to have had little liking. He was the warlike spirit deified, rather than a war god such as Mars was for the Romans; Ares was usually named as the god worshipped by other people, such as the Amazons, and held in favour by foreign races, such as the Trojans.

In the *Iliad* (Book XIII) one of Ares' sons, Ascalaphus, as violent a character as his father, is killed by Deiphobus (son of Priam) by accident. When Hera tells Ares, with some malice, of his son's death, he is ready to destroy the Achaean fleet. He is prevented by Athene, who warns him of the consequences of their father's wrath. Homer actually has Zeus declare that he hates his son *(Iliad,* Book V) for his perpetual violence and aggression. In the same part of the story Ares fights on the side of the Trojans and helps Hector to inflict heavy losses on the enemy, but is bested by Athene, who wounds him severely. Ares is forced to leave the field, his bellows of pain and rage striking terror into the hearts of soldiers on both sides.

Plainly Homer disliked Ares. In the *Odyssey* he tells the story of Ares and Aphrodite caught and humiliated by the net of Hephaestus with great gusto, and his dislike of the warlike spirit was shared by most Greeks. He was, however, honoured in Thebes as the father of Harmonia, who became the wife of Cadmus, the city's founder.

Ares' most interesting part in mythology, apart from his lusty encounters with Aphrodite, is his appearance among his fellow gods in a matter of justice – the first trial for murder. Ares was the father of Alcippe, who was raped by Halirrhothius, Poseidon's son. Ares killed Halirrhothius, and was called to account at the insistence of Poseidon. Ares was heard and, supported by his daughter's testimony, was acquitted. The proceedings took place on a hill in Athens which became known as the Areopagus, the hill of Ares. In historical times the Areopagus had particular importance as the place where trials for murder took place.

See also Aphrodite, Otus and Ephialtes.

Arethusa A beautiful nymph, one of the Hesperides. She went to bathe in the river Alpheus, whereupon the river god fell in love with her. She fled from him and sought sanctuary from the goddess Artemis on the island of Ortygia. Artemis transformed her into a fountain and Alpheus, not to be denied his beautiful nymph, directed his course under the sea. In this way he was able to surface on Ortygia, his waters joined to those of the fountain of Arethusa.

See also Alpheus, Hesperides.

Argonautica An epic in four books by Apollonius Rhodius, the best known version of the adventures of Jason and the Argonauts. The story was old long before Apollonius, and there were many variants and peripheral incidents of which the poets made good use. It was known to Homer, who mentions Jason and the Argo in the *Odyssey* (Book XII), to Hesiod and Pindar; to Aeschylus (the plays in which he uses ths stories no longer exist) and Euripides, whose *Medea* is one of the most famous plays in history. The theme was also used by writers who came after Apollonius.

Like many writers of his time Apollonius presumed that his audience knew much of what happened both before his story opened and after it ended: rightly, since this was an oft-told tale and the Greeks loved the story-tellers. The *Argonautica* might be called a novel based on a familiar theme. A summary is given below, and the list of entries following it will show the reader where to turn for the opening or further adventures of some of the principal characters.

BOOK I The Argonauts gather at Pagasae in Iolcos, to accompany Jason on the voyage to Colchis in quest of the Golden Fleece – the fleece of the golden-winged ram on which Phryxus escaped from death as a sacrificial victim. The fleece hangs in the temple of Ares in Colchis, guarded by a dragon. Among the Argonauts are Orpheus, Heracles, Admetus, Mopsus the seer, Telamon and Peleus, Hylas, Nauplius, Polydeuces and Castor, Idas and his brother Lynceus of the keen sight, Meleager, Zetes and Calais (wing-footed sons of the North Wind)

Acastus (Jason's half-brother) and Argos, who built the ship *Argo* to the instructions of Athene.

The ship carries an oracular beam in her stem, from Zeus' oak at Dodona, placed there at Athene's order, which gives the *Argo* the power of speech. The people gather to see the ship launched, and the women voice their sympathy for Aeson and Alcimede, Jason's parents. Aeson has been King in Iolcos but his half-brother Pelias had usurped the throne and killed any children who might prove a threat to him: but Alcimede had managed to save her son's life and get the child out of the kingdom. Many years later, an oracle warns King Pelias that the deeds of a man with one bare foot would bring about his death, and at a feast to honour the gods, such a man appears. He is Jason: he had lost a sandal while crossing the river Anaurus. He wants his throne – but agrees to go to Colchis for the Golden Fleece first.

Pelias hopes that Jason will be killed on the expedition. But Jason, who is already befriended by Athene, now has another Olympian on his side – the goddess Hera, whom Pelias has stupidly not included in the honours at his feast.

The *Argo* is sucessfully launched and sacrifice is made to Apollo. Heracles modestly yields his place as leader to Jason, and the Argonauts enjoy a farewell feast. At dawn the oracular beam wakes them and they take their places at the oars: to the music of Orpheus they row for the open sea. They hoist sail, and a steady breeze carries them to the island of Lemnos.

Lemnos, a rich island and a favourite of the god Hephaestus, is populated entirely by women, who the year before had murdered every man on the island. They had aroused the wrath of Aphrodite by neglecting to honour her; in revenge she had made them undesirable to their husbands and lovers. The men of Lemnos found their Thracian slave girls more attractive and made love to them instead, and the Lemnian women, after their rage had smouldered for a while, fell on both men and slave girls and slaughtered them. Only one man, King Thoas, had escaped. His daughter Hypsipyle had put him in a boat to drift away over the sea. He reached land alive at the island of Oenoe.

The Lemnian women live in fear of being invaded from Thrace, and when they see the *Argo* they swarm down to the beach carrying the arms left by their men. A herald from Jason reassures them, and Hypsipyle's old nurse, Polyxo, advises the women to make the Argonauts welcome. The island, she points out, is vulnerable, and what if the men of the *Argo* had proved to be the savage Thracians? They had made a brave show – but how long would any army of women last? They needed children, and here was a shipload of men. Make them welcome: they might even stay. Hypsipyle follows this advice, and Jason is made welcome at the palace by the King's daughter. He knows nothing of what has happened, and Hypsipyle's story that the men had become besotted with their Thracian captives and let the island go to ruin – and were turned out by the women – is easily believed.

Heracles and a few others stay on the ship but the rest of the Argonauts enjoy a wild time on Lemnos, an island full of man-hungry women. It is Heracles who calls Jason and the Argonauts to order, and eventually the *Argo* sails away.

Their next call is at Samothrace, where Orpheus is anxious that they land and learn something of the rites of the Cabeiri, the servants of Persephone, who protect sailors from danger at sea. This done, they sail on with more confidence, navigate the Hellespont sucessfully and enter the Propontis (the Sea of Marmara), where they make landfall at the country of the Doliones. The King, Cyzicus, makes them welcome and invites them to take the ship into the harbour of Chytus. Cyzicus is a young man and just married, and is worried by an oracle which has warned him never to raise arms against noble mariners who call at his country. A man of peace, he wonders what the oracle can mean. Now he feasts with Jason and tells him all he can about the Propontis and the surrounding country. Of the land which lies beyond, to the east, he knows nothing.

The next day some of the Argonauts climb to the high ground to survey the sea to the east, while others take the ship into the harbour of Chytus. There they are attacked by six-armed monsters from the mountains, who try to block the mouth of the harbour with boulders to trap them. Heracles and those on board make short work of them, and the rest of the Argonauts hurry to help them. The monsters are driven off and the *Argo* is able to sail again. But the wind freshens and veers against them, so they are glad to find shelter back in the country of the Doliones that night. King Cyzicus is alarmed at the arrival of what he thinks is a strange ship – only a raider would land at night. He and his men attack, and the King is killed in the fight. The oracle is fulfilled.

The Argonauts stay and mourn the dead King and his men for twelve days and wait for a favourable wind. Then Mopsus sees a kingfisher fly around the ship; it hovers over Jason's head, and then flies to the prow where it alights. Mopsus moves nearer to listen to its twittering, and when it flies away he knows what the Argonauts must do. He wakes Jason and tells him they must sacrifice to the goddess Rhea, mother of Zeus, and mistress of the earth, winds and sea. They row the *Argo* back to Thrace, where there is a sanctuary of Rhea on Mount Dindymum. On the way up the mountain, Argos comes across an ancient withered vine, which he carves into an image of the goddess.

The sacrifice is offered, and the image is placed in the sanctuary. Rhea signifies her pleasure by making a spring of fresh water flow from the mountain. It is the only one on Mount Dindymum, and is called Jason's spring. The Argonauts return to the ship and find the contrary wind has now dropped. They take the oars and go on their way. During the day Heracles' oar breaks in his hands from the mighty strain he puts on it, and when the *Argo* pulls in near the mouth of the Rhyndacus in the evening he goes ashore to find a suitable tree to tear up and make into a new oar. His squire, Hylas, goes to look for a spring of fresh water.

Heracles finds a suitable pine tree, and Hylas finds a fresh water spring, in the woods of Pegae. The naiad of the spring sees Hylas approach and finds him beautiful, and when he bends down to draw some water she puts her arms round his neck and pulls him down into the water to keep him for herself.

The next morning brings a breeze and Tiphys, the helmsman, urges the Argonauts to waste no time taking advantage of it. The sail fills and soon they are far out to sea, and it is after dawn before they discover that they have sailed without Heracles and Hylas. A quarrel breaks out when Telamon accuses Jason and Tiphys of deliberately leaving without them through jealousy of Heracles' fame. Glaucus, spokesman of the sea god, rises from the waters and tells them what has happened. Heracles will search for Hylas and forget the *Argo*. The Argonauts must go on.

BOOK II The *Argo* reaches the country of the Bebryces in Bithynia, where Polydeuces fights and kills the bullying King, Amycus. The Bebryces attack, but the Argonauts win a pitched battle and are left in peace when their enemies break and flee. The Argonauts help themselves to anything useful, and after feasting listen to Orpheus' song in praise of Polydeuces. The next day they enter the Bosporus and Tiphy's skill as a helmsman brings them through safely.

Their next stop is the country of blind Phineus, the King of the land on the western shore of the Bosporus. Phineus is a prophet and many people come to consult the oracle of Apollo in his city. Phineus has been careless with Apollo's gift of prophecy and told too many of the god's secrets he learned through it: Zeus struck him blind as a punishment and also sent two Harpies to plague him. They are the swift-winged daughters of Thaumas. Whenever Phineus sits down at table they swoop down and snatch the food from his hand, and foul the dishes as well. He is very weak and ill and tells the Argonauts that his case is hopeless – he has consulted his own oracle and learned that help will only come from the children of the north wind. He is overjoyed when Calais and Zetes make themselves known. They drive away the Harpies and the Argonauts look after Phineus, who is near to death from privation.

Phineus tells them what to expect on their further journey. They will come to the Symplegades (the Clashing Rocks) and they must send a dove to fly through as the rocks crash together. As the rocks separate again they must row like madmen to get through before they crash together again. This they do, and the dove only loses its tail feathers: the Argonauts, in spite of great work by the skilful Tiphys, nearly fall victims to the rocks because the sea runs against them when the rocks separate. Athene has been watching: she uses her divine power to drive the *Argo* through, and then fixes the rocks apart forever. They are in the Black Sea.

Following the route described by Phineus, the exhausted Argonauts reach the island of Thynias. Here they see a vision of Apollo, travelling north to the Hyperboreans. They build a temple to Apollo of the Dawn, and Orpheus sings a hymn in his honour. They sail on, encouraged by Phineus' declaration that the Symplegades was the hazard they would most have to fear. They reach the land of the Mariandyni where King Lycus welcomes them as his deliverer from the brutal Amycus, who was always raiding his lands. But their pleasure in his welcome is marred when one of their number is killed by a boar: worse is the death of Tiphys, the matchless helmsman, who succumbs to a short and severe sickness. Ancaeus, a son of Poseidon, becomes helmsman in his stead, and the Argonauts sail on to Sinope, where they collect three recruits, the sons of Deimachus. These had accompanied Heracles during his adventure against the Amazons, and unaccountably got left behind.

Farther on, they reach the Isle of Ares, where the birds of the war god have brazen feathers. They loose these on the *Argo* as the ship approaches and the first missile to fall wounds one of the Argonauts on the shoulder. The Argonauts shelter under their shields and helmets, and when they reach the shore they make a deafening noise by well-timed shouting and banging on their shields. The noise is something the birds have never heard before and they fly off in panic.

The Argonauts make camp on the island and are just in time to escape a violent storm. While it rages four shipwrecked men, clinging to a beam, are blown ashore near the camp. Jason and the others give them food and clothing, and find out that they are none other than the sons of Phryxus, the children of his marriage to Chalciope, daughter of the King of Colchis. They are Argos, Phrontis, Melas and Cytissorus: as Phryxus is dead, they are returning to Orchomenus, their father's home. They feel uneasy about the coming encounter with the formidable King of Colchis, but they decide to join the Argonauts.

Two nights later the Argonauts reach Colchis. They stow the sail and row up the river Phasis: on their right they see the plain and grove sacred to Ares, on their left the city of Aea and the mountains of Caucasus. On the advice of Argos, Jason has the ship rowed into the reed-filled marshes and anchored there.

BOOK III Athene and Hera have been watching the progress of the expedition, and they debate how best Jason can carry out his plan to steal the Golden Fleece from King Aeëtes. They consult Aphrodite, who sends Eros to awaken love in the heart of Medea, the King's daughter; they know that Medea is a witch – and this is the only way to weaken her.

Jason, meanwhile, has decided to approach Aeëtes and simply *ask* for the Fleece to be returned. He takes with him the four sons of Phryxus, and Telamon and Augeias. They approach the gleaming palace: Aeëtes is the son of Helios, and Hephaestus built the palace as a favour to Helios. They are received by Aeëtes, his Queen Eidyia, his son Absyrtus (by his wife Asterodeia), and Chalciope, his daughter. Chalciope hurries to her sons, overcome with joy at seeing them returned, and then Medea, Aeëtes' younger daughter, joins the royal party. She sees Jason and Eros does his work.

Argos, son of Phryxus, has been chosen as spokesman. He tells Aeëtes why Jason has come and what he seeks. The expedition was commanded by an oracle, and in return for the Fleece Jason will add the lands of the savage Sauromatians to Aeëtes' kingdom. The King listens to Argos and then erupts in rage: he insults them and their ancestors and reviles them for abusing his hospitality. He believes that what they really want is his kingdom. Jason assures him that this is not so – has he not promised to extend it? Aeëtes decides to test the claims made for Jason by his comrades in another way.

On the plain of Ares, he explains, he keeps two monstrous bulls, brazen-hoofed and fire-breathing. Jason must yoke them to a plough in the morning. Then he must sow the dragon's teeth, which will rise as armed men. These he must kill. The task must be done before night falls. If Jason refuses the challenge, Aeëtes makes it plain that the Argonauts' fate will be made an example to deter anyone else from coming to Colchis and making rude demands of its King. Jason has no choice but to accept the challenge. Medea retires, her heart aching for Jason and what may happen to him.

Jason returns to the *Argo* and tells his men what must be. Argos, son of Phryxus, tells them that his aunt, Medea, is a priestess of Hecate and can – if she will – help them. Rather than seem to be hiding, the Argonauts move the ship from the reeds and haul it on to the shore for all to see. Argos hurries back to the palace where Medea, in a dream, learns that her father has no intention of keeping his word.

Argos goes to his mother Chalciope who, in fear for the lives of her sons, agrees to approach Medea. She finds her half-sister willing to help Jason: Medea has endured a night of torment – she knows that to help Jason will extend the bloodshed she fears is coming, but she also knows that she cannot help herself. The alternative is suicide, and the watchful Hera drives that thought out of her mind.

Medea goes to the shrine of Hecate escorted by her twelve attendants. Jason goes from *Argo* accompanied by Mopsus, and by Argos to show him where to find the shrine. They wait for him at the edge of the plain, and he goes to meet Medea, who has dismissed her attendants. Medea gives him a salve which he must wear for his encounter with the fire-breathing bulls, and instructions for the sacrifice he must make that very night to the goddess Hecate. She asks that he remember her when he goes from Colchis. He replies that she would never be forgotten – indeed, if she left Colchis with the Argonauts she would be the most honoured woman in Hellas, and Jason's wife. Medea has what she wanted.

The next day Jason sows the dragon's teeth, and with the help from Medea carries out the challenge of King Aeëtes. The King watches, his bitterness growing. He turns from the field, determined to destroy Jason and the Argonauts that night.

BOOK IV Medea knows that for her there is no turning back. She slips out of the palace as soon as darkness falls and hurries down to the ship. She tells Jason that her father has discovered every thing – if Jason will keep his promise she will gain the Fleece for him at once. Jason swears that he is bound to her by love. She takes him to the grove of Ares, where the serpent guards the Golden Fleece.

At the great oak in the grove there is an altar, and the Fleece hangs above it. But at the approach of Jason and Medea the great serpent comes forward on gigantic coils, threatening the intruders: Medea invokes the god of sleep and the wandering moon and soon it is asleep and harmless. She calls to Jason to seize the Fleece while she puts a magic salve on the serpent's head to stop it awakening. Then they make for the *Argo* as fast as the weight of the Fleece will allow them.

The triumphant Argonauts set sail, armed and ready for trouble they know will come from Aeëtes and the Colchians. Hera gives them a fair wind and the *Argo* speeds down the Phasis, Jason near the helmsman and Medea at his side.

Medea has been missed from the palace. Aeëtes summons his army, and, with Absyrtus as his charioteer, drives down to the river bank in an attempt to cut off the ship. By then the *Argo* is already sailing out to sea. Aeëtes orders every ship and boat in Colchis to pursue the Argonauts: he will have revenge on his treacherous daughter somehow.

Following the instructions of Phineus, the Argonauts seek another route home. Argos explains what Phineus meant: they must seek the mouth of the Ister (the river Danube) and sail up it. Tributary rivers will take them to the Ionian Sea and they can sail home to Iolcos around Hellas. They make the mouth of the Ister only to find that Absyrtus, Medea's half-brother, has reached it before them – the Colchians first thought had been to block all the ways out of the Black Sea, and Absyrtus had made straight for the Ister.

The Argonauts and Colchians try to parley. Absyrtus agrees that Jason has earned the Fleece by fulfilling the task set by Aeëtes. But Medea must be handed over. The Argonauts return that a fair judgment must be made by a third party: they will escort Medea to the Sanctuary of Artemis where she will remain in safety until this can be arranged. The truce is a breathing space for the Argonauts, who are hopelessly outnumbered by the Colchians: but Medea turns on Jason in a fury and threatens to set fire to the ship if he goes on with the plan. She tells him that for her there is no going back and Jason can plan nothing that does not take her into account. She will dispose of her half-brother herself; then the Argonauts can defeat the leaderless Colchians. Jason agrees, appalled by her outburst: he is beginning to fear her.

Medea arranges a trap, which Absyrtus walks into so that Jason can murder him. Like all murderers, Jason licks up the blood of Absyrtus three times, and three times spits it out, and cuts off the victim's limbs in the hope that his guilt can be set aside. The Argonauts break the truce and in a surprise attack slaughter the Colchian guard of Absyrtus. The Argonauts set their course up the river Ister and the goddess Hera lets a thunderstorm loose on the rest of the Colchian fleet. The Argonauts are no longer pursued.

When they regain the sea the Argonauts are struck with terror when the oracular beam of the *Argo* speaks. The blood of Absyrtus stains the hands of Jason and Medea, it tells them. If they are not purged of that guilt they, and the rest of the Argonauts, will never set foot in Hellas again. Castor and Polydeuces pray to the Olympians, who send the *Argo* scurrying before a fierce wind to the mouth of the river Eridanus (Po). From there they reach the Rhône, and then they sail back to the sea to the haven of Aeaea on the west coast of Italy, where Circe, sister of Aeëtes and sorceress aunt of Medea, has made her home. Circe purges them of the blood guilt, but refuses them hospitality and any further help. They return to the ship, and the Argonauts set sail once more, heavy-hearted at the thought that they must now face the dangers of the Sirens, and of Scylla and Charybdis. The Sirens are strange creatures, half birds, half women: Orpheus saves the Argonauts from their fatal enchantments by singing a sweeter song than theirs, and Hera gives her help when they reach Scylla and Charybdis. Scylla is a monster living in a sea cave, opposite the whirlpool of Charybdis. When sailors try to avoid the whirlpool they expose themselves to the monster, who devours them. Hera sends Thetis and the Nereids to guide the *Argo* through safely.

Across the Ionian Sea the Argonauts reach the island of Drepane (Corfu), and are given a good welcome by the King, Alcinous. But their pleasure comes to an abrupt end when a large force of Colchians reach the island also – the Colchians knew that the *Argo's* route would take them back to Hellas from this direction. They want Medea, and threaten to destroy the island if she is not handed over. Alcinous manages to keep the peace for the time being and Medea takes care to remind the Argonauts how much they owe to her. Then she appeals to Arete, Alcinous' Queen. Arete prevails upon her husband far enough to make him agree to hand over Medea only if Jason has not first claim on her as her husband.

While Alcinous sleeps Arete hurries out of the palace and goes to the Argonauts' camp. She warns Jason and Medea to be married at once – if they are not married already. They do marry, though they had wanted to celebrate the event in Jason's home at Iolcos. The Argonauts stay on guard, not sure how the Colchians will react when Alcinous tells them that Medea will not be handed over. After some threatening noises the Colchians accept the decision – but they plead with Alcinous to let them stay in his kingdom. They know their lives are forfeit if they return to King Aeëtes without his daughter. Alcinous agrees, and the Argonauts set sail once more.

Trouble overtakes them again. Just as they hope to turn east at the Peloponnese a northerly gale blows them off course. It lasts for nine days and the *Argo* is blown as far as Libya into the Gulf of Syrtis (Sydra). They are blown far up on a barren desert and the sea recedes, leaving them stranded and without hope. They lose several men, including Mopsus the seer, but they are saved from death by the nymphs of the Libyan shore and by the Hesperides, who tell them how Heracles stole the golden apples. The Argonauts eat and drink and, sad at the loss of so many of their friends, mount the *Argo* on rollers and push her back into the sea.

Not certain where they are, Orpheus reminds Jason of the tripod from Delphi which is his prized possession and a gift from Apollo. They return to the shore and set up the tripod, and at once, Triton, the son of Poseidon and Amphitrite, appears. He shows them their course, and accepts the gift of the tripod. Jason gratefully offers a sheep as a sacrifice to him, and as a further gesture Triton tows the *Argo* into the open sea. Jason sets his course for Crete, where there is another menace to overcome. This time Medea demonstrates her powers.

Crete is guarded by Talos, a bronze giant created by Hephaestus. His life depends on a single vein, which is sealed by a membrane in his ankle. Medea hypnotises him, and he staggers even while he reaches for huge rocks to throw down on the ship. Not in control of himself, he grazes his ankle and ruptures the membrane that holds his life's blood. It flows away and he falls dead on the shore.

That is the last of their troubles. Apollo gives them light to find their way at night through the islands of the Aegean, and Jason and the Argonauts bring their marvellous ship *Argo* and the Golden Fleece home to Hellas. Jason has also brought Medea, the royal sorceress from Colchis, to Hellas as his wife. But that is another story.

See also Admetus, Athamas, The Dioscuri, Idas, Ino, Lynceus, Medea, *Medea* (Euripides), Meleager, Mopsus, Peleus, Pelias, Phryxus.

Argos 1. A city in the Peloponnese, about three miles from the sea at the Gulf of Argos. It was settled as early as the beginning of the Bronze Age and became the centre of a Mycenaean empire. The city then fell to the Heraclids, Dorian Greeks who raised it to even greater eminence as the most powerful city in Greece. After the seventh century BC the power of Argos was successfully challenged by Sparta. The territory of Argos, in classical times, included Nauplia, Tiryns and Mycenae. The name Argos means 'the plain' and describes the area in which the city stood.

In mythology Argos was the realm of Agamemnon and the city was the setting for Aeschylus' tragedy of that name. From pre-Hellenic times the principal deity was Hera (often called Argive Hera). Her shrine was the Heraeum, which lay six miles north of the city.

Argos 2. A name which turns up frequently in Greek mythology – there are two characters of that name in the *Argonautica* alone – but probably best known as the one commanded by Hera to watch the priestess Io when Zeus fell in love with her. This was Argos of the Hundred Eyes. Hermes killed him at the order of Zeus, and a later tradition says that Hera put his hundred eyes into the peacock's tail as a perpetual reminder of his murder.

See also Io.

Ariadne The heroine of Theseus' adventure in Crete, when he succeeded in killing the Minotaur. She was the daughter of King Minos
and Pasiphae, and fell in love with Theseus. She gave him the ball of
thread that enabled him to find his way out of the Labyrinth, and fled
with him and the other Athenians. Theseus abandoned her on the island
of Dia (Naxos), where they landed during the journey home. One
version of the story says that the god Dionysus found her there and
fell in love with her: another that Theseus left the island, and Ariadne,
at the god's command because he wanted her for himself. These are,
however, attempts to explain the inexplicable – a hero could never
behave so shabbily. Scholars now believe that some part of the original
myth has been lost.

A believable interpretation is offered by Mary Renault in her remarkable novel, *The King Must Die*. Miss Renault's Ariadne is, cor-
rectly, a priestess – being a princess – and the events on Naxos follow
inevitably upon this.

See also Minos, Theseus.

Arion The swiftest of all horses, he was born of the union of Demeter
(as a mare) and Poseidon (as a stallion). He turns up in the myths of
Poseidon, Heracles and Adrastus.

Aristaeus The son of Apollo by Cyrene, daughter of King Hypseus
of the Lapiths. Apollo carried Cyrene off to Libya, where Hermes
attended the birth of her son. The nymphs of Hermes taught Aristaeus
the arts of bee-keeping and cheese-making and the cultivation of olives.
As a man he went to Boeotia where the Muses, at Apollo's bidding,
taught him healing, hunting and the care of herds and flocks.

He was guilty of trying to force his attentions on the Dryad, Eurydice, who trod on a poisonous snake while running away from him.
Virgil, the Latin poet, extends the story by telling how, in revenge,
the Dryads destroyed the bees. Aristaeus was advised by his mother
Cyrene to propitiate the Dryads with sacrifices of cattle – but to leave
the carcasses on the ground. After nine days he was to return. When
he did he found swarms of bees in the rotting carcasses.

Aristaeus was honoured as a god in many parts of ancient Greece,
in return for having passed his knowledge on to man.

See also Orpheus.

Artemis The daughter of Zeus and Leto and the twin sister of Apollo. (For the mythology of her birth see the entry for Apollo.) In Homer she is Mistress of Beasts, Lady of all Wild Things, and a Lion unto Women – one of her titles is Eileithyia 'who is come to aid women in childbirth'. All these descriptions combine with her function in the care of small children, and seem to look back to origins in the very old, pre-Hellenic times, when the great fertility goddess of the eastern Mediterranean would have been a single deity, overseeing all the functions of fertility and motherhood which were divided among the Olympian goddesses of later times.

In keeping with the character of the Great Mother, from whom she undoubtedly derived, was the worship accorded Artemis in Ionia. Her cult centre was at the great seaport of Ephesus, where her temple was of such magnificence as to become known as one of the wonders of the world. There she was the 'giver of fertility' and the multibreasted image of Artemis of Ephesus looks very different from the more familiar one of her as a chaste huntress. Phocaean Greeks took the cult to the west and established it at Massilia (Marseilles). From there it found its way to Rome, where it soon absorbed the cult of Diana.

From her ancient lineage Artemis kept a strange cult which had its centre in Brauron in Attica, where her votaries dressed as bears (in the story of Callisto there is a strange echo of the bear connection). There was a precinct sacred to Artemis Brauronia on the Acropolis. She was not, in Greek mythology, a goddess of the moon.

Nevertheless, Artemis was a firm favourite with women, particularly with the ordinary wives and mothers who honoured her in her original form.

See also Actaeon, Callisto, Diana, Eileithyia, Hippolytus, Orion.

Asclepius According to Hesiod, the son of Apollo: but in Homer a mortal who was instructed in the art of healing by the wise centaur, Chiron. Generally Asclepius is the Greek god of healing and medicine, having inherited this gift from Apollo.

The myth of his birth makes his mother the Princess Coronis, daughter of Phlegyas, King of the Lapiths. Apollo saw her bathing her feet at the edge of a lake and fell in love with her. She was quite willing to have him – until she got the man she really wanted, Ischys the Arcadian. When Apollo returned to Delphi he left a white bird, a crow to watch over her. Coronis was successful in her pursuit of Ischys, and when the crow saw them making love he sped off to Delphi to tell Apollo. Coronis was already pregnant by this time, and even before the crow arrived in Delphi, Apollo knew that she was carrying his child. He turned the crow black for failing to attack his rival.

Artemis, meanwhile, outraged on her brother's behalf, killed Coronis with her arrows. But Apollo wanted his child, and sent Hermes to snatch the unborn baby from Coronis' funeral pyre. The people of Epidaurus claimed that their city was the scene of the birth of Asclepius.

In the *Iliad,* Books II and IV, Asclepius is referred to as the father of the physicians Podaleirus and Machaon, who use his gifts – and Chiron's – in their care of the wounded Achaeans. Also in the *Iliad* is the mention of Tricca, in Thessaly, as the sons' home, and it is possible that the cult of Asclepius originated there. L.R. Farnell suggests that he was originally a hero, who was elevated to godlike status.

In mainland Greece itself – there were great cult centres at Pergamum and Cos – the centre of his cult was at Epidaurus. Patients could sleep in the sanctuary of Asclepius and this in itself was often sufficient to effect a cure. Snakes, the symbols of renewal, were his emblem and roamed freely, unmolested, in the precinct. (They were quite harmless and the ones that can occasionally be seen there today, small, yellow-ochre coloured, are probably the same ones described by Pausanias.) When a new shrine was dedicated to Asclepius elsewhere, a young snake was taken there from Epidaurus.

See also Aesculapius for the god's Roman form.

Atalanta In Greek mythology the daughter of Iasus, King of Arcadia. She was a chaste huntress – one authority sees her as a version of Artemis – whom her father, hoping for a son, left to die on Mount Parthenion. She was suckled by a she-bear sent by Artemis, and cared for by a band of hunters who found her. She joined the band of hunters from all over Greece who gathered to kill the Calydonian boar; the presence of a woman was objected to by some, but Meleager, the leader, fell in love with her and insisted on her inclusion. She was the first to wound the boar and was present at the kill: Meleager, infatuated, gave her the pelt.

Her fame, after this exploit, led her father to recognise his daughter, but Atalanta was displeased by his insistence that, as a princess, she must marry. She set an inflexible condition: anyone who sought her hand must enter a foot race against her; if he lost, his life would be forfeit. So she stayed single, as might have been expected, until Melanion, an Arcadian prince, fell in love with her, and went to the goddess of love, Aphrodite, to plead for help. Aphrodite gave him three golden apples, and during the race, at careful intervals, Melanion threw them in the path of Atalanta. She was unable to resist picking them up, and Melanion won the foot race and the prize.

See also Meleager.

Ate A definition rather than a deity, Ate in Greek myth is the personification of moral blindness in which the sense of natural values is destroyed. It can happen in love or war, through physical passion or envy – any emotion strong enough invokes Ate. In Homer she is the daughter of Zeus, blamed by Agamemnon for provoking the conduct which led to his fateful quarrel with Achilles (*Iliad*, Book XIX).

Athamas One of the sons of Aeolus, and King of Orchomenos, Athamas stands at the beginning of the cycle of myths that became the quest for the Golden Fleece. He married Nephele, the woman created by Zeus in the shape of Hera to trick the lustful Ixion. (Nephele's name means 'cloud', and Athamas means 'reaper'. Robert Graves' speculation on the sky god, Zeus, and a rain goddess, Nephele, combined with a reaper king, Athamas, gives a fascinating glimpse of the ancient past where myth originates.)

Phryxus and Helle were the children of Athamas and Nephele. Athamas fell in love with Ino, daughter of Cadmus, and made her his second wife. Ino hated her stepchildren and was determined to remove Phryxus, the firstborn of Athamas. She persuaded the women of Boeotia (both Thebes and Orchomenos were cities of Boeotia) to roast the seed corn; then, when the harvest failed, prevailed upon Athamas to consult the oracle at Delphi. When his emissaries returned, the King heard the dreadful news that he was required to sacrifice his children by Nephele to propitiate the gods. He did not know that Ino had bribed them to lie to him.

At this point Nephele appealed to Hera, who sent Hermes to her with a winged ram which had a fleece of gold. Nephele explained that the horrible sacrifice was to take place on Mount Laphystium: the golden ram arrived there as Athamas raised the knife. The creature spoke to Phryxus and Helle, commanding them to mount on his back: then it bore them away from danger, flying east to the land of Colchis.

Hera re-enters the story. Ino's children by Athamas were two sons, Learchus and Melicertes, and her sister was Semele, the mother of Dionysus. Ino and Athamas sheltered Dionysus but Zeus' jealous wife came to know; Athamas had already offended Hera by spurning her likeness, Nephele. Hera smote him with madness: he saw his son Learchus as a white stag and shot an arrow into him, then began to eat the still warm flesh. Ino fled with her other son, Melicertes, and the people of Orchomenos drove Athamas out of the kingdom.

His mind healed when he became a wandering outcast, and he went to Delphi to ask for advice. The oracle told him to settle in the place where he was nourished by wild beasts. He wandered north, into Epirus, and there disturbed some wolves feeding on a flock of sheep. The wolves ran off at his approach and he found himself with food to eat and to spare. He settled there and founded a city called Alos.

See also *Argonautica*.

Athene   The patron goddess of Athens and guardian of the city. She was the daughter of Zeus by his first wife, Metis, who personified wise counsel. Zeus was warned by Gaia (Mother Earth) that his children by Metis would surpass him in wisdom and could usurp his place as king of the gods; whereupon Zeus (himself a usurper), when he found that Metis was pregnant, swallowed her whole and absorbed all wisdom to himself. In the version told by Hesiod, Athene was simply born from Zeus himself, and she is first called *Tritogeneia* – an epithet which suggests an association with water. The myth was embroidered and from it developed the story of Zeus suffering from violent headaches that made him howl with pain and rage. Hermes found him on the banks of the Triton river and, knowing what the trouble was, summoned Hephaestus. The smith god, with a mighty blow of his hammer, cracked Zeus' head and Athene, fully armed, sprang forth with a shout that shook the heavens.

It oftens occurs in mythology that one story conveniently explains another, and it seems likely that the location of the Triton for the birth of Athene was invented to dispose of the inconvenient *Tritonegeia*. In the days of formalised religion the waters were the domain of Poseidon, who will be seen to have been Athene's rival in some respects.

Athene's cult was not confined to Athens and she was, like her Olympian sisters, a goddess of many aspects; she may have been a mariner's goddess in archaic times. As a guardian goddess, *Polias,* she has been identified with those of Crete and Mycenaean Greece and this points to her origins in the original mother goddess – it would have been many centuries before one particular aspect of a universal goddess emerged as the preference of any community, and there was civilised life in Crete 1500 years before the time usually called 'classical' in the history of Greece. What became her most famous cult centre, on the Acropolis, was built on the site of a Mycenaean palace.

Like Artemis she was a virgin goddess, hence the Parthenon – the temple of *Athene Parthenos* (Athene the Virgin); but she was also a state goddess and thus concerned with fertility in all respects since the well-being of the state depended on it. Appropriately as the goddess of busy, thriving Athens where so many skills were practised, she was the patroness of all crafts – *Ergane,* the work woman – but this, again, was not confined to Athens; the potters of Samos worshipped her as the teacher of their craft.

But she was firmly claimed by the Athenians as their very own goddess and this claim brings Athene's ancient origin to our attention again. The people of Arcadia and Attica (the region where Athens stood) claimed that they alone, of all the people of Greece, were *autochthonous,* 'of the soil', people who had always been there – never displaced by the waves of migrant peoples from the north. Athene's name is pre-Greek, and the dispute with Poseidon (who was Greek, and a later arrival) for the possession of the Acropolis was probably a memory of the collision between new people with new gods and the original people with their ancient, well-loved ones. Athene kept possession of the Acropolis by convincing the other Olympians that she could give the greater benefits to her people. Poseidon struck the rock with his trident and at once a spring began to flow: Athene planted the first olive tree beside the spring, and the gods acknowledged her claim.

Athens also acknowledged her as the ancestress of their first King, Erichthonius. Athene was wooed by Hephaestus but she did not want him: he tried to force his attentions on her but she had no trouble in repulsing him. However, he got so excited while they were struggling that he ejaculated and his seed fell on the ground: Earth nourished it and in due course a boy was born. Athene gave him to the daughters of Cecrops to bring up. He became one of the earliest Kings of Athens and instituted the cult of Athene. (Erichthonius is often confused with Erechtheus and the myths are tiresomely alike.)

Athene's association with birds is believed to stem from her Cretan associations. The owl is most familiar but she takes the form of a sea-eagle in the *Odyssey* (Book III). She was generally a formidable goddess, with a tendency to turn into one of war as in the *Iliad* and the *Heraclidae* of Euripides. She is frequently the goddess who offers particular help to heroes such as Jason, Diomedes and Odysseus.

See also Arachne, Cecrops, Erechtheus, Erichthonius, Metis, Pallas Athene.

Atlas A Titan, the son of Iapetus and Clymene. In Hesiod he is the supporter of the sky, appointed (or ordered) by Zeus. In the *Odyssey* (Book I) he supports the pillars of heaven: both functions are in any case a punishment for taking Cronus' part in the war against the Olympians. He is also the father of Calypso in the *Odyssey,* and a prominent figure in one of the Labours of Heracles.

Atreus The son of Pelops and brother of Thyestes, he was the father of Agamemnon and Menelaus. Atreus and Thyestes are the victims of the curse brought on their house by the actions of Pelops, a curse which carries its shadow on through his descendants until Orestes, his grandson, is absolved by the grace of Apollo.

See the entry for Pelops for the cycle of myths of which the story of Atreus and Thyestes is part.

Augeas The King of Elis who owned great herds of cattle – and very dirty stables which only a hero of great strength could clean.

See also Heracles, Labours of.

Aurora In Roman mythology the goddess of the dawn. For her stories, which all belong to her Greek original, see under Eos.

Autolycus The son of Hermes and Chione, daughter of the north wind. His father Hermes, cleverest of thieves, bestowed those gifts on his son and also gave him the gift of making himself and his booty invisible when necessary. The only man who outwitted him was Sisyphus. Autolycus is mentioned in the *Iliad* (Book X) as the man who stole the helmet of Eleon which Odysseus was given: Odysseus is in fact his grandson (his daughter Anticleia is Odysseus' mother). In the *Odyssey* (Book XIX) he helps to nurse his grandson when Odysseus suffers the wound in his thigh after the boar hunt.

See also Odysseus, Sisyphus.

B

Bacchae, The A tragedy by Euripides, produced after his death in 405 BC. Chronologically it is the last of the great Greek tragedies of which most of the text has survived (there are a number of lines missing near the end of the play, just before the last appearance of Dionysus).

The scene is the forecourt of the palace of King Pentheus of Thebes. On one side of the court is the tomb of Semele, overgrown with wild vines, Semele was the mother of the god Dionysus: her sister Agave is the mother of King Pentheus.

Dionysus is alone in the forecourt. He recalls that here in Thebes his mother died from a moment's glimpse of the glory of his father, Zeus. He has returned to his birthplace after wandering, in danger from the hatred of Hera, in distant countries. He speaks warmly of Cadmus, the founder of Thebes and father of Semele, for honouring his mother's tomb. But the benefits that Dionysus can bring to Hellas are scorned – here, in his own city. They even deny his godhead.

Dionysus relates how he has touched the women of Thebes with a Bacchic madness (Bacchus – *Bakchos* – is another of the god's names, meaning 'the shoot' – or tendril of the vine). They have forsaken the palace and their homes and turned to the mountain's wooded slopes, where they exist in a trance of delight which they do not question – they only know the irresistible attraction of the wild world. Pentheus hates and fears the delight of the Theban women in something he cannot understand. He will destroy the influence of this new 'god', if he can. Dionysus announces that he will appear in Thebes as a stranger: he will exact from everyone the honour due to his mother and the worship due to himself. He leaves, to join the women on Mount Kithaeron.

Reports of the stranger's activities reach Pentheus, who orders his arrest. The stranger acknowledges that he serves Dionysus: his attitude enrages the King, who orders that his long hair be shorn. The stranger warns him that his hair, thus worn, is sacred to Zeus. Pentheus scoffs at this, and the shearing proceeds. Pentheus demands the ivy-wreathed wand the stranger carries; the stranger replies that it cannot be given: Pentheus snatches it from the stranger and his offence is complete. The stranger is bound and imprisoned – then a great voice announces the coming of the god, and the stranger returns to the courtyard unharmed.

Pentheus is provoked by further news from Kithaeron and orders that the Bacchae, among whom are the Queen Mother, Agave, and her sisters Ino and Autonoë, shall be surrounded and taken. The stranger tried to dissuade him from this course – and the King insults him: Dionysus begins the punishment of the man who denied his godhead. In the god's power Pentheus, without knowing why, agrees to go along to Kithaeron, in woman's clothes. The stranger assures him that his mother Agave will bring him back to Thebes. She does: a great voice tells the Bacchae that their god's persecutor is among them. The women find Pentheus and tear him to pieces. Agave, quite mad, returns to Thebes in triumph carrying her son's head. Dionysus appears in full majesty at the end of the play, to pronounce the end of the royal house of Thebes.

See also Cadmus, Dionysus, Euripides.

Bacchus The name by which the Romans knew Dionysus. The orgiastic side of Dionysian religion spread to Italy in the second century BC and led to excesses which alarmed the state. The Roman senate suppressed the rites in 186 BC, according to an inscription which survives, but the cult of Bacchus soon gained a firm hold on the Roman imagination. He became identified with the ancient Italian god Liber, and eventually obscured and superseded him.

See also Liber.

Bassarids Another name for the votaries of Dionysus. Scholars give the meaning as 'wearers of fox skins'.

Bellerophon The hero of an ancient Greek myth which exists in versions widely separated in time. The story appears in Homer (*Iliad*, Book VI), where there is no mention of the winged horse, Pegasus, and in Hesiod, where there is. A later version, in Pindar's Olympian odes, also includes the winged horse and gives different names to some of the characters, and that version is the most familiar one.

Bellerophon, a young man of Corinth, is at the court of the Argive King, Proetus. He is very beautiful, and the King's wife, Stheneboea, wants him. She tells Bellerophon that she loves him and that he must satisfy her longings – it will, of course, be a secret between them. Bellerophon declines to bring dishonour on the house where he is a guest, so Stheneboea decides that he will pay for spurning her. She goes to her husband and tells him that his guest has tried to seduce her. Proetus cannot murder his guest, so he sends him to his father-in-law, Iobates, King of Lycia, with a sealed letter. Iobates receives the young man hospitably and later, when he opens the letter, finds that his guest has brought his own death warrant – Iobates is expected to kill him. But Iobates, no more than Proetus, can bring himself to descend to so mean a crime as murdering a guest under his roof. He sends him to kill the Chimaera, a fire-breathing monster with the head of a lion, the body of a goat, and a serpent's tail.

Bellerophon gains help from the seer, Polyeidus, who advises him to catch the winged horse, Pegasus, and from the goddess, Athene, who gives him a golden bridle. With this he is able to tame the winged horse when he catches him drinking at the spring of Peirene, in Corinth. He is able to kill the Chimaera with the help of the wonderful horse, who flies above the monster, enabling Bellerophon to hurl lumps of lead into the Chimaera's mouth. The monster's breath melts the lead, which runs down its throat and kills it.

Iobates tries again to put Bellerophon out of the way. He sends him to fight the savage Solymians and their Amazon allies: Pegasus flies over their heads, too, and Bellerophon rains down rocks and sharp stones on their heads. Their arrows cannot reach Pegasus and, demoralised, they retreat from the field.

Iobates, at last won over, shows the letter from Proetus to Bellerophon and asks him for his side of the story. He believes Bellerophon, and adopts him as his heir to the throne of Lycia, with his daughter Philanoë as Bellerophon's consort.

Bellerophon's fortunes seem to be made, but he makes his first and irrevocable mistake by deciding that he will ride Pegasus up to Olympus. But Pegasus flings him off; Bellerophon tumbles to earth and spends the rest of his life alone, a lame outcast who shuns the company of men. (Homer's version, without the winged horse, simply says that he incurred the displeasure of the gods, and ended his days as a solitary wanderer. Obviously, Homer's audience would have been able to supply the necessary link in the story.)

See also Pegasus.

Bellona The Roman goddess of war. There is uncertainty about her origin – whether she was an offshoot of Mars or a complementary deity, but she has been traced back to early times in Roman religion. Her temple stood outside the city walls at the Colline Gate and was the traditional place where returning generals or ambassadors were received. Near the temple was the small column over which the priest of Jupiter *Feretrius (Fetiales)* threw a spear on the declaration of war.

See also Jupiter.

Bendis The moon goddess of Thrace, in the north of Greece. Her worship was orgiastic, like that of Cybele, but appeared in a more subdued form when her cult appeared in Piraeus, taken there by Thracian immigrants and sailors.

Bona Dea A Roman goddess who was worshipped exclusively by women. She has been identified with Fauna, the consort (or perhaps mother) of Faunus, the Roman god of fertility, and certainly the secrecy of her annual rites, which took place early in December, suggest another version of the timeless Mother Earth. A political crisis was caused by the violation of the secrecy of the rites by Publius Clodius in 62 BC when they were held in Caesar's house (Caesar was *Pontifex Maximus*), and Clodius attended disguised as a woman.

Boreas The North Wind in Greek mythology. He fell in love with Oreithyia, daughter of King Erectheus of Athens, and carried her off from the bank of the Ilissus river to be his wife. This made him 'brother-in-law' to the Athenians, as Herodotus puts it, and they were quick to appeal to him during the Persian invasion. Boreas obligingly destroyed a Persian fleet off Artemisium for them. He was the father of the winged-footed Calais and Zetes, who sailed with Jason on the quest for the Golden Fleece.

Britomartis A goddess of Crete, probably of fertility, who became identified with Artemis. Her name meant 'sweet maid', and King Minos fell in love with her. She managed to elude him until one day – there being no other way of escape – she threw herself into the sea. She was rescued by some fishermen who hauled her aboard in their nets, an adventure which accounts for another of her names, Dictynna – 'fishing net'. Britomartis reached the island of Aegina safely and was worshipped there as Aphaea. All her names, and associations, seem to have some connection with the moon and fertility, and are probably variations of the eternal mother goddess figure.

Bromios One of the names of Dionysus, derived from the Greek word meaning 'to roar'. Dionysus was sometimes manifest as a great voice, as in *The Bacchae* of Euripides.

Busiris In Greek mythology the son of Poseidon by either Lysianassa or Anippe. King of Egypt, he sent to Greece for a seer to advise him what to do when his country was stricken with drought. The Cyprian, Thrasios, advised him that the sacrifice of a stranger each year would keep drought away. So Busiris promptly sacrificed the seer. He made a habit of sacrificing strangers until Heracles passed that way, looking for the Garden of the Hesperides. Busiris tried to sacrifice him, too, but Heracles killed him on his own altar.

C

Cabeiri, The The gods of fertility who were worshipped particularly in the Greek parts of Asia Minor (Phrygia), Lesbos and Samothrace, where there is evidence of phallic rites and sacrificial pits. Tradition says that the Cabeiri were four in number, and in various places they were identified with other gods of the earth, such as Demeter and Dionysus. From about the sixth century BC they were also worshipped as protectors of seamen, and Samothrace became the centre of the cult and its mysteries. In the *Argonautica* (Book I) Orpheus persuaded the other Argonauts to take the ship there to enable him to learn the mysteries and so be able to help them face unknown seas with greater confidence.

Cacus A Roman intrusion into the cycle of myths concerning Heracles (Roman *Hercules*) who, when he sought the Oxen of Geryon (one of his Labours) travelled to the west. Cacus appears in the *Aeneid* (Book VIII) and is described as the son of Vulcan, a savage, fire-breathing monster who lived in a cave on the Aventine hill. He terrorised the countryside, and even stole some of the cattle from Hercules when the hero was herding them back to Argos. Hercules traced them to the cave and there he killed the monster and retrieved his cattle.

It is generally believed that Cacus was an ancient fire god of the region where Rome was founded.

Cadmus The founder of Thebes. He was the son of Agenor, King of Tyre, and the brother of Europa who was carried off by Zeus in the form of a white bull. Agenor sent Cadmus and his brothers, Phoenix and Cilix, to search for Europa when she was carried off and told them not to return to Tyre without her. Cadmus crossed the sea with a few companions and went to Delphi to consult the oracle, and was told that he would found a city. He was to give up the search for his sister, and follow in the tracks of a cow. Where the cow sank down from weariness would be the site for his city.

Cadmus left Delphi and the first creature he encountered on the road was a cow, walking eastward from Delphi. Cadmus and his friends followed, and the cow walked deep into Boeotia before she rested. The site already made plain to him, Cadmus planned to build a citadel, but first he intended to sacrifice the cow to Athene. His companions found a spring and were about to draw some water when the guardian of the spring, a dragon, attacked them. Cadmus ran to help them, and managed to crush the dragon's head with a rock; but his companions were all dead.

Alone, he proceeded with the sacrifice, and was rewarded by a visit from Athene herself. The goddess advised him to sow the dragon's teeth.

Cadmus hacked out the teeth, buried them in the ground, and waited. His harvest came almost at once – armed men, fully grown, rose from the ground. The dragon was sacred to Ares, the war god, and at once the *Spartoi* (the sown men) looked around for someone to fight. Cadmus threw a stone into the midst of them. The men were soon fighting, each accusing the other of throwing the stone. When the fighting stopped, five weary survivors were left, and these helped in the building of the citadel, the Cadmea. It was to be the citadel of the new city, Thebes, and the Spartoi were to be the ancestors of the Theban nobility.

Cadmus married Harmonia, the daughter of Ares and Aphrodite. The Olympians attended the wedding, and Aphrodite gave her daughter a fateful necklace, which conferred beauty on its wearer. The children of Cadmus and Harmonia were all daughters: Ino, Agave, Antonoë and Semele. Agave married Echion, one of the Spartoi, and eventually Cadmus resigned the throne to their son, Pentheus.

In their old age, after the revenge of Dionysus destroyed the royal house of Thebes, Cadmus and Harmonia were exiled and made their way to Illyria, where they turned into serpents.

The strange ending of the story of Cadmus and Harmonia is argued about amongst the scholars and interpreted in various ways. The most simple one is that they simply returned to the earth – that they in fact died. Serpents were essentially earth creatures. But in myth simple endings were rarely granted to heroic figures and the founders of cities.

Cadmus is traditionally credited with the introduction of writing into Greece, an arresting idea since he came from Tyre (in Phoenicia) and early alphabets in Greek were derived from Phoenician.

See also Amphiaraus, *The Bacchae* (Euripides), Dionysus.

Caenis The daughter of Coronis the Lapith, and one of the many women in Greek mythology who attracted the roving eye of a god. In this case the god was Poseidon, who, feeling generous after enjoying Caenis, asked her what she would like as a gift. She promptly said that she would like to be a man, for a change. Differing interpretations have been put on this: that she really did want a change, or that she wanted no more of the sort of experience to which Poseidon had subjected her. Whatever her reason, the request pleased Poseidon, since it meant that no other man could have her. So he made her into a man, from then on to be known as Caeneus, and also bestowed the gift of invulnerability in battle. As Caeneus, he was present at the savage fight with the centaurs at the wedding of Peirithous, and killed several of them before being hammered into the ground. The centaurs then piled earth and rocks on him and he died.

See also Lapiths, Peirithous.

Calchas In the *Iliad,* the seer who accompanied and advised the Achaeans on the expedition to Troy. He is called the son of Thestor, and is a priest of Apollo. He appears quite early in the *Iliad* (Book I) and advises Agamemnon to give up the girl he stole from Achilles (Chryseis) because she is the daughter of a priest of Apollo: the plague that has striken the Achaean camp is a punishment from the god. In Book II Odysseus relates how Calchas divined that it would take the Achaeans ten years to capture Troy.

Calchas also appears in the myths leading up to the events of the *Iliad*: it is he who persuades Agamemnon to sacrifice his own daughter in exchange for a fair wind at Aulis, and he who makes it clear that there is no hope of victory without Achilles. In the play by Sophocles it is Calchas who demands the use of Heracles' bow and arrows from Philoctetes, during the siege.

He is a sinister figure, his every appearance heralding death or grief for someone. Some versions make him a renegade Trojan, who went over to the Achaeans because he foresaw that Troy would fall. His death, in a later story, is attributed to mortification when another seer, Mopsus, proves himself the better.

See also Agamemnon, *Iliad*, Iphigenia, Mopsus, Philoctetes.

Callisto   The subject of a myth connected with the goddess Artemis, whose handmaiden Callisto was, and written down in later classical times. However, its other connection, with astronomy, suggests an ancient source and the story as we have it is confused. Zeus falls in love with Callisto and she bears a son, Arcas, the ancestor of the Arcadians. Artemis is furious at Callisto's departure from chastity and she (or Hera) changes the girl into a she-bear. Arcas, grown up, is out hunting one day and encounters a she-bear and is about to kill her when Zeus, to prevent Arcas from killing his mother, changes them both into stars: Callisto becomes Ursa Major, the Great Bear, and Arcas becomes Arcturus, Guardian of the Bear.

Camenae   In Roman religion every body of water – every river, lake or spring – had a deity of its own. The Camenae were the goddesses of a sacred spring in a grove outside the Porta Capena in Rome, traditionally believed to have been dedicated by King Numa, the legendary successor of Romulus. The Camenae (foretellers) had the power of prophecy.

Camilla   The warrior maiden of the *Aeneid* (Book XI). Her father, Metabus, was driven from his city during the Volscian Wars and escaped with his baby daughter. His flight was checked by the flooded River Amisenus, and to save his child he dedicated her to the goddess Diana, tied her to a javelin, and hurled it across the water. Then he was able to swim across himself. Camilla grew up as a virgin huntress, like Diana, and then joined Turnus in the struggle against Aeneas.

See also *The Aeneid*.

Capitol   One of the hills of Rome, and the site of the citadel rather than a part of the city itself. There are two 'peaks', and in ancient times the temples of Jupiter, as guardian of the city, and Juno Moneta (giver of counsel) stood upon them. Victorious generals sacrificed there at the conclusion of a Triumph, as did magistrates when taking office. The oldest shrine in Rome stood on the Capitol, that of Jupiter Feretrius: the meaning of 'Feretrius' is lost but it could have some ancient association with the sacred oak tree that grew there, the tree on which Romulus hung the spoils of war.

The incident of the geese which saved the Capitol dates from 390 BC, when Rome was attacked by the Gauls. The geese, birds sacred to Juno, were kept in the Capitol and were there when the citadel was besieged. The Gauls attempted a surprise attack one night and the cries of the geese awoke the commander, Marcus Manlius, enabling him to rouse the garrison in time and repel the attackers. Thereafter, the care of the geese became a charge of the city of Rome, and Manlius was known as Manlius Capitolinus.

Carmentis In Roman religion a goddess who protected women in childbirth. In mythology she is a prophetess, and the mother of Evander of Arcadia who founded a city on the Tiber. She was believed to have brought the art of writing to Italy. As a goddess of prophecy she was sometimes spoken of in the plural, as Carmentes – *antevorta,* who knew the past, and *postvorta,* who knows the future. Carmenta is the Greek form of her name.

Carnea A festival in honour of Apollo held at harvest time, particularly in Sparta, at which races were held and musicians competed for prizes. The races were run by youths carrying bunches of grapes on their heads, and omens for the future were seen in the results. The Apollo honoured in the festival was the protector of the flocks, but there was probably a more ancient deity in the original rites.

Caryatids 'Maidens of Caryae'. Caryae was a town in Laconia in the Peloponnese where maidens performed ritual dances at the annual festival of the goddess Artemis. The attitudes of the girls in some part of the dances were reproduced in sculpture, and the motif found its way into the supporting columns of the entablatures of temples. The most famous caryatids are those in the southern portico of the Erectheum on the Acropolis.

Cassandra The daughter of Priam, King of Troy. She is first mentioned in the *Iliad* (Book XIII) as his loveliest daughter. At the very end (Book XXIV) she is the first of the Trojans to see Hector's body as it is brought back to Troy. But Homer tells us no more than that, and the frequent appearance of this princess in Greek mythology, and her fatal prophetic gift from Apollo, cannot be definitely stated as being before or after Homer. It is found in Pindar (fifth century BC), and at about the same time in Aeschylus.

In the first part of the *Oresteia,* Cassandra relates how she asked Apollo (as Loxias, the prophetic god) for the gift of prophecy; how he gave it to her to win her love, and was then spurned by her. He left her with the gift – her punishment was that she would never be believed. Another version of Cassandra's prophetic gift tells how she and her brother Helenus, when small children, fell asleep in the sanctuary of Apollo. The sacred serpents found the children and began to lick their ears with their forked tongues. Hecuba came upon them, looking for her children, and gave a scream of terror; the serpents at once slid away into the darkness, and the children, their ears 'cleaned' by Apollo's agency, thereafter possessed prophetic powers.

See also Agamemnon, Ajax, *Iliad, Oresteia* (Aeschylus).

Castalia A nymph who excited the lust of Apollo. Surprisingly, since he was held to represent the perfection of masculine beauty, she fled from him, and threw herself into a spring on Mount Parnassus. The spring is still there; the pool is for many people the starting point of their visit to the site of Delphi and lies just off the road, a little to the north-east of the sacred precinct.

Cecrops The mythical first King of Athens, who grew from the soil itself and for that reason was sometimes represented as being a serpent from the waist down – serpents were regarded as the essential earth creatures in ancient times. The claim was made more than once in Greek mythology that founding fathers, or noble families, were part of the very soil they ruled (see the entry for Cadmus for another example); but in the myths of the founding of Athens there are several strands hopelessly entangled and Cecrops is just one of the characters encountered in them who claims to be the first king. Erechtheus and Erechthonius are others, and one version names Cecrops as one of the sons, and the successor, of Erechtheus; another has Athene give the infant Erechthonius into the care of the daughters of Cecrops,

In straightforward terms Cecrops is the son of Mother Earth, and the good he brought to his kingdom (this is found in the writings of late classical times, the second century BC) included a rejection of blood sacrifice, the principle of monogamy, the invention of writing and the practice of burying the dead. The Athenians identified a spot on the Acropolis, near the Erechtheum, as the tomb of Cecrops.

See also Erechtheus, Erichthonius.

Centaurs In Greek mythology, the centaurs' origins lay in the unlawful passion of Ixion of Thessaly for the goddess Hera. Zeus observed this and fashioned a false Hera from a cloud: Ixion was delighted to find 'Hera' compliant, and was having a wonderful time until Zeus appeared and caught him in the act. His punishment was ordered but Zeus apparently forgot to do anything about the cloud woman, Nephele, who continued to exist. She gave birth to a son, Centaurus. This son mated with the mares of Thessaly and brought into being the centaurs, the strange creatures who were men down to the waist – and horse from the waist down.

The centaurs are probably part of the myths of Greece that stem from the time of the migrations and the coming of the horse – which was unknown in Greece before the second millennium BC. The memory of the horse as a cult animal (it would have been of enormous importance to migratory nomads) persisted and occurs frequently in Greek myth. In remote regions, in Thessaly particularly and in Thrace, there were probably communities of semi-primitive people whose livelihood was in the catching and taming of wild horses; their skill would have been impressive to outsiders and in many people's minds made an inseparable connection with the creature.

The centaurs' foes, the Lapiths, may represent rival tribes in the regions where the centaurs lived. Centaurs were generally wild, lustful, and strongly attracted to wine, which they could not hold and which made them uncontrollable.

For the myths concerning the most notable centaur see Chiron.

See also Heracles, Migrations, Theseus, Prometheus.

Cephalus A hero of Greek mythology who was loved by the goddess Eos (the dawn). He married Procris, the daughter of Erechtheus, who was a favourite of the goddess Artemis. Artemis gave Procris two gifts; a spear which never missed its mark, and a wonderful hound called Laelaps who caught whatever he pursued. Procris, to regain the affections of her husband from Eos, gave him the hound and the spear, and it seemed that all was well between them. But Procris remained jealous and one day followed her husband into the forest when he went hunting. Eos, also afflicted with feminine jealousy, saw her opportunity for revenge. She made the bushes stir where Procris was concealed, and Cephalus hurled the spear, thinking an animal was there. The spear never missed its mark, and killed Procris.

See also Eos.

Cerberus The hound of Hades, a monstrous dog that guarded the entrance to the nether world. Cerberus was the offspring of Typhon and the half-woman, half-serpent Echidna, descendant of Medusa. Heracles, in his Eleventh Labour, stole Cerberus from Hades at the order of King Eurystheus. Hesiod describes Cerberus as bronze-voiced, with fifty heads: representations in art are generally less extravagant and show him with three.

See also Echidna, Heracles, Labours of, Medusa, Typhon.

Cercopes The clever twin thieves of Ephesus, sons of Oceanus and Theia. Theia warned her sons to avoid Heracles, at that time undergoing a period of servitude to Omphale, Queen of Lydia, a punishment for his desecration of the shrine of Delphi. The Cercopes found the great hairy hero an irresistible target for their tricks and eventually enraged him by keeping him awake at night, buzzing like flies. When they tried to steal his weapons he sprang up and seized them, tied their feet together, and hung them at each end of a strong pole. Then he trudged off to deliver them to justice, the pole across his huge shoulders. Heracles had gone a little way when he heard them whispering to each other; thinking they might be planning to escape, he listened carefully, and when they started laughing he realised that they were laughing at him. The lion's skin he wore only came to his waist – the rest of him was constantly exposed to the sun. The twins were chortling at the only thing they could see, and exchanging jokes about the big black bottom that obscured the sun. Their laughter was infectious, and Heracles enjoyed the joke so much he let them go.

See also Heracles.

Ceres The ancient corn goddess of Roman mythology, often identified with Demeter. Her cult centre was at the foot of the Aventine hill. It was established in the fifth century BC and by then had acquired strong

Greek overtones, the more so since Ceres became associated with the Roman earth god, Liber, and his female counterpart, Libera. The three thus presented a similar trio to that of Demeter, Persephone and Iacchos at Eleusis. Like Demeter, Ceres had a connection with the earth, and sacrifices were made to her to purify a house where death had occurred. She was popular with the common people, who celebrated her rites in April of each year.

See also Demeter.

Chaos 'The gap' which came into being when all the elements, hitherto blended in fusion, separated and formed heaven and earth at the beginning of time. In Hesiod, Earth appears once the gap has come into being; then come Tartarus (a sunless abyss below Hades) and Eros (love) – after which all things followed.

See also *Theogony* (Hesiod).

Charon In Greek mythology the ferryman who carried the dead to Hades across the river Styx. His fee for the service was one obol, and it was customary to place the coin in the mouth of the dead person before burial. The tradition persisted in Greece until recent times and is probably as ancient as Greece herself, though the first mention in literature is not found until the time of Aristophanes (*The Frogs*) in the late fifth century BC. Virgil brings Charon into *The Aeneid* (Book VI), and Dante, thirteen centuries after Virgil, makes powerful use of the idea in *The Inferno*.

Charon is not mentioned by Homer, probably because the Achaeans, who invaded Troy from Greece, belonged to a different tradition and burned their dead.

Charybdis The dangerous whirlpool of Greek epic, traditionally placed in the Straits of Messina. It lay opposite the lair of the monster Scylla: to be 'between Scylla and Charybdis' was to be in danger from both, since measures taken to avoid one drove you into the other. The *Argo* sailed between Scylla and Charybdis on the long voyage home, as did Odysseus.

See also *Argonautica, Odyssey,* Scylla.

Chiron A centaur, of great wisdom and kindness, friend of both man and gods, the source of the arts of healing and music, and in some versions the king of the centaurs. The education of Asclepius, Jason and Achilles was entrusted to him. A late tradition made him the son of Cronus who, to deceive his consort, Rhea, turned himself into a horse to go off and make love to Philyra. This would, however, have made Chiron the half-brother of Zeus and older tradition made no attempt to specify his divine origins, though there is an underlying assumption that he was immortal. He was, simply, the repository of ancient wisdom in a particular form: the horse, untamed, was dangerous; but it could be tamed, and be of enormous help to man, and not all the centaurs were wild and uncontrollable. Chiron was an extension of the ancient tribal medicine-man.

The centaurs themselves play a part in the heroic exploits of Heracles – and also in his death – and both subjects in Greek myth seem to have a bearing upon one another. Quite why this is so is obscure; the connections are ancient – both Heracles and the centaurs appear in Homer – but there is no clear statement. Heracles, unwittingly, brought about Chiron's death. On the way to his Third Labour, the capture of the Erymanthian boar, he stopped at Pholoe in Arcadia and was given hospitality by the centaur, Pholus, in his cave. Heracles asked for wine, and as a host Pholus was obliged to open the communal wine jar to give him some. The other centaurs caught the scent of the wine, and furious that it was being given away, attacked Heracles and Pholus. Heracles met the attack, and killed some of the centaurs; the rest of them fled to the cave of their king, Chiron, who came out to see what was happening. Just at that moment Heracles loosed an arrow, which missed its target and hit Chiron in the knee. Chiron, in agony, stumbled back into his cave and Heracles rushed to help him. But nothing he could do, nor all the healing arts that Chiron possessed, were any help: the arrow had been dipped in the blood of the Hydra, the many-headed water serpent, and the wound would never heal. And Chiron was immortal – he would suffer eternal pain.

Eventually the cruel impasse was resolved. Zeus allowed Chiron to surrender his immortality to Prometheus, and die in peace.

See also Centaurs, Heracles, Prometheus.

Cimmerians In the *Odyssey* (Book XI), the people at the frontiers of the world, on whom the sun never shines. Circe directs Odysseus to go there to find the entrance to Hades.

Circe The witch-goddess of the *Odyssey* (Books X–XII). Homer calls her the daughter of thè sun god, Helios, and sister of the King of Colchis, Aeëtes. Post-Homeric stories make her the mother of a son (Telegonus) by Odysseus: in the *Odyssey*, however, the year she spent with Odysseus was unproductive. She appears in the story of Jason, purifying him and Medea for the murder of Absyrtus.

See also *Argonautica, Odyssey*.

Clytemnestra The daughter of Tyndareus, King of Sparta, and Leda, who was loved by Zeus in the form of a swan. Clytemnestra was therefore the half-sister of Helen, following the tradition that Helen was the result of Leda's encounter with the swan.

Clytemnestra married Agamemnon, King of Argos. Helen married Agamemnon's brother, Menelaus, who became King of Sparta.

With the departure of Agamemnon for the attack on Troy, his wife was courted by his cousin Aegisthus, and Clytemnestra yielded. Any feelings she may have retained for Agamemnon turned to hatred when he persuaded her to send their daughter Iphigenia to Aulis, where the Achaean fleet was halted for the lack of a favourable wind. The pretext was that Iphigenia was to be a bride for Achilles – so Clytemnestra let her go. The true reason was that the Achaeans needed a sacrifice to procure a wind to enable them to sail. Calchas pointed out to the leaders that Agamemnon had offended the goddess Artemis; therefore his daughter would be an appropriate offering. The wretched Agamemnon agreed, Iphigenia was sacrificed, and the fleet sailed for Troy and ten years of war.

Clytemnestra, meanwhile, was living with someone who also had reasons for looking forward to Agamemnon's return. Aegisthus was a member of the accursed house of Pelops, and of the opposing branch to Agamemnon. (For the story of Pelops, and the curse laid on his house, see the entry for Pelops.)

When Agamemnon returned from Troy he brought the Princess Cassandra with him as part of the spoils. He and Cassandra were murdered by Clytemnestra and Aegisthus almost as soon as they entered the palace.

The story continues with the characters of Electra and Orestes, the children of Agamemnon and Clytemnestra who themselves avenge their father's murder.

Clytemnestra is a remarkable figure who, though she has little mythology of her own, has nevertheless become a major character in any consideration of Greek mythology. This is due to the tragedians, who found her irresistible, and used the fragmentary references in Homer (*Odyssey*, Books III and XI) to construct striking dramatic pieces where Clytemnestra is the central figure. Aeschylus, Sophocles and Euripides all wrote plays in which she has an important part.

See also *Electra* (Euripides), *Electra* (Sophocles), *Iphigenia at Aulis* (Euripides), *Oresteia* (Aeschylus).

Cocytus One of the rivers of Hades in Greek mythology. Geographically it is a tributary of the Acheron in Epirus (north-west Greece).

Colchis The country at the eastern end of the Black Sea, where Jason and the Argonauts travelled on their quest for the Golden Fleece.

See also *Argonautica*.

Concordia In Roman religion the spirit or personification of harmony in the community. A temple was dedicated to Concord in the fourth century BC, near the Forum, and there was a shrine to her on one of the peaks of the Capitol. Her temple was dedicated to Concordia *Augusta* in AD 10 by the Emperor Tiberius and she was so called from that time on. Tiberius sought to promote harmony in the imperial family, notorious for its murderous hatreds.

Consus A Roman god, originally of agriculture and, as with most gods of fertility, connected with the nether world. His festival, the Consualia, was celebrated in August during the harvest, and the rites were held at an underground altar in the Circus Maximus which was only uncovered at that time. The site of his altar, in a place where chariot-races were held, led to Consus also being worshipped in connection with horses; on the day of his festival horses and asses were allowed to rest and they were garlanded with flowers.

Creon A name which means 'ruler' or 'prince', it belongs to more than one character prominent in Greek mythology and in each case the bearer is a member of a royal house. The name occurs once in Homer (*Iliad*, Book IX), where he is simply referred to as the father of 'the noble Lycomedes'. The only version of a 'death' of Creon is in a Latin epic about Thebes by the poet Statius in the first century AD.

For the stories of which Creon is part see the following entries: Amphitryon, *Antigone* (Sophocles), Heracles, Jason, *Medea* (Euripides), *Oedipus* and *Oedipus at Colonus* (Sophocles), The Seven Against Thebes.

Crete The original inhabitants of Crete have so far remained unidentified, in spite of the island's brilliant civilisation and its place as a power in the Aegean. It is known that they were *not* Semitic, from the Near East, nor part of the waves of Indo-European migrants who eventually occupied the whole of Greece. The civilisation of Crete was called Minoan by Sir Arthur Evans, who excavated the site of Cnossos and the 'Palace of Minos' at the beginning of this century. It was a useful label since the rulers of Crete were called Minos in mythology and it may have been a title rather than a name. Crete was the centre of a thriving maritime empire and her influence was strong enough to reach as far north as Thebes. The civilisation suffered a crippling blow about 1400 BC, when Cnossos was destroyed by invaders and the royal line extinguished. The myth of Theseus and the Minotaur is almost certainly concerned with this destruction and the dubious honour therefore falls to Athens. A further invasion, by Dorian Greeks, occurred about 1200 and this was fatal: the glory of Crete was extinguished for ever. Crete is often mentioned in Greek mythology: apart from Minos and Theseus it had a strong connection with Zeus, and claimed Mount Dicte as his birthplace.

See also Daedalus, Mount Dicte, Europa, Minos, Minotaur, Theseus.

Cronus The son of Heaven and Earth (Uranus and Gaia) and the father of Zeus. Cronus and his brothers and sisters were called Titans: the exact meaning of that word, and therefore its implications, is unknown. The Titans belong to a very remote past and there is no record of their ever having been worshipped as gods.

There are various versions of the story of Cronus but the oldest written source is Hesiod. Uranus and Gaia had many children but Uranus was jealous of them and confined them in the earth, i.e. in the body of Gaia. She found the burden intolerable and encouraged her bravest son, Cronus, to put an end to her suffering. She gave him a sickle, and the next time Uranus approached his consort Cronus castrated him. From the drops of blood which fell on earth came the Furies and the Giants; from the genitals, which Cronus flung into the sea, was born the goddess, Aphrodite. Uranus, defeated, left the earth to the Titans, and Cronus and his sister-consort Rhea became the rulers of the world. But Uranus warned his victorious son that Cronus, in his turn, would be overthrown by one of his sons.

Cronus, to ensure his supremacy, swallowed his children as soon as

Rhea gave birth to them – Hestia, Demeter, Hera, Hades, Poseidon, Rhea, in despair, asked Gaia to advise her: she told her to give Cronus a stone to swallow when her next son was born. This she did, and hid her son away in safety. The son was Zeus.

When Zeus had grown to maturity Rhea persuaded Cronus to forget his fears and vomit up his children. He did so beginning with the stone he had swallowed in place of Zeus, then he disgorged the other children and Zeus and his brothers gave battle. The struggle lasted for ten years, many of the Titans fighting on the side of Cronus. For allies Zeus and his brothers had the Cyclopes and the Hecatoncheires, and he was eventually victorious. He imprisoned his defeated kinsmen in Tartarus, a place in the underworld, and entered upon his kingdom, ruling from Olympus.

Cronus was probably a corn god in very ancient times. The only festival known of his was the Cronia, a harvest festival celebrated in Athens, Thebes and on the island of Rhodes, where there is evidence that he was offered human sacrifice. This could accord with a primitive, or unenlightened, worship of a fertility deity. The sickle, which he carries in the few representations of him known in art, and which the myth says he used to castrate his father, could well have been both a harvesting tool and the implement used to kill those sacrificed to him.

See also Cyclopes, Hecatoncheires, Titans.

Cupid The Roman god of love and the son of Venus. He was an adaptation of the Greek god Eros but quite unlike his counterpart, who was the personification of a timeless impulse. The Roman god, by contrast, is an insipid boy-god of no great importance even to the Romans. Writers made use of him: Virgil in the *Aeneid* (Book I), and Lucius Apuleius in *The Golden Ass*.

Curetes The guardians of the infant Zeus. When his mother Rhea hid him from his father Cronus, she took him to Crete, where the goat Amalthea brought him milk, and bees brought him honey. (The Cretan tradition says that Zeus was born in a cave in Mount Dicte.) To prevent the cries of the infant being heard, the Curetes, young men who were semi-divine, would dance and clash their weapons. There was probably a cult in Crete devoted to the god as a youth (*kouros*); the Curetes may have been derived from the young men who would have been his votaries. An inscription has been found in Crete, at Palaiokastro, containing the Hymn of the Curetes to Zeus *Kouros*.

Cyclopes The sons of Uranus and Gaia, the Cyclopes (according to Hesiod) were three in number. They had one eye each, set in the middle of their forehead, and their names were Brontes (thunderer), Steropes (lightener), and Arges (bright). They were craftsmen and made thunder bolts, and helped Zeus in his battle with Cronus and the Titans. Later writers credited them with the building of the tremendous (cyclopean) walls of Tiryns and other fortified cities of ancient times.

Cyclops The savage one-eyed giant of Homer, of whom only one is ever named. In the *Odyssey* (Book IX) the Cyclops, Polyphemus, catches Odysseus and his companions in his cave and makes a meal of two of them before Odysseus succeeds in blinding him and making good his escape. The island of the Cyclops became identified with Sicily, and it was there that Virgil placed them in the *Aeneid* (Book III).

D

Daedalus In Greek mythology the epitome of the great craftsman or artificer. The son of Metion, an Athenian, he was a descendant of Hephaestus, the divine artificer himself. Daedalus was credited with the invention of the plumb-line, the axe and the saw, and with the discovery of glue: he was the first man to understand the value of sails and masts. His statues were so skilfully fashioned that they were said to move like living creatures.

In his native Athens Daedalus had for apprentice his nephew, Talos, and became jealous of his skill – fearing that Talos would surpass him. In one version of the story, Talos invented the saw and it was this that drove Daedalus to murder him. He threw his apprentice down from the Acropolis, and the gods changed the boy into a partridge – *perdix* (he was also called Perdix).

His fear of retribution drove Daedalus away from Athens. He fled to Crete, and entered the service of King Minos and his Queen, Pasiphae. Pasiphae had an unnatural lust for a fine bull sent to Minos by the god Poseidon, so Daedalus constructed a false cow in which the Queen could conceal herself – only Daedalus could have made it sufficiently lifelike for her purpose – and remain among the King's herds. The trick worked and Pasiphae was mounted by the bull; the offspring of this union being a creature who was half man and half bull – the Minotaur.

To hide the result of the Queen's lust, Minos commissioned a maze in which the Minotaur could live unseen. Daedalus constructed the labyrinth for him – and found himself imprisoned there too, with his son, Icarus, borne him by Naucrate, one of Minos' slaves. The King had not forgiven Daedalus for his help to Pasiphae in the matter of the bull. To escape from the prison he had made himself, Daedalus constructed two pairs of wings on which he and Icarus flew away from Crete. But Icarus flew too near the sun and the heat melted the wax which held the feathers in place: he crashed into the sea and was drowned. Daedalus flew on, and landed safely in Sicily.

In the meantime, Minos, determined to recapture his prisoner, had arrived in Sicily. He brought with him a triton shell, and offered a rich reward to anyone who could pass a linen thread through it. Eventually he was received at the court of King Cocalus. The King was interested in Minos' shell, and declared that he knew a man who could do it – Minos thought there could be only one man in the world who could do it, and he waited to see if the King's clever man was the one he wanted.

Cocalus took the shell to Daedalus, who by his talents had secured an honoured place at court. Daedalus bored a tiny hole in the point of the shell, then he attached a gossamer thread to an ant, and put it into the hole. The entrance to the shell he smeared with honey, and the busy ant hurried through the spirals to get at the sweetness. Daedalus now had a triton shell threaded with gossamer; it was more difficult to attach a linen thread to the gossamer and pull that through as well – but he managed it, to the delight of Cocalus, who hurried off to show it to Minos.

Minos' demand for the surrender of Daedalus upset his host. It also upset his host's daughters, who had grown very attached to their guest. They warned him that Minos was at the palace, and willingly helped him plot the murder of his persecutor. This was done by the installation of a duct in the ceiling of the palace bath. Minos was conducted there, and while he was luxuriating in the steamy warmth the hidden duct opened and boiling water gushed forth. Minos was suffocated, or boiled, and his body was solemnly conveyed back to the Cretans as the result of a tragic accident.

The story of Daedalus ends there, though there was a later tradition that he settled on the island of Sardinia with some colonists from Greece. It is a matter for argument whether there ever *was* a Daedalus so skilful that myths grew around his memory, or whether he was entirely the product of imagination. It could be either – his name means 'cunningly wrought', which could also be applied to clever works, or workmanship.

See also Minos.

Danae One of the girls upon whom the roving eye of Zeus rested. She was the daughter of Acrisius, King of Argos, who had been warned by an oracle that he would die at the hands of his daughter's son. Acrisius had quarrelled with his twin brother, Proetus, and he knew that Proetus had seduced Danae. Fearing the worst, Acrisius locked his daughter in a prison secured with brazen doors: Danae confirmed his fears by giving birth to a son. Acrisius naturally believed that Proetus was the father – not knowing that Zeus had been visiting Danae in a shower of gold.

Rather than kill his own daughter, Acrisius put mother and son into a wooden chest and pushed it out to sea. The chest drifted south and was then borne eastward, to be washed ashore on the island of Seriphos. The King's brother, Dictys, found the chest and rescued Danae and her baby, taking them to his brother Polydectes. Polydectes gave refuge to Danae and her son grew up in the palace. His name was Perseus.

See the entry for Perseus for the adventures of the young hero and the fate of Acrisius.

Danaus The brother of Aegyptus and the son of Belus, Danaus was a descendant of Zeus by his union with Io. After a quarrel with his brother over their inheritance, Aegyptus suggested the marriage of his fifty sons to the fifty daughters of Danaus. Danaus did not like the proposal – neither did his daughters – and consulted an oracle, which confirmed his uneasiness by revealing that Aegyptus intended to destroy him and his family. So Danaus and his daughters fled on a ship that took them, by way of Rhodes, to Lerna in Argos.

The King of Argos, Gelanor, gave Danaus his throne – not because he liked him, but because an event occurred that seemed to guide him to it. A wolf came down from the wild hills to the very walls of the city, where the royal herd was grazing: it killed the leader bull of the herd, and the King saw this as a sign that the stranger could, if he wanted to, take the throne by force.

Danaus built a shrine when he became king, and dedicated it to Apollo Lykeios, convinced that the wolf had been sent by Apollo. He also set out to cure the drought which was plaguing Argos, and sent his daughters to search the countryside for new springs and streams. One of the girls, Amymone, was saved from rape by a satyr by the timely arrival of the god Poseidon, who hurled his trident at the satyr. The trident struck a rock, and an idea struck Poseidon: Amymone was a very pretty girl. She was also a sensible girl, and knew that Poseidon was the very god to please if water was what she needed. So Poseidon got the girl, the girl got an eternal spring of fresh water, and Argos got the river Lerna. Eventually the girl got a son, Nauplius.

But the kingdom of Danaus was not yet secure. Aegyptus had not given up. He sent his fifty sons to Argos to pursue the marriage project. They besieged the citadel of Argos, and Danaus found himself cut off from the precious water of the Lerna. Eventually he submitted, and the sons of Aegyptus thought they had achieved their goal. A mass marriage was arranged – but Danaus gave orders to his daughters to kill their husbands on the wedding night. He gave each one a weapon, a long sharp pin to conceal in her hair.

Only one of the bridegrooms escaped, Lynceus. His bride, Hypermnestra, could not bring herself to kill him and helped him escape. The other daughters, for their crime, were condemned to spend the after life in Tartarus, carrying water in perforated jars.

The people of Argos, the descendants of Danaus, are the Danaans of Homer's *Iliad*.

See also Aegyptus, Amymone.

Daphne A mountain nymph, daughter of the river Peneus in Thessaly. She was loved both by Leucippus, a mortal, and the god Apollo. Daphne was a priestess of Mother Earth, and she and the other nymphs conducted celebrations which were forbidden to men. Leucippus disguised himself as a girl and followed the nymphs to their sacred ground: the jealous Apollo advised the nymphs to bathe naked to keep their rites undefiled – they could be sure then that all the celebrants were female. So Leucippus was discovered, and the furious nymphs tore him to pieces. The way was clear for Apollo, who lost no time in telling Daphne what he had in mind. She declined: he persisted. She took to her heels, determined to remain chaste. Apollo chased her. He caught her without much trouble, whereupon she cried out to Mother Earth, who turned her faithful priestess into a laurel tree.

Apollo is often represented in art as wearing a laurel wreath, and it was the leaves of this tree which the Pythoness or Pythia at Delphi, Apollo's priestess of the oracle, chewed to induce the divine ecstasy during which the prophecies were uttered. The laurel was sacred to Apollo.

Daphnis The son of a Sicilian nymph and the god Hermes, Daphnis was a shepherd who, in turn, was loved by another nymph, Echenais. In one version of the story he is unfaithful to her and in a jealous fury she blinds him. After that he sings unhappy songs, and is traditionally the originator of pastoral music. Eventually Hermes takes his son up to Olympus, and causes a stream of fresh water to flow where he was last seen. Another version makes Daphnis immune to love, and thereby arouses the wrath of Aphrodite. The goddess afflicts him with a longing for an unattainable ideal, and it is from the longing that he dies.

Dardanus According to Homer (*Iliad,* Book XX), the founder of Troy. The story is told to Achilles by Prince Aeneas. Dardanus was the son of Zeus (later writers give his mother the name of Electra) and he founded 'Dardania': there was as yet no city. Dardanus' son was Erichthonius, the richest King on earth, with three thousand fine mares and three beautiful foals: the North Wind fell in love with the foals and sired twelve superb horses on them. Erichthonius' son was Tros, who gave his name to the race, and Tros had three sons, Ilus, Ganymede, and Assaracus. Priam was of the line of Ilus, and the reigning King: Aeneas was a prince of the royal house through his descent from Assaracus.

See also Aeneas, Ganymede, *Iliad,* Priam.

Deianira The daughter of Oeneus, King of Calydon, and sister of Meleager, she became the second wife of Heracles and, unwittingly, the agent of his death. There were many suitors, but they all retired when Heracles and Achelous sought her hand: Heracles was a renowned hero, and Achelous was the god of the river of that name. The two contested for Deianira, and Achelous, who could assume three shapes – a bull-headed man, a serpent, and a bull – fought Heracles – only to be beaten in all three.

Deianira is the principal character of Sophocles' play, *The Women of Trachis*.

See also Heracles.

Deiphobus One of Priam's sons. He appears frequently in the *Iliad* as a fighting man and is said by writers later than Homer to have quarrelled with Helenus after the death of Paris – both of them wanted the beautiful Helen. She wanted neither of them but Deiphobus took her by force. In the *Odyssey* (Book VIII) it is told how Menelaus and Odysseus made straight for the house of Deiphobus when the city fell . . . but the storyteller's next verse is unheard when the attention shifts back to Odysseus, one of those listening. No more is heard of Deiphobus in Homer but, again, a later story says he was stabbed in the back by Helen when the fighting began in his house.

See also Helen, *Iliad, Odyssey*.

Delphi The most venerated shrine in ancient Greece, and probably the oldest. It lies on the south-west spur of Parnassus, about 2000 feet above the blue waters of the Gulf of Corinth, and seems to hide against the side of the mountain in a natural cleft. Probably the nature of the site led to Delphi being called the navel of the earth.

The oldest objects found at Delphi give a date of at least 1600 BC and the precinct, with its oracular chasm, was probably sacred long before that. The ruins of the temple of Apollo, the presiding god, can still be seen, above the Sacred Way that winds up from the road and passes the remains of the twenty-three treasuries built by the Greek states to house their sacred vessels. Above the temple is the theatre – Dionysus presided in Delphi when Apollo was absent among the Hyperboreans during the winter months – and above that again is the stadium, where the Pythian Games were held in the third year of each Olympiad.

Below the road is the precinct of the third deity of Delphi, the goddess Athene *Pronaia* – the guardian of the sanctuary. The famous circular temple, the Tholos, is to be found here, and speculation continues as to what its purpose was: it is not known to whom it was dedicated. The Castalian spring lies above the road, but below and to the east of Apollo's precinct.

The preservation – and presentation – of this wonderful site is a triumph of archaeological skill and a fitting memorial to Théophile

Homolle and the École Française, who began excavations there in 1892. Before work could begin the whole village of Kastri had to be evacuated and its people rehoused and re-landed a short distance away. An enlightened French government contributed much to the success of the archaeologists, paying the huge sum necessary for the move.

There is a magic about Delphi that cannot be expressed. It has to be experienced, and it is impossible to say how much its glorious past contributes to the effect. The situation itself is striking, with the Phaedriades, the 'shining' rocks of Parnassus, dominating the scene: the Pleistos valley and the sea of olive trees stretching away to the Gulf of Corinth; and, to the east, the harsh road through the mountains from Athens and Thebes. The road which Oedipus followed, away from the oracle, leads to the place where three roads met.

See the entry for Oedipus, and the following one for the oracle whose every utterance was heard with profound respect for centuries.

Delphic Oracle In Greek mythology the origin of the oracle at Delphi came about through the agency of Zeus, who sent two eagles to fly from the opposite extremities of the earth. They met at Delphi, and established that the spot was the centre of the world, the navel. A stone marked like a navel – *omphalos* – existed near the fissure in the rock from which the oracle spoke – the *adyton*. In classical times the *adyton* was an underground rock chamber in the temple of Apollo.

Originally, the site of the oracle was sacred to Mother Earth (Gaia) and Delphi was called Pytho. It was guarded by a serpent, the creature of the earth, and the mythology of Apollo tells how he slew the serpent and made the oracle his own. In time the serpent became known as Python and was accredited with crimes against Apollo's mother. Henceforth it was the shrine of Pythian Apollo, called Loxias, the god of prophecy. There are several versions; one gives the name of the serpent as Delphyne – while the term for womb is *delphys* – to explain the name of Delphi (*Delphoi*, strictly speaking – the familiar Delphi is the Latin form).

The oracle was pronounced by a priestess of Apollo, the Pythia, in a state of possession. The inducement of her condition has been argued over for a long time and no satisfactory conclusion has been reached. There was a theory that the tripod on which she sat was, in its position in the rock chamber, conveniently placed to surround her with mephitic vapours from the depths of the earth, though this has been largely disproved by the excavations. Largely, but not completely: the region is subject to earthquakes and much could have changed since classical times. Another theory is that the Pythia chewed laurel leaves – the plant was sacred to Apollo, and the leaves contain cyanide.

However, as H.J. Rose points out, no 'explanation' of this kind is really necessary: spiritual possession is a well-attested fact and there are thousands of recorded cases of a voice 'speaking through' someone else. There would have been no lack of priestesses for the oracular shrine.

The decline of Delphi and the oracle of Apollo, or, to put it another way the decline of this centre of moral excellence and guidance in personal and political integrity, can be seen in history as parallelled by the decline of Greece herself. The rise of Macedon and the crushing of the Greek city states; the advent of the Romans – Sulla plundered the shrine in 86 BC – and the fashion for astrology; the old times were gone and the world was the darker for it.

The enlightened Emperor Hadrian tried to re-establish Delphi's influence, but his efforts failed, and the Christians were growing in numbers. The oracle was to all intents and purposes dead by the time Constantine made Christianity the official religion of the empire in AD 313. The last effort was made by Julian the Apostate (*c.* 331–363 AD), whose life's dream was the restoration of the old Greek religion. But the Pythia herself told him that the oracle's days were over, and in AD 385 the Emperor Theodosius, in the name of Christianity, silenced the voice of Apollo for ever.

Demeter The sister of Zeus, Hera, Poseidon and Hades; the daughter of Cronus and Rhea. This is according to Hesiod, and it makes the Olympians a peculiarly incestuous family. But it must be remembered that the gods were older than the recorders, and Demeter may well have been the oldest of all.

She was the goddess of the fruitful earth, a concept more ancient by far than that of a sky god such as Zeus. Demeter was worshipped throughout mainland Greece and her festivals were enormously popular; her mysteries were celebrated twice a year at Eleusis and were held in such honour that no one was ever known to break the vow of secrecy required of an initiate.

In mythology Demeter is best known as the sorrowing mother, whose daughter was stolen from her by Hades and carried off to the nether world to be his Queen. The kidnapping was witnessed by the sun god, Helios, who told Demeter: she, in an agony of grief, left Olympus and abandoned her duties, and the world grew desolate without its mother goddess.

(Demeter's daughter, later called Persephone, was originally referred to as *Kore* – the maiden. As Persephone she has a mythology of her own so she will be referred to as Kore in this entry.)

Demeter's wanderings eventually took her to Eleusis, not far from Athens, and there she rested in the guise of an old woman. She was treated with kindness by the King, Celeus, and given the care of his baby son. She was amused by the bawdy humour and jesting of Iambe, a maid in the King's household, and, while she refused wine, enjoyed a draught of *kykeon,* a sort of barley water with mint flavouring. Grateful for the goodness shown to her, Demeter decided to make the King's son immortal. She rubbed ambrosia into his limbs and then laid him in the fire to burn away his mortality. But the Queen, Metanira, came upon her and gave a scream of terror at what she saw. Demeter, to assure the frightened mother, revealed herself. She declared that Eleusis would be eternally honoured, and she would reveal to the people there the mysteries of the fruitful earth over which she presided.

In the meantime, Zeus, while he knew full well what his brother Hades had been up to, could not persuade his sister Demeter back to Olympus to restore the earth to fruitfulness. She refused, famine or not, until her daughter was returned to her. Zeus was obliged to demand of Hades that Kore be given up, although Hades was loth to surrender his chosen Queen. Finally he agreed – but it was then discovered that Kore had eaten of the food of the dead, some pomegranate seeds in the nether world. This bound her to the kingdom of Hades for ever. But the Olympians forced a compromise on Hades: Kore would spend most of the year on earth with her mother, and four months with Hades in his kingdom.

Demeter at once set about bringing the earth back to fruitfulness. To the young prince of Eleusis, Triptolemus, she gave ears of corn, and the knowledge of its cultivation. He carried it to the Greeks and on to the rest of the world. The Athenians often boasted that they were the first to receive the knowledge.

Demeter and Kore are really two aspects of the same goddess, a goddess who was in fact the eternal woman. The mother goddess –and

Demeter is, unmistakably, the mother goddess as well as the ancient corn goddess (inevitably, one might say, since the ancient earth mother was both) – was usually seen in three aspects: maiden, wife and mother. She was eternal because her functions never ceased – the maiden became the wife, who became the mother, who bore the maiden and attended at other births, and laid out the dead as an old woman; who died in time and was renewed as the maiden, who became a wife . . .

As a fertility goddess, Demeter, concerned with what the earth brought forth, was connected with the dead – hence the myth of Kore and her sojourn each year in the nether world.

Apart from her renowned cult centre at Eleusis, the great festival of Demeter was the Thesmophoria, held in the autumn (about the end of October) to honour her as Demeter *Thesmophoros,* the bringer of riches (of the earth). In Arcadia in the Peloponnese she was regarded as the consort of Poseidon, in his aspect as earth-holder (he was, as the entry for him shows, rather more than the god of the sea), and there is a story of Demeter's unsuccessful attempt to escape his attentions. It may have been because Poseidon was (says Hesiod) her brother, or it may have been that she was more concerned with the loss of Kore. Whatever the reason, she changed herself into a mare and slipped in among the horse herds of Arcadia. Poseidon, however, was as adept as his brother Zeus at getting what he wanted and his keen eye had spotted the transformation. He turned himself into a horse and joined the herd as well, and the outraged Demeter soon found herself mounted by a triumphant Poseidon. This equine union produced the wonderful horse, Arion, who became the steed of Adrastus, King of Argos.

See also Eleusinian Mysteries, Hecate, Persephone.

Deucalion The son of Prometheus, and the equivalent in Greek mythology of the Old Testament hero, Noah. Zeus, disgusted with the behaviour of King Lynceus of Arcadia, decided to destroy the whole race of men. Lynceus had instituted the worship of Zeus in Arcadia – but had offered up human sacrifice. The furious god turned Lynceus and his family into wolves, and retired to Olympus to plan the annihilation of the human race.

Prometheus warned his son Deucalion, King of Phthia, to be ready for the Deluge that was to come. Deucalion built an ark, stocked it with food, and went aboard with his wife, Pyrrha, daughter of Epimetheus and Pandora. The rain began to fall at once, and lasted for nine days, until all that could be seen were the mountain tops. When Zeus was satisfied the rain ceased, and the waters began to subside. Deucalion and Pyrrha found their ark resting on Parnassus, and when they disembarked they offered sacrifice to Zeus, and then went down to visit the shrine of Themis. (This was equated with Delphi by some mythographers: Themis, the personification of order, was occasionally named as one of the original deities, like Gaia.)

The prayers of Deucalion and Pyrrha were answered by the appearance of Themis herself. She instructed them to re-people the earth with the bones of their mother, which they should sow by casting them over their shoulders. They pondered this strange advice for a while before understanding what Themis meant: then they realised that the stones which lay all round them were the bones of their mother (Earth).

The stones which Deucalion cast grew into men, those cast by Pyrrha into women. Of their own children, the eldest son of Deucalion and Pyrrha was Hellen, the ancestor of the race of Hellenes.

The Deluge of this myth is without doubt the familiar one of the Old Testament and the Gilgamesh Epic of Babylon, and reflects a dim memory common to all the peoples of the Mediterranean.

See also Themis.

Diana A Roman goddess often identified with the Greek Artemis, though the resemblances are superficial and Diana's mythology speaks strongly of an original Latin deity going back to primitive times: she has no 'parentage' such as that contrived for Artemis by Hesiod, and was probably a fertility goddess, especially of human fertility. Diana was commonly worshipped in groves and wooded places, and the reverence shown her by women confirms her function as the guardian and protectress of women in childbirth. In that aspect she did resemble Artemis, and to a certain degree also in her being worshipped as a goddess of wild places. But Diana's antiquity on her native ground, and her original character, is best seen in the myth of the Golden Bough.

On the north shore of Lake Nemi, not far from Rome, there existed a grove of oak trees sacred to Diana *Nemorensis* (of the wood). Somewhere in the grove there was a particular tree – in the centre? the myth is tantalisingly inexact – and it bore the mistletoe. A runaway slave could, if he reached the grove, break off a mistletoe bough – if the priest of the grove did not kill him first. The bough gave the fugitive the right of combat: if he killed the priest he succeeded him, and succeeded also to the horrible, endless vigil, waiting for another who might, in turn, manage to reach the Golden Bough. The *Rex Nemorensis* was a doomed priest-king.

The Golden Bough was the point of departure for Sir James Frazer in his great study of religion and magic of that name. He concluded that the 'king' who served Diana was her consort as well as her priest: the equation to Aphrodite-Adonis and Cybele-Attis is plain, in principle if not in detail.

The mistletoe was sacred in many places in ancient times. It was believed, in classical Rome, that the Sibyl sent Aeneas (*Aeneid*, Book VI) to pluck the mistletoe, the Golden Bough that enabled him to descend to the nether world – and safely return.

Dicte, Mount In the eastern part of the island of Crete. In a cave of Mount Dicte Zeus was born, according to Hesiod. Identified as the modern Mount Lasithi, it was carefully investigated by D. G. Hogarth in 1900. He found a huge grotto, and in it a great number of votive offerings to the god, testifying to the strong belief in the myth which existed in historical times.

See also Zeus.

Dido The Queen of Carthage who loved Aeneas. The best known version of her story is the one told by Virgil in *The Aeneid,* but the legend is much older and was familiar to the Romans in the second century BC.

Elissa (Dido was a later name) was the daughter of Belus, King of Tyre, and the wife of Sychaeus (sometimes called Acerbas). When Elissa's brother Pygmalion succeeded to the throne he coveted the wealth of Sychaeus, and murdered him. Elissa fled from Tyre with a small band of followers and her husband's treasure safely intact. Arriving on the coast of Africa, Dido (our heroine has this name at Carthage; a possible meaning is 'the wanderer') obtained a grant of land – as much as could be covered with the skin of a bull. She chose a spot on a peninsula jutting into the sea, and then had a bull's skin cut into thin strips. Joined together, the strips enclosed the space which became, eventually, the great city of Carthage.

See also *The Aeneid* (Books I,II and IV) for the rest of Dido's story.

Diomedes 1. One of the Achaean heroes at the siege of Troy. He was the son of Tydeus and Deipyle, daughter of Adrastus, and at Troy was favoured by the goddess Athene, who helped him in battle (*Iliad*, Book V). Among those he defeated was Ares himself, and Aphrodite – who got her own back on him at a later date. In Book VI he is notably chivalrous to Glaucus, the Lycian prince fighting on the Trojan side, because of an hereditary friendship existing between their two families.

Other adventures in which Diomedes takes part are perhaps better known for his companions in them, and will be found in the entries listed below. His part in the second attack on Thebes (which was an inevitable event since his father, Tydeus, was one of the original Seven Against Thebes) is mentioned by Homer in Book IV.

Diomedes is a prominent character on the Achaean side, a man of valour as the Achaeans saw themselves – and in those terms rather more likeable than Achilles or Ajax the Locrian. He is bold, and a good strategist, whose advice is sound, and offered freely and frankly to Agamemnon. He kills without compunction, and that it hardly likeable – but it has to be seen in its context of military glory being the thing that mattered. He survives the Trojan War, and makes his last appearance in Homer in the *Odyssey*, Book III, where Nestor relates how Diomedes got safely home to Argos.

Apart from his adventures in Homer, the rest of his life is an anticlimax, as for so many of the Achaean leaders. He returns home to find that his wife, Aigialeia, has turned to another man – Aphrodite had brought this about – so he leaves Argos and sails away, eventually landing in Italy. Tradition makes him the founder of several cities, including Brundisium.

See also Epigoni, *Iliad*, Odysseus, Palamedes, Philoctetes, Rhesus.

Diomedes 2. The King of the Bistones in Thrace, who kept the fierce horses that lived on human flesh. See the entry for Heracles – the capture of the Thracian horses was his Eighth Labour.

Dionysus The son of Zeus and Semele, according to Hesiod. Homer hardly mentions him, though there is a brief reference to his persecution in the *Iliad* (Book VI).

In the most familiar version of his origins he is the son of Zeus and Semele, the daughter of Cadmus, King of Thebes. Zeus fell in love with her and visited her in the guise of a mortal. The jealous Hera, consort of Zeus, when she learned that the princess was six months with child, decided to adopt a guise of her own and appeared to Semele as an old woman of Thebes. Gaining the girl's confidence, she questioned her about her lover. Who was he? She advised Semele to demand the truth – to be *shown* his real identity. Hera then departed, satisfied that her rival would demand visible proof from her lover of who he really was.

When Zeus came again, Semele extracted a promise from him to grant her one request, and he agreed. When she made her request he knew that it would result in her death – no one, as Hera well knew, could look on the king of the gods in the full blaze of his divinity and survive. Semele persisted, and he yielded; she had a moment's glimpse of Zeus in his glory before she was consumed by the divine fire. But the same fire made her son, yet unborn, immortal. Zeus snatched the child from the fire and concealed him in his thigh, to be born at the proper time.

Zeus entrusted the care of the newborn baby to Semele's sister, Ino, and her husband, Athamas. But this had not escaped the watchful eye of Hera who, seeking to destroy the child, visited madness on his foster-parents. Dionysus survived, and Zeus gave him to Hermes to take to the nymphs of Nysa, a mountainside near Helicon. Some versions of the myth say that Hermes transformed the baby into a lamb or a kid to deceive the vengeful goddess; at all events he was delivered safely and grew to manhood on Nysa. Possibly it was there that he divined the properties of the vine and the benefits that the juice of the grapes could bring to man.

The young Dionysus was not honoured as a god, indeed he was persecuted by those who refused to recognise his divinity. So he left Greece and travelled into Asia, where none knew him, and there he learned to use his divine power. He commanded allegiance, and inspired devotion – everywhere men and women followed him. He returned to Greece in his full godhead as the son of Zeus, and Apollo admitted him to his shrine at Delphi. Thus Dionysus joined the company of the Olympians.

To the north of Greece, in Thrace and Macedonia, there was in very ancient times a powerful cult of the spirit of nature and fertility that found expression in human sacrifice, nature worship and orgiastic rites. It probably existed long before the Dorian Greeks made their way down into the peninsula. The newcomers brought their own gods but the ancient deities kept their strength, and the people continued to worship them. It was only a matter of time before the ancient cults had to be recognised and the acceptance of Dionysus into the Greek pantheon is a striking instance of this.

Scholars say that the cult of which Dionysus is the divine manifestation had its true beginnings farther east. It has been identified in Phrygia, in Asia Minor, and it has been proved that the peoples of Thrace and Phrygia were of the same race. The cult found its way into Greece about 1000 BC and made an irresistible appeal with its ecstatic character. At its centre was Dionysus, who represented the force of life in all growing things, animal and vegetable; eventually he was regarded as the god of the vine. But in earlier times his followers (most women, the guardians of fertility) did not need to drink; their frenzies were self-induced, and uncontrollable. It was dangerous to encounter a band of women in a Dionysiac frenzy: animals, and sometimes children, were torn to pieces and eaten – in the belief that to devour part of an animal was to partake of the god himself, a true sacramental meal.

The votaries of Dionysus – the women followers – were called maenads, 'mad women', a description of their behaviour during their frenzied worship. During the older, more bestial orgies the maenads often wore masks, and the god was also represented by one, carried on a pole. The pole was draped in an animal skin but the mask always bore a human face, and this simple form of representation in a religious ceremony developed until it reached a sophisticated stage which saw the beginning of the drama as an art form.

The admittance of Dionysus to the precinct of Apollo at Delphi during the winter months shows how completely the worship of the 'young god', Dionysus, was recognised and took its place among the more ordered forms of state religion. By the fifth century BC the principle expression of the worship of Dionysus could be seen in the dramatic festivals which were an essential part of Greek culture. The most famous was the great Dionysia – the spring festival of Dionysus.

The followers of the god were known by many names. Apart from maenads they were variously called Sileni, Satyrs, Bassarids, and perhaps most familiarly of all *bakchoi*, from one of the names of the god. It was as Bacchus that he was known to the Romans.

Dionysus is in many ways the most arresting of the Greek gods. In modern times, with the development of psychological enquiry, the personification of a god – or force – that makes us acknowledge our basic instincts and desires is intensely interesting. There are counterparts of Dionysus in other ancient religions but we in the West, who regard ourselves as the inheritors of Greek culture, lost sight of the idea for centuries. The Greeks, with their marvellous sense of proportion, re- alised that instincts could not be denied; but at the same time they were well aware that the dangers of denial were equalled by the dangers of excess. This philosophy is finely expressed in one of the greatest of all Greek plays, *The Bacchae*.

See also *The Bacchae* (Euripides).

Dionysus Zagreus Another version of the Dionysus story makes him the son of Zeus and Persephone. Hera, once more, brings about the near-destruction of the divine child, but in this case by making him the victim of the Titans, traditionally the enemies of the gods. The Titans nearly devoured the body of Zagreus (his name in this version), but Athene managed to snatch up the heart and took it to Zeus, who hurled his lightning at the Titans and destroyed them. From their ashes was born the race of men, who have therefore a divine element mixed with their base nature.

Zeus then swallowed the heart of Zagreus, and he was eventually reborn as the son of Semele.

This is probably an older version than the one already given: the name Zagreus is not Greek – probably Phrygian or Thracian, and the connection with the later version is plain. *Zagreus* means 'torn in pieces' which, as Dionysus, manifest in living things, he frequently was. This was the form of the story most favoured by the followers of the religion called Orphism.

See also Persephone.

Dioscuri, The Castor and Polydeuces (Pollux is the Latin form), the sons of Zeus according to one of the Homeric hymns. But elsewhere in Homer, and in Hesiod, they are the sons of Tyndareus and Leda and therefore brothers of the beautiful Helen.

In the *Iliad* (Book III) Helen looks for them among the Achaean leaders: the following lines state that, unknown to her, they have died at home in Sparta. In the *Odyssey* (Book XI) they are mentioned again as having died – but are honoured like the gods and each one lives

every other day. Pindar, in one of his Nemean odes, tells that Castor
was mortally wounded in the fight with Idas and Lynceus, that Polydeuces implored Zeus to be allowed to share his brother's suffering,
and that life on alternate days for them was granted by Zeus – they
had to share a single life. Pindar also states that Castor was the son of
Zeus, and Polydeuces the son of Tyndareus: they were borne as twins
by Leda.

Pindar wrote at a much later date than Homer but he may have been
writing down a story that was part of an already accepted tradition; he
may, on the other hand, have been explaining the suggestion in the
Odyssey in poetic terms. The origin of the Dioscuri probably lies in
heroic myth, and like many heroes they were favoured by the gods,
eventually becoming honoured as divine.

In mythology they take part in heroic adventures; they sail in the
Argo, they rescue their sister Helen from Theseus, and in their last
adventure come face to face with a rival set of twins, Idas and Lynceus.

See also Amycus, *Argonautica,* Helen, Idas and Lynceus, Leda,
Theseus.

Dirce The wife of Lycus, who was the brother of Nycteus and therefore the son of one of the Spartoi. Nycteus killed himself when his
daughter Antiope, pregnant by Zeus, fled for refuge to Sicyon; but
before dying he charged his brother to punish Antiope. Lycus made
war on Sicyon and captured Antiope, and ordered that the twin sons
she had borne be left to die on Mount Kithaeron. Dirce was Lycus'
wife, and she took pleasure in being cruel to Antiope at every opportunity, knowing that Antiope was a prisoner and at the mercy of Lycus.

However, the twin sons of Antiope survived their exposure. they
were rescued by shepherds and grew up to take revenge on Dirce for
the way she had ill-treated their mother. One of Dirce's threats had
been that she would have Antiope roped to the horns of a wild bull:
she was given this treatment herself by Amphion and Zethus and was
soon dragged and stamped to death.

See also Amphion and Zethus, Antiope, Lycus.

Dis The Roman god of the nether world, loosely the equivalent of
Hades. His name is believed to be from the Latin for Pluto (one of the
names of Hades), originally *Dives* – the rich. Dis and Proserpine

enjoyed a cult in Rome for some centuries but the name, Dis, gradually became a symbolic term for the nether world.

See also Hades, Persephone, Pluto.

Dodona, Oracle Of Sacred to Zeus, it was situated in the mountains of Epirus in northern Greece. The myths of its origin tell of a pigeon that flew from Thebes in Egypt and alighted on an oak tree at Dodona. It spoke to the people and ordered the founding of a sacred precinct where the oracle of Zeus would be heard. The oracle was centred on the oak tree – the will of Zeus was divined from the rustling of the leaves (Herodotus calls it a beech tree). The sanctuary at Dodona was shared with Dione, the mother of Aphrodite according to Homer.

It is known that the questions were written by the enquirers themselves, upon lead tablets, though there were both priests and priestesses in attendance. It is believed that the oracle was interpreted by other means as well as the rustling of the leaves; by the flight of the pigeons kept there, and possibly by the use of a bronze gong. Some of the lead tablets have been discovered and can be seen in the museum at Iannina – in all of them the questions are of a personal nature, unlike those concerning statecraft and morality so often asked at Delphi.

The oracle is referred to three times by Homer. In the *Iliad* (Book XVI) Achilles prays to Dodonean Zeus, and calls the priests of Dodona 'The Helli, who go with unwashed feet and sleep upon the earth'. In the *Odyssey* (Book XIV) the hero himself, in disguise, tells of 'Odysseus' going to Dodona to discover the will of Zeus from the mighty oak tree. He speaks in the same terms to his wife, Penelope, in Book XIX.

The presence of Dione at Dodona suggests that the oracle was, like the more famous one at Delphi, of great antiquity, and taken over by a male god in the course of the Indo-European migrations.

See also Aphrodite, Zeus.

Dorians The wave of invading migrants – and the last – who followed the Achaeans into the Greek peninsula and islands. They were of the same stock as the Achaeans and spoke the same language, but brought little with them apart from a powerful weapon – the cutting sword made from iron. They were believed to have come down by way of Epirus and western Macedonia.

The arrival of the Dorians brought Achaean – Mycenaean – civilisation to an end, and from about 1100 BC there followed a three-century Dark Age. It was during this period that the ancient heroic tales were told and re-told, and probably acquired the numerous versions familiar to us from mythology.

Eventually a new culture arose and, blending with the art of Ionic Greece, produced the great flowering that represents what most of us recognise as Greek art. In some places it also produced the remarkable advance in ideas that led to democracy: but in others, particularly in Sparta, the Dorians continued to think of themselves as conquerors, and therefore as an élite, with the original people serving them.

See also Heraclidae.

Dryads The nymphs of trees, who came into being when the tree was born and ceased to be at its death.

E

Echidna The daughter of Phorcys and his sister Ceto (they were, according to Hesiod, children of Gaia (Earth) and Nereus, the ancient sea god). Echidna was half-woman and half-snake and ate men raw. She mated with Typhon, another monster produced by Gaia by mating with Tartarus, and gave birth to, among others, Cerberus, the Hydra, the Chimaera and the Nemean lion. Hesiod calls her immortal, but in one story she is killed by Argus, the hundred-eyed, while asleep.

See also Cerberus, Gaia, Heracles, Typhon.

Echo A nymph who appears in two separate myths. In one the god Pan falls in love with her, and is repulsed. In revenge he endows her with a voice that can do nothing but repeat the last word she hears. In another she falls in love with the beautiful Narcissus, and is herself repulsed in turn. She pines away, until she is nothing more than a lonely disembodied voice.

See also Narcissus, Pan.

Egeria A Roman goddess with two particular associations – childbirth, and fountains. Women made sacrifices to Egeria when they were pregnant, hoping for an easy delivery when their child was born. This made a connection with the goddess Diana, and both deities were worshipped at Aricia. Egeria's association with water was at the spring of the Camenae, outside the Porta Capena of Rome: the connection is obscure, however, though Roman legend says that it was here that Egeria gave wise counsel to Numa Pompilius, the successor to Romulus as King of Rome.

See also Camenae, Diana.

Eileithyia The daughter of Zeus and Hera, according to Hesiod. She is a goddess with a function but very little mythology, though she is met in extended accounts of the births of Heracles and Leto's delivery of her divine twins, Apollo and Artemis. She was probably a pre-Olympian goddess (or goddesses – she is sometimes referred to in the plural, as Eileithyiae). Sometimes Eileithyia is identified with Artemis, sometimes with Hera, and her function as the nurse-goddess of women in childbirth is sometimes attributed to her Olympian sisters. Unlike them, she had no other function.

See also Artemis, Hera, Juno (Lucina).

Eirene One of the Horae (the seasons), according to Hesiod. She was the personification of Peace: her name is perhaps more familiar in its more common form – Irene.

Electra Like that of Antigone, the character of Electra is the creation of the poets as far as can be gathered from the sources available to us. The first mention of this daughter of Agamemnon and Clytemnestra is in Stesichorus, who wrote an *Oresteia* in the fifth century BC; but only fragments survive, and the development of this remarkable conception of an avenging fury can be found in Aeschylus, Sophocles and Euripides.

A basically repellent character, Electra is presented differently by each of the tragic poets, who saw the implications of the story in different ways. In Aeschylus she is a small part of a great design; Euripides uses her to utter his incisive comments on human responsibility – but always within the limits of the traditions from which the character arises. Sophocles offers no comment: his play is a high-voltage shocker and he leaves judgement to his audience.

All the tragedians keep Electra's aims in mind. She is perhaps a shade more sympathetic in Aeschylus but she remains guilty of a pathological nursing of her grievances. She is given a form of happy ending in the two plays of Euripides in which she appears, bestowed as a wife on Pylades, the faithful friend of her brother Orestes.

See also *Electra* (Euripides), *Electra* (Sophocles), *Oresteia* (Aeschylus), Orestes.

Electra A tragedy by Sophocles. The date is uncertain: it may have been produced before the play of the same name by Euripides – or just after it. Scholars are, however, reasonably sure of the dates of Sophocles' birth and death (496–406 BC), and it is unlikely that he was less than eighty years old at the time. In the light of this the sheer force of the play is astonishing.

For the background and the events leading up to the play, see the entries for Agamemnon and Clytemnestra. The action takes place in Mycenae, before the palace of Aegisthus and Clytemnestra, formerly the palace of Agamemnon.

Three men enter: Orestes, the son of Agamemnon and young brother of Electra, his tutor and Pylades, Orestes' friend. Orestes' sisters, Electra and Chrysothemis, have lived on in the palace under the harsh eye of their mother Clytemnestra, and Aegisthus the usurper. Electra had saved the infant Orestes, the true heir, and entrusted him to his tutor, who has served him faithfully and brought him to manhood. Orestes has returned to claim his kingdom, and the Delphic oracle has told him that he must punish his father's murderers alone, without help. He and the tutor must plan very carefully – if Orestes is recognised he will be killed without compunction. (In this play Pylades is present but never speaks.)

The tutor will enter the palace as a stranger – his hair has turned white in the meantime, and the Queen will hardly remember what a servant looked like. He will tell that Orestes is dead, and he will just be a messenger, bringing the news. Meanwhile, Orestes and Pylades will visit Agamemnon's tomb where Orestes will leave a lock of hair. They are about to separate when they hear a wild, keening cry from the palace. Orestes wonders if it can be his sister Electra: the tutor warns him he cannot risk making himself known, and the three men hurry away.

Electra emerges from the palace. The chorus, the women of Mycenae, listen uneasily while she rails at her condition. They remind her that her sister Chrysothemis is facing life as best she can; nothing can bring their dead father back and Orestes will, surely, return one day.

Chrysothemis appears, carrying offerings to her father's tomb – Clytemnestra has tortured dreams and seeks to placate the dead. Electra cuts off a lock of her hair and gives it to her sister – it is the only offering she has. But she quarrels with Chrysothemis and taunts her with being the Queen's true daughter. Her sister warns her that her behaviour will lead to her permanent confinement; then she proceeds to her father's tomb.

Clytemnestra enters the courtyard to place offerings on the altar of Apollo and Electra confronts her. A stormy exchange follows during which Electra questions her mother's true motive for the murder of Agamemnon: it is brought to an end when Clytemnestra turns her back on her and goes on to the altar. She is there when the tutor enters, and brings news of Orestes' death. Clytemnestra is exultant; Electra is crushed – the return of her brother was all that sustained her. But now Chrysothemis hurries back from the tomb, excited. Orestes is alive! On their father's tomb was a lock of hair; not her's, or Electra's, certainly not the Queen's.

Orestes returns, with Pylades, and the tutor admits them to the palace. Electra waits in the courtyard, her excitement mounting to frenzy when she hears her mother's death screams. Then she waits for Aegisthus, soon to return. Orestes will kill him too.

Electra A tragedy by Euripides, first produced about 413 BC. The story and the course of the action differ in detail from Sophocles' treatment of the same subject, and Euripides introduces a character – probably found in another version of the myth – who appears neither in Aeschylus nor in Sophocles. This is the husband of Electra, a man of common birth to whom Aegisthus has married her, to ensure that she cannot bear a son of royal lineage. In the manner of the times a claimant to the throne of Mycenae would need an unassailable pedigree as well as direct descent. In most translations this character is called 'the peasant', a description which, as Gilbert Murray points out (though he, oddly enough, calls him a peasant also) does him less than justice. He is a man who owns land and cultivates it to provide his livelihood. A fairer description would be 'the farmer'.

In Euripides the characters of Electra and Orestes are far from heroic. The sister is a creature of inexhaustible self-pity; the brother a young man with apparently no will of his own and the victim of ever-present fears. He is totally insecure, driven along by forces stronger than himself. The oracle which commands him to kill is, to Euripides, too base (no matter how tradition describes it) to be regarded as an order from the gods. To him it is merely a response to ancient and savage demands for revenge. Orestes' sister, too, is older and far stronger than her brother, and there is the faint, desperate hope of a prince without a birthright who knows that usurpers often succeed. All these factors drive Orestes far beyond his natural capacity and, in a later play (*Orestes*) are shown by Euripides to have done serious damage to his already precarious balance.

The setting of Euripides' play is a mountainside in Argos, near Mycenae, in front of the farmer's modest home. It is dawn, and the farmer is about to start his day. He reflects on his strange situation, married to a princess of Mycenae – a royal wife whom he has never touched, honouring both her and the memory of her father, Agamemnon. Electra appears from the house and the farmer tries to persuade her that menial work is not required of her. She replies that she goes to draw water from the well, so that all may see the condition of Agamemnon's daughter now that Aegisthus rules and her mother Clytemnestra is his wife . . . Orestes and Pylades make their entrance when the farmer and Electra leave the scene, and the story of blood vengeance gets under way.

As well as the character of the farmer, Euripides introduces a *deus ex machina* to bring the play to a close (both of the Dioscuri appear but only Castor speaks). The murder of Aegisthus has taken place off stage – Orestes and Pylades present themselves as strangers from Thessaly, and strike Aegisthus down while he is at the altar making a sacrifice. Electra has sent a message to the palace saying that she has given birth to a son, knowing that such news will bring her mother to her side. Clytemnestra is thus decoyed into visiting the farmer's house not knowing that her husband is already dead. Electra wants her mother to be *her* victim, solely. But when Clytemnestra is within the house it falls to Orestes to commit that murder, too. And the second murder nearly destroys him and his sister – suddenly they realise what will follow. They are guilt-stained, they have no future; no man will ever look at Electra kindly, and Orestes – where will he be welcome?

But there has to be an end, Euripides implies, and he brings the divine twins on to the scene to make order of the horrible condition that the ancient thirst for vengeance has brought about. Electra will be taken as wife by Pylades, himself the son of a king (of Phocis). Orestes' future is harsher: he cannot set foot in Argos or Mycenae – he is a matricide and his inheritance is poisoned. Worse, the Furies have been aroused and are already winging their way to his side. He will know their torments and he must make his way, with all possible speed, to Athens, where he will be judged, and be shown how to expiate his crime. His guilt, Castor says, belongs to Apollo, who commanded these killings. Apollo will take the guilt upon himself – Justice will order that.

Brother and sister part – neither will see Argos again. Electra goes to Phocis with Pylades, and the farmer, who will have an honoured place in a new kingdom. Orestes turns towards the Isthmus road, to make his way to Athens and seek the promised absolution, the beatings of the Furies' wings already sounding in his ears.

Eleusinian Mysteries Eleusis was a city that stood by the sea about ten miles north-west of Athens. The road to Eleusis went on to the Isthmus and so to the Peloponnese. The city stood on a very ancient inhabited site and was independent until about the seventh century BC when it became part of the Attic confederacy and so under the leadership of Athens. The antiquity of the site was probably one of the reasons for the reverence with which it was held, but the city's unique place in the ancient world was due to its connection with the goddess Demeter, and the celebration of her Mysteries there, at the very place she rested when searching for her daughter, Persephone. The Great Mysteries were celebrated in early autumn, the Lesser Mysteries in the spring.

The Mysteries were connected with the birth and death, annually, of the corn, and H.J. Rose points out that the rituals are more ancient than the goddess herself – that is, before Demeter was named there was an ancient festival there, pre-Hellenic, of the same kind, to the ancient Earth Mother. Both Demeter and Persephone, two aspects of the same goddess, were honoured at the Mysteries. Later a third deity was added, Iacchos, variously said to be the consort, or son, of Demeter. Robert Graves suggests that his name arose from the riotous hymn, the *Iacchos,* that was sung on the sixth day of the Mysteries.

See also Demeter, Persephone.

Elysium A conception of the after life, found in both Homer and Hesiod, for those favoured by the gods. Also called the Isles of the

Blest, Elysium was believed to be somewhere at the ends of the earth – this was before the Pythagorean theory, later proved by Aristotle, that the earth was a sphere. So Elysium would have been situated at the ends of a flat earth, surrounded by Ocean, under the vault of heaven. Those translated to Elysium were usually exempted from death, it being supposed that they were to enjoy a blessedly happy 'life' – not oblivion.

Endymion The son of Zeus and the nymph Calyce who became King of Elis (the part of Greece where Olympia is situated). He was very beautiful, and was observed by Selene, the moon goddess, when he lay asleep on Mount Latmus. She fell in love with him, and contrived that he should sleep forever. Every night she descended to embrace him while he slept.

Enyo A minor deity in Greek religion, associated with Ares and hence with war. She has no mythology of her own, though her brother deity, Enyalios, makes a brief appearance in the *Iliad* (Book XX). However, H.J. Rose points out that the name Enyalios is probably an epithet –if not another name of Ares himself.

Eos The goddess of the dawn, as described by both Hesiod and Homer. In Hesiod she is the daughter of the Titans, Hyperion and Thea, and it is interesting to note that while Hesiod gives those same parents to Helios (the sun) and Selene (the moon), Homer uses the name of Hyperion for the sun in the *Odyssey* (Book XII).
See also Cephalus, Tithonus.

Ephesus The great city of Ephesus in Ionia was founded by colonists from Athens about 1100 BC. The site, ideal at the time, was at the mouth of the River Cayster, and not far from the spot hallowed, in ancient tradition, by a goddess whom the Greeks identified as Artemis. Both factors contributed to the city's ancient glory: Ephesus was one of the great seaports and trading centres of the ancient world, and the temple built to her patron goddess was one of the wonders of the world.
Ephesus declined only in the early centuries of the Christian era, when the famous harbour was choked by silt brought down by the river. The ruins are now far from the sea – the once famous road that led to the harbour simply dwindles away into the country.
See also Artemis.

Epidaurus A city on a peninsula in the Saronic Gulf, Epidaurus was celebrated in ancient times for the sanctuary of the god Asclepius. The ruins have been carefully excavated, and they lie in a small green valley of pleasant restfulness. Perhaps an even more famous, because better preserved, feature of Epidaurus is the magnificent theatre, which dates from the fourth century BC. A dramatic festival is held there annually and attended by thousands of visitors making use of a unique opportunity to attend performances of the Greek tragedies in the correct setting. There are seats for 12,000 spectators.

See also Asclepius.

Epigoni The sons of the Seven who marched against Thebes. The name means 'those who came later' or the younger generation. When the expedition of Adrastus and Polynices failed the only survivor was Adrastus, King of Argos. In his old age he rallied the sons of the fallen champions – with his own son, Aegialeus – for a new attack, which succeeded. Thebes was destroyed, an event which probably occurred in fact and which scholars believe took place just before the Trojan war (early twelfth century BC). The expedition of the Seven is mentioned in the *Iliad* (Book IV), during a confrontation between Agamemnon and Diomedes, one of the Epigoni.

The names of the Epigoni differ in the principal versions but the one which fits best with what is known from the Theban epic cycle is as follows: Alcmaeon and Amphilochus, sons of Amphiaraus; Aegialeus, son of Adrastus; Diomedes, son of Tydeus; Promachos, son of Parthenopaeus; Sthenelus, son of Capaneus; Thersander, son of Polynices; and Euryalus the son of Mecisteus.

See also Adrastus, Alcmaeon, Amphiaraus, Diomedes.

Erebus The primeval darkness which, according to Hesiod, emerged from Chaos. The brother of Night, he became the father of Day and Sky by her.

Epona A goddess worshipped by the Romans as the deity associated with horses and mules. There may have been a pre-Roman goddess with her functions but the name itself is Celtic and the deity seems to have found her way back to Rome, so to speak, from Gaul. Some authorities believe that she was merely the personification of the old horse cult common to the migratory peoples who moved into Europe from the grasslands of central Asia. The many surviving monuments to her were dedicated chiefly by Roman soldiers.

Erectheus There is a confusion of myths about the founders and first kings of Athens. Erechtheus, often confused with Erichthonius, was a legendary King who, in response to the Delphic oracle, was required to sacrifice one of his daughters to save Athens from the Eleusinian invaders. The name of the daughter is Chthonia in some versions, Otionia in others; one account tells how all the King's three daughters agreed to die together. Erechtheus won the battle, and thereafter Eleusis was subject to Athens.

See also Cecrops, Erichthonius, Ion, Poseidon.

Erichthonius The son of Hephaestus and Earth, who grew out of the seed spilt on the earth by the divine artificer when he tried to force his attentions on Athene. Earth nourished the seed and when the child was born Athene put him into a wooden chest and gave it to the daughters of Cecrops to look after. She forbade them to open the chest, and this, inevitably, was what they could not help themselves from doing, to see what was inside. When they did see the contents they rushed off and hurled themselves off the Acropolis. They may have been infected with madness by Athene, angry at being disobeyed: or they may have been horrified by the sight of a child who was half-serpent, having been born from the earth. (See the entries for Cecrops and Cadmus for a comment on the earth-serpent tradition.)

Other traditions make Erichthonius the father of Pandion, who was the father of Erechtheus.

See also Athene, Hephaestus.

Eris The personification of strife. In Homer she is the sister of Ares, and is to be found with him when he takes part in battles (*Iliad*, Book IV). In Hesiod she is the daughter of Night and the mother of battles, quarrels and lawlessness.

Eris was present at the marriage of Peleus and Thetis, the parents of Achilles, and provoked the quarrel among the goddesses which led to the Judgment of Paris and so to the Trojan War. But this story is a later addition and not part of the original myth.

See also Judgment of Paris, Paris, Peleus, Thetis.

Eros Traditionally, the god of love, but in origin something rather different and more profound. In Homer there is no god as such; *eros* is the irresistible attraction between two people, which can deprive them of their sense of proportion and, taken further, can destroy them. Hence the attraction felt for each other by Paris and Helen and what it led to. In Hesiod Eros is a god; but he is not an overfed baby boy flitting around with a bow and arrow – he is one of the oldest of the gods, as old as Gaia (Earth) herself. Nor is he the son of Aphrodite, merely her constant companion.

Eros was a force to be feared for the havoc he could cause, and neither gods nor men were immune from him. Out of these conceptions a god of love emerged, though as late as Euripides he is recognised as dangerous, in one of the choruses in *Iphigenia in Aulis*; it is here also that his arrows are mentioned – though in metaphor, not in fact.

Eros inspires love, nevertheless, and for the Greeks this had no boundaries; he was as much the agent of the love that men and women could feel for a member of their own sex as the love of man for woman. Thus Eros enjoyed a cult among the soldiers of the Sacred Band of Thebes.

He is sometimes called the son of Aphrodite by Hermes. Hermes was himself a god of fertility in origin, and Eros, in his cult centre at Thespiae, was so worshipped.

Eteocles The elder son of Oedipus. In the Theban tradition, Oedipus did not leave the city after blinding himself, as in Sophocles' famous tragedy; he shut himself up in one of the inner chambers of the palace while his sons grew to maturity. The late Queen Jocasta's brother, Creon, administered the kingdom in the meantime. Eteocles and his brother Polynices insulted their father in various ways: they served him with inferior food at table, and against his expressed wish made use of the vessels which had belonged to King Laius, Oedipus' father. Oedipus had unwittingly murdered Laius on the road from Delphi, and had ordered that the vessels should be shut away for ever. The blind King erupted in rage: he cursed his sons, calling down eternal disunity between them, and praying that they would die at each other's hands.

How the curse was fulfilled is part of the Theban epic cycle. For the other strands of the story see the following entries: Antigone, Adrastus, Epigoni, Oedipus, Polynices, The Seven Against Thebes.

Eumolpus In mythology the ancestor of the clan, the Eumolpidae, who officiated at the celebration of the Eleusinian Mysteries. He was believed to be the son of Poseidon. His story is confused and probably the remnant of a local tradition, since it was generally believed that the goddess Demeter instituted the Mysteries, whereas Eumolpus in one version was himself the founder. He was defeated and killed in the war against Athens when that city was defended by Erechtheus.

Euripides The latest born of the three great tragic poets of ancient Greece, though he and Sophocles were contemporaries. It is believed that he was born in 486 BC in the region, or on the island, of Salamis, and some of his contemporaries maintained that his parents were shopkeepers. Euripides' beginnings may have been humble – there is no certain documentation – but he is one of the great names of European literature, and in his own time he earned the admiration of no less a man than Socrates. As far as our information goes, Euripides seems to have been a retiring man by nature, though he held the priesthood of Zeus at Phyla for a time, and was a member of an embassy sent to Syracuse by Athens. He lived to the age of eighty, and was the father of three sons, one of whom arranged the posthumous production of some of his father's plays. Euripides left Athens in the later years of his life, and there is no exact information about the reason. He spent a little time at Magnesia in Thessaly, where he was much honoured, and spent his last years at the court of King Archelaus of Macedonia. One of the plays he wrote there was *The Bacchae*.

Euripides was as unlike Aeschylus and Sophocles as could be imagined. They worked within the framework of accepted beliefs; Euripides questioned them – and often found them wanting. The scientific curiosity of the Greeks led them to search for natural reasons for what had been, hitherto, supernatural phenomena, and Euripides' inherent scepticism could not tolerate for long the idea that gods maintained the order of the universe: or, if they were responsible for it, he saw that they were not doing a very good job. Even in the beliefs which his fellow Athenians accepted without question Euripides found the Olympians often cruel, stupid and prompted by desires that would be shameful in a human being. The gods, to him, were far less noble than a noble man or woman. He used them in his plays, frequently; sometimes to make a point of devastating truth, as in *The Bacchae*, sometimes to resolve a situation beyond the wit of the characters he had created, as in his *Electra*; in his *Hippolytus* he uses two of them as opposing forces, jealous of their due.

His characters – his people, are the great thing in the plays of Euripides. His consuming interest in humanity, in the motives of men and women, gives his plays their force, and their timelessness. Medea may be a sorceress; she is also a woman deeply wronged, and her persecutors are contemptible. Pentheus foolishly opposes Dionysus, but he is a man afraid of his own nature, and that additional conflict is what makes *The Bacchae* a play for all time.

Euripides lived during the period of the Peloponnesian War and, like Aristophanes, hated it and what it was doing to his city and to the character of his fellow citizens. His indictment of man at war, *The Trojan Women*, is an imperfect play, being a succession of tragic scenes on a single theme. But the impact is profound, and it will never cease to be read.

Of the ninety-two plays he wrote only seventeen survive: *Alcestis, Andromache, The Bacchae, Electra, Hecuba, Helen, Heracles, The Heraclidae, Hippolytus, Ion, Iphigenia in Aulis, Iphigenia in Tauris, Medea, Orestes, The Phoenician Women, The Suppliant Women, The Trojan Women*. A play whose authorship is in doubt but is believed by some to have been written by Euripides is *Rhesus*, dealing with an episode of the Trojan War. Another play, *Hypsipyle*, exists only in fragments.

Europa The daughter of Agenor, King of Tyre, and the sister of Cadmus, the founder of Thebes. Europa was beautiful, and it was not long before Zeus spotted her, with her handmaidens, when she went each day to her father's fields near the sea. One day Europa was arrested by the sight of a fine white bull grazing close by. The creature was plainly of a gentle disposition and seemed to encourage her to stroke his spreading horns and beautiful white coat. Europa was delighted, and climbed on the bull's back. At once the bull turned towards the sea and plunged into the waves, the terrified girl clinging desperately round his neck.

Zeus, in his assumed bull shape, swam to the island of Crete, where he was able to enjoy his captive. Some versions say he took the form of an eagle for this exercise but it is more likely that he kept his bull form, since a strange echo of the myth occurs in the story of Pasiphae and her passion for another bull.

Europa bore three children to Zeus: Minos, Rhadamanthus and Sarpedon. Then she married Asterion, King of Crete, who adopted her sons. She was worshipped as a goddess after her death.

The story of Europa is very old, and probably looks back to a time when the bull, a symbol of strength and fertility, was the principal cult animal of the eastern Mediterranean: Homer and Hesiod give it passing mention, no more, and it was left to later story-tellers to adorn it. Crete, and its Minoan civilisations, are famous for the bull cult that existed there and it is possible that the figure of Zeus was grafted on to an ancient tradition, making the king of the gods the principal in a ritual of fertility. The same theme occurs in the stories of Io and Pasiphae, and an essential part of them is that the female figure is always a member of a royal or priestly family.

See also Agenor, Cadmus, Io, Minos, Pasiphae, Rhadamanthus, Sarpedon.

Eurydice The wife of Orpheus, who died from the bite of a poisonous snake while fleeing from the advances of Aristaeus. Her story is really a part of the myths surrounding Orpheus, who almost succeeded in rescuing her from the world of the dead.

See also Orpheus.

Evander 1. A minor god in Greek mythology, worshipped in Arcadia and connected with Pan. Tradition made him the son of Hermes and a nymph, daughter of the river god, Ladon. He was probably an aspect of Hermes, who was in origin an ancient god of Arcadia before being given a place among the Olympians.

Evander 2. In Roman mythology the grandson of Pallas of Tegea in Arcadia. He plays a large part in the later events of the *Aeneid,* when he becomes the ally of Aeneas in Italy, having left Arcadia himself and founded his own city on a hill by the river Tiber. He called the city Pallenteum, after his grandfather; the site is known to us today as the Palatine Hill.

Evander was believed to have introduced the cults of Faunus (the Roman equivalent of Pan) and Hercules, and to have established the festival of the Lupercalia.

See also *Aeneid* (Books VII–XII), Lupercalia.

F

Fates, The The idea of each man's destiny being ordained and controlled by forces beyond his control is as old as man himself. The Greeks used various terms to describe these forces, and *aisa, moira* and the *daimon* are frequently encountered in Homer. The notion of a 'thread' of life inevitably gave rise to the notion of a 'spinner' and three spinners (*Klothes*) are mentioned in Hesiod, the first personification in Greek literature that we have. Hesiod's naming of the forces is also the earliest; Lachesis, who allots each man's portion; Clotho, who spins the thread of life, and Atropos, who will sever it at the appointed time. They are the daughters of Zeus and Themis but a later poet, Pindar, makes them bridal attendants of Themis upon her marriage to Zeus. The Fates frequently appear to function against the will of Zeus himself, but the gods have to obey them, since their very existence is part of the order of the universe and this the gods cannot gainsay.

See also Themis.

Faunus A Roman god of nature, Faunus evolved into a single deity from the original idea of the Fauni – spirits of the countryside. Faunus was worshipped as the guardian of crops and herds, and believed to possess oracular powers. His festival was celebrated in rural communities on 5 December, an occasion for dancing and general high spirits. As a promoter of fertility in herds he was referred to as Inuus; as an oracular god he was Fatuus. He had female counterparts, Fauna and Fatua, and in historical times was identified with the Greek god, Pan.

The shepherd, Faustulus, who found the twins Romulus and Remus being suckled by a she-wolf, is believed by some scholars to be a derivation of Faunus, given human identity in the evolution of the myth.

See also Lupercalia, Romulus and Remus.

Feronia A Roman goddess, believed to have been Etruscan in origin, about whom little is known though inscriptions show that she was popular in central Italy. She was probably an ancient goddess of fertility, and Virgil (*Aeneid,* Book VIII) mentions her as a goddess of childbirth. This little-known deity has a particular interest in that her shrine near Terracina was used for the ceremony of bestowing freedom on slaves; unfortunately no details of her connection with the ceremony are known.

Fetiales Members of a priestly college, twenty in number, who in Roman history were entrusted with the conduct of treaties and negotiations with other nations. They also made formal declarations of war in a simple ceremony (see the entry for Bellona). They made no decisions themselves but acted as advisers and ambassadors, as well as officiating in the religious formalities that attended international occasions.

Flamens The special priests of the Roman gods – and only of the true Roman gods; there were no *flamens* of the many deities worshipped in Roman history who were imported from the conquered countries.

The chief priests of the Roman gods supervised the daily sacrifices, and they were exempted from taxation and military duties. There were fifteen, three major and twelve minor: the major ones being those of Jupiter, Mars and Quirinus (who was often identified with Romulus). A peculiar conceit of Roman dicators and emperors was the aceptance of deification during their lifetimes – and the appointment of a *flamen* of their own. Thus Mark Antony was *flamen* to Julius Caesar.

See also Pontifex Maximus.

Flora The Roman goddess of flowering plants. She was possibly the same goddess as Feronia but her cult was more widespread and she had a *flamen,* which Feronia, as a more localised goddess, did not. Flora's temple was near the Circus Maximus and her festival day was 28 April, when games were held and farces of a lewd character were performed. Flora was a goddess held in high regard by courtesans and prostitutes.

Fortuna The Roman goddess of destiny and chance – not of luck, as her name might suggest in modern times. She was also the 'bringer' of fertility or increase. There is confusion about the place assigned to her in formal Roman religion, since one of the centres of her cult at Praeneste displayed the contradictory identifications of her (on an inscription) as 'child of Jupiter' and (on a statue) as a mother suckling both Jupiter and Juno.

Fortuna was a goddess of great antiquity, much older than the Roman state, and it is strange that so venerable a deity had neither a *flamen* nor a fixed festival.

Her cult centre at Praeneste boasted an oracular shrine, where consultants were given a flat piece of oak wood drawn at random from a vessel by a boy. Each piece bore an advisory inscription, and the 'chance' that led to its selection showed the consultant which course to follow.

Furies The primeval beings who were, according to Hesiod, born of the blood of Uranus when he was castrated by his son, Cronus. They are the avengers of crime, particularly crimes which offend against the tie of kinship, and as such play a large part in the story of Orestes. They were sometimes referred to as *Eumenides*, as in the title of the third part of the *Oresteia*: this is a propitiatory term meaning 'the kindly ones'. They could be likened, in their incessant, tormenting presence, to a tortured conscience.

G

Gaia The personification of Earth in Greek mythology. The name is sometimes written as Ge or Gaea in English. In Hesiod she is born of Chaos: she is both mother and mate of Uranus (the sky), and thus the mother too for the seas, mountains and all the natural features of the world. She is also the mother of the Titans, the Cyclopes and the Hecatoncheires (hundred-handed worker giants). Her youngest child, Cronus, overthrew his father and castrated him, and Gaia took the blood that fell on her and bore the Giants and the Furies. Later she bore Typhon to her brother Tartarus.

Gaia is the nearest equivalent to Mother Earth in Greek mythology, though almost every goddess who watches over the fertility of man and beast is a development of the ancient idea. This primeval deity – born of Chaos – is an early expression of a cosmogonic theme. Her subjection, as mate, to a sky god reflected new ideas as new people made their way into Greece during the migrations. It is notable that her offspring are often the enemies of the gods – and in each of those cases one finds an expression of Earth's wrath at offences committed against her.

Gaia's creatures (chthonian – of the earth) were probably the original holders of oracular shrines – Apollo had to kill one, a serpent, at Delphi to supplant the ancient goddess. It is very likely that before Greek religion was formalised any piece of ground that responded to cultivation was recognised as having power resident in it; pre-Hellenic Greece was largely an agricultural land and the cult of Mother Earth would arise naturally from that. Hesiod wrote many centuries after the arrival of the new gods.

Gaia is found in Homer, and she is a witness to oaths taken since she is always aware of what happens on her (Earth).

See also Cyclopes, Cronus, Furies, Giants, Hecatoncheires, Titans, Typhon, Uranus.

Galatea 1. A sea nymph. The name is first found in Homer (*Iliad,* Book XVIII) but the myths about her lover Acis and the Cyclops, Polyphemus, are of later date. They were a favourite subject of the Greek pastoral poets of Sicily.

Galatea was loved by the huge one-eyed Polyphemus but she disliked his uncouth attentions. Besides, she was herself in love with Acis, son of Faunus (the version given here is from Ovid, the Roman poet – Acis may have been, originally, a son of Pan). One day, while Polyphemus was singing of his love for Galatea, the two lovers were in earshot; they had hidden themselves hastily when the giant came on the scene. Unfortunately Polyphemus caught sight of them: Galatea dived into the sea and escaped but Polyphemus felled Acis by hurling a huge rock at him. As he lay dying, Galatea turned him into a river which bore his name for ever.

Galatea 2. The statue that came to life and fulfilled the love of its creator.

Pygmalion, the King of Cyprus, repelled by the loose behaviour of the women around him, carves an ivory statue of a beautiful girl. He falls in love with his creation, and at the festival of Venus prays to the goddess to be granted a wife like the ivory girl he has carved. Venus, touched by his appeal, gives a sign that she has heard his prayer. Pygmalion hurries back to his palace and, upon embracing the beautiful image, finds it warming to life. Venus herself attends the marriage of the happy couple.

This story is, like that of the other Galatea, best known in the version written by Ovid in his *Metamorphoses.*

Ganymede The great-grandson of Dardanus, the founder of Troy, according to Homer (*Iliad,* Book V). Zeus steals the prince, and to compensate his father, Erichthonius, gives him a herd of superb horses (the event is related by Diomedes). Zeus wants the beautiful young man to be cup-bearer to the gods Book XX. The *Iliad* does not relate how Zeus carried off Ganymede but the Homeric Hymn to Aphrodite says that the god came in a storm wind.

The first statement that Zeus stole Ganymede because he fell in love with him comes in the work of a poet of the sixth century BC, Theognis. But the poet may have been following a traditional interpretation of the myth, since Hebe, the daughter of Zeus and Hera, was already known as the gods' cup-bearer *(Iliad,* Book IV).

See also Dardanus, Zeus.

Giants According to Hesiod the giants of Greek mythology were borne by Gaia from the blood of the castrated Uranus. The giants of Homer are given passing mention in the *Odyssey* (Book VII), as the subjects of King Eurymedon, who led his subjects and himself to destruction through headstrong foolishness.

The myth of the struggle between the gods and the giants was a familiar one in the ancient world, and probably reflected a struggle either between barbarism and order, or between man and the violent forces of nature. It was a favourite theme with artists and poets, though most scholars believe it to be a tradition that found its way to Greece – the Greeks simply dressed it in more familiar clothes.

Gaia prompts the giants to attack the gods, in revenge for some slight she has suffered. She has given them a plant that makes them invincible. Furthermore, they are bound to win as long as they are fighting gods alone. Zeus discovers the secret of the plant; he orders the Sun, Moon and Dawn to find it and, when it is located, gathers it all himself. Then he calls his son Heracles to his side for the fight, since the presence of a mortal will frustrate the designs of Gaia.

The battle was finally won by the gods, Heracles accounting for some of the giants, Alcyoneus and others, by his skill with a bow. One giant, Porphyrion, tried to take advantage of the confusion of the battle to rape the goddess Hera: Zeus got him with a thunderbolt. Athene killed Enceladus, and Hephaestus proved invaluable with his ready supply of red-hot iron, which he used as deadly missiles. Dionysus used his vine as a snare, trapping and killing a number of the enemy. Apollo, Hermes, and Poseidon accounted for many more, and in the end the giants were completely defeated. Traditionally, those who were not killed in the battle were believed to have been buried under volcanoes – and the dangerous nature of volcanoes was thus explained.

Glaucus 1. One of the heroes of the *Iliad,* he was, with his friend and co-ruler Sarpedon, the leader of the Lycian forces who fought on the side of Troy. He is met by Diomedes, of the enemy forces, for combat (Book VI) and Diomedes demands his name. He learns that Glaucus' family and his own enjoy a hereditary friendship: Glaucus is descended from Bellerophon; Diomedes from Oeneus, who had once been Bellerophon's host. The two warriors agree to honour the friendship and will avoid encounters in the war. Then they exchange armour – Glaucus gives his golden suit to Diomedes and is happy to receive a bronze one in exchange.

Later in the *Iliad* (Book XII), Glaucus and his friend Sarpedon lead an attack on the Achaean camp which enables Hector to breach the defences and push them back to their ships. In this engagement Glaucus suffers a wound from an arrow shot from the camp by Teucer: he conceals the severity of it so as not to give encouragement to the enemy. Sarpedon is killed by Patroclus while Glaucus is recovering from his wound (Book XVI), and Glaucus, anguished at the loss of his friend, implores Apollo to heal him and let him return to the field. Apollo answers his prayer and Glaucus is able to rally the Lycians, enlist the help of Hector, and renew the battle over the body of Sarpedon. The fate of Glaucus is not recorded in Homer, but later writers say that he was killed by Ajax, son of Telamon. Apollo then took his body from the funeral pyre and bore it home to Lycia, where the nymphs brought a river to life around his grave.

See also *Iliad*, Sarpedon.

Glaucus 2. The son of Sisyphus, and the father of Bellerophon. He was the proud owner of a team of fine mares – and refused to let them breed, hoping to make them unbeatable in the chariot races at the games. He also fed them on human flesh.

He attended the funeral games ordered by Jason upon the death of Pelias but, meanwhile, Aphrodite had been watching him. She was growing angry because her creatures, the mares, were being denied their natural function. The night before the games she led the mares out of their stable to drink at her sacred well, knowing that a herb grew around it that would make them uncontrollable. At the games on the next day Glaucus succeeded in yoking his team, but they bolted the moment he mounted his chariot. He was dragged the length of the stadium, unable to disentangle himself from the reins: the mares at last came to a halt and Glaucus lay on the ground, broken and bleeding. The mares ate him alive.

Glaucus 3. One of the sons of Minos and Pasiphae. While a boy he was lost in his father's labyrinthine palace, and Minos almost gave up hope of ever finding him. An oracle told him to look for a man who could offer the best simile for a strange, tri-coloured calf that had been born in his kingdom. Such a one would restore his son to him. The seer, Polyeidus, described the calf as being like a ripening mulberry, and Minos decided he had found his man. Polyeidus was sent in search of the boy – and found him in a vat of honey, into which the boy had fallen and drowned. He had yet to restore the boy to his father; there was no point in taking Minos a dead body. While he was pondering on this he was alarmed to see a snake approaching the body and he promptly killed it. Almost at once another snake appeared, and Polyeidus watched while it seemed to examine the dead one. Then it glided away – to return a few minutes later carrying a herb in its mouth which it laid on the body of the dead snake. Polyeidus, astonished, saw the dead snake come to life and both creatures glide away. He picked up the herb at once and applied it to the dead boy, who, after a while, opened his eyes and sat up.

Minos showered honours and gifts on Polyeidus, who returned to his home in Argos a rich man. But he never divulged the secret of the herb of life.

Glaucus 4. A son of Poseidon, who also became a sea god like his father and is encountered in the *Argonautica*. A story was told of him that he owed his immortality to a herb of life – but there may well be some confusion in the strands of the ancient tales, leading to the adventures of one Glaucus being mixed up with those of another.

Gordian Knot, The In a time of trouble in Phrygia, an oracle told the leading citizens that peace would return to their country when they made a king of the first man they met approaching the temple of Zeus in a wagon. This man proved to be a peasant named Gordius, driving an ox cart, and he was at once given the kingdom. His son was Midas.

Gordius dedicated his ox cart to Zeus, and eventually housed it on the acropolis of his new city, Gordium. The yoke and pole of the cart were joined in a peculiar knot that Gordius had invented, and since he wanted his offering to remain intact he never explained the knot to anyone. The ox cart remained at Gordium for centuries and a legend grew up about the knot: whoever untied it would become the lord of Asia.

It was never untied. Robert Graves has pointed out that Gordium was the key to Asia, lying as it did across the trade route from Troy to Antioch, and that the famous mystery was probably a religious one – a knot-cypher containing the ineffable name of a god. The god could have been Zeus, or possibly Dionysus, whose worship in Phrygia was promoted by Midas when he succeeded to the throne. Alexander the Great, faced with the mystery, drew his sword in irritation and slashed through the knot. This brought about the end of an ancient belief by placing the power of the sword above that of deeply revered religious mystery. The power of his sword made Alexander the lord of Asia.

See also Midas.

Gorgons, The Phorcys and Ceto were brother and sister, Children of Gaia and Pontus (the sea), and the parents of both the Graiae and the Gorgons. One of the Gorgons, Medusa, was mortal and is the only one with a mythology – the others are merely named as Sthenno and Euryale.

The three were once beautiful, and Poseidon fell in love with Medusa. Unwisely, they retired to a temple one night to enjoy each other – and incurred the wrath of Athene, whose temple it was. She changed Medusa into a monster with glaring eyes and serpent hair. Her gaze could turn men into stone.

When she was eventually killed by Perseus, Medusa was carrying the children of Poseidon and these arose from her headless body: Pegasus, the winged horse, and Chrysaor, who is encountered in the story of Heracles as the father of Geryon.

Perseus eventually gave the head of Medusa to Athene, who fastened it to her shield.

See also the Graiae, Heracles, Perseus.

Graces, The Daughters of Zeus, and, from the time of Hesiod, three in number. Their mother was Eurynome. They were the personification of the joy and well-being produced by fertile nature, beauty, love – everything that contributed to happiness, and were present at the celebration of human and divine marriages. They also represented grace itself *(charis)*: grace in giving and gratitude in receiving, and true grace in behaviour.

The names given them by Hesiod are as follows: Thalia, the flowering; Euphrosyne, joy; and Aglaia, the radiant.

Graiae, The The three sisters of the Gorgons, children of Phorcys and Ceto. The Graiae are a curious conception, the personification of age (their name means the grey ones), with a single eye between them. Their names are given as Dino, Enyo and Pemphredo by Hesiod. They were the sentinels of the lair of the Gorgons: in the story of Perseus he stole their single eye from them to make them divulge the whereabouts of the helmet, sandals and wallet he needed for the completion of his quest.

See also Perseus.

H

Hades One of the sons of Cronus and Rhea, and brother to Zeus and Poseidon. His realm was the nether world, the portion he drew when the three brothers cast lots after the overthrow of Cronus (Homer, *Iliad,* Book XV).

Hades was implacably just: he should never be thought of as the Devil, a concept alien to Greek thought which believed that man committed evil or good deeds himself, without any prompting from a good or evil force. Nor was Hades a punisher: he was never feared in that way because the Greeks never thought in that way. Any man who was arrogant or stupid or foolhardy enough to offend the gods was punished by the gods, the lord of the nether world having no more, or less, to do with it than the other Olympians.

Hades means 'the Unseen': he was also called Pluto, meaning 'the Rich'. Both words are descriptions, so the third son of Cronus had no real name. As Pluto, the richness he represented may have been that of the productive earth since it was commonly believed that his realm was somewhere in its depths. As Hades, he was the god to whom all must go, sooner or later, but the living shrank from giving a name to one who became their lord upon death. Hades was accorded universal respect, and given reverence by those who cared for the condition of the departed.

In early tradition his realm was in the West *(Odyssey,* Book X) and this was a frequent belief among ancient people since the sun set there. Later it was placed underground and everyone, after being properly buried, arrived at one of the rivers of Hades, Styx or Acheron, to be rowed across by Charon. The destination of most of the dead was the Plain of Asphodel (asphodel is a wild flower that grows in barren places in the eastern Mediterranean). There they continued a shadowy existence in continuance of their former lives since they were bodiless and outworn.

The fortunate few, who had earned the gods' favour, went to Elysium, or the Islands of the Blest. Those who had offended the gods (and, interestingly, very few are named) went to Tartarus, their punishment already decreed.

Hades and his consort, Persephone, were supreme in their kingdom but they shared Olympus with the other gods. In the nether world there were three judges, just men of former time, who allotted to each arrival their place. These were Minos, Rhadamanthus, and Aeacus, though the role of the last is rather vague.

Hades was rarely depicted in art but on the rare occasions when he was shown he looked rather like his brother Zeus.

See also Aeacus, Charon, Islands of the Blest, Minos, Persephone, Pluto, Rhadamanthus.

Harmonia According to Hesiod, one of the children born of the love of Ares and Aphrodite. She was given as wife to Cadmus, the founder of Thebes, and all the gods attended the wedding. Among the marriage gifts she received was a necklace fashioned for Cadmus by Hephaestus. It was placed round her neck by Aphrodite, and she bestowed on it the power of bringing beauty to its wearer. The necklace was to play a grim part in the later history of Thebes.

See also Adrastus, Alcmaeon, Amphiaraus, Cadmus.

Harpies, The The 'snatchers'. The supernatural winged beings of Greek mythology were probably, in origin, winds that carried off people. The idea that winds and spirits were in some way allied was very common in ancient times, and the step to a belief in malevolent wind spirits was inevitable. They are numbered as two and named in Hesiod, who refers to their beautiful hair and their powerful flight. They are Aello and Ocypete, descended from Gaia and Oceanus. Virgil gives us the name of a third in the *Aneid* (Book III), Celaeno. They are described as 'storm winds' in Homer (*Odyssey*, Book XX), in Penelope's prayer to the goddess Artemis, when she recalls how they stole the daughters of Pandareus to make them servants to the Furies. The

Harpies also appear in the *Argonautica* (Book II), as the tormentors of King Phineus.

Hebe Daughter of Zeus and Hera, Hebe is mentioned by Hesiod and appears in Homer as the cup-bearer of the gods (*Iliad,* Book IV). In Book V she bathes her brother Ares after his encounter with Diomedes. She is the wife of Heracles in the *Odyssey* (Book XI) but the passage in which she is mentioned is of doubtful authenticity according to some scholars. The tradition is nonetheless followed by Euripides in his play, *The Heraclidae.*

She has no mythology apart from this, and only one cult centre, at Phlius, has been identified.

Hecate An ancient fertility goddess much honoured in Greek-speaking Asia Minor and in Boeotia, Hecate has no mythology and in the progress of Greek religion undergoes an odd metamorphosis. In Hesiod she is called a daughter of the Titans – but much respected by Zeus, the Titans' supplanter – and one who retained her great powers for good in the fortunes of mankind. Hesiod's genealogy makes Hecate cousin to Artemis, and like her she has the care of children among her functions. The high place given her by Hesiod is found in no other ancient authority (Homer does not mention her), and, being a goddess of the earth, she became inevitably connected with the dead. This became her portion, eventually, and more and more she was the goddess associated with witchcraft: in both Euripides' play and in the *Argonautica* she is the goddess of the sorceress, Medea, and resident in Hades' kingdom.

Robert Graves has pointed out that Hecate and Persephone represented the ancient, pre-Hellenic hope of regeneration. Aspects of the recurring cycle of death and fertility, they are joined by Demeter in the more developed myth, and it is tempting to see Hecate as the goddess allotted the third aspect of the ancient triple goddess, maiden, mother and crone. See the entry for Demeter for further information.

See also *Medea* (Euripides).

Hecatoncheires The 'hundred-handed' giants, children of Uranus and Gaia, according to Hesiod. They were imprisoned in Tartarus by their brother Cronus, and fought against him with Zeus when that god overthrew his father. They were named Cottus, Briareus and Gyes. One of them, Briareus, was hurried to the aid of Zeus by Thetis, when

Athene, Hera and Poseidon, exasperated by the sky god's caprices, tried to overthrow him. The tale is told in the *Iliad* (Book I), by Achilles when he calls on his mother, Thetis, for help during his quarrel with Agamemnon.

Hector The eldest son of Priam, King of Troy, and Hecuba; the husband of Andromache and the father of Astyanax. Hector's name was Greek, meaning 'holder' or 'stayer', and H. J. Rose suggests that the Trojan hero could have been invented by Homer. If this is so Homer was completely successful in portraying a warrior in complete contrast to his opposing champion, Achilles.

Achilles was a better fighter, for what that was worth: Hector emerges from the pages of the *Iliad* as a sympathetic and warm-hearted man; brave in battle, certainly, but an honourable foe, and an affectionate father and husband. Helen honours him as one who, in the course of the war, was never unkind to her.

Unlike Achilles, Hector has almost no mythology outside of the part he plays in the *Iliad,* and the epic comes to a close with his funeral. His first appearance is in Book II, when he leads the Trojan army to the battlefield, and he is in the forefront of events until the fatal confrontation with Achilles in Book XXII. His scene with his wife Andromache and his baby son Astyanax in Book VI is a justly famous passage.

Hector is favoured by Zeus (Book XV), and his character – whether a complete invention or based on an ancient story – left a powerful impression. He was the centre of a hero cult in several places, notably at Troy and, in Greece, at Thebes. There was a tradition at Thebes that his bones had been taken to that city at the command of an oracle.

See also Achilles, Andromache, *Iliad,* Patroclus, Priam.

Hecuba The wife of King Priam of Troy (strictly speaking, *Hecabe;* Hecuba is the Latinised form but the more familiar). Hecuba was the daughter of the King of Phrygia in the *Iliad* (Book XVI); she bore Priam fifty children, eighteen sons among them, of which the most renowned were Hector, her first born, and Paris, whose love for Helen was to prove so fatal to the royal house of Troy.

Hecuba, in Homer, is a tragic figure, a Queen who sees her sons destroyed one by one. Her lament for Hector (Book XXIV) is a fine presentation of regal dignity harrowed by grief.

After Homer the tragedian Euripides placed her in the centre of two plays, *Hecuba* and *The Trojan Women,* and she is also found in other myths dealing with the time before the Trojan War. One of these makes her Priam's second wife; another tells of her dream while she carried Paris in her womb – she gives birth to a flaming torch, which the seers tell her means that the child she carries will be the cause of Troy's destruction.

See also Cassandra, Hector, *Hecuba* (Euripides), Paris, Priam, *The Trojan Women* (Euripides).

Hecuba A tragedy by Euripides. The date is uncertain but it is believed to have been written about 425 BC.

The scene is Thrace, on the opposite shore to Troy, and the action takes place before Agamemnon's tent. Troy has fallen, and the women of the royal house have been divided like chattels among the Achaean leaders – Hecuba is now a slave belonging to Odysseus. She tells her women of her fears for her youngest son, Polydorus, sent to the King of Thrace for safety; and her daughter Polyxena, whose life is demanded by the ghost of Achilles. This appallingly cruel sacrifice was promised to the dying Achilles as his share of the spoils of Troy: now the homeward bound fleet is becalmed in Thrace and Neoptolemus, Achilles' son, is impatient to make the sacrifice and appease his father's restless shade.

Odysseus comes with the news that the pledge must be honoured. He will take Polyxena away and he is unmoved by the despair of Hecuba. He remains unmoved when Hecuba reminds him that she, the Queen of Troy, once saved his life. Polyxena intervenes: she does her best to console her mother and insists that death is preferable to the lot of a slave. She goes to her death with dignity, leaving her stricken mother with the prospect of preparing for her burial.

On the heels of this blow comes another: Polydorus, her only surviving son, is murdered. The King of Thrace, Polymestor, has accepted the care of the boy who had been sent to the court at Thrace with a large part of Priam's treasure. When Troy fell, Polymestor, greedy for the treasure, had murdered the Trojan prince and had his body thrown into the sea. The sea had returned the corpse to land, near the Achaean camp, and now it is brought to his mother.

Hecuba, at this new cruelty, demands one thing only – vengeance. She has no other feeling left. She demands help from Agamemnon; but he hedges, giving her nothing but sympathetic words: he points out that the Thracian King is the ally of the Achaeans. Seeing that Agamemnon will not help her, Hecuba is content to gain a safe conduct through the camp for one of her women, whom she sends with a message for Polymestor and his two sons. Agamemnon leaves the scene.

When Polymestor arrives, Hecuba quickly establishes that he is lying to her – he does not know that the sea has washed up the body of her son, and declares that the boy is alive and well. Hecuba tells him of further treasure, buried in the ruins of Troy, which the King and his sons must also secure. Polymestor's greed leads him into the trap, and he listens carefully while she tells him where the treasure is 'hidden'. She explains further that she has contrived to bring away from Troy certain things which he must have if his search is to be successful. They are in her tent, where the Achaean soldiers never go. Polymestor leads the way, followed by his sons, while Hecuba's women gather round her. They follow the Thracians into the tent.

Polymestor is fully paid for his treachery. Hecuba and her women kill his two sons: then they blind him. They watch him calmly while he crawls out of the tent, screaming imprecations. He curses Hecuba, saying she will find a dog's grave – Dionysus has told him what the future holds in store. Agamemnon, who arrives on the scene, is told of his forthcoming murder – but he prefers to see that Polymestor is out of his mind: he orders his men to take the blinded King to a deserted island – and leave him there.

Hecuba turns away. She has her vengeance, and now she will go and bury her children.

This grim play exposed to an Athenian audience two aspects of war to which they, for all their qualities, could become as subject as any state. Every speech made by Odysseus, Agamemnon and Polymestor reeks of hypocrisy, of the politicians' justification of the things they do. And Hecuba, the victim of their justified cruelty, becomes an avenging fury herself. The complete destruction of an opposing city and the enslavement of its people was well known among the Greek states and Athens was to commit exactly that crime nine years later, in Melos. Euripides wrote another play on the same theme the following year, in 415 BC. See his *The Trojan Women*.

Helen The most famous woman of Greek mythology was the daughter of Zeus and Leda, the wife of Tyndareus, King of Lacedaemon. Zeus seduced Leda in the guise of a swan and Helen and her brother

Polydeuces were born in an egg. No mention is made in any of the stories of any reaction on the part of Tyndareus; but the kings of mythology were usually quite tractable if the other father should prove to be a god.

Helen was the most beautiful woman in the world and seems to have been endowed with a quality over and above that which made her physically desirable. She belongs properly to the *Iliad* and the *Odyssey*, but such a figure was inevitably used by poets later than Homer. She is included in the adventures of Theseus, who kidnaps her in the hope of making her his wife. His plans go awry and he spends four years in Tartarus for his pains. Other stories seek to anticipate the part she plays in Homer: the Judgment of Paris makes Helen (the most beautiful woman in the world) the prize offered to Paris by Aphrodite, who discloses Helen's identity and guarantees that Helen will return Paris' love.

When Helen grew to womanhood all the princes of Greece wanted her. Her father, Tyndareus, was disconcerted not only by their number but also by the lavish gifts they pressed on him – he knew that any preference he made would also make him the enemy of the rest. Odysseus advised him to insist on an oath of loyalty from the suitors to whomever Helen married. They agreed, and Helen eventually chose Menelaus who became King of Sparta. Her sister Clytemnestra married Agamemnon, Menelaus' brother and High King of Argos.

Helen, in the *Iliad,* has already eloped to Troy with Paris. She is regarded as his wife, not his mistress, and throughout Homer her uneasy feelings are expressed more than once. Significantly (Book III) none of the Trojans seem to express resentment of her at the beginning of the war – it is only as the dreadful toll continues that she becomes the object of dislike and unkindness. She is quite definitely, in Homer, the reason for the war.

Menelaus and Helen are reconciled after the death of Paris and the fall of Troy and appear to be living quite happily in his kingdom when encountered in the *Odyssey*, though this return to a calm domestic life was probably not without its early trials and Euripides makes a fine scene of their re-encounter in *The Trojan Women*.

A strange variant of the story of Helen appears in Stesichorus. Helen herself did not go to Troy with Paris: Zeus commanded Hermes to steal his daughter and entrust her to the care of King Proteus of Egypt; then Hera fashioned a false Helen from clouds – it was this Helen who went to Troy. After Troy fell Menelaus retrieved his true and faithful wife. This silly story was useful to Euripides, who based a play about Helen on it.

See also The Dioscuri, *Iliad*, Leda, Menelaus, Paris, *The Trojan Women* (Euripides).

Helenus One of the sons of Priam and Hecuba, Helenus possessed the gift of prophecy, like his sister Cassandra. He fights staunchly with his brothers in the *Iliad* and gives Hector good advice on two occasions (Books VI and VII). He is badly wounded by Menelaus in the attack on the Achaean ships (Book XIII), and thereafter plays no part in the story. The tragedians gave Helenus further adventures. In his play *Philoctetes*, Sophocles makes Helenus the prisioner of Odysseus, who forces from him the secret of the arms of Heracles which will decide the fate of Troy. (Another version tells that he knew Troy was doomed and in return for the secret asked for a safe home in a distant land.) Euripides, in his *Andromache*, makes him the husband chosen by Thetis for Andromache upon the death of Neoptolemus (Euripides seems to be picking up the story where someone else laid it down). Virgil, in the *Aeneid* (Book III), has Helenus and Andromache usefully settled in Chaonia; Helenus offers his brother Aeneas hospitality, and makes the prophecy that Aeneas will found his new Troy in the west, in Italy.

See also *Aeneid*, Andromache, *Andromache (Euripides)*, Cassandra, *Iliad*, Philoctetes.

Helicon, Mount The highest mountain in Boeotia, and celebrated in Greek mythology as the haunt of the Muses, whose sanctuary lay in a high glen near Thespiae. Hesiod lived at Ascra, on the slopes of Helicon. Just below the summit was the spring of Hippocrene, the inspiration of poets, said to have been born when Pegasus stamped his hoof on the rock. This is, however, a legend of a much later time.

Helios The sun god of the Greeks – but not a particularly important god to them since the heavenly bodies, generally, were too remote. He was strongest on the island of Rhodes, which he chose himself as a home, and where he mated with Rhodos, the nymph of the island. Their children were the first inhabitants of Rhodos. His festival was the Halieia.

Helios was generally conceived as a charioteer, who drove the sun across the earth from east to west each day. Because he saw everything, e.g. the abduction of Persephone by Hades, he was often called upon to witness oath-taking and solemn promises, as in the *Iliad* (Book III). His oxen, in one of the most celebrated episodes of the *Odyssey* (Book XII), fall victim to Odysseus and his hungry companions when they reach the island of Thrinacia. Homer calls him Hyperion in this book and it is believed that it was another name for the sun. Hesiod gives Helios Titan parents, Hyperion and Thea; sisters in Selene (the moon) and Eos (the dawn), and a consort in Perseis. Helios was the father of Circe, Aeëtes and Phaethon.

There was a tendency, in historical times, to identify Helios with Apollo but the sun, as a cult in the ancient world, did not receive wide acceptance until the late Roman empire when, as Sol Invictus, he became in many ways its principal god.

See also *Argonautica,* Circe, *Odyssey,* Phaethon.

Hellenes   The name by which, around the seventh century BC, the Greeks as a whole were calling themselves. Their country was Hellas. The name of 'Hellenes' came from one of the tribes that settled in Thessaly during the time of the migrations, and a myth of ancestry made the Hellenes the descendants of Deucalion through his son, Hellen. There is no good explanation of why the name Hellenes should have been the one to fall on the people of ancient Greece: it was probably fortuitous, and as likely as that we should know of them as Achaeans, or Argives, or Danaans.

The word *Greek,* paradoxically, is not Greek at all: it comes from the Latin, Graecia, the country in which lay Graia. It was from Graia that the settlers known as the Graii came to live in Italy in the region of Cumae.

See also Deucalion.

Hephaestus   The divine artificer, god of craftsmen, god of fire – and particularly of the crafts in which fire was employed. His cult centres were always found in those places where heavy industry, such as the forging of metals, was practised, and volcanic regions such as Sicily and the Lipari Islands. His origins probably lay in Asia where, the Greeks knew very well, metalwork and armour was fashioned with a skill far superior to theirs.

Hephaestus is older than Homer, who makes him the child of Zeus and Hera. He is lame and in the *Iliad* waits on the Olympians (Book I) to keep the peace between his parents. He refers to an occasion when his father Zeus, furious at his intervention in an earlier quarrel, flung him from Olympus: Hephaestus fell on the island of Lemnos, where he was kindly received. Later, in Book XVIII, he is visited by Thetis, who pleads with him to make armour for Achilles, and he relates how his mother Hera, disgusted with the appearance of her new child, dropped the infant from Olympus – he was succoured by Eurynome and Thetis, hence his eagerness to be of help to the latter.

However, neither of his parents' cruel deeds made Hephaestus lame – he was lame from birth and this was an important part of his mythology; a lame man with strong shoulders and skilful hands was a very useful member of the community. Most men could fight but not many commanded the skill to become armourers. Hephaestus makes wonderful – magical – things: in the mythology of all nations this is a recurring theme – a smith was often a magician.

Hesiod's account differs from Homer's. There he is the son of Hera but not of Zeus. The Queen of Olympus, after a quarrel with her lord, conceived Hephaestus by an effort of will. Hesiod gives him no wife but in Homer he has two: in the *Iliad* she is Charis (Book XVIII), and she is described as beautiful; in the *Odyssey* (Book VIII), she is the goddess Aphrodite, and while she is beautiful, too, she is a faithless wife.

See also Aphrodite, Athene, *Iliad*, *Odyssey*.

Hera In mythology the daughter of Cronus and Rhea and the sister and wife of Zeus. She was the mother of Ares, Hebe, Hephaestus and Eileithyia.

Hera's origin was ancient – she was there before the time of the migrations and there is no trace of her having a consort of any kind. In Olympian religion she was the patroness of marriage, the goddess most concerned with the life of women, and the guardian of children: all those attributes would certainly have been part of her original character in pre-Hellenic Greece. Her original name, incidentally, is unknown – Hera is more a title ('lady') than a name. It is believed that her original cult was so strong that it had to be acknowledged by the newcomers from the north, who absorbed it into their own religion at the highest level. Thus she became the consort of the king of the gods.

The marriage was not, according to mythology, a happy one, and Hera seems to have had no affection for her children. The stories give a remarkable picture of an unhappy wife, quarrelling ceaselessly with a husband she did not choose; bitterly jealous at the same time of his endless sexual adventures, which made her spitefully cruel to her rivals and their children.

Hera's cult centres, in historical times, were on the island of Samos and in Argos. Samos claimed to be her birthplace, and the scene of the early love of Hera and Zeus (Homer's story, in the *Iliad,* Book XIV). Cronus still ruled, and the couple made love in secret on the island. Argos also claimed to be Hera's birthplace and may have had a stronger claim than Samos, since her ancient shrine, the Heraeum, stood about six miles north of the city. Argos, too, was the setting of her seduction by Zeus: one day Zeus' roving eye caught sight of the splendid figure (all the mythographers grant Hera magnificence of face and form) and was determined to have her. He changed himself into a cuckoo, and got himself thoroughly drenched in a rainstorm on the mountain in Argos where Hera liked to walk. After the rain she duly appeared, and sat down on the spot where a temple was later dedicated to Hera *Teleia* (fulfilled). A sad bedraggled cuckoo crept on to her lap for warmth. At once she found herself wrestling with Zeus, who had promptly resumed his true shape. He got his way in the usual manner of seducers: he insisted that he wanted her to be his wife.

Hera and Zeus bicker all the way through the *Iliad* – they are on opposing sides, in Hera's view. She is firmly on the side of the Achaeans, Paris and Helen having offended against her laws. Zeus tries hard to remain uncommitted but he has an obligation to Thetis and Hera regards this as opposing her. (Thetis had once helped Zeus when all the gods on Olympus had turned against him.) On occasions she borrows the girdle of her Olympian colleague, Aphrodite: with this weapon she seduces her husband and weakens his will.

Her festival, The Heraia, was held at Argos and was accompanied by athletic contests.

See also Io, Leto.

Heracles The great hero of Greek mythology, Heracles and his adventures are probably the memory of some great figure of earlier times. Both Argos and Thebes claimed him as their son, and the most familiar story of his birth is laid in Thebes; but the indications point strongly to Argos as the true background, though it is impossible to say which is the true period. There is no unbroken line of tradition that gives us his life story from beginning to end: what we have is a sort of patch-work, though this does not detract in any way from the eternal fascination of a great heroic figure who is very human and believable in spite of being the son of Zeus and abnormally strong.

Heracles' mother was Alcmene, the wife of Amphitryon. While Amphitryon was at war Zeus visited Alcmene in the guise of her husband. The king of the gods wanted to sire a champion for both gods and men, and he made one night last as long as three, to be certain of his design succeeding. When Zeus departed Amphitryon returned, successful in war and looking forward to rejoining his wife. So Alcmene bore twin sons, Iphicles and Heracles.

Like all the bastard children of Zeus, the hero incurred the hatred of Hera, and was soon exposed to danger. Zeus sent Hermes to bring the baby to Olympus: in the meantime he lulled his wife to sleep. When Hermes arrived Zeus took the baby and laid him at Hera's breast. The lusty infant woke Hera, inevitably, and she pushed him away from her angrily, her milk spraying across the heavens to become the Milky Way. Zeus retrieved the baby and returned him to Alcmene, pleased that his trick had worked. His mortal son had been suckled by a goddess. He would become immortal.

Hera bided her time. Heracles and Iphicles were still babies when she tried again, sending two serpents to kill them in their cradle. The screams of Iphicles brought their parents, who arrived in time to see Heracles strangle the serpents. One version of the story says that the serpents were harmless, and put there by Amphitryon, who wanted to be certain which of the two was the child of Zeus. He had been puzzled by his wife's behaviour on the night he returned from the war – Alcmene had seemed to think that he had returned the night before. Amphitryon consulted the seer, Tiresias, who had told him the truth.

Amphitryon brought up Heracles with care, bringing the best trainers and tutors to Thebes. As a boy he did not know his own strength, and actually killed one of his tutors, who was trying to teach him music, by striking him with his lyre. To give Heracles an outlet for his strength Amphitryon sent him to a cattle farm in his lands, and there Heracles acquired a taste for living out of doors. He stayed on the farm until he was eighteen, his strength growing all the time. He was believed by many to have grown into a man of huge size but there is a persistent note in the myths that suggests he was no bigger than the average man, which was the way the Greeks always portrayed him. The presentation of Heracles (Hercules) as a muscle-bound heavyweight is a Roman idea.

His first adventure was to kill the lion of Mount Kithaeron, which was ravishing the herds of Amphitryon. He skinned the lion, and thereafter wore the pelt over his brief tunic, the lion's head making a sort of helmet. While he was away Thebes had become embroiled in a war with Orchomenus – and been defeated. Heracles arrived to find the city disarmed and paying extortionate tribute. He at once armed every man of fighting age by stripping the temples of all the spoils dedicated there as trophies in the past. The goddess Athene observed all this and approved such resolution; she was to prove a valuable ally to Heracles.

The war resumed and the Thebans, led by Heracles, turned the tables on Orchomenus. One ruse he employed was to dam the river Cephissus, which then overflowed and flooded the Orchomenians' cornfields. He demolished the dam as soon as the war was over – Heracles was not vindictive, though Amphitryon himself lost his life in the fighting.

Creon, King of Thebes, showered honours on Heracles and he became the idol of the city. He was appointed the city's protector, and given the princess Megara as his wife. Her younger sister was bestowed on Iphicles. The brothers became the fathers of numerous children – Heracles had eight – and Iphicles' eldest son, Iolaus, became Heracles' favourite.

Hera struck again. Heracles was suddenly afflicted with madness: he attacked his beloved Iolaus one day and would have killed him if Iolaus had not been strong enough and nimble enough to escape Heracles' arms. Heracles then seized his bow and began to look for imaginary enemies: he shot down six of his own children and two of Iphicles' before the madness lifted. When his mind cleared, and he saw what he had done in his madness, Heracles shut himself away in a dark underground room, refusing all human contact, and grieving for the children he had killed. After some time Heracles was persuaded to see his friend, the King of Thespiae, who performed a ritual purification which enabled him to visit Delphi and consult the oracle. He sought some means of atonement, and was prepared to accept any orders the oracle might utter. The result was his servitude to Eurystheus, King of Argos, and the Labours which that King ordered him to undertake. (See the entry for Heracles, Labours of.) The Labours all had a fixed object but many other adventures are recorded which were not connected with them.

When his servitude was over and his Labours accomplished, Heracles returned to Thebes. But there was a shadow over his marriage after the dreadful events of his madness, and he separated himself from Megara, who later married Iolaus, and looked around for a new wife. He heard that Eurytus, son of the King of Oechalia, wanted a husband for his daughter Iole. Eurytus was a renowned archer and promised Iole to anyone who could shoot better. Heracles did shoot better than the King – so much better that Eurytus was furious, and accused Heracles of using magic arrows: worse, he was no better than a slave to King Eurystheus. Heracles departed – he could have killed Eurytus but he was content to wait.

Eurytus then discovered that twelve brood mares and twelve foals had been stolen from his stables, and the thief was presumed to be Heracles, whose departure had been remarkably quiet for one notoriously easy to rouse. Iphitus, Eurytus' eldest son, refused to believe the charge and set out to find the mares himself. (They had in fact been stolen by Autolycus, the prince of thieves, who had sold them to the unsuspecting Heracles.) Iphitus' heart sank when his search took him to Tiryns, where Heracles had gone after dissolving his marriage to Megara. He told Heracles that he was looking for the mares stolen from his father: Heracles promised to help him find them, and made Iphitus his guest. But over dinner that night Iphitus' manner betrayed what was really in his mind, and the enraged Heracles hurled him to his death from the top of his house.

His temper had led Heracles to commit an almost unforgivable crime. He had murdered a guest in his own house, (Homer, in the *Odyssey*, Book XXI, has a damning reference to the murder), and he had to seek the ritual of purification once more. But most refused to help him, since there was no madness to excuse him this time. Eventually he was helped by Deiphobus of Amycale, but he was a prey to evil dreams that plagued him so badly that he was forced to go to Delphi again to seek absolution. But there, to his dismay, he found no comfort; the Pythoness of the oracle denounced him and declared that she had no words for such as he. Heracles' dismay developed into a new rage – he plundered the shrine and seized the sacred tripod, declaring that he would have an oracle of his own. The Pythoness invoked Apollo, who hastened to Delphi to find out who was desecrating his sacred ground. He confronted Heracles, who promptly attacked him, and they fought so furiously that Zeus himself was obliged to go and separate his sons. He left the Pythoness to pronounce the punishment for both the murder of Iphitus and the desecration of Apollo's sanctuary.

Heracles became a slave once more. Omphale, the Queen of Lydia, bought him for one year and the price was donated to the children of Iphitus. The Queen, however, had taken a long hard look at Heracles, and he was not long in her household before she was commanding services he was well able to perform. She bore him three sons according to one account, and the year of his servitude passed pleasantly enough to be extended. Heracles performed numerous services to the kingdom, and put an end to the tricks of two clever thieves (see Cercopes).

Eventually Heracles returned to Tiryns, but is was not long before he was off on another adventure. Laomedon, King of Troy, had incurred the wrath of Poseidon, who had sent a sea monster to plague the people and destroy their food crops. Laomedon consulted the oracle of Zeus, and learned that he was required to sacrifice his daughter Hesione to the monster. It would then withdraw and leave the people in peace. Heracles arrived to find the hapless girl chained to a rock by the sea, waiting for a horrible death. He wasted no time in freeing her, and restored her to her family. To King Laomedon, her father, he offered the destruction of the monster – in return for two mares from the marvellous herd that Zeus had given to Laomedon when he fell in love with Ganymede, the King's son, and took him to Olympus. The King agreed.

At this point in his adventures he received the help of the goddess Athene, who inspired the Trojans to build a stout, high earthwork along the shore. Heracles lay in wait for the monster behind it, and succeeded in killing it when it lifted its head from the waves and blew its foul breath over the land. The earthwork was made strongly enough to last for many years: it was there during the Trojan Wars, and provided a vantage point for Poseidon, Hera and Athene to watch the advance of Aeneas under the protection of Apollo (*Iliad,* Book XX).

Laomedon, however, cheated on the agreement, and tried to foist two ordinary mares on Heracles. The King's son, Podarces, protested to his father, who silenced the boy and ordered him from the scene. This confirmed Heracles' suspicions that he was being deceived and he stormed out of the city, first warning Laomedon to prepare for a war.

Heracles returned to Greece in haste, to recruit allies. He collected soldiers in Tiryns, and those who joined him with their forces were his beloved Iolaus, Oicles of Argos – father of Amphiaraus, and the sons of Aeacus, Peleus and Telamon. Telamon was at Salamis, his kingdom, awaiting the birth of his first child, and it was then that the child, a boy, was wrapped in Heracles' lion skin in the hope of making him immortal. His name was Ajax, and one day he would also go to war at Troy.

Laomedon was defeated and killed with all his family except for Hesione and Podarces who was made a prisoner – Heracles spared his life for his honesty in the matter of the reward for his services to Laomedon. Hesione accepted the hand of Telamon in return for the privilege of ransoming a single captive. Heracles agreed, and she gave him her golden veil to secure the freedom of her brother, Podarces. She sailed away from Troy with Telamon, and bore him a son, Teucer, at Salamis. But she was an unfaithful wife and as soon as her son was weaned she deserted Telamon and his court.

Her brother, meanwhile, inherited the devastated kingdom. His name was changed after his sister ransomed him, and Podarces became Priam, 'the redeemed'.

The adventure at Troy had given Heracles a taste for war. He attacked Elis, to pay off an old score against King Augeas, and, successful there, went on to capture Pylos. This became the kingdom of Nestor: Heracles bestowed it on him when he proved a fearless soldier and a man of wisdom. In his later years, at the Trojan Wars, Nestor recalls the adventures of his youthful days (*Iliad*, Book XXIII).

Heracles eventually settled down in Aetolia, where he sought the hand of Deianira, daughter of the King of Calydon. He won her by fighting and defeating his only serious rival, the river god Achelous. The marriage was successful and Heracles seemed content, but a tragic accident occurred that drove him and Deianira away from Calydon. One evening at table a young kinsman of the King's was acting as cup-bearer, and, told to pour water on Heracles' hands after the meal, was so careless that much of it splashed on Heracles' knees. In his quick-tempered way Heracles boxed the boy's ears. But he hit him too hard, and the boy died.

Heracles and Deianira set out for Trachis to make a new home. On the way they came to a river in full flood, and Deianira hesitated: she could cross on Heracles' back – he was strong enough to swim the swollen river, but the day was cold and she would be thoroughly drenched. While she hesitated a centaur who had been watching them approached, told them that his name was Nessus, and guaranteed a safe and dry crossing for Deianira on his broad horse's back. They agreed and Heracles, after hurling his bow and his club to the far bank, swam across. The centaur, as soon as Heracles reached the other side, seized Deianira and galloped away with her. Heracles heard her screams, and looked back to see Nessus some distance away, attempting to rape his wife. He seized his bow and loosed an arrow, aiming carefully over the long distance, and managed a brilliant stroke: the centaur fell, an arrow through his heart.

Nessus knew he was dying. He told the trembling Deianira that he had a secret to impart which all women would wish to know – he knew how she could always ensure that Heracles would never leave her for another. Deianira saw Heracles hurrying back across the flood as fast as he could and she remembered his reputation; she bent to listen. She must gather the blood from his wound, said Nessus, and the semen he had spilt in his haste to possess her. Mix them with oil, and anoint a shirt of Heracles' when he looked like straying. With his last breath, the centaur promised her that if she did those things no rival would ever possess her husband. Deianira took the small oil jar she carried and hastily collected drops of blood and semen before Heracles rejoined her. They continued their journey to Trachis.

It was from this city that Heracles was finally revenged on King Eurytus of Oechalia, who had insulted him when he won the Princess Iole in fair competition, and had refused to acknowledge Heracles' right to her hand. He decided to make war on Eurytus but first he consulted the oracle of Zeus at Dodona. He told Deianira what the answer was: the venture against Eurytus might be his last exploit and be followed by a peaceful life – or it might be the reason for his death. As it was, he defeated his old enemy and killed him and all of his family with the exception of Iole, whom he sent to Deianira in Trachis.

Deianira received the princess with uneasy feelings: the venture had succeeded and all should be well. But why had he spared Iole? News from the fighting had told Deianira that Iole had attempted to kill herself, rather than be taken. What did Heracles want with her? He, meanwhile, was preparing a sacrifice on the Cenaean headland to celebrate his victory, and had sent his herald Lichas to ask Deianira to send him fresh clothing, a new shirt and a short tunic of the kind he usually wore. The request seemed to point the way for Deianira: she gave Lichas a new tunic for her husband, and a new shirt. The shirt was anointed with the blood of the dying Nessus. Lichas hurried away with them to deliver them to Heracles.

The centaur had his revenge. He knew that Heracles' arrows had been dipped in the blood of the Hydra and carried fatal poison: even while he was dying he could feel it racing through his own blood. Heracles dressed in his fresh clothes, and went about his sacrifices –and was suddenly gripped with agony. The poison charred his flesh and he knew he would soon die. He called his son, Hyllus, and begged him to make a funeral pyre on the summit of nearby Mount Oeta. Hyllus did what his father asked, and promised to make Iole his wife.

The pyre was ready, and Heracles, writhing in agony, was carried there by Hyllus and Iolaus. But neither of them could bring themselves to kindle the flames. In the end Heracles called on a passing shepherd boy, who obeyed him without hesitation. The grateful hero, at last able to die and escape his pain, gave the boy his bow, his quiver and his arrows, and mounted his funeral pyre. He used his club of olive wood for a headrest, and spread his lion skin cloak over his chest, while the grieving Iolaus, his son Hyllus, and the shepherd boy stood by. The boy's name was Philoctetes. Suddenly the flames themselves were blasted by thunderbolts and the pyre and its burden reduced to ashes. Zeus had claimed his son, and taken him to Olympus before he died.

Iolaus instituted the worship of Heracles, and Hyllus duly married the Princess Iole. But they returned to Trachis to find that Deianira, in anguish at what she had unwittingly done, had hanged herself. On Olympus, Hera was at last reconciled to Heracles, and adopted him as her son. The Olympians gave him a great welcome, and he became the husband of Hebe.

Heracles' name, 'glory of Hera', suggests an origin among people who revered the goddess Hera. This could have been Argos, and Heracles was also associated with the city of Tiryns which is in Argos. Eurystheus, King of Argos, could well have been his overlord.

The stories of Heracles and his servitude are pre-Hellenic and his birth is recounted in the *Iliad* (Book XIX). The Dorian invaders of the

Peloponese found the cycle of hero-myths already in existence, and lost no time in adapting them to fit their own ancestry. The term Heraclidae was used in describing how the seed of the mighty hero was connected with the royal house of Argos.

See also Alcmene, Cercopes, Chiron, Heraclidae, Laomedon, Nestor, Peleus, Philoctetes, Priam, Theseus.

Heracles, Labours of I The Nemean Lion Heracles' First Labour was to kill and flay the gigantic lion which was the offspring of Selene, the goddess of the moon. When the creature was born she regarded it with horror – and then dropped it on earth. It fell near the city of Nemea in Argos and made its home in a cave with two openings. Selene was content to leave it there, until her wrath was aroused by the denial of a sacrifice to her by the local people; then she let it loose to prey on them. The lion proved invulnerable to all weapons, so Heracles blocked up one opening of the cave and entered the other, and used his club to fight the beast with. When it showed signs of weakening he dropped his club and choked it to death. He flayed it with one of its own claws, and bore the pelt back to King Eurystheus. Some versions say that this was the lion's skin he habitually wore, others that his cloak came from the lion he killed on Mount Kithaeron.

II The Hydra of Lerna The Hydra was a serpentine monster, the offspring of Typhon and Echidne, and nurtured by Hera in the hope of defeating Heracles. Lerna stood near the sea about five miles from the city of Argos; it later became famous as sacred ground, revered by the worshippers of Dionysus and Demeter. In Heracles' time the Hydra had its lair in a grove of plane trees near the source of the river Amymone, and it haunted a nearby swamp. Heracles called in the help of his nephew Iolaus, and first tried driving the nine-headed monster from its lair by firing burning arrows in; but Hera intervened by sending a huge crab to worry at Heracles' legs. He managed to crush the crab by stamping on its shell – then the Hydra emerged, and charged at Heracles. The monster's breath was deadly and Heracles had to work at furious speed to cut off its heads. But the heads grew again, until Iolaus brought firebrands and cauterised the stumps as the heads fell. Eight of them were disposed of in this way, but the ninth – the principal head – was immortal. Heracles took the evil thing, still hissing, and buried it deep in the ground. Before leaving the scene, he dipped his arrows in the Hydra's blood to make them more deadly.

III THE ERYMANTHIAN BOAR Heracles' Third Labour was to capture alive the great boar which terrified the people who lived near the wooded slopes of Mount Erymanthus in Arcadia. He drove the creature into deep snow on the higher slopes of the mountain, and when it could no longer run he leapt on to its back and chained its legs together. He carried it back to Argos to show it to King Eurystheus and prove that the Labour had been carried out. The sight of it, struggling in its chains and snorting with fury, terrified the King, who climbed into a deep bronze jar and hid there until the beast was taken away.

IV THE HIND OF CERYNEIA The hind of Ceryneia was one of five; the goddess Artemis had run down four of them in Thessaly, and harnessed them to her chariot. The fifth escaped and ran free on a hill near Ceryneia; it had brazen hooves and strangely – for a hind – horns, which shone like gold. It was sacred to Artemis and Heracles, while he was required to capture it and take it alive to Argos, could not harm it in any way. He simply ran it to exhaustion, and then, carrying it across his shoulders, set off for Argos. Heracles had not gone far before he encountered Artemis – in an angry mood. What was he doing to her creature, and where was he going with it? Heracles explained what was required of him: the one responsible was really Eurystheus. Artemis then allowed him to proceed, on condition that, once the Labour was proved to have been performed, the hind was set free.

V THE STYMPHALIAN BIRDS The woods around Lake Stymphalus in Arcadia had become infested with noisy birds, which plundered the cultivated fields and plagued the people with their unceasing noise. In this Labour Athene came to the help of Heracles. She persuaded Hephaestus to make a rattle out of bronze, and gave it to Heracles. He stood on Mount Cyllene, overlooking the lake, and swung the rattle. The noise was shattering – and totally unfamiliar. The birds rose in alarm, clouds of them. Heracles repeated the noise, and the birds panicked, flying in circles and blundering into each other. Heracles kept up the dreadful noise until the birds, terrified, flew away to the east. They were never seen again.

VI THE AUGEAN STABLES Augeas, King of Elis, possessed more flocks and herds than any man on earth; by a divine dispensation his livestock was immune from disease and Augeas did not waste time or labour, therefore, in keeping his stables and byres clean. His own animals were not affected, and Augeas had no care for the swarms of flies and the stench of dung that tormented everyone else. Eurystheus ordered Heracles, for his Sixth Labour, to clean out the Augean stables in a single day. Heracles breached the walls of the royal enclosure, which stood knee-deep in filth. Then he feverishly dug a channel to the walls from the river Alpheus and diverted the course of the waters. The river cleansed the stables and, resuming its normal course farther on, carried all the filth down to the sea.

VII THE CRETAN BULL Eurystheus next sent Heracles to the island of Crete, where a great bull roamed at liberty, terrifying the people and trampling vines and crops wherever it roamed. In some versions the bull is identified with the one sent by Poseidon, which sired the Minotaur on Queen Pasiphae. King Minos offered any help that he could give, but Heracles managed to capture the bull himself, single-handed, and then took it across the sea to Argos. Eurystheus was as frightened of the bull as he had been of the boar, so he dedicated it to Hera – the great goddess of Argos – and then set it free. Hera was not pleased: the bull really came from Heracles, as she knew very well. She drove it out of Argos and it made its way across the Isthmus to Marathon, where it was later captured again by Theseus.

See also Theseus.

VIII THE HORSES OF DIOMEDES This Diomedes, not to be confused with the Achaean hero of the *Iliad*, was the son of the god Ares and the nymph Cyrene, and King of the Bistones in Thrace. He kept a team of war horses which he fed on human flesh – usually that of wayfarers who fell into his hands. It was Heracles' task to bring the horses back to Argos. When he arrived in Thrace Heracles went to Diomedes' stables and overpowered the grooms; then he made a single halter to which he tied all four horses, and hauled them, rearing and kicking, out of their stable. The noise was considerable and the alarm was raised; Diomedes and his guards were soon on the spot to see what the disturbance meant. The King attacked Heracles, who let go of the horses and felled him with his club, and then dealt with the guards.

While he was thus engaged the horses ate their master – and at once became quite tame. They followed Heracles all the way back to Argos and gave him no more trouble.

See also *Alcestis* (Euripides).

IX THE GIRDLE OF THE AMAZON In the temple of the goddess Hera in Argos there was shown, in classical times, an article which was known as the girlde of Hippolyta, the Amazon Queen. The Amazons were purely creatures of imagination and Eurystheus' demand that Heracles bring him the girdle of Hippolyta can be likened to the familiar folk-tale motive of such things as the search for a talisman which is the property of some strange, not quite human, race of people. But one version of the story says that when he arrived in the Amazons' country Heracles found himself as much admired by Hippolyta as he was later to be by Omphale, and was *offered* the girdle. Another version says that the Queen's name was Antiope, in another she is Melanippe. At all events Heracles did succeed in stealing the girdle, whereupon the Queen made war on Athens because Theseus – the King – had been Heracles' ally in the theft. Theseus captured Hippolyta and made her his wife.

See also Amazons, Antiope, Hippolyta, Theseus.

X THE CATTLE OF GERYON Geryon's father was Chrysaor, the son of Medusa and Poseidon who was born at the moment of Medusa's death. His mother was Callirhoë, father of the Titan, Oceanus. Geryon had three heads and was the strongest man on earth; his kingdom was in the most westerly part of the world and his fine red cattle were the envy of everyone – including Eurystheus, who sent Heracles to steal them. Heracles set out for the far west in a great golden cup given him by Helios, the sun god, and when he reached the extremity he erected the Pillars of Heracles where Europe and Africa face each other across the straits (the Pillars are now identified as the mountains on either side of the Straits of Gibraltar). When he got to Geryon's kingdom he had first to kill Eurytion, Geryon's herdsman, the monstrous two-headed dog, Orthrus, and finally Geryon himself. Hera herself tried to help Geryon, but she fled when an arrow from Heracles wounded her in the breast. He loaded the cattle into the golden cup, made a sail of his lion skin, and made his way safely back to Argos, where he was able to return the gift of Helios and deliver the cattle to Eurystheus.

XI THE STEALING OF CERBERUS Eurystheus may have wanted to dispose of Heracles once and for all in setting him this terrible task – he ordered him to go to the kingdom of Hades and steal the fearful watchdog of the infernal regions. But this time both Athene and Hermes gave him help. Hermes, the conductor of souls, showed him the way, and Athene stayed close by to reassure him. When he arrived at the Styx, Heracles succeeded in bullying the scowling Charon into rowing him across, and when he stepped ashore in the nether world he saw a shade approaching him. He drew his bow, but Hermes told him that it was Meleager's shade, and that he had nothing to fear from the dead. Out of the meeting with Meleager came Heracles' eventual marriage to Deianira, who was Meleager's sister.

Heracles next encountered Hades himself, who denied him any further passage and challenged his right to be there at all. A struggle followed, in which Hades was wounded and left lying inside the gate of his own kingdom. He told Heracles to take Cerberus – if he could. Heracles found the great dog on its chain and seized it by the throat. At once the three heads tried to attack, and Cerberus lashed about with his powerful tail. Heracles hung on grimly, and Cerberus relaxed into unconsciousness. Athene was ready to help him back to the Styx with his burden, and rowed him across to the other side.

Eurystheus may have been surprised to see Heracles alive – when he saw the three slavering heads and the huge dog they belonged to he was frightened out of his wits, and leapt back into the safety of his great bronze jar.

See also Meleager.

XII THE APPLES OF THE HESPERIDES In a garden in the far west, on Mount Atlas, there was an apple tree that bore golden fruit. It was a present from Gaia to Hera on her marriage to Zeus, and she planted it in the garden to be cared for by the Titan, Atlas, and his daughters, the Hesperides. Hera also set the dragon, Ladon, to guard the precinct – the whereabouts of which was unknown to mortals. Heracles' last task for the hated Eurystheus was to collect some of the golden apples. Atlas, meanwhile, had taken part in the Titans' rebellion against the Olympians, and his punishment was to support the vault of heaven on his shoulders. The dragon, and his daughters, still guarded the golden apples.

Heracles had first to find out *where* the garden was, so he went to

Nereus, the ancient god of the sea. Nereus refused to tell him – he was a mere mortal. Heracles seized the god and swore he would not let him go until he delivered the information. Nereus finally yielded, but advised him that it would be better if he asked Atlas, who knew where to find the tree, to gather the fruit for him. So Heracles made his way to the garden of the Hesperides. He asked Atlas to get the apples for him – but Atlas told him of the dragon, which he feared. Heracles took his bow and was able to kill the dragon – a deed for which Hera would certainly make him pay.

Atlas then protested that someone would have to relieve him of his burden while he gathered the golden fruit: Heracles shouldered the mighty weight and Atlas went off for the apples. He returned with three of them – but he was reluctant to resume the burden of the sky. He undertook to go to Argos himself with the apples – Heracles could carry the weight while he was gone. Heracles was alarmed by the proposal, feeling certain that Atlas would never return. He pretended to agree, and asked Atlas to take the weight while he adjusted his lion skin on his shoulders to carry it more comfortably. Atlas put down the three apples' and Heracles put the sky back on the Titan's shoulders. Then he made off with the apples as quick as he could. The apples were shown to Eurystheus and the Labours were complete. Eurystheus knew better than to keep the apples, and handed the golden fruit back to Heracles, who gave them to Athene, who sped back to the Hesperides and restored them to Hera's garden. Hera, however, was by no means mollified; Heracles had killed her dragon and despoiled her garden, and some versions of the stories about the hero say that his madness was inflicted *after* he had performed the Twelve Labours.

See also Atlas, Hesperides, Nereus.

Heraclidae The descendants of Heracles, as conceived by the Dorian invaders of the Peloponnese to give support to their contention that the royal house of Argos was connected with the great Argive hero. After the defeat and death of Eurystheus by Iolaus at Athens, Hyllus consulted the oracle at Delphi to discover when the children of Heracles could return to their home in Argos. The oracle told him at the time of the third harvest. Hyllus understood this to mean in the third year, and followed the advice. He entered the Peloponnese at the head of an army, but was defeated and killed in a battle near the Isthmus of Corinth. The Heraclidae withdrew.

A hundred years later a descendant of Hyllus, Temenus, consulted the oracle again, and received the same reply. Temenus was puzzled at first but then understood; the 'third harvest' was the third harvest of men – the third generation, of which Temenus was one. The Heraclidae tried again, this time following the oracle's advice to enter by way of Elis, and taking a 'three-eyed man' for a guide. When they landed in Elis they met an Aetolian, Oxylus, who was riding a mule. The mule had only one eye, and Oxylus guided them on their quest for the lands of their fathers. They succeeded this time, and divided the land between them. Argos went to Temenus, Messene to Cresphontes; the twins Procles and Eurysthenes took possession of Sparta, where they founded the dual kingship for which Sparta was known in historical times.

Hercules   The Roman form of Heracles. The Argive hero's cult found its way to Rome by way of the Greek colonists of Sicily and Magna Graecia. The appearance of Hercules in the *Aeneid* (Book VIII) is almost certainly an invention of Virgil's and without a true mythological base, though it is possible that the Romans also had a folk memory of a great hero of giant strength. Hercules' altar in Rome, the Ara Pacis, stood in the Forum Boarium, between the Palatine Hill and the Tiber, a spot connected with the story of Hercules and the giant, Cacus.

Hermaphroditus   The son of Hermes and Aphrodite. The nymph Salmacis fell in love with him when she saw him bathing in her spring but he rejected her advances. She prayed to be united with him eternally in one body, and when he next came to the spring wound herself around his limbs. Her prayers were answered, hence the use of the name Hermaphroditus to describe one person in which the two sexes were united. Salmacis' spring was near Halicarnassus in Asia Minor.

Hermes   In mythology the son of Zeus and Maia, daughter of Atlas. He was born in a cave on Mount Cyllene in Arcadia, and soon after his birth was able to leave his cradle and walk. His first steps took him to the entrance of the cave, where he met a tortoise (they are common in Arcadia to this day). He took the tortoise into the cave and killed it; he wanted its shell for making music. It became the sounding board for a lyre – the first one ever made.

Hermes' next adventure (he was still a baby) was to discover a fine herd of cows, the property of Apollo. He stole the herd, making the cows walk backwards: he also made a pair of shoes out of twigs and wore those back to front, so that the tracks he left baffled Apollo when he tried to discover where his cows had gone. However, an old man had seen Hermes driving the cattle away backwards, and he told Apollo the story.

Apollo, in a great rage, stormed off to the cave – and found an infant Hermes sleeping peacefully in his cradle. In spite of Maia's angry protests he woke her son, and demanded that he bring the cows back. Hermes blinked his baby eyes and asked what cows were. Apollo would have been even more furious if he had known that Hermes had killed two of his cows to obtain strings for his lyre. As it was he was quite angry enough to haul him off to Olympus and complain to Zeus.

Zeus was amused, and encouraged his baby son's impudence. But after a while Hermes got tired of the game and owned up. He produced the lyre he had made, which so charmed Apollo that he gladly gave Hermes the rest of his herd in exchange for it. Zeus, watching his two sons, felt a thrill of pride at the quick wits of the younger, and made him his envoy, herald, ambassador, the guardian of the roads and the patron of travellers. Apollo gave him his herald's staff of gold, the *kerykeion* which he always carried. Hermes was messenger of all the gods, including his uncle Hades, who sent him to lay his golden staff on the eyes of the dying and conduct them in a gentle sleep to the next world.

Hermes was a young god always, and was indulged by the older Olympians. Apollo taught him how to prophesy and treated him with the affection of an older brother. Artemis took him hunting with her. Pan taught him to play the pipes. But he soon grew up, and became the father of sons himself. Autolycus, the greatest of thieves, was his son by Chione; Daphnis, the poet, by a Sicilian nymph; Hermaphroditus by the goddess Aphrodite; Myrtilus by a mortal woman.

Hermes, born in Arcadia, was in origin a pastoral god of that region, and much worshipped there as a patron of the ancient form of richness – of herds, flocks and their continuing increase. He was older than Apollo, also a pastoral god in origin, and long established before Apollo ever came to Greece. Hermes was, inevitably, connected with human fertility as well as with animal – increase was essential in both fields – and in his oldest monuments is represented simply as a phallus. This device developed into the *hermai,* the simple columns tapering towards the ground and surmounted by a head of the god. From the centre of the column an erect phallus protruded, perpetuating Hermes' ancient origins and giving the Greeks a feeling of reassurance, since he was also the god of luck. Both the phallus and the *hermai* developed from the simple idea of stones endowed by country people with magical properties.

His connection with fertility and the earth also associated him with death, and we have seen how, in myth, he became the conductor of souls *(Psychopompos)* for Hades. In his original form this function would have been part of the powers naturally attributed to him, and it fitted well with the formalised Olympian pattern.

He was a favourite with young men, being always regarded as a young god. Every gymnasium contained a *herm,* and every portrayal – like the celebrated statue at Olympus – shows Hermes as a young, athletic and graceful man.

See also Autolycus, Daphnis, Hermaphroditus, Pelops.

Hero and Leander The two lovers are best known from a poem by Musaeus, who wrote in the fourth century AD. Hero was a priestess of Aphrodite at Sestos; Leander was a youth of Abydos, on the opposite shore of the Hellespont, who fell in love with her. At night Hero would carry a torch on the seashore and Leander would swim across to her, guided by its light. One night, in a stormy sea, the light was extinguished by the waves, Leander was drowned, and Hero threw herself into the waves to be with him in death.

The story was known before Musaeus (Ovid was familiar with it) but his version has survived complete.

Hesiod A Greek poet, whose work is usually dated 800 BC, a little later than Homer's. He was the son of a merchant of Aeolis, who was forced by poverty to move to Boeotia, where he farmed at Ascra on the slopes of Mount Helicon. Hesiod became a farmer too and his poem, *Works and Days,* gives a remarkable description of a year in the life of a farmer of those days. It also refers to a legal dispute with his brother, Perses, about their inheritance of the land. Hesiod won the poetic prize at Chalcis with his composition of a hymn, and it is as a poet that he is remembered by posterity. His death was violent, according to Plutarch. He was murdered by the brothers of a woman at whose seduction he conspired or was guilty of himself.

Hesiod's claim to fame is a sound one. First, *Works and Days* is the earliest Greek poetry concerned with the day-to-day life. Second, he wrote the first consciously religious poem in Greek, the famous *Theogony*, from where much information is derived about the Greeks' beliefs concerning the origins of the universe and the gods who arose during its formation. Every account of Greek myth and religion in modern times relies to some extent on what Hesiod has to say.

Hesperides, The The daughters of Night, according to Hesiod, who lived far to the west in the garden of the golden apples of the sun. The far west, where the sun set, was often equated with the land of the dead and some myths place the entrance to Hades' kingdom there. It is possible that the Hesperides, three in number, were originally connected with the dead, though some later writers make them the daughters of Atlas.

See also Heracles, Labours of.

Hestia A Greek goddess who represented the priceless life-giving necessity of fire. The deity of the hearth, she was unknown to Homer, but was called by Hesiod the daughter of Cronus and Rhea.

She has almost no mythology, though the Homeric Hymn to Aphrodite makes her refuse both her brother Poseidon and her nephew Apollo as consorts, insisting on remaining a virgin. Hestia was really a sacred principle personified and much honoured as such. She kept apart from disputes on Olympus, and was represented in the city, which maintained a public hearth, as well as in the home. She was invoked before all sacrifices, and colonisers from Greece took fire to their new lands from their native city hearth, the *prytaneia*.

Hippolyta The Queen of the Amazons, whose girdle Heracles was required to secure as his Ninth Labour. In the myths surrounding Theseus she appears at the head of an Amazon army which invades Athens, where Theseus is king. Theseus defeats the Amazons and makes Hippolyta his first wife, and she bears him a son, Hippolytus.

See also Hippolytus, *Hippolytus* (Euripides), Theseus.

Hippolytus The son of Theseus and Hippolyta, the Amazon Queen. For the best known version of his story see the following entry, which concludes with his death. Further legends say that he was restored to life by Asclepius at the behest of Artemis: the stories go on from there to equate him with the consort of the Roman 'Artemis', Diana, as Virbius, her consort.

See also Diana, Theseus.

Hippolytus A tragedy by Euripides, first produced in 429 BC. It follows the myth of Hippolytus and the fatal love of Phaedra, daughter of King Minos, very closely, and once again presents an Olympian, the goddess Aphrodite, in an unflattering light. Her spiteful resentment of Hippolytus sets the story in motion – the goddess of love makes love a destroyer.

The play takes place before the palace of Troezen, where Theseus, King of Athens, is spending a year of voluntary exile to atone for a crime. With him are his wife, Phaedra, and his son by Hippolyta, called Hippolytus. Two statues can be seen in front of the palace: that of Artemis on the right, and of Aphrodite on the left. The goddess Aphrodite herself stands before the palace. It is evening.

Aphrodite speaks of Hippolytus, the chaste son of Theseus who will have nothing of love and cares for nothing but the hunt. He gives all his devotion to Artemis, goddess of the chase, and spurns the gifts that Aphrodite alone can bestow. To Artemis her due, Aphrodite implies – but man cannot spurn any one of the gods without risk, and Hippolytus is completely unaware that his father's wife is sick with love for him. He will pay – his narrow devotion to one pursuit and one patroness cannot be condoned. Aphrodite, before she leaves the scene, recalls that Theseus was awarded three prayers by his father, the god Poseidon – the mere utterance of one will bring an immediate response. The gift of Poseidon will play a part in the events the jealous goddess sets in motion.

Hippolytus and his companions return from the hunt as Aphrodite retires. They pass her statue without notice and go straight to the altar of Artemis, where they make offerings and sing her praises. An old huntsman joins them, and asks Hippolytus why he always ignores the worship of the other goddess whose image is there. Hippolytus replies that he cares nothing for Aphrodite's grace – his life is clean. The old huntsman is disturbed by his presumption and warns him of his debt to all the gods; Hippolytus turns to the statue of Aphrodite and makes a perfunctory gesture of reverence, and then follows his friends into the palace. The old huntsman, appalled, prays to the goddess to forgive him his youth and irreverence. Gods should be more kind and wise than poor mortals.

The old man's plea comes too late. Aphrodite has afflicted Phaedra, Theseus' wife, with a hopeless love for her stepson. Her nurse, unwisely, tells Hippolytus, who is outraged; the despairing Phaedra hangs herself. But first she ties a letter to her wrist which accuses Hippolytus of dishonouring her.

Theseus finds the letter when he returns to the palace. When he confronts his son he finds no comfort; he does not know that Phaedra's nurse had sworn Hippolytus to secrecy before telling him of the Queen's love. Theseus denounces his son as a hypocrite and banishes him; he has already invoked the wrath of Poseidon, the sea god and his patron. The unhappy Hippolytus and his companions travel along the shore road to Epidaurus, and it is there that Poseidon honours his promise to Theseus. He sends a great bull from the sea and the horses panic; Hippolytus is dragged and trampled when he loses control of his team. The companions bear him, dying, back to Troezen, where the goddess Artemis appears to Theseus. She tells him the truth, and is unsparing in her reproaches – he was very quick, was he not, to use the weapon Poseidon placed in his hands? Theseus is completely broken; but Hippolytus dies content, in his father's arms.

Homer The great epic poet of ancient Greece, and Greek literature's most famous name. But almost nothing is known of his life – even his birthplace is disputed, though the island of Chios has the strongest claim. He was probably an Ionian Greek; that much can be concluded from the *Iliad*, where he several times mentions the westward-facing shore. For a Greek this could only have meant Asia Minor (Ionia), since Greece herself is almost surrounded by the sea. The claim of Chios to have been his birthplace is reinforced by the presence there of a society of *rhapsodes* (story-tellers) called Homeridae, who lived on the island and spread the knowledge of his works. Originally, the Homeridae were believed to have been Homer's descendants.

As uncertain as the place of his birth is the time, but the general opinion, in spite of endless arguments among scholars, inclines to some time in the ninth century BC. The Mycenae of the *Iliad,* the city of Agamemnon who lead the Achaeans to Troy, had its greatest days some time around 1200–1000 BC, and it is thought that the *Iliad,* and the *Odyssey* were based on heroic saga hitherto transmitted orally –

there are examples of that sort of story-telling in Homer's work – and modelled by Homer into epics of tremendous power. The 'authorised' texts which we possess derive from the time of Pisistratus, the autocrat of Athens in the sixth century BC who ordered the works to be written down.

Apart from his genius as a poet, Homer has unique value for historians, archaeologists and students of comparative religion. The great German archaeologist Heinrich Schliemann proved, in his excavations of Troy and Mycenae in the nineteenth century, the historical basis of Homer's epics and it is now agreed that he preserved for us with complete fidelity the late Bronze Age society of the Achaeans who invaded Troy. The Achaeans fell from power when the Dorians in turn moved down from the north, and the succeeding three or four centuries are usually described as the dark ages of Greece – before the great flowering of culture familiar to us as the legacy of classical Greece. The gap between the fall of Mycenaean (Achaean) Greece and classical Greece is illuminated only by Homer. It is to him that we owe our knowledge of the Greeks' attitude to their gods in the heroic age, and, more important perhaps, their moral code and their notions of honour.

Homer was first translated into Latin in the third century BC (the *Odyssey*); the *Iliad* followed during the first century. Fittingly, Homer was the first Greek Poet whose works were *printed* in Greek, in Florence in 1488. Modern prose translations of both the epics by E. V. Rieu have proved enormously popular since they first appeared: the *Odyssey* in 1946 and the *Iliad* in 1950. A verse translation by Richard Lattimore, the American scholar, was published in 1962 and has been accorded the highest praise.

Hyacinthus   In Greek mythology a young man of Amyclae near Sparta, of exceptional beauty, who was loved by both Apollo and the god of the West Wind, Zephyrus. Hyacinthus preferred Apollo, and the rejected Zephyrus took his revenge one day when the two were playing with a discus. When Apollo threw, the West Wind deflected the discus so that it struck Hyacinthus on the head and killed him. The hyacinth first grew where the young man's blood fell on the earth.

Hyacinthus was in fact a pre-Hellenic fertility god – his death nourished the earth and flowers grew where his blood fell. A cult-statue has been preserved of the true Hyacinthus, and it shows a bearded, fully mature man, not the youthful-looking beauty the myth suggests.

Apollo was a later arrival among the Greek gods and the cult of Hyacinthus was one of those he absorbed into his own worship.

Hygeia One of the daughters of Asclepius, the god of healing and medicine. She represented Health; others were Iaso (Healing) and Panacea (Cures All).

See also Asclepius.

I

Iacchos A Greek god about whom almost nothing is known beyond the fact that he was honoured during the celebration of the Eleusinian Mysteries. One theory suggests that he was only known as more than a name to those who were initiates – and therefore bound to secrecy. It is unlikely that he was connected, as some have suggested, with Dionysus (Bacchus).

See also Eleusinian Mysteries.

Iapetus A Titan, one of the sons of Uranus and Gaia. He was the father of Prometheus, Epimetheus, Atlas and Menoetius. His name is not Greek and scholars suggest that it could be a version of Japhet, like the son of Noah in the Old Testament.

Ida, Mount 1. A range of mountains in Phrygia which formed the southern boundary of the lands of Priam, King of Troy. In the *Iliad* Zeus watched the progress of the Trojan War from its summit.

Ida, Mount 2. A mountain in Crete where, according to some traditions, Zeus was born.

See also Mount Dicte, Zeus.

Idas and Lynceus A famous pair of twins, Idas and Lynceus were the sons of Aphareus, King of Messene, and their story was known to Homer, who refers to Idas as the strongest of men (*Iliad*, Book IX) and one who challenged Apollo himself. Lynceus, according to Pindar, had the sharpest sight of any man (*Nemean Ode* X).

The quarrel between Idas and Apollo was over the hand of the beautiful Marpessa, daughter of the river god, Euenus. Idas stole a march on Apollo by securing the help of Poseidon (in some versions of the story Idas is Poseidon's son), who gave him a winged chariot.

When Apollo arrived to pay court to Marpessa she had already gone – Idas had whisked her off in his chariot and carried her home to Messene. Apollo went storming after him, outraged that a god's wishes had been thrust aside. But when he arrived in Messene he had to fight Idas, who was determined to keep his lovely Marpessa. The fight went on all day – until Zeus made them stop, and called Marpessa to appear before him. Which of them would she choose? Marpessa was quick to make up her mind. She would have Idas – she had heard too much about Apollo and his love affairs. Zeus ordained that it should be so, and Apollo was obliged to withdraw.

Idas and Lynceus sailed with the Argonauts, where they encountered another pair of twins, Castor and Polydeuces. Both sets of twins also took part in the Calydonian boar hunt but they were never friends. Another myth told how Castor and Polydeuces had carried off the two daughters of King Leucippus who were promised to Idas and Lynceus: the two sets of twins became bitter rivals from that moment on in spite of shared adventures.

The last adventure was a cattle raid in Arcadia, which was successful and yielded a fine herd. However, Idas cheated over the division of the spoils, and Castor and Polydeuces were left with nothing. They bided their time, and later went to Messene to steal the whole herd back; they also determined to settle their rivals once and for all, and lay in ambush for them. But Lynceus, with his remarkable eyesight, spotted them from Mount Taygettus; Idas raced down the mountainside and hurled his spear at the hollow tree where Castor was hiding. The mighty throw killed Castor, and Polydeuces rushed to avenge him: Idas broke a stone over his head, but not before Polydeuces had managed to kill Lynceus with his spear. Idas would have certainly finished off Polydeuces then – but Zeus had been watching, and Polydeuces was his son. Idas died from one of Zeus' thunderbolts.

In some versions of the story it is Castor who is the son of Zeus, but the outcome of the fight is always the same for Idas and Lynceus, since none could survive a blast from one of Zeus' thunderbolts.

See also the Dioscuri (for Castor and Polydeuces).

Idomeneus   According to Hesiod a descendant of King Minos, and one of the original suitors of the beautiful Helen. In Homer Idomeneus is also the King of Crete, and leads his army in eighty ships to the siege of Troy (*Iliad*, Book II). One of the senior Achaean leaders, he is as valiant as the younger ones, in the forefront of the action when Hector attacks their ships (Book XIII).

A later myth relates that, returning from Troy, his ships met a severe storm. He swore to sacrifice to Poseidon the first living thing he encountered when he landed safely in Crete. The first living thing proved to be his son, who had hurried down to the shore to welcome his father home. Some versions say that he kept his oath; others that he attempted to – whichever it was, a plague broke out in his kingdom. The people, completely against him by this time, drove him out of Crete. He died in exile in Italy.

Iliad, The The name of Homer's epic poem derives from Ilion, one of the names of Troy, which in turn derives from the city's founder, Ilus. The division into twenty-four books is believed to have been made by Aristarchus of Samothrace in the edition he produced in the second century BC.

Homer's poem describes some episodes in the long, dreary siege of Troy, but not the events which led up to it, though they are discussed and referred to in the narrative. At the end of the *Iliad* Troy has not fallen, though Hector has been killed. The poem ends with the return of Hector's body and the funeral rites, with Achilles victorious and the war continuing. The Wooden Horse and the fall of the city are part of the story told in the *Odyssey*, and details have been added by many ancient writers. An outline of the *Iliad* follows, and the reader should study the entries for the major figures under their own names.

BOOK I After nine years of fruitless siege the Achaeans have left part of their army to patrol the approaches to Troy, and used the rest to make raids on neighbouring cities. They have taken and plundered the city of Lyrnessos, and from the spoils Agamemnon is awarded Chryseis, daughter of a priest of Apollo. Achilles is given a beautiful slave girl, Briseis.

Apollo's priest offers gold to Agamemnon to ransom his daughter: Agamemnon treats the old man rudely and drives him out of the camp, declaring that Chryseis will end her days in Argos, serving in the palace – and serving Agamemnon in his bed. The shocked and grieving old man goes at once to his temple and implores Apollo's help and the god, furious at the treatment of his priest, sends a plague that decimates the Achaean camp. Men die like flies.

At last, in desperation, the Achaeans consult Calchas, the seer, who declares that Apollo's wrath was provoked by Agamemnon's behaviour – he will just have to return the girl to her father. And he'd better send a propitiary gift to Apollo, as well. Agamemnon is forced to yield; he will send the girl back, he says, but – he adds – he will require compensation from one of the other Achaean chieftains to make up for his loss. This brings an angry comment from Achilles on Agamemnon's mendacity; the other Achaeans are there as his allies to avenge the dishonour done to Menelaus, Agamemnon's brother. If greed is going to dictate their behaviour Achilles will leave them to it, and retire from the field with his Myrmidons. Agamemnon, stung, declares that Achilles can leave if he wants to: Agamemnon is the leader of the expedition, and will command. And he commands Achilles to surrender his beautiful captive, Briseis. Achilles finds this order, delivered as to a common soldier, more than he can endure. He draws his sword – but the goddess Athene speaks to him: Agamemnon will pay dearly for his shortcomings, she says. She and Hera will see to that.

Achilles surrenders the girl. His beloved friend Patroclus escorts her to the heralds who will accompany her to Agamemnon's tent. Chryseis is restored to her father and the plague ceases. Achilles broods for a while and then calls on his mother, the goddess Thetis. Zeus is indebted to Thetis (see the entry for Hera), and Achilles asks her to seek his help for the other side – the Trojans. Then Agamemnon will learn how weak he is without Achilles in his army. Thetis does as he asks, and Zeus agrees to grant her request – a little reluctantly, because he knows Hera will be furious. But he does give his word, and when Hera accuses him of plotting something with Thetis he frightens her into silence.

Book II   Zeus sends Agamemnon a dream, which persuades him that he can capture Troy himself – he has only to rally his armies for battle. The next day he assembles the other leaders and tells them of it. Nestor, King of Pylos, agrees that the armies must be assembled. Agamemnon says he will test their spirit, and when the Achaean host is gathered he announces that Zeus has deserted him. When he suggests that their cause is certainly lost and the armies might as well return home, he is mortified at how eagerly they take up his suggestion and make for their ships.

But they are observed by Hera, who has been nursing her suspicions of Zeus and his meeting with Thetis. Hera goes at once to Athene who, like her, is on the side of the Achaeans. Athene in turn goes to Odysseus, who has witnessed the exodus with dismay. She heartens him, and he manages to save the day. His fiery words and the support of Nestor bring the armies back, except for the soldiers of Achilles who stay with their brooding leader and take no part in the action.

The Trojans have also assembled, and the two armies advance across the plain to confront each other.

BOOK III The armies meet. Paris steps forward from the Trojan ranks and offers single combat to any of the Achaean leaders. This is rash of the Trojan prince: he is a great archer but the Achaean leader who accepts the challenge is none other than Menelaus, King of Sparta, a veteran warrior who is, moreover, the man whom Paris has personally wronged. Paris had stolen Menelaus' wife, Helen, and that was the cause of this dreadful war. Paris is paralysed with shame and fear together – and flees back to the Trojan line. His brother the great and noble Hector, heir of Troy, gives him a verbal thrashing and tells him that the Achaeans should have stoned him to death, like a criminal. Paris regains his self-control: he acknowledges Hector's words, and will make amends. He will meet Menelaus in combat: whoever wins shall keep Helen. A truce must be proclaimed.

Menelaus agrees, and asks that Priam, King of Troy, shall join him in a sacrifice to seal the agreement. Priam leaves the city and joins the warriors for the sacrifice, and when he returns to Troy he finds the Trojan elders watching Helen; she is alone and has grown uneasy and restless for her homeland. They speak of her beauty and of the harm she has done, but Priam is wise enough to know how little she is to blame. He calls her to his side, and engages her attention by asking her to name the Achaean leaders for him.

The combat takes place, and Menelaus looks like winning. He is stronger and more experienced than Paris, and believes he has right on his side. At the last moment Paris is saved – by the goddess Aphrodite who favours him. The Trojans are unmoved by the outcome. They loathe Paris for the harm he has done: but when Menelaus prowls in front of the Trojan ranks looking for his enemy no one can tell him where Paris is. Aphrodite has spirited him away to the safety of the city.

Menelaus, with reason, declares himself the victor. He demands Helen, and enormous reparation.

BOOK IV The Trojans are glad of the truce, uncertain how to proceed since Paris has not been killed, though it seems plain that Menelaus has won the combat. Athene, impatient with the stalemate, decides to provoke action. She visits Troy in the guise of one of Priam's many sons, and approaches Prince Pandarus of Lycia, one of Troy's allies and a famous archer. The 'boy' points to Menelaus in the Achaean ranks, glowering with rage at the tardiness of the Trojans in keeping to the agreement, and declares that whoever killed the King of Sparta would be honoured by every Trojan who ever lived. Could Pandarus kill him at that long range? Pandarus, the great archer?

The prince falls for the flattery. He takes careful aim, and shoots an arrow at Menelaus. Athene deflects the arrow so that the stroke is not lethal – just enough to wound Menelaus, and break the truce with dishonour to the Trojans. Agamemnon rallies the Achaean forces again; the Trojans are advancing to the attack now that the truce is broken. Ares, the war god son of Zeus, fights on their side, while Athene gives her support to the Achaeans.

BOOK V Diomedes, son of Tydeus, now comes to the fore among the Achaeans. Athene inspires him to great deeds in battle; she also persuades Ares, her half-brother, that they should both withdraw from the field and let the mortals fight on until the best side wins.

The Achaeans have the best of the day. Apart from Diomedes, Agamemnon, Idomeneus and Menelaus distinguish themselves. Diomedes leads the assault again and again – until Pandarus, in a chariot driven by Aeneas, brings him down with an arrow in his shoulder. Athene is false to the declaration she made to Ares, and appears at Diomedes' side to heal him with her divine art. He returns to the battle on foot, having fallen from his chariot, and encounters Pandarus and Aeneas. He kills Pandarus with a spear throw: Aeneas stands his ground, shield and spear ready. Diomedes hurls a huge stone at Aeneas, which would have killed him but for Aphrodite, who favours him, no less than Athene favours the Achaeans. Aphrodite is no warrior goddess, but she is Aeneas' mother. She throws her veil over her son and bears him from the field, Diomedes in pursuit. He lunges with his spear and wounds Aphrodite in the wrist: she screams with pain and her son falls from her hands. But Apollo, who favours the Trojans, catches up the unconscious prince and delivers a warning to Diomedes that he is presuming to fight with gods. Diomedes falls back in fear, and Apollo takes Aeneas to safety. The rest of the Achaeans fight furiously to kill someone they believe to be Aeneas, not knowing that Apollo has left them a phantom to keep them busy.

Hector, meanwhile, enters the battle with Sarpedon, and Aeneas returns to the field, completely restored and accompanied by Ares, Aphrodite's lover. The war god has come to put fresh heart into the Trojans. Sarpedon, in combat with a son of Heracles, kills his opponent but is himself wounded and carried from the field by his captains. The Trojans, led by Hector and inspired by Ares, drive the Achaeans back steadily.

This is too much for Hera and Athene. Hera rallies the Achaeans by proclaiming the valour of Achilles: Athene takes the place of Diomedes' charioteer, wearing the cap of Hades which makes her invisible. She charges straight at Ares and guides Diomedes' spear so that it flies straight into the war god's belly. Ares leaves the field, and the Trojans find the battle turning against them. But Hector and Aeneas manage to hold the line, while Nestor exhorts the Achaeans to forget everything but the need to kill and kill and kill.

BOOK VI Helenus, the young seer and brother of Hector, advises the Trojan leader to slip back to the city and offer sacrifice to Athene to stop the havoc wrought by Diomedes. Hector hurries into Troy, and there is a brief lull in the fighting. Diomedes sees a single Trojan advancing to meet him in combat. Impressed by the courage shown he asks the Trojan to tell him his name. He proves to be Glaucus, Sarpedon's cousin – and no combat takes place because their two families enjoy an old friendship which they decide to honour.

In the city, Queen Hecuba offers her finest robe as part of the sacrifice to Athene. It is in vain. Athene will never help the Trojans.

While the ceremony proceeds Hector goes in search of Paris, and finds him with Helen, polishing his armour. He rebukes him, and Paris returns to the battlefield. Helen confesses to Hector that her mind is in a turmoil – she would rather have died than have caused the bloodshed men blame her for. Hector speaks kindly to her, and leaves to snatch a moment with his wife, Andromache, and his baby son. But Andromache is at the city wall, regarding the distant field with terror. When she sees her husband she hurries to him, weeping with relief to see him safe. She implores him not to return to the field. Hector tells her that she must remember who her husband is: he has no choice in the matter and he will die when the Fates decide.

BOOK VII Hector, Glaucus and Paris put fresh heart into the Trojans and the indefatigable Athene comes scurrying down to see what else she can do for her Achaeans. But she finds Apollo already there, and yields to his suggestion that a champion from either side should fight. Apollo inspires Hector himself with the idea, and the Trojan prince advances between the lines to make the challenge. There is no response – no one is eager to try conclusions with him. At length Menelaus, ashamed of the timorous Achaeans, is prepared to offer himself. Agamemnon dissuades his brother: Achilles himself, he points out, has not met Hector alone. Then Nestor, the ageing King of Pylos, shames the Achaeans into accepting the challenge and lots are drawn: it is great Ajax who must fight. The combat lasts until nightfall and is inconclusive. But Hector honours Ajax as a great fighter and the two part after exchanging gifts. A truce follows, so that both Achaeans and Trojans can collect the dead and bury them honourably.

BOOK VIII Zeus orders the rest of the Olympians not to help either side, but Athene asks his permission to at least advise them. He grants that, and then flies to the top of Mount Ida to watch the course of the battle. He has a debt to pay to Thetis, mother of Achilles, and now he creates fear and confusion on the Achaean side with his thunderbolts. The Trojans advance, and soon even Odysseus leaves the field, convinced of the uselessness of trying to prevail against the power of Zeus.

Old Nestor is alone on the field in his chariot, grimly unyielding. Paris fires an arrow that kills one of Nestor's horses, so that his team is crippled: Nestor soon has Hector bearing down on him but he is rescued by Diomedes. At Nestor's advice, Diomedes turns his back on Hector's charge of cowardice and races off the field in the general rout. The old King knows that Zeus is against them that day.

The Trojans pursue the enemy to their camp. Hera taunts Agamemnon so effectively that he manages to rally the Achaeans, and their finest archer, Ajax's brother Teucer, takes deadly toll from the walls of the stockade. He kills Hector's charioteer – whereupon Hector uses Diomedes' trick and hurls a stone. He smashes Teucer's shoulder and collar bone, and he is out of the fight. The Achaeans are driven back on to their ships.

Hera and Athene, watching the retreat, are driven to join the fight against the Trojans. Zeus, all – seeing, orders them back and they retire to Olympus, sullen and resentful. Later he joins them, and tells them that they can sulk as much as they like: but if they lift a finger to help the Achaeans he will blast them into Tartarus. Hector, he says, cannot be halted save by Achilles. That is decreed. Darkness falls on the earth and the Achaeans leaders are wearily grateful for a respite.

BOOK IX The perilous position of the Achaeans moves Agamemnon to call a council. He suggests that their cause must be lost if Zeus has turned against them, but Diomedes tells him he is a coward – he can go home to Argos, if he wants to. Nestor supports Diomedes, and advises Agamemnon to listen to the other leaders before displaying his weakness again. Then Nestor recalls to him his foolishness in the matter of Achilles and the girl Briseis: that mistake should be rectified without delay. Agamemnon agrees, and says he will not only restore the girl but will make generous gifts to Achilles if it will help mend the quarrel. He will also offer Achilles one of his daughters in marriage. Nestor commands his decision; Odysseus, great Ajax and Phoenix, an old and honoured soldier who helped to care for the growing Achilles, will form the deputation that will treat with the absent champion.

The three proceed to the camp of Achilles and find him with Patroclus, absently plucking a lyre. Achilles' quarrel is only with Agamemnon and he receives them courteously. Odysseus tells him how badly things have gone: the Trojans are likely to win and Hector is carrying all before him. If Achilles' quarrel is only with Agamemnon, could he not think of the other Achaean leaders, who have never offended him? They need him now.

Achilles replies that there was a time when battle was the greatest thing in life to him. But he is beginning to find peace attractive – now that his glory as a warrior has been sullied by Agamemnon. He refuses to help the Achaeans and says he will sail for home on the next day. He asks Phoenix to stay: he has an affection for his former guardian and will try to persuade him to accompany him home. Ajax turns to Odysseus and tells him they might as well go, since Achilles is determined to forget all his comrades and nurse his grievance. Achilles acknowledges the justice of Ajax's words: but says that Agamemnon shamed him in the presence of the Achaean army, and he will not lift a finger unless Hector threatens the safety of his own ships and men. Odysseus and Ajax leave to take the news back to the Achaeans.

Agamemnon and the others hear Odysseus in silence. Then Diomedes declares angrily that Achilles can be left alone with his pride since it means so much to him. The rest agree, and prepare the defence of their ships.

BOOK X That night Agamemnon, sleepless, hears the sound of feasting behind the walls of Troy. He calls the other leaders and suggests a spying exercise – any kind of information may prove useful to them in their present straits. Diomedes volunteers to go, and selects Odysseus to go with him. Meanwhile, in the city, Hector has had the same idea, and while Diomedes and Odysseus are picking their way silently through the unburied corpses of the battlefield, a spy is found for the Trojans. He is Dolon, one of the heralds: he wears a wolfskin cap and is famous for his speed. He leaves the city, and the total silence convinces him that his quest will be easy. But he soon finds himself pursued: Diomedes and Odysseus were lying among the corpses. They cut off his retreat.

Dolon is threatened with death. The two Achaeans want to know where the sentries are positioned and where the allies' camps are. Dolon weakens, and tells them what he knows, but Diomedes and Odysseus murder him anyway, not interested in having him as a prisoner. Then they act on the information they have wrung from him, and go to where King Rhesus of the Thracians is encamped by the city walls. The Thracians are sleeping, with their fine horses tethered nearby. Diomedes and Odysseus fall on the sleeping men and slaughter them and their King. Athene warns them that Apollo is rousing the Trojans, so they mount two of the captured horses and escape back to the Achaean camp.

BOOK XI The fighting is resumed at dawn. Almost all the Achaean leaders suffer badly: Diomedes is seriously wounded and Odysseus is only saved from death by Menelaus and great Ajax. Nestor sees the physician Machaon felled by another of Paris' arrows: Idomeneus implores him to get Machaon back to the camp – a good physician is worth many men. Ajax has to fight his way back to the camp a foot at a time.

Achilles watches the fighting from his ship. When he sees Nestor's chariot race into the camp carrying a wounded man, he sends Patroclus to find out who it is. Patroclus visits Nestor's tent, and the wise old

King makes use of the occasion. He points out that Achilles is the stronger, and the more nobly born: but Patroclus is older, and he could give his friend good counsel. Why, if Achilles will not fight himself, does he not send his Myrmidons with Patroclus? He could also give Patroclus his armour to wear – the Trojans will believe that Achilles is inside it, and it will make them hesitate.

(See the entry for Aeacus for the origin of the Myrmidons.)

BOOK XII The Achaeans are now on the defensive behind their great stockade, built and strengthened throughout the long war with Troy. In front of it is another line of defence, a deep trench filled with sharpened stakes.

Hector and the Trojans leave their chariots and cross the trench to storm the walls on foot. Among the commanders are Sarpedon and Glaucus. From Mount Ida, Zeus sends a strong wind to blow the dust of the battlefield into the faces of the Achaeans. Hector is leading the attack on one gate when he sees in the sky an eagle, carrying a snake in its talons. The great bird is still in flight when its prey suddenly twists and strikes with its fangs at the eagle's breast. The eagle gives a harsh cry and drops the snake. One of the older Trojans sees a bad omen in this: the apparent victor did not win, after all. Hector disregards his words and leads the attack on the gate.

At another gate Sarpedon and Glaucus nearly force an entry: they are only held by the arrival of great Ajax and Teucer. The issue is decided for the time being when one of Teucer's arrows brings Glaucus down. Hector, meanwhile, determined to get to the Achaean ships, manages to smash in a gate bar with a huge stone, given extra strength for the deed by Zeus. He leads his Trojans into the camp of the Achaeans, who retreat in a panic to their ships.

BOOK XIII Zeus is not the only Olympian watching the battle. His brother Poseidon watches too, from a peak on the island of Samothrace. He favours the Achaeans, and is enraged by Zeus' apparent alliance with the Trojans. In the guise of Calchas, the seer, he appears at the side of great Ajax, and touches him with his staff. He tells him not to fear for the other gates but to concentrate on the one by which Hector and his men have entered. Then he turns away and fades from sight, and this is seen by Ajax the Locrian, who turns to great Ajax and tells him that it was a god that spoke to him.

Poseidon goes through the camp and speaks to the other leaders also: Hector finds the Achaeans' resistance strengthened and the fight no longer in his favour.

BOOK XIV Hera is watching, too. She is delighted to see Poseidon rallying the Achaeans and decides to keep Zeus from attending too much to what his brother is doing. She borrows the girdle of Aphrodite, and enlists Sleep (*Hypnos*) as her ally with the promise of one of the Graces to be his bride. She goes to Mount Ida, and Zeus suddenly finds his quarrelsome wife irresistible. After making love to her his eyes are closed by Sleep, who then hurries off to Poseidon and tells him to do what he likes for the Achaeans while he can.

Poseidon rallies and renews in turn Menelaus, Diomedes, Agamemnon, Idomeneus and Odysseus; Ajax the Locrian and great Ajax, meanwhile, decimate the Trojans near the breach made by Hector. Hector himself is knocked senseless by a great blow and carried off the field. The Trojans, stunned by this reversal, are driven from the stockade and back across the trench, pursued to deadly effect by Ajax the Locrian, the fastest runner and greatest spearman of the Achaeans.

BOOK XV Zeus awakens, and sees what has happened. He turns a thunderous brow on Hera, and asks if all this is her doing. She answers meekly that it wasn't her – it was his brother, Poseidon. Zeus renews his warning about interference: he tells her of his design to bring Achilles into the fight – that is his promise to Thetis.

Zeus sends Iris with a message for Poseidon, warning him to stay out of the war, and Poseidon yields with bad grace. Then Iris goes to Apollo, whom Zeus wants to make aware of Hector's plight. Apollo goes at once and revives Hector – to the dismay of the Achaeans, who had believed him to be dead. They had been advancing – now they pause.

Inspired by Apollo, the Trojans follow Hector in his tremendous charge back to the Achaeans' stockade. Teucer takes aim at Hector but his bowstring snaps: this omen disheartens the Achaeans even more. They retreat to the ships, where great Ajax stands on a prow and calls on them to save themselves by their own courage – there is no longer any place to where they can retreat.

BOOK XVI Patroclus asks Achilles to lend him his armour and his Myrmidons. Achilles agrees, but insists that they must only be used to drive the Trojans from the Achaean ships – Hector has already managed to set one on fire. The appearance of someone in the armour of Achilles, in Achilles' chariot, turns the tide yet again. The Trojans are driven back from the ships and Patroclus, forgetting his promise to Achilles, pursues them on to the battlefield with his Myrmidon army.

Sarpedon is mortally wounded, to the grief of Glaucus, and a fierce fight takes place around the fallen prince. The Achaeans strip the dying man of his armour but Apollo carries him away from the blood and filth of the battlefield and gives him to Sleep and Death (*Thanatos*) to take to his home in Lycia. Patroclus fights his way to the walls of Troy, the idea of victory growing stronger in his mind. There he leads the Myrmidons in an attempt to scale the walls – an attempt which ceases abruptly when Apollo speaks directly to Patroclus. Apollo tells him he will never take the city, nor will Achilles: the Fates have decreed otherwise.

Patroclus withdraws, and returns to the battlefield. But his brief glory is over: Apollo goes to the battlefield and deals him a mighty blow on the back with the palm of his hand. The helmet of Achilles rolls in the dust and Patroclus lies on the ground, stunned. He tries to get back to the Myrmidons but Hector sees him, and kills him. Hector wants to secure the chariot with Achilles' superb horses and gives chase: but Patroclus' charioteer has no trouble outstripping him.

BOOK XVII Menelaus has seen Patroclus fall and he goes to guard the body from capture by the Trojans. Apollo calls Hector back from his pursuit: Hector charges back to the field and Menelaus is forced to leave the body he was guarding. Hector strips the armour of Achilles from Patroclus but when he tries to take the body as well he finds great Ajax barring his way. Hector abandons the corpse of Patroclus and leaves the field: when he returns he is wearing Achilles' armour. Zeus observes this, and shakes his head over such behaviour. But he knows what will be: his design has succeeded and his promise to Thetis is fulfilled. Achilles will not be absent from the fight for much longer.

Meanwhile, Menelaus and Ajax and their men fight desperately to stop the Trojans from taking the body of Patroclus. They send a runner to Achilles with the news of what has happened.

Book XVIII Achilles' grief alarms his friends. Nestor's son, Antilochus, who has brought him the news, seizes his hands in fear that he may kill himself. Achilles' great cry of grief brings Thetis to the scene. He tells her that all he wants is to kill Hector – after that he cares little about living or dying. Thetis knows that her son's death will follow on Hector's – but for now he must have arms and armour. She promises that he will have them the very next day, from the divine artificer himself.

On the field the Achaeans are driven back, pursued by Hector and the Trojans, who are only prevented from seizing the body of Patroclus by the stubborn fighting of great Ajax and Ajax the Locrian.

Hera sends a message to Achilles. If he cannot fight he must at least appear – the Achaeans are now fighting with their backs to the stockade. Achilles hurries to the wall, and Athene clothes him with radiance, so that his appearance is almost godlike. His presence stuns the Trojans: three times he gives his battle-cry, which Athene echoes from a distance. The Achaeans take advantage of the confusion and drive the Trojans back: the body of Patroclus is safe behind the Achaean lines. Hera orders Helios, the sun, to set, so that darkness comes early.

In the Trojan camp, Hector decides against advice from Polydamas to withdraw into the city, now that Achilles is back in the war. The Trojans will prepare for the morning, he says, and fight again at sunrise.

On Olympus, Thetis is given new armour for Achilles by Hephaestus.

Book XIX Thetis finds Achilles with the body of Patroclus in his arms. He takes the armour gratefully, and she promises him that the body will not decay – he can go to war and do what he must, and then come back and give Patroclus his funeral rites.

Achilles and Agamemnon have ended their quarrel. Odysseus tells the other leaders that the army must eat before going to battle and orders are given. But Achilles remembers that it was always Patroclus who prepared their food, and refuses to eat. Zeus observes this, and tells Athene that her favourite is fasting before battle – is that wise? Athene goes to Achilles and gives him divine strength.

In his chariot Achilles murmurs to his horses: will they bring him back from the battlefield – or leave him dead on it, like Patroclus? One of the horses, given a voice by Hera, answers him: it was Apollo that killed Patroclus, though Hector is credited with the deed; Achilles too will die at the behest of a god. Achilles retorts that he knows his life is drawing to a close: meanwhile, there is a battle to be fought and a Trojan prince to be killed.

BOOK XX Zeus summons the gods to Olympus. He will simply watch the fight now, he says: Achilles is at war. The rest of them may do what they will. The gods lose no time: Hera, Athene, Hermes, Poseidon and Hephaestus go to help the Achaeans; Ares, Artemis, Apollo, the river god Xanthus, Aphrodite and Leto go to the side of the Trojans.

Apollo goes to the Trojan prince Aeneas, who had once fought Achilles: Aeneas hesitates to face him again because he knows that Athene is Achilles' alley. Apollo reminds Aeneas that he is the son of Aphrodite, and gives him courage to challenge Achilles. Achilles, with his divinely-wrought armour, is unharmed by Aeneas' deadly spear throw and almost kills his challenger. But Poseidon himself intervenes and carries Aeneas off the battlefield: the Fates have a new life in store for Aeneas.

Apollo also speaks to Hector, telling him not to seek Achilles for direct combat: Achilles is the stronger and will surely kill him. Hector is depressed by the warning but takes heed of it – until he sees his brother Polydorus fall in the battle, killed by Achilles. He rushes to the field to challenge the man who has sworn to kill him. Achilles exults – and Athene helps him. Hector hurls his spear with lethal accuracy: the goddess turns it aside. Achilles hurls himself at Hector: Apollo snatches the Trojan prince out of harm and leaves a column of mist in his place – and Achilles screaming with rage that Apollo has helped his enemy. He says nothing, of course, about Athene's help to him. Robbed of his chosen victim, Achilles kills like a madman. He is protected by the armour made for him by Hephaestus.

BOOK XXI Achilles' fury divides the Trojan forces and half of them are pressed back to the river of Xanthus, the Scamander, where he and his Myrmidons slaughter them in the shallows. Xanthus rises in wrath and sends great waves crashing down in the Myrmidons. Achilles is forced back by the great waters, which knock him off his feet again and again as he retreats through the corpses on the battlefield. Hera appeals to her son Hephaestus, who sends his divine fire to scorch the field. The corpses burn on the field and in the river, which heats dangerously; the fish and river creatures start to die. Xanthus rolls his waters back into their course and Achilles is saved.

The gods, meanwhile, are fighting too. Athene manages to fell Ares with a heavy rock. The war god's paramour, Aphrodite, comes to help him off the field – whereupon Athene turns on her and strikes her a mighty blow in the breast. Then she rejoins Hera – both women are well pleased with the way things are going. Poseidon challenges Apollo, who tells him coldly that gods should not fight each other. Artemis hears this, and jeers at her brother for not taking up the challenge: whereupon Hera emulates Athene, and attacks Artemis without warning. Artemis, demoralised, runs from the field.

Apollo is busy elsewhere. King Priam has been watching the battle with increasing anxiety: he sees the Trojans being driven back to the city and orders the city gates to be opened for them – but somehow, he knows, Achilles will have to be kept out. Apollo inspires Agenor, a young Trojan nobleman, with the courage to face Achilles. Agenor places himself in the path of Achilles and hurls a spear at him. The divinely-wrought armour saves Achilles once more and he hurls himself at Agenor whom he sees turn and run. Achilles gives chase and the Trojans get safely into the city and close the gates behind them. Only Hector stays outside, at the Scaean Gate, knowing that he will have to fight Achilles sooner or later. Priam implores his son to save himself: Hector hears his words and his mother Hecuba's weeping, but he waits for Achilles.

BOOK XXII Achilles is halted abruptly when his quarry stops and turns on him. It is not Agenor, but Apollo: Apollo has placed the gallant Trojan safely inside the city and runs instead of him, knowing that Achilles will follow. Achilles wastes no time but races back to the city walls where Hector waits for him.

Hector sees Achilles charging straight at him in his invulnerable armour, and his heart fails him. He turns and runs round the city walls, Achilles pounding after him. The gods watch, and Zeus knows what the Fates have planned for both men. He does not prevent Athene from weighing the scales further against Hector. She assumes the form of Hector's brother Deiphobus, and persuades him to stop and fight after the chase has taken the two men three times round the walls.

The victory is an easy thing for Achilles, since he does not fight alone. He reviles the dying Hector, and swears that the Trojans will never have the body of their prince for decent burial. With his last breath Hector warns Achilles that his hour is not far off, that Apollo and Paris will soon bring him to account, here at the Scaean Gate.

The royal family of Troy, watching from the walls, see Hector die. Their grief is turned to horror when Hector's body is despoiled: Achilles pierces Hector's heels and ties the feet to his chariot. Then he drives back to the Achaean camp, dragging Hector's body through the blood and dust of the battlefield. The aged Priam, almost mad with grief at his son's death and the outrage done to his body, rushes to the city gates to go after Achilles: the people have to hold him back.

BOOK XXIII Achilles throws the body of Hector down in the dust beside the bier of Patroclus. Agamemnon sends for him to dine with the other Achaeans in his tent and prepares a great cauldron of steaming water so that he can wash off the blood of the fighting. Achilles swears he will not bathe until Patroclus is given a hero's funeral rites, and he falls asleep from exhaustion. The ghost of Patroclus appears to him, and asks him to make sure that their ashes lie in the same urn – for Achilles will be with him soon. In his sleep Achilles reaches out to embrace his beloved Patroclus – only to wake to the bitterness of finding himself alone.

At the funeral pyre Achilles calls to the dead Patroclus, telling him that the man who killed him will never be honoured. Hector's body will be thrown to the dogs.

BOOK XXIV Achilles' madness continues. Between lamenting in solitude and dragging Hector's body around the tomb of Patroclus, he hardly lives at all. Hector's body stays miraculously bright and undulled by death: Apollo makes sure of that. On Olympus the gods are watching grimly – except Hera, who still cannot forgive Paris and the Trojans. Hermes offers to steal Hector's body; but they do nothing, until Apollo upbraids them and a quarrel breaks out between him and Hera. Zeus intervenes. He sends for Thetis, and tells her that her son's behaviour is displeasing to the gods: Achilles must return Hector's body to Priam, who will dare Achilles' wrath in his enemy's own camp. Thetis bows to Zeus' words and goes to her son. Iris, the gods' messenger, is sent to Troy, where she puts it into King Priam's head that he must go and ransom Hector's body.

Priam tells Hecuba what he is going to do. She is horrified – certain that Achilles will kill him. Priam says he will go nonetheless. Achilles can kill him if he wants to, he would rather that than do nothing, and he may at least be able to hold his son's body in his arms before he dies. He orders his other sons to provide him with a chariot, and to fill it with treasure. Hecuba brings her husband a gold cup of wine, so that he can pour a libation to Zeus in hope of a safe return. Zeus sends his eagle to fly over the city as a sign that he accepts Priam's prayer, and the King sets out full of hope. Hermes, in the guise of a Myrmidon soldier, guides him to Achilles' tent.

Achilles, impressed by the noble old King's courage in coming alone to the enemy's camp, treats him honourably. He will give him the body of Hector – since Thetis has bidden it; but the Trojan King's behaviour moves him deeply. When Priam tells him he has not slept since his son died, Achilles persuades him to rest.

But in the night Hermes wakes Priam – he must not sleep among his enemies – and conducts the sad procession back to Troy. They reach the gates at dawn, and Cassandra sees them from the walls. She rouses the city, and a funeral pyre is prepared for the noble Hector, prince of Troy.

The *Iliad* ends with the funeral rites for Hector. The fate of Achilles, foretold in Homer, does not occur in that writer's work, though he is encountered in Hades in the *Odyssey* (Book XI). His shade tells Odysseus that he would rather be a servant on earth than a King among the dead. In Book XXIV the shade of Agamemnon describes to Achilles how the Achaeans buried his ashes with those of Patroclus under a mound on a headland on the Hellespont, and what a fierce struggle ensued over his body when he fell; Zeus himself let loose a storm under cover of which the retreating Achaeans removed the corpse.

The most familiar version of Achilles' death tells that Apollo, after Achilles' treatment of Hector's body, guided the arrows of Paris on the battlefield when the fighting resumed. One of them struck Achilles in the right heel, his only vulnerable spot, and he died in agony. Another version – more in keeping, since the vulnerable heel is a later tradition – tells that Apollo himself killed Achilles.

Io The daughter of Inachus, a river god of Argos, one of the judges when Hera and Poseidon disputed for the possession of Argos. Inachus decided in favour of Hera, and introduced her cult, his daughter Io becoming one of her priestesses. Poseidon retaliated by ensuring that the rivers of Argos run dry throughout the summer.

Io, unfortunately for her, was noticed by Zeus. He decided that he wanted her badly enough to violate his consort's shrine. But Hera was constantly jealous of Zeus and her suspicions were hard to escape, so Zeus turned Io into a white heifer when it seemed that his latest dingy escapade was about to be discovered. Hera, undeceived, blandly admired the heifer – and asked Zeus to make her a present of it. Zeus could hardly refuse, without betraying himself, and the hapless Io was led away with a halter round her neck. Hera had her tethered to an olive tree in Nemea, and set Argos of the Hundred Eyes to watch her.

Zeus at last bestirred himself to do something for the victim of his lust, and sent Hermes to Nemea to steal the white heifer and bring her back. Hermes knew that Argos never slept completely – some of his eyes were always open – so he took his flute with him and charmed Argos into total sleep with divine music. That done, he cut off his head, and released Io. But he wasn't quick enough.

Hera had, by divine means, heard of the plot to release Io, and no sooner was the heifer-priestess untethered than a vicious gadfly appeared and stung her, again and again. The terror-stricken Io fled, the gadfly in pursuit.

Io's wanderings (which Aeschylus, in his *Prometheus Bound*, used to devise a memorable encounter with Prometheus) took her eventually to Egypt where Zeus restored her to true shape. She then gave birth to his son, Epaphus, the ancestor of Danaus and Aegyptus.

The strange story of Io has a possible origin in pre-Hellenic religion. She could have been a moon goddess (they were often depicted in ancient religion as being horned – the Egyptian goddess Hathor, for instance). Or she could have been a form of Hera as the ancient goddess of Argos, and her dispossession by the Olympians could be seen in her being driven out as Io, a horned moon maiden. In Homer the goddess Hera is often described as 'ox-eyed'.

See also Argos, Aegyptus, Danaus, Prometheus.

Ion The Athenian prince who became the mythical ancestor of the Ionian race. Euripides' play is perhaps the form in which the story is best known.

Creusa, daughter of King Erechtheus, was loved by Apollo and she bore him a son. In fear of her father's wrath, she abandoned the baby in a cave below the Propylaea (the entrance to the Acropolis) in Athens. Hermes took him to Delphi, where the priests gave him a name, Ion, and brought him up as a temple servant.

Creusa, meanwhile, was married to Xuthus, one of the sons of Hellen. Their marriage was not fruitful and Xuthus decided they must go to Delphi and consult the oracle. Apollo told him to accept as his son the first person he met upon leaving the temple, and this proved to be Ion. The young man accepted his newly-found 'father', but longed to know who his mother was, and if she still lived. Creusa was bitterly angry because the oracle had not promised her a child. Apollo had once had his way with her – what of *that* child?

The conviction grew that Ion was some bastard of her husband's that he was trying to pass off as his heir, and so Creusa attempted to poison Ion. But the attempt failed and her murderous intention was exposed.

Creusa claimed sanctuary at the altar of Apollo but Ion denied her right to it and was only prevented from killing her by the priestess of the oracle. The priestess carried a cradle, one she had kept in her possession from the time that Ion was brought to Delphi by Hermes. She told Ion that he was no longer a servant of Apollo's – he had a new life to begin in Athens. She gave him the cradle and told him that the contents would help him find his mother.

Creusa recognised the swaddling clothes in which she abandoned her baby, and told Ion the truth about his birth. He was the son of Apollo. They were now faced with a dilemma – if he was the son of Apollo he could not be the son of Xuthus.

The goddess Athene, at the command of Apollo, went to Delphi to resolve the matter. Ion was the god's son, she proclaimed: he was also of the royal house of Erechtheus. Therefore he was the rightful heir, a gift from Apollo to Xuthus. She prophesied a peaceful and prosperous reign, and that Ion and his sons would rule in lands across the sea (Iona).

Iphigenia The daughter of Amagemnon and Clytemnestra. She does not appear in Homer, where a daughter with a similar name (Iphianassa), but with no part in the mythology known to us, is mentioned Iphigenia is first mentioned in a poem of the seventh century BC and, like her sister Electra, became a subject for the tragedians. Euripides wrote two plays about her, dealing with different aspects of the story, and she is mentioned by Sophocles in his *Electra,* where her death is the motive proclaimed by Clytemnestra for the murder of Agamemnon. See the next two entries for the story of Iphigenia as told in the best known versions.

Iphigenia in Aulis A tragedy by Euripides, first produced about 406 BC. It was written after the *Bacchae* and some scholars believe that he left it incomplete when he died, the completion being the work of his son. The action of the play takes place at Aulis, in front of Agamemnon's tent. The fleet bound for Troy is halted there, waiting for a favourable wind that never seems to come.

Agamemnon relates to his elderly slave the events that led to the Trojan War and how he was chosen as the leader of the expedition. He declares he wishes it had been someone – anyone – else: the fair wind will never come until Agamemnon sacrifices his own daughter, Iphigenia, to the goddess Artemis. Calchas, the seer, has consulted the oracle and proclaimed this, and Menelaus and the other war leaders have insisted that the awful deed be carried out.

Agamemnon, yielding to their bullying, has sent for his daughter: the pretext is a marriage to Achilles. Only Calchas, Odysseus and Menelaus know of the pretext. But Agamemnon declares he will reverse the decision – he was written a letter to Argos warning his Queen, Clytemnestra, not to send Iphigenia to Aulis. The slave will carry the letter to her at once, and turn back the Queen if she has already set out. But Menelaus has been watching the road from Argos and he sees Agamemnon's messenger. He stops the old man and seizes the letter.

A bitter scene between Menelaus and Agamemnon follows. Agamemnon still refuses to sacrifice Iphigenia, and Menelaus says, darkly, that he has other, more resolute friends to whom he can turn, and he reminds Agamemnon that the war was undertaken because of the injury done to him, Menelaus. The two Kings are interrupted by a messenger who announces the arrival of Clytemnestra, Iphigenia and Agamemnon's baby son, Orestes.

Agamemnon's despair touches his brother, and Menelaus is moved to say that his second decision must stand: he will spare his daughter. Agamemnon says it is too late – now that his family are here: if he should stand by his decision Calchas will publish the oracle to the whole army. Menelaus offers to kill Calchas to prevent it: Agamemnon replies that Odysseus knows of Agamemnon's first decision, and of the pretext. And Odysseus is capable of anything.

Agamemnon cannot bring himself to tell Clytemnestra the truth. He lets her talk about the proposed marriage and then suggests that she would be better off in Argos caring for her other children – she can leave Iphigenia here. Clytemnestra refuses point blank: she will not be absent from her daughter's marriage to Achilles.

A chance encounter with Achilles reveals to Clytemnestra that he knows nothing about the proposed marriage: then Agamemnon's slave, in an attempt to save Iphigenia, tells them the whole truth. Achilles is outraged, both by the decision to sacrifice the girl, and the pretext of offering him, Achilles, as bait. Clytemnestra sees Achilles as her only hope, and agrees to abide by what he decides.

When next Agamemnon appears he is met by his wife and his daughter in a superbly written confrontation. (The seeds of his eventual murder are sown here.) They both know the truth now. Agamemnon, cornered, reveals his irresolute character and tells them that he cannot control the army if they find he has changed his mind. They would destroy him, his family and his kingdom. He leaves his wife and daughter and returns to the army.

Achilles comes back: the whole army is against him, even his Myrmidons – but he will stand against them. He hurriedly buckles on his armour as the mass of soldiers approach, led by Odysseus. Iphigenia, now, makes a decision for herself.

She will die. She has seen what is at stake. The war is a just war and she will not endure her position as a hazard to so many. Achilles says he will go to the altar and wait for her: if she should give him any sign that her resolution has weakened, he will save her. He walks away, and Iphigenia takes leave of her mother, sending her into the tent so that she will not have to see her daughter taken away.

Later, a messenger comes looking for Clytemnestra. He tells her of a strange scene at the sacrifice. Iphigenia stood before the altar and Calchas came forward to perform the sacrifice; the assembled army, standing with lowered eyes, heard the stroke of the axe – then silence. The messenger says that when he looked again, Calchas and the leaders were staring at the altar in astonishment. Iphigenia had vanished, and a fine stag lay on the altar in its death throes. Artemis had taken the girl to herself.

A fair wind is blowing, and the fleet will sail.

Iphigenia in Tauris This is an earlier play than *Iphigenia in Aulis*, but this time Euripides deals with a later part of the myth of Iphigenia. The date of the first performance was somewhere between 414 and 412 BC.

The scene is Tauris (the Crimea), before a barbaric temple. A blood-stained altar is visible, and the roof is hung with the possessions of those sacrificed there. The time is long after the Trojan War. Iphigenia, the priestess, emerges from the temple, which is sacred to Artemis. The Taurians sacrifice all male Greeks who set foot on their shores; the women are kept as slaves and temple attendants. Iphigenia, as priestess of Artemis, prepares the victims for sacrifice.

To this place comes Orestes. The Delphic oracle has told him that his blood guilt, and torment by the Furies, for the murder of his mother, Clytemnestra, will finally be purged when he brings to Athens the image of the goddess Artemis from the temple in Tauris. His faithful friend Pylades is with him. They examine the temple and leave to make their plan for breaking in.

A herdsman has observed a Greek ship on the sea, and two young Greeks have been seen making for the shore of Tauris. He calls Iphigenia from the temple to tell her of the two sacrifices she will soon be offering: the men have been captured, and the Taurian soldiers are bringing them to her while he speaks.

The story's resolution lies in the recognition, by stages, of Iphigenia by her brother. She is in the habit of questioning all Greeks, in the event that one of the victims may come from Argos: it is this persistence that puzzles Orestes and Pylades and leads to their reunion. But they have to escape from Tauris – and Orestes must not leave without the image of Artemis.

Iphigenia finds a way. She tells the King of Tauris, Thoas, that the two intended victims clung to the image in their terror – it is now defiled. She, as priestess of Artemis, must order the ritual purification –

in sea water. And the two victims – she was prompted by the goddess to question them and she has discovered that they both carry blood guilt. They must be purified too – or Tauris will bear the wrath of Artemis.

The King yields to Iphigenia's wishes. She is given a small guard, and falls in behind Orestes and Pylades, carrying the image of Artemis. Her brother leads the way to his ship, and the three manage their escape, largely through Iphigenia's order to the guards to turn their backs on the sacred mysteries of purification.

Thoas, enraged, is ready to pursue them with his army and fleet, but Athene appears on the scene and tells him of the gods' wishes. Orestes will take the image to Halae, in Greece, and a temple will be built there: Iphigenia will become priestess of Tauronian Artemis. The sorely-tried children of Agamemnon will at last find peace. Thoas bows to Athene's commands, and the play ends on a joyful note when he releases all the Greek women who are slaves in Tauris, and puts his ships at their disposal to take them to their homes.

See also Agamemnon, Clytemnestra, *Electra* (Sophocles), Orestes.

Iris The goddess of the rainbow and often the messenger of the gods – Zeus, particularly, in Homer. Later writers make her the messenger of Hera, and she sleeps under Hera's throne.

According to Hesiod Iris was the daughter of Thaumas, the Titan, and sister of the Harpies. She was also the rainbow itself, which was probably what gave her, in men's minds, the function of messenger – the rainbow appearing to touch both earth and heaven. There is no record of any cult of Iris.

Islands of the Blest Sometimes called Elysium, the Islands of the Blest were conceived as the resting place of those especially favoured by the gods. Life continued there – those being so favoured were exempted from an ordinary death. The idea is honoured by both Homer (*Odyssey,* Book IV) and Hesiod (*Works and Days*), and the location was somewhere at the ends of the earth. Elysium, in later writers, is in the nether world within the domain of Hades.

Ixion The son of the Lapith King, Phlegyas, Ixion was betrothed to Dia, daughter of Eioneus. He had promised to pay a generous price to Dia's father and invited him to a banquet: but Ixion had no intention of keeping his side of the contract and had only invited Eioneus so that he could murder him. For this crime Ixion was actually forgiven, and purified by Zeus.

Later, Zeus invited him to eat at his table. Ixion conceived a passion for Hera and this did not escape the eye of his host, so Zeus fashioned a cloud into the shape of Hera. Ixion, drunk, lost no time in taking advantage of the false Hera (Nephele) and was surprised in the act by Zeus. He was punished with a merciless flogging by Hermes; then he was bound to a fiery wheel which rolled across the sky eternally.

Ixion is sometimes named as the ancestor of the Centaurs; Nephele continued her life as the wife of Athamas.

See also Athamas, Centaurs.

J

Janus One of the principal Roman gods, and always the first to be mentioned in prayers, even before Jupiter. There is some argument still about whether the god was named after the principal door to a house – *ianua*, or whether the door was named after the god. He was the custodian of the universe, according to Ovid, and this was probably the reason why his image was commonly placed at the entrance: he was the opener – and fastener – of all things and he looked inwards as well as out, hence the presentation of Janus as a god who looks both ways.

There was a shrine in the Forum in Rome with doors on the eastern and western sides, and these were kept closed in time of peace. In time of war they were opened for the formal setting out of the army, the ritual implying that the city's forces were proceeding in the right way.

Roman tradition said that Janus was an early king, who settled on a hill on the west bank of the Tiber – the Janiculum. He developed, in religion, as the god of beginnings; for example, the first hour and the first month were his. In time, his two faces were believed to represent wisdom – seeing both ways he knew the future as well as the past.

Jason The hero of the quest for the Golden Fleece is best known from the carefully presented account by Apollonius Rhodius (see the *Argonautica*) but the story of Jason and the voyage of the *Argo* was an ancient one and known to Homer.

Jason was the son of Aeson, the Aeolian King of Iolcos. Aeson's half-brother Pelias usurped the throne, and would have slaughtered every member of the royal house when an oracle told him he would be killed by a descendant of Aeolus, the founder of the kingdom. However, in answer to his mother's plea Pelias spared Aeson's life and shut him up in prison. The Queen, Alcimede, hid the infant Jason (the rightful heir) and smuggled him to safety, entrusting him to the care of Chiron, the centaur. Many years passed, and Jason grew to manhood. Pelias believed himself safe on his usurped throne – until another oracle told him to beware of a man wearing one sandal.

Jason made his way back to Iolcos to regain his father's kingdom. He found the river Anaurus in flood, and on its banks an old woman, pleading for help to cross the waters. Jason carried her across, and lost a sandal on the way. But his kindness would bring a reward because the old woman was Hera in disguise: she would always be Jason's ally from that time on and, moreover, she had a score to settle with Pelias, who had been neglecting her worship. Jason reached Iolcos, and Pelias recognised his enemy in the one-sandalled man. The meeting resulted in the expedition for the Golden Fleece.

The *Argonautica* ends with Jason triumphant, his course safely set for home. But he has brought with him Medea, the royal sorceress of Colchis and Medea's story, from the time they land, overshadow's Jason's. His was one of increasing disillusion and, finally, of a lonely and unhappy death. Trying to rid himself of Medea he brought about disaster, and wandered about Hellas from city to city, shunned by those who once regarded him as a hero. He made his way to the seashore below Corinth, where the *Argo* now lay, and sat in the shadow of the prow, remembering his days of glory. And there he died, when the prow of his rotting, once-proud ship fell on him and killed him.

For Jason's life after the return of the *Argo* see the entry for Medea. See also *Argonautica, Pelias.*

Judgment of Paris, The

The story of the awarding of the golden apple of discord first appears a long time after Homer. Zeus, believing Earth to be overburdened with people, allows Eris (strife) to be present at the marriage of Peleus and Thetis, the parents of Achilles. Eris makes the goddesses quarrel among themselves about which of them is the most beautiful, and then throws a golden apple among the guests. It is inscribed 'For the fairest'. Zeus sees the quarrel developing into a three-cornered contest between Hera, Athene and Aphrodite – and loftily refuses to give a verdict. They decide to have an independent arbiter, and Hermes takes them and the apple to Mount Ida, where Paris, the most handsome of men, is watching his flocks.

Paris' award of the prize is secured by Aphrodite, who bribes him with the promise of Helen. Hera and Athene become the enemies of Troy on that day.

See also Eris, *Iliad*, Paris.

Juno one of the great deities of ancient Rome, Juno came to be identified with Hera though she was certainly, in origin, a goddess of her own particular place – Italy – and of the moon. The latter aspect makes the antiquity of her cult more apparent since the moon, as Stewart Perowne points out, was the only calendar that primitive people possessed.

She was also Juno *Moneta* (she who warns), after her sacred geese gave the alarm when the invading Gauls tried to take the Capitol in 390 BC. The coins of Rome were minted in her temple after the Roman victory over King Pyrrhus of Epirus in 275 BC and the word for money in our language derives from *moneta*.

As a moon goddess, Juno was inevitably associated with the sexual life of women and in time assimilated the characters of the minor goddesses of marriage and childbirth. But the association with the state – which started with the title of *Moneta* – became more pronounced as time went by until we find Juno *Regina*, protectress of the state. This was her title as a member of the Capitoline triad with Jupiter and Minerva. The women of Rome, however, remained faithful devotees to the Juno who was also *Lucina*, goddess of childbirth, and *Sospita*, who protected them in confinement. There was a temple to Juno *Lucina* on the Esquiline Hill as long ago as 735 BC, where her festival, the Matronalia, was celebrated on 1 March.

With the closer identification of Jupiter with Zeus, Juno became more identified with Hera, and so regarded as the sister and consort of Jupiter.

See also Capitol, Mars.

Jupiter The ancient sky god of Italy, Jupiter became a personalised deity with the coming of the Etruscan Kings of Rome. They grouped the three (to them) most important figures of the pantheon – Jupiter, Juno, Minerva – as a triad in a great temple on the Capitol. This began the cult in Rome of Jupiter *Optimus Maximus* (best and greatest), and it was to this temple that generals proceeded when honoured with a triumph.

Jupiter's functions covered a wide field. He was god of light – *Lucetius,* the stayer of defeat – *Stator* – and giver of victory, and as *Feretrius* the force of union in the community. Thus he protected the state during war and maintained its well-being in peace.

Jupiter, like most of the Roman gods, has no mythology of his own. When became identified with the sky god of the Greeks, Zeus, his name became attached to stories in which the true Roman Jupiter played no part whatever: even in the *Aeneid* the gods and goddesses with Roman names palpably display the characters of their more interesting Greek equivalents.

Juturna A Roman goddess associated with springs and waters. A temple was dedicated to her in 241 BC, after a vow by Lutatius Catulus, the victor over the Carthaginians, during a sea battle near the Aegatian Islands. There was a fountain at her spring in the Forum, where legend said that Castor and Pollux watered their horses after fighting on the side of Rome at the Battle of Lake Regillus.

Juturna is also the name given by Virgil to the sister of Turnus in Book XII of the *Aeneid*.

Juventas A Roman goddess of youth, sometimes identified with the Greek goddess Hebe. In Juventas' case 'youth' applied to men who had reached military age, and had nothing to do with a cult of youth, or youthful well-being. Her shrine was in the hall of Minerva in the temple on the Capitoline Hill.

L

Labyrinth The origin of the word labyrinth is uncertain, but it is believed to have been derived from a non-Greek word, *labrys,* meaning a double-headed axe. The symbol of the double-headed axe occurs frequently on columns and stone-work of Minoan Crete and probably had some religious significance. Daedalus built a labyrinth for King Minos – a complicated building of tortuous corridors in which the Minotaur could be concealed and from which no one could could escape. Thereafter the word labyrinth was used to describe any kind of architectural maze. One theory says that the King's house, which Daedalus built, was the house of the Double Axe (*labrys*), hence labyrinth, often identified with Cnossos.

See also Daedalus, Minotaur, Theseus.

Laius One of the Kings of Thebes in the cycle of myths about that city. He was a baby when his father Labdacus died, and the throne was usurped by Lycus. Laius did not gain his throne until after the deaths of Amphion and Zethus, who had themselves disposed of the usurper.

Laius became King with a burden of guilt on his shoulders. While in exile he had been befriended by Pelops, King of Elis. Laius fell in love with Pelops' bastard son, Chrysippus, and when he regained his throne he kidnapped Chrysippus and took him to Thebes. Worse was to follow: Hippodameia, the wife of Pelops, had feared that the sons of her marriage might be passed over in favour of Chrysippus, and she seized her opportunity. Now that the deed could be done far away and unseen by Pelops she either had Chrysippus murdered or killed him herself.

His throne secure nevertheless, Laius married Jocasta, sister of Creon of one of the noble families of Thebes. The marriage was childless, and eventually Laius consulted the oracle at Delphi – to be told that he would be killed by his son, if he sired one. He turned away from his wife after that but one night Jocasta got him drunk, and into her bed – and a son was born. His name was to be Oedipus – but his father was never to know that.

For the rest of the story, see Amphion, Antiope, Oedipus, *Oedipus* (Sophocles), *Oedipus at Colonus* (Sophocles), Pelops.

Laomedon King of Troy and father of Priam and Hesione. He built the walls of Troy, obtaining from Zeus the services of Apollo and Poseidon, who were at that time being punished for attempting to revolt against the authority of the king of the gods. The walls completed, Laomedon earned the wrath of Poseidon by refusing to pay, and the sea god sent a monster to plague the kingdom. Apollo, apparently, bore him no malice; but Poseidon was the enemy of Troy from that time on. Pindar gives another version of the story: the two gods were helped by Aeacus, and since he was mortal, the part of the wall he built was the first to yield to the assault of the Achaeans during the Trojan War.

Laomedon and all his sons, with the exception of Priam, were eventually killed by Heracles, whom he also tried to cheat when Heracles came to Troy and killed the monster sent by Poseidon.

See also Heracles, Priam.

Lapiths The people of northern Thessaly, and neighbours of the Centaurs. Their most famous king was Pirithous, who became the friend of Theseus and at whose wedding with Hippodamia (*not* the wife of Pelops, who bore the same name) the Centaurs got so drunk and violent that a murderous fight broke out.

See also Pirithous, Theseus.

Lares In Roman religion, spirits. Originally, the Lares were probably the spirits of ancestors, whose special care was the home – Lares *Familiares* – and who were regularly worshipped. The Lares *Compitales* were the spirits of the crossroads, and were propitiated to guard wayfarers from danger. The Lares *Praestites* were the spirits (guardians) of the state, and a temple sacred to them stood at the head of the Via Sacra in Rome.

Leda The daughter of King Thestius of Aetolia and the wife of Tyndareus, King of Sparta, Leda had the dubious pleasure of being made love to by Zeus in the form of a swan. That same night her lawful husband made love to her, too, and when these couplings bore fruit one of them, inevitably, resulted in Leda laying an egg. The egg contained Helen and Polydeuces; Castor and Clytemnestra arrived by normal delivery.

The story of the egg was apparently never completely disbelieved and Pausanias (second century AD) was shown an egg suspended from a temple ceiling in Sparta – declared by the people to be the one that Leda bore which contained Helen and Polydeuces.

The story of Helen's birth from an egg does not appear in either the *Iliad* or the *Odyssey*. H. J. Rose points out that, while the story is probably older than Homer, the poet seems to have had a dislike of the grotesque and the re-telling of such tales is notably absent from his work.

Lethe   The river of forgetfulness in the nether world of the Latin poets. There is a celebrated passage in the *Aeneid* (Book VI) where Aeneas watches the souls who drink the waters of Lethe, and thus forget their former lives in readiness for being born again.

   In Greek poetry Lethe seems to have been a plain in Hades, so called by Charon in Aristophanes (*The Frogs*). The word lethe means forgetfulness; in Hesiod, Lethe is the child of Eris (strife).

Leto   The mother of Apollo and Artemis, Leto was a Titaness according to Hesiod, and noted for her gentleness. Zeus fell in love with her and Leto, when she was pregnant with the divine children, had to suffer the inevitable spite of Hera.

   See also Apollo, Artemis.

Liber   An Italian god, also called Liber *Pater,* of fertility and the vine – the latter aspect leading to his identification with Dionysus. He was a god of country communities and his festival, the Liberalia, was an occasion for pleasure and relaxation. He had no temple in Rome itself but the date of his festival, 17 March, was traditionally the one when boys assumed the *toga virilis* and entered upon their manhood.

Linus   1.   The character seems to have arisen from a harvest or vintage song, which marked the closing of the old year and bewailed the passing of Linus, whose name was possibly a derivation from some older word that described either the time which had gone or the sorrow to be expressed. The song of Linus is mentioned in the *Iliad* (Book XVIII), in the description of the armour forged by Hephaestus for Achilles.

Linus   2.   The chief character of a myth from Argos known to us from the writings of Pausanias. Apollo took his pleasure with Psamathe, daughter of the King of Argos. Psamathe gave birth to a son and, in terror of her father, exposed the child, Linus, on a mountainside. Linus was cared for by shepherds but was later killed by the King's dogs during a hunting party. Psamathe's grief betrayed her and the evil King put his daughter to death.

   Apollo sent a winged monster to Argos, and many children were carried off. Then an Argive named Coroebus killed the monster, whereupon Apollo sent a plague to devastate the city. The plague was not lifted until Coroebus went to Delphi and confessed to killing the monster. The oracle ordered Coroebus to institute the worship of Apollo at Megara, and the plague at Argos was lifted after the propitiation of the ghosts of Linus and Psamathe.

Linus 3. This Linus was also an Argive, the son of the Muse, Urania, and Amphimarus, son of Poseidon. Linus was a musician of superb skill and, according to some versions, taught Orpheus and Thamyris. He also invented rhythm and melody, and was eventually killed by the jealous Apollo for declaring that he was Apollo's equal as a musician.

See also Muses, Orpheus, Thamyris.

Lityerses The son of King Midas of Phrygia, Lityerses prided himself on his skill in the harvest. He grew so arrogant that he would challenge all visitors to compete with him – and then maltreat them when they lost. Eventually he was beaten by someone stronger and more skilled – Heracles in some versions – who cut his head off with the sickle and threw the body into the river Meander.

Lityerses is in some respects a parallel myth to that of Linus in the Homeric version: a harvest dirge commemorating Lityerses was sung by the reapers of Phrygia.

Lupercalia The Lupercal was a cave below the west-facing corner of the Palatine Hill in Rome. There, on the 15th day of February, was held the annual festival called the Lupercalia during which two youths, called *luperci,* ran through the bounds of the Palatine naked except for belts of animal skin and carrying strips of goat hide. They struck everyone they could with the strips as a form of fertility magic.

The god honoured at the Lupercalia was, strictly speaking, Faunus; but there was a strong association with Romulus and Remus, the city's mythical founders, who were suckled by a she-wolf, allegedly in the Lupercal cave. There was also a possible placatory theme, inasmuch as Faunus was the ancient nature god and wolves would have been an ever-present danger to a primitive rural community.

It was during the Lupercalia of 44 BC that Mark Antony offered a crown to Julius Caesar, which Caesar refused.

See also Faunus, Romulus and Remus.

Lycaon A king of Arcadia, Lycaon founded the cult of Zeus *Lycaeus* on the mountain of that name. But he presumed upon the god's favour by sacrificing a child to Zeus instead of an animal. In some versions the child is Lycaon's own son, Nyctimus. Zeus, in disgust, blasted the King and his family with his wrath, turning them all into wolves. Then he returned to Olympus and prepared the flood that was to wipe out the whole race of men.

The story of Lycaon has echoes of the traditions surrounding the Lupercalia and some scholars have tried to find a connection between the two. Certainly Arcadia was a pastoral country of remote valleys and high hills, and the wolf would have been a menace there. The sacrifice of a child on Mount Lycaeus (wolf mountain) may have been a propitiatory one.

See also Deucalion, Lupercalia.

M

Maia 1. The daughter of Atlas and the mother, by Zeus, of the god Hermes. The story is found in Hesiod, and is her only appearance in myth.

Maia 2. A Roman goddess, much like Fauna, the feminine counterpart of Faunus, the nature god. Her festival was held on 1 May, when the *flamen* of Vulcan offered the sacrifice to her (her association with a fire god remains unexplained – she was principally a goddess of increase and fertility). The time of her festival – when all plants were growing – undoubtedly gave the month its name.

Manes The spirits of the dead in Roman religious thought. In early times the dead were believed to be a single entity and regarded with a certain dread that led to them being called euphemistically 'the kindly ones', in the same placatory way as the Greeks referred to the Furies. Collectively, the dead were worshipped as *Di Manes*.

In later Roman times family tombs became more widespread and *Di Manes* more personalised, identified with the dead of the family: eventually *manes* came to be used for a single spirit. The collective *Di Manes*, by another process of thought – and the spread of Greek ideas – became identified with the underworld deities Dis, Proserpina and Hecate. A pit was dug in Roman cities, known as the *mundus*, which symbolised the abode of the three, and the stone which covered the pit was removed three times each year when the gods of the underworld came forth.

See also Dis, Hecate.

Mars The most important god of Rome next to Jupiter, Mars is best known as the god of war. But he was originally a spirit of vegetation and a farmer's prayer to him was written down by Cato and so preserved for us.

Mars (he should not be identified with Ares, though the Romans themselves did, inevitably, when they identified Jupiter with Zeus) became the high god of an agricultural people who were often obliged to be at war. He would thus have had an overall function, protecting the work of the fields and promoting fertility; protecting the men who fought for their community and promoting in them a warlike spirit. His priest was the *flamen Martialis* and the creatures sacred to him were the wolf and the woodpecker.

In the formalised religion of the Roman state Mars was the god of war and elaborately honoured during his month of March. There were further celebrations in October and February, and every five years a purification ceremony at his altar in the Campus Martius accompanied the census (the registration of citizens for taxation).

Marsyas A satyr who was also the god of the river Marsyas, a tributary of the Meander.

The goddess Athene, according to Pindar, invented the flute. But she disliked the way they contorted her face when she played them – they were played in pairs – and threw them away. Marsyas picked them up, and this annoyed Athene, who beat him for his presumption. The flutes fascinated him, however, and he retrieved them when the goddess's back was turned. He played them so well that people flocked to hear him and declared that he played better than Apollo himself. Marsyas should have contradicted them, but he did not.

Apollo heard about Marsyas and (in some versions) challenged him to a contest. (Other versions say it was Marsyas who issued the challenge.) However it was, the challenge was offered and accepted, the victor to do as he liked with the loser. Apollo won, and took a vicious revenge on Marsyas, tying him to a pine tree and flaying him alive.

Medea The royal sorceress of Colchis, Medea was the daughter of King Aeëtes and the niece of Circe, the witch goddess of the *Odyssey*. Hera and Athene commanded Eros to make Jason fall in love with her, so that she would help him to succeed in his quest for the Golden Fleece. The goddesses' design was carried out and Jason sailed off in the Argo with both the Fleece and Medea, whom he married during the long voyage home.

When, after many adventures (see *Argonautica*), the two arrived safely in Iolcos, Medea's first deed was to destroy the usurping King, Pelias. She showed the King's daughters how to rejuvenate their ageing father by cutting up an old ram into thirteen pieces and boiling them in a cauldron with magic herbs. The ram stepped forth as a new lamb. The daughters, convinced, jointed their father and boiled him, too – but Medea had carefully withheld the essential herbs. Unfortunately Medea had so horrified everyone by her deed that Acastus, Pelias' son, roused the people without difficulty and Jason and Medea had to flee the country.

They made their way to Ephyra, near Corinth. Jason beached the *Argo* on the Isthmus of Corinth as an offering to Poseidon: the Golden Fleece was hung in the temple of Zeus at Orchomenus. Jason and Medea settled down with their two sons, but Medea's security was shattered when Jason decided that he could no longer endure his outcast status and would have to put Medea aside: he planned to marry the daughter of the King of Corinth. This callous rejection (as a non-Hellene, Medea had no rights) drove her to an orgy of murder in revenge: she killed their sons as well as the Corinthian princess. Then she fled to Athens, to the court of King Aegeus, from whom she had already secured a promise of sanctuary. (See the next entry: Euripides' celebrated play deals with that part of Medea's adventures.)

In Athens all was well until the arrival of Theseus, come to be acknowledged by his father, Aegeus, and to secure his succession. Medea, fearful for her position in Athens, persuaded Aegeus that the young man was a mere pretender hoping to gain a throne. Aegeus allowed her to prepare a poisoned cup of wine for Theseus; but the King recognised his son by the tokens he had brought, and dashed the cup from his hand in time.

Medea was obliged to flee Athens, just as she had fled from Colchis, and Iolcos, and Corinth.

Unfortunately, the myths become vague after this point and a believable conclusion to Medea's story is not to be found. A later version (second century AD) returned her to Colchis with Medus, her son by Aegeus. The throne of Colchis had been usurped by Perses, Medea's uncle. Her father Aeëtes, the rightful King, apparently forgave his daughter her desertion, her treachery and her fratricide when she managed to restore him to his throne; her son Medus proved himself useful by killing Perses. When Medea extended the kingdom of Colchis the new lands were called Media, after her son.

See also Absyrtus, Aegeus, Jason, Theseus.

Medea A tragedy by Euripides, first produced in 431 BC. The scene is Corinth, before the house of Jason, and the play begins with the Nurse reflecting on Medea's plight.

Her mistress, the Nurse says, is beside herself at the news that Jason now rejects her. She has even turned against their sons who have also been rejected by Jason now that he has married Glauce, daughter of the King of Corinth. The Nurse is uneasy about Medea's brooding – she knows her mistress can be a formidable enemy.

The children and their Tutor come back to the house from a walk in the city. The Tutor alarms the Nurse by telling her what he has heard in the market place – that King Creon intends to banish Medea from Corinth. The Nurse implores the Tutor to keep the rumour to himself – such news would drive her mistress to some terrible deed.

The women of Corinth await Medea. When she emerges from the house and addresses them they understand her anxiety more clearly. She is not just being abandoned by a faithless man; she is not a Hellene and neither she nor her children will have any rights or protection. The King arrives with his guard to banish Medea himself; he knows that she is a sorceress and wants her out of Corinth that very hour. Medea pleads on her children's behalf and gains a small grain of compassion. Creon gives her one more day; after that her life is forfeit. After Creon has left Medea recalls her own royal blood; she is a king's daughter, of the line of the sun god, Helios. And she is more than a match for Jason, who arrives next. He has brought money for her and the children to make their journey easier; he bears her no ill-will, he says. Medea's scorn leaves him thoroughly mauled, and he leaves with her curse on his marriage bed ringing in his ears.

Medea is certain of refuge in Athens with the King, Aegeus; her magic arts can help him sire a badly-needed heir. She plans her revenge on Jason and the royal house of Corinth. First she persuades Jason that he should take the children, and he agrees to her suggestion that he plead for them through his wife, the Princess Glauce. To her Medea sends gifts, carried in the children's hands; a golden coronet and a mantle from the royal house of Colchis, gifts from the sun god. When the children return the future seems promising for them – the Princess was pleased with the gifts and had been kind to the children.

Then dreadful news comes from the palace: the coronet and mantle were impregnated with a deadly acid, and when she put them on the Princess was consumed by it. Creon died, too, trying to save her. Medea is satisfied; it only remains for her to settle her account with Jason. He, anxious to save his children from the wrath of Creon's family, arrives at the house. He is too late; Medea has murdered the children, and she leaves Corinth in a sun chariot, taking the bodies with her. She will bury them in Hera's temple, and go on to sanctuary in Athens. Her last words to Jason foretell his death.

See also Aegeus, Jason.

Melampus   One of the seers of Greek mythology, Melampus was descended from Aeolus, one of the sons of Hellen. He is sometimes credited with being the first mortal to possess prophetic powers. His story is laid in Pylos, the home of King Nestor who is one of the principal characters of the *Iliad*.

Melampus was devoted to his brother, Bias, who was in love with their cousin, Pero, daughter of King Neleus of Pylos. Being a King's daughter Pero had many suitors, and her father made the condition that whoever wanted her would first have to steal the highly-prized cattle of his neighbour, King Phylacus. Melampus had been taught the art of divination by Apollo, and one day had saved the lives of a nest of small snakes after his servants had killed the parents, with the result that they had gratefully 'cleaned his ears' with their forked tongues. From that day Melampus could also understand what birds and animals said to each other.

Bias appealed to Melampus to help him win the hand of Pero, and Melampus decided to steal the cattle of King Phylacus for him. But Phylacus' herds were guarded by a dog that never slept, and Melampus was caught and thrown into prison. There he heard two woodworms gnawing through the roof beams, and heard one tell the other that the beam would collapse at the next dawn. Melampus at once demanded another cell, and was given one, though Phylacus was sceptical about the reason Melampus gave him – that the roof was about to collapse. When it did fall the astonished King sent for Melampus and told him of his son, Iphiclus, who was impotent. The King promised both freedom and cattle to Melampus if he could cure Iphiclus.

His understanding of the speech of animals came to the aid of Melampus once more. He heard two vultures speak of the time when King Phylacus was gelding his rams: he had paused in his work and stuck his knife into an oak tree – and magically gelded his son, possibly by cutting the sacred mistletoe by mistake. Melampus recovered the knife, from the tree where it had stuck fast for years, and used the rust from the blade to cure Iphiclus. He returned to Pylos in triumph, driving the cattle of King Phylacus before him. Bias delivered them to Neleus and got his bride in return.

Melampus' next adventure was in Argos, where King Proetus was suffering from the behaviour of his three daughters. They had refused to honour Dionysus, so the god had inflicted them with madness. They lived wild on the hillside, the terror of travellers whom they regularly assaulted. Proetus became alarmed when their Maenad (frenzied) condition began to infect the other women in his kingdom. He was more alarmed when Melampus stated his terms – he wanted a third of the kingdom for himself and another third for Bias. But Proetus had to yield, since no other cure could be found.

Melampus and Bias gathered a band of sturdy companions and they drove the King's daughters out of the hills away from Argos, making sure that their course was northward to Sicyon on the Gulf of Corinth. There they forcibly immersed them in a holy well, and their madness was cured. Melampus himself married one of them, and he and Bias returned to Argos to enjoy their well-earned good fortune.

The gift of extra understanding, bestowed by a serpent's licking a mortal's ears 'clean', occurs more than once in Greek mythology – see the entries for Cassandra and Tiresias.

Meleager One of the descendants of Aeolus, son of Hellen, Meleager was the heir of King Oeneus of Calydon. The Fates appeared to his mother, Althaea, when Meleager was seven days old: they pointed to a stick burning in the fireplace and told her that her son's life would last for as long as the stick would burn. Then they departed, and Althaea at once leapt up and snatched the stick from the fire: she put out the flame and hid the stick away.

Meleager grew to young manhood. His father Oeneus, meanwhile, had incurred the wrath of the goddess Artemis; in his yearly sacrifices he had, one summer, forgotten to make an offering to her, and to punish this slight she sent a great fierce boar to Calydon. The beast ravaged the crops and killed men and cattle alike.

Meleager, determined to destroy the boar, sent heralds to all parts of Greece asking for those bold enough to take part in the hunt. Whoever delivered the death thrust would be awarded the boar's pelt and tusks as testimony of his skill and valour. Soon there were gathered in Calydon the bravest men in Greece – and one woman. Among the men were Castor and Polydeuces, Idas and Lynceus, Theseus, Pirithous, Jason, Nestor, Peleus, Amphiaraus, Telamon and the brothers of Althaea. The woman was Atalanta, the virgin huntress. Artemis, unseen, was also present and spitefully determined to make trouble.

Meleager himself was the unwitting instrument of the trouble when it came – he fell in love with Atalanta, though he was already married to a daughter of Idas.

When the boar was finally cornered Atalanta was the first to wound it, but the huge creature nevertheless killed several of the men. Amphiaraus succeeded in blinding it with a finely cast arrow and the actual death thrust was delivered by Meleager himself.

The award of the tusks and pelt was not a matter for argument – they plainly belonged to Meleager: but he was so besotted with Atalanta by this time that he insisted on the prize going to her. Everyone was offended, and his uncles upbraided him for his folly. Meleager's temper rose, a quarrel broke out, and he killed them both. The hasty, stupid murders proved fatal to Meleager as well: his mother, Althaea, saw her brothers' corpses brought from the hunt, and when she learned how they died she searched out the stick she had hidden away at Meleager's birth. She threw it into the fire, and Meleager's life drained away.

The story of Meleager and the Calydonian boar hunt was known to Homer, and he refers to it in the *Iliad* (Book IX). But there is no mention in Homer of how Meleager died; he earns his mother's curses through the death of her brother, but the visit of the Fates is not part of Homer's tale.

See also Althaea, Atalanta.

Memnon The son of Eos (dawn) and Tithonus, the brother of King Priam, Memnon became King of Ethiopia and was his uncle's ally in the Trojan War. He killed Antilochus, the son of Nestor, and was killed by Achilles when he returned to the fight after the death of Patroclus. The story is referred to in the *Odyssey* (Books III and IV).

See also Tithonus.

Menelaus The brother of Agamemnon, Menelaus was King of Sparta and the husband of the beautiful Helen. The stealing of Helen by the Trojan prince, Paris, was the cause of the Trojan War.

Menelaus is a prominent character in Homer, younger than Agamemnon and inclined to be self-effacing, but he is a good soldier and enjoys fighting and killing as much as the other Achaeans. He gets the better of Paris in single combat (*Iliad*, Book III); is the Achaean leader wounded by Pandarus when that Trojan prince breaks the truce (Book IV); defers to Agamemnon, and is uncomfortably aware that the long war is being fought for his sake (Book X); and fights with great tenacity to prevent the body of Patroclus from falling into Trojan hands (Books XVII).

Menelaus is always referred to in terms that give the impression of a tried and trusted veteran who deserves respect. In the *Odyssey*, when visited by Telemachus and Peisistratus, he is celebrating the wedding of his daughter Hermione to Neoptolemus, son of Achilles. In spite of his years and adventures he is described as 'red-haired', but here again Homer gives the impression of a man who was never, so to speak, *young* (Book IV). He tells Telemachus of his adventures on the way home, and of his encounter with Proteus, who prophesied that Menelaus was destined for Elysium. Menelaus and Helen appear to be very contented and domestic in this scene.

The Spartan King, like the other Achaeans at the Trojan War, turns up in other stories outside Homer, notably in Euripides, who gives him a remarkable scene of reunion with Helen in *The Trojan Women*. In *Iphigenia in Aulis* and *Andromache* he is both villainous and mean; in *Helen* he is treated more kindly – but it is plain that Euripides has little liking for the character frequently referred to in complimentary terms by Homer.

See also *Iliad, Odyssey, Iphigenia in Aulis* and *The Trojan Women* (Euripides).

Mercury The Roman god of traders and merchants, Mercury was almost certainly a Latinisation of the Greek god, Hermes, who was the patron of merchants among other things. Mercury's temple stood on the Aventine Hill and was of comparatively late date, 495 BC. He was worshipped there with a goddess who was in essentials the Greek Maia (Hermes' mother) and not the Roman goddess of the same name who was connected with plant life.

Mercury was never an important state god – he had no *flamen* – but his popularity was considerable and spread with the extension of Roman power and trade. His festival was celebrated on 15 May.

Metamorphoses A series of mythological stories conceived as a whole and presented in fifteen books, the *Metamorphoses* is the most famous work of the Latin poet, Ovid, of the last century BC and the first years AD. The title refers to the recurrent theme of transformation, e.g. the transformation of Chaos into an ordered universe, with which the book begins. The intention of the *Metamorphoses* is purely and simply to tell stories; the result a fascinating and varied collection ranging through the legends of early Rome, Greek mythology, and even Babylon, whence comes the story of Pyramus and Thisbe.

See also Ovid.

Metis According to Hesiod the first consort of Zeus was Metis (counsel), the wisest of all among both mortals and gods. When Metis was pregnant Zeus was advised by Uranus and Gaia to swallow her, lest she bear a son who could overthrow him – uniting his power with her wisdom. Zeus took their advice, and in due course a child (his daughter, Athene) was born from his head. The wisdom of Metis thus stayed with him forever.

See also Athene, Zeus.

Midas A mythical King of Phrygia (in fact, all the kings of Phrygia were called Midas in ancient times – it was a title, like *Pharoah,* rather than a name).

The myths surrounding Midas have two locations, Macedonia and Phrygia, and H.J. Rose points out that the people of the two countries were in fact of the same race and shared the same traditions. However, the most familiar version is the one given by Ovid, who sets the scene firmly in Phrygia.

In the train of Bacchus (Dionysus) there was an old satyr, Silenus, who found it hard to keep up with the rout of revellers who attended the god. Some Phrygian peasants found him and bound him with garlands; then they took him off to their King, who had been instructed in the mysteries and was a devotee of Dionysus. Midas recognised him as one of the god's companions and treated him as an honoured guest. When he restored Silenus to his master, the grateful god offered the King a gift of his own choosing.

Midas chose the golden touch. His divine benefactor kept his word, though he shook his head over the King's ill-considered choice. Midas returned to his palace, testing his gift on the way: stones turned to gold as he picked them up, his finger tip turned a spider's web into exquisite gold tracery. He sat down at table well pleased with his choice – and then discovered what a terrible mistake he had made. Not even a king could eat gold bread, or drink gold water. What if he touched one of his children?

The King, completely humbled, prayed desperately to Dionysus to relieve him of the fatal golden touch. The god responded, touched by the immediate appeal, and the admission of stupid greed. He told Midas to go at once to the source of the little river Pactolus, near the city of Sardis, and to immerse himself in the waters where they bubbled out of the earth. So King Midas lost the golden touch, which passed from him into the river. Now the traces of gold can still be found in the sands of the river Pactolus.

But Midas was to make another mistake in an encounter with gods. His unpleasant experience with the golden touch turned him from luxury and he spent more time in the fields and woods; he became a devotee of the god Pan, and loved to hear him playing his pipes. One day, on the slopes of Mount Tmolus, Pan was playing his pipes to an admiring circle of nymphs and boasted that he could make better music than Apollo. The spirit of the mountain shook when it heard the boast, and told Pan to justify it – let them all, nymphs, mountain and King Midas, hear both gods play. Apollo at once appeared, and played his lyre after Pan played his pipes. Tmolus and the nymphs, enchanted, gave the palm to Apollo: Midas alone declared for Pan. Apollo promptly gave him donkey's ears to wear instead of his own.

Midas covered his shame as best he could, wearing a head cloth of royal purple from that day on. But his barber had to be told, and was sensible enough to know that he'd better keep the secret. He was bursting to tell someone and the need grew dangerously stronger with each passing day. At last the barber went into a field, and dug a small hole, and told the earth that his master, King Midas, had donkey's ears. Then he put the earth back into the hole, burying the secret forever.

The earth itself gave the secret away to anyone who knew how to listen. A carpet of reeds grew in the freshly-turned ground, and when the south wind blew through them they told again the secret of King Midas and his donkey's ears.

See also the Gordian Knot.

Migrations The original inhabitants of Greece are often given the name Pelasgians (sea people), though there is no general agreement among the scholars about exactly who they were, whether the original inhabitants, or themselves part of an earlier movement, possibly from the Near East, which took them westward to settle in the fertile islands and mainland. Whoever they were, the early inhabitants were displaced by peoples who moved down into the peninsula from the north in the great movement called the Indo-European Migrations – some time near the end of the third millennium (about 3200–2800 BC). The new people brought with them the Indo-European language which became Greek.

See also Achaeans, Dorians, Hellenes, Ion.

Minerva The Roman goddess of war and of artisans probably evolved from the fusion of two deities: the ancient Italian goddess (Menerva) of handicrafts, and the Minerva of the Etruscans who brought her cult to Rome as one of the Capitoline triad with Jupiter and Juno. Some scholars assert that the Etruscans' Minerva was in fact Athene, borrowed from the Greeks – certainly the character of Minerva as a Roman state goddess was very like that of Athene *Promachos* (champion). The feast of the Quinquatrus (the fifth day after the Ides of March, the 15th), originally devoted solely to Mars, was celebrated on the same day as the birthday of Minerva, and it later became devoted solely to her, enhancing her identity as a goddess of war.

Minos In Greek mythology the great King of Crete, son of Zeus and Europa. In history he is impossible to place: scholars often take his successful demand for tribute from Athens to be a memory of hostility between the Greeks and Minos' island kingdom. His name may have been a title, or a dynastic name.

In the mainstream of mythology he is a just and wise ruler – at his death he was made one of the three Judges in Hades – but there is an attribute of cruelty in the myths which stem from Attic Greece (the region of Athens) and this may, again, reflect the memory of hostility mentioned above.

On the death of Asterion, King of Crete and stepfather to Minos and his brothers, the succession was in dispute. Minos claimed the throne, and to demonstrate his right he built an altar to Poseidon on the sea shore: then he prayed to the god to send him a bull for sacrifice. Poseidon answered his prayer and Minos became king – but the bull sent by the sea god was so magnificent that Minos could not bear to sacrifice it; he turned it loose among the royal herds. Poseidon was very angry, and took a cruel revenge by having Minos' Queen, Pasiphae, develop an overpowering lust for the bull.

The result of her unfortunate passion was the birth of a son who was half-man, half-bull – the Minotaur. Minos ordered the great craftsman, Daedalus, to build a place where the Minotaur could live unseen, and the result was the labyrinth, the great maze which was later to challenge Theseus.

During his reign Minos imposed his authority on the nations around him. He made war on Megara, where the King, Nisus, was blessed with a bright lock of hair which was the source of his life and power. When the army of Minos approached, Nisus' daughter, Scylla, was watching from a tower in the fortress, and she fell in love with Minos when she saw him ride up to prepare for a siege. That night she stole into her father's room and cut the bright lock of hair from his head; then she took the keys of the city from her father's body and stole out to Minos' tent. She offered him the keys of the city; in return she wanted his love.

The city was taken, and Minos gave Scylla his love – once. He had fulfilled his part of the bargain but had no intention of taking a murderous daughter back with him to Crete. Scylla, demented, tried to swim after his ship and drowned. (For a parallel story, see Amphitryon.)

Minos also made war on Athens, where his son, Androgeus, was murdered at the instigation of King Aegeus, a crime for which the Athenians had to pay a tribute, every year, of seven youths and seven maidens. These young people were to be the prey of the Minotaur, and one year Theseus went with them as one of the seven youths.

See also Androgeus, Pasiphae, Theseus. For the death of King Minos, see Daedalus.

Momus According to Hesiod the personification of blame and fault-finding. He was the son of Night.

Mopsus The name of two characters in Greek mythology, both of them seers. One of them sailed on the *Argo,* and died of a serpent's bite in Libya during the journey home (see *Argonautica*, Book IV). The other Mopsus was the son of Manto, daughter of another seer, Tiresias. He was connected with the oracle of Apollo at Claros, and thence, after the fall of Troy, came Calchas, the seer of the Achaean forces who was very vain of his powers. Mopsus was challenged by Calchas to a contest of powers and Mopsus proved the better man. Calchas died of mortification.

See also Calchas.

Morpheus According to Hesiod dreams were the daughters of Night. The idea of a god of dreams is much later, and usually attributed to Ovid, who named three sons of Sleep: Morpheus, who sends dreams of human form; Phobetor, who sends dreams of beasts, and Phantasos, who sends dreams of inanimate things.

Muses, The Personifications of the highest aspirations of artistic and intellectual minds, the idea of the Muses was a remarkable and attractive conception in Greek mythology. The conception seems to have emerged with the formalisation of religion in ancient Greece: it is honoured by Homer in the *Odyssey* (Book VIII) and given shape by Hesiod, who gives the number of the Muses as nine and also their names. The separation of their fields of inspiration is a Roman fancy of a much later date.

The Muses were the daughters of Zeus and Mnemosyne (memory), and sang and danced, led by Apollo, at celebrations by the gods and heroes. The academies of the Pythagoreans, of Plato and Aristotle were organised as associations for the cult of the Muses – hence the word, museum, originally a place of education and research.

The Roman separation of the Muses' function was as follows: Calliope of epic poetry, Clio of history, Euterpe of flute playing, Erato of lyric poetry and hymns, Terpsichore of the dance, Melpomene of tragedy, Thalia of comedy, Polyhymnia of mine, and Urania of astronomy.

Mycenae A city of ancient Greece which stood at the north-east corner of the plain of Argos, nine miles from the sea and six miles from the city of Argos. The name is not Greek and the original settlement there was probably of people who came from Crete or the islands. In mythology the founder of the city is named as Perseus, and Mycenae is the city of the High King, Agamemnon, in Homer.

The modified form of Minoan (Cretan) civilisation came to be called Mycenaean: it spread to many parts of Greece and testifies to the high place the city held at the time, 2000–1200 BC. By then it was certainly under the rule of Achaean invaders from the north; this was the Mycenae of Homer, and its proud position was only lost when the Dorians, in turn, moved down into Greece and became the chief power. The archaeological evidence shows that Mycenae of the great days was destroyed by fire.

What remains of former glory is a site of impressive and – because of its associations with Agamemnon, Clytemnestra, Electra, Orestes – haunting ruins. Archaeology has upset romantic notions in the naming of the great beehive tombs and the bodies found in the shaft graves (the beehive tombs were *not* the Treasury of Atreus and the Tomb of Clytemnestra; Agamemnon was *not* buried in the shaft graves). But Mycenae knew greatness, nonetheless, and there are few places to be seen that suggest so vividly the proportions and placing of a city which existed in a world which can only be recalled through the magic of epic poetry.

N

Narcissus A beautiful youth, son of the nymph Liriope and the Cephisus river in Boeotia. He was loved by the nymph, Echo, but he played with her affections and did not really want her; she wasted away with grief, only her sad disembodied voice remaining. Narcissus had often been guilty of this behaviour and one day another whose love he had trifled with prayed to Nemesis that he be punished. Narcissus got his deserts: one day he saw his reflection in a forest pool, and fell in love with that. He pined away, too, and died by the forest pool. The flowers that grew where he died were named after him.

See also Echo.

Neleus One of the sons of Tyro and Poseidon (his brother was Pelias), Neleus became King of Pylos and was the father of Nestor, Pero, and many other children. In one version of the myths surrounding Heracles, he incurs that hero's wrath by refusing to give him ritual purification after the murder of Iphitus. His son, Nestor, was kind to Heracles, and so was spared when Heracles made war on Pylos and killed Neleus and his other sons.

See also Nestor, Pelias, Tyro.

Nemesis One of the children of Night, Nemesis is described by Hesiod in vague terms, almost as a perpetual irritation, to both gods and men. Traditionally, the figure of Nemesis was an abstraction, the retribution that was certain to follow evil deeds and was inescapable.

That there was also once a goddess called Nemesis is proved by both the shrine to her which existed at Rhamnus in Attica, and by her appearance in mythology as one of the reluctant partners in the sex games of Zeus. She tried all sorts of tricks to avoid his favours, at last turning herself into a wild goose and taking to the air. Zeus promptly turned into a swan and overtook her, grounding her eventually at Rhamnus. Nemesis, in due course, laid an egg which she abandoned; it was found by a shepherd who took it to Leda, the wife of King Tyndareus of Sparta. In this version of the story Leda merely nurses the egg, from which Helen is eventually born.

See also Helen, Leda.

Neoptolemus The son of Achilles by Deidamia, daughter of the King of Scyros. In the *Odyssey* (Book XI), Odysseus tells the shade of Achilles how he went to Scyros, after Achilles' death, to bring Neoptolemus to the Achaean army at the siege of Troy; how brave and handsome Neoptolemus was; how he was one – the most gallant one – of the group inside the Wooden Horse.

Odysseus' words help to reconcile Achilles to the dreariness of the after-life and Homer may simply have been giving them to Odysseus to console Neoptolemus' dead father: apart from his mention in Book III by Menelaus as the husband of Hermione we learn no more about him from Homer.

However, the son of the great Achilles inevitably plays a part in other myths and some of them may stem from a tradition as old as that drawn on by Homer. Pindar relates how Neoptolemus killed King Priam at the altar of Zeus, and as a punishment was doomed never to reach his home again. He was driven by contrary winds to the country of the Molossians, which he ruled for a time. The people there claimed to be descended from Neoptolemus through the Trojan Princess Andromache, who was part of his share of the spoils when Troy fell. Later he went to Delphi where he was killed in a squabble over precedence.

In Sophocles' play, *Philoctetes*, Neoptolemus' presence at the siege is made a condition of victory, as is also his mission to the hapless Philoctetes on the island of Lemnos. In Euripides' *Andromache* Neoptolemus is killed at Delphi by Orestes: the tradition that he did, in fact, die there was a persistent one and there was a hero-cult in Delphi devoted to him.

See also *Andromache* (Euripides), *Odyssey*, Philoctetes.

Neptune In Roman religion Neptune was originally a god of water – but not of the sea. It was not until he became identified with Poseidon that his dominion was extended. His festival was of great age in the Roman religious observances and he may have been an Etruscan deity in origin. The festival, appropriately for a god of water, was held at the hottest time of the year, on 23 July.

Nereus The old sea god, particularly of the Aegean, and father of Thetis. He was a different god from Poseidon, whose functions were broader and who was probably a later arrival. Nereus was called the son of Pontus (the personification of the sea) by Hesiod, and in myth he is generally credited with great wisdom and the gift of seeing what is to be. Though he is frequently encountered, he has almost no mythology of his own. His daughters were the Nereids, sea nymphs.

See also Heracles, Labours of, Thetis.

Nestor The son of Neleus, Nestor was King of Pylos and sixty years old when he went off to the Trojan War.

In Homer, Nestor is a vigorous man for his years and much respected though inclined to talk a great deal and offer advice which nobody takes very seriously. He could have emerged from the *Iliad* as an old bore but he has a sense of humour and enough intelligence not to mind when his counsel is not followed.

In the *Odyssey* he must be a venerable old King indeed, about eighty in the chronology of the poems, but he emerges more clearly than in the *Iliad* and gives a strong impression of a King who now possesses the wisdom he once aspired to. He is one of the Achaean leaders who sails for home without delay after the taking of Troy and reaches his kingdom safely. He welcomes Telemachus, who is in search of his father, Odysseus (*Odyssey*, Book III), and tells him something of what befell the other Achaean leaders on their homeward journeys. In Book XXIV the shade of Agamemnon relates how Nestor stopped panic spreading among the Achaeans at the funeral of Achilles when Thetis rose from the sea to mourn her son, the Nereids rising from the waves to mourn with her. A tradition, not in Homer, gives Nestor the decisive voice in the bestowal of the arms of Achilles on Odysseus, which leads to the madness and suicide of great Ajax.

The supposed grave of Nestor was known in late classical times but there is no mention in the myths of his death. The successful location and superb excavation of the site of Pylos was the work of the American archaeologist, Carl W. Blegen.

See also Heracles, *Iliad*, Neleus, *Odyssey*.

Nike The goddess of victory, or perhaps the personification of it, Nike is described by Hesiod (the earliest known mention of her) as the daughter of a Titan, Pallas, and honoured by Zeus for her part in the battle between gods and giants. Her most famous temple in Greece was at Athens.

Niobe The daughter of Tantalus and wife of Amphion, Niobe was the mother of six sons and six daughters of whom she was inordinately proud. She was foolish enough to boast that she was superior to Leto, the mother of Apollo and Artemis – Leto had, after all, only borne two children. Her boast enraged Apollo and Artemis, who killed her children. They lay unburied for nine days, the people of the land having been turned to stone by Zeus. Niobe sat mourning her children all that time until she too turned to stone, a marble woman on Mount Sipylon in Lydia. On the tenth day the gods buried the dead children.

The story is told to Priam by Achilles in the *Iliad* (Book XXIV).
See also Aedon.

Nymphs In Greek mythology nymphs were the personification, always female, of various aspects of the natural world. No definite statement can be found that endows them with immortality, though they are the children of Zeus with the exception of the Nereids, the sea-nymph daughters of Nereus, and the Oceanids, daughters of Oceanus. Generally, nymphs were rather like the fairies of another tradition.

The nymphs of the mountains were the Oreads, of springs and pools the Naiads, of trees the Dryads.

O

Oceanus In Hesiod the son of Uranus and Gaia, and the brother and husband of Tethys; in Homer the river encircling the world, the source of all waters including the rivers of Hades. In mythology, where his appearances are few, Oceanus is kind, as in Aeschylus' *Prometheus Bound*, but he never became personalised in the same way as the sea god, Nereus, or the Olympian god, Poseidon.

Odysseus The son of Laertes, King of Ithaca, and Anticleia, daughter of Autolycus. One of the most famous characters in literature, Odysseus plays a large part in the *Iliad* and is the central character of the *Odyssey*: in Greek myth generally his deeds and adventures are also concerned with events which take place both before and after those related in Homer's two great works.

His first appearance, chronologically, is as one of the suitors of Helen, though he knows his little island kingdom makes him no match for the rich and powerful princes of the mainland. It is Odysseus who gives Tyndareus, Helen's father, the idea of making the suitors swear loyalty to one another, thus averting a quarrel among them when Helen's choice was made known, and ensuring that Helen's abduction would embroil them all in a long and disastrous war.

Odysseus marries Penelope, niece of Tyndareus, and returns to Ithaca where his son, Telemachus, is born. It is while Telemachus is still a baby that Menelaus and Agamemnon arrive, accompanied by Palamedes. Odysseus, reluctant to go to war, feigns madness and is seen ploughing his own fields and sowing them with salt, the plough yoked to an ox and a donkey. His deception is exposed by Palamedes, who takes the baby Telemachus from Penelope and puts him on the ground in the path of Odysseus' ill-assorted team. Odysseus of course has to stop to save his child: but he nurses a grievance against Palamedes and later takes a particularly mean revenge on him. In the muster of forces, it is Odysseus himself who finds Achilles at Scyros, disguised as a girl by his mother, Thetis.

At Troy Odysseus proves to be resourceful and courageous and just as ready to kill as the other Achaean leaders (for his part in the story see the *Iliad*). He also plays a large part in the myths which connect the *Iliad* – it closes with the funeral of Hector, not with the fall of the city – with the *Odyssey*.

He and great Ajax fight desperately to prevent the body of the fallen Achilles from being captured by the Trojans. It is because they succeed that they are claimants to Achilles' divinely-wrought arms and armour, which are eventually awarded to Odysseus. Ajax's jealousy robs him of his reason.

Later Odysseus enters Troy disguised as a beggar; but Helen recognises the spy and gives him shelter, confiding to him that with Paris and Hector both dead, her life in the city has become unendurable. Helen and Odysseus are surprised by the entry of Hecuba – and Odysseus flings himself at her feet. The Queen of Troy finds the King of Ithaca dressed in filthy rags, grovelling on the floor. She allows him to escape; but she will earn no gratitude for her disdainful mercy to him (see the entries for Hecuba and the *Iliad*).

Odysseus is sometimes credited with the idea of the Wooden Horse, but there are conflicting versions, and his status as the centre of an epic poem is to be found in the *Odyssey* (see the following entry).

Like many of the principal characters in Homer the figure of Odysseus was to be of great value to both Euripides and Sophocles, who emphasise the sinister aspects of his character already seen in the myths separate from Homer. He is treacherous (in his dealings with Palamedes), completely callous (Iphigenia), totally inhuman if it will further his design (Hecuba, Polyxena).

Signs of these characteristics can be discerned in Homer's Odysseus. Alone among the Achaean leaders he is *clever*; he will survive anything and everything, and his courage and resourcefulness are completely believable. Likeable he is not, any more than Achilles or Agamemnon, but Homer makes no effort to draw a sympathetic hero. Odysseus, as we see, inspires love and unswerving loyalty, as such men often do, and it is Homer's genius that makes him a completely rounded character, the first such creation in Western literature.

How Odysseus died is not recorded in Homer but in a separate myth which was recorded in an epic poem, the *Telegonia*, now lost to us but known from references in classical writers. In the *Odyssey* (Book XI) the shade of Tiresias tells Odysseus that he has offended Poseidon by his treatment of Polyphemus: when he reaches his home he must placate the god – but on land, away from the salt sea air, and he must carry an oar. He will know he has reached the right spot when the people, knowing nothing of the sea, believe his oar to be a winnowing flail such as farmers use.

After his home and kingdom are restored Odysseus duly sets out from Ithaca carrying an oar. All goes to plan and Odysseus makes his sacrifice, appeases the sea god, and makes his way home. In Ithaca, he finds that his son, Telemachus, has left the island. An oracle had predicted that Odysseus' son would kill him, so Telemachus is in self-imposed exile on the island of Cephallenia, nearby. But in this version Odysseus has another son, unknown to him, by the witch-goddess, Circe, with whom he spent a year during his wanderings. This son, Telegonus, is now sailing the seas in search of his father. One day an alarm is sounded in Ithaca, and King Odysseus and his men hurry down to the sea where men are landing from a strange ship. A fight ensues and Odysseus is killed by the strangers' leader, none other than his son Telegonus.

See also Achilles, Ajax, *Hecuba* (Euripides), *Iliad*, Palamedes, Philoctetes, *The Trojan Women* (Euripides), and the separate entries for the characters named in the *Odyssey*.

Odyssey, The An epic poem by Homer dealing with the adventures of Odysseus after the fall of Troy; his tortuous journey and the way he restored order to his kingdom which was in danger from usurpers. The division of the *Odyssey* into twenty-four books is credited to Aristarchus of Samothrace, who was also responsible for the division of the *Iliad*. It is generally believed to be a later work than the *Iliad*, and though the behaviour of the gods is different, the poem is believed by most scholars to be by the same author.

In the *Odyssey* Odysseus has the benefit of a special relationship with the goddess Athene, who favoured him in the *Iliad*, but he incurs the enmity of Poseidon who, also in the *Iliad*, favoured the Achaean cause as a whole. In the same way he incurs the wrath of Helios (Hyperion) – but in both cases it is for a particular offence and due punishment is given.

The action of the *Odyssey* covers a short period – no more than six weeks, though ten years' adventures are related in the course of it. So Odysseus, when he reaches Ithaca once more, has been away for nineteen years (Book II) and is probably a man in his middle forties. He has chestnut hair.

BOOK I The story opens on Olympus where the gods discuss the fate of the Achaean leaders after the fall of Troy. Athene seizes the opportunity to remind her father Zeus of the fate of Odysseus, who has not reached home yet: the war has been over for ten years, and after many perilous adventures he is even now held captive on the island of Ogygia by the beautiful nymph, Calypso. Zeus reminds Athene that his brother Poseidon was offended by Odysseus' treatment of Polyphemus, the Cyclops. However, he will send Hermes to Ogygia, and Calypso will have to let Odysseus go. In the meantime, Athene will be at Ithaca to prompt Telemachus to search for his father.

Disguised as a chieftain, Athene calls herself Mentes and arrives at Odysseus' house. Neighbouring princes and chieftains, coveting the island kingdom, pay suit to the Queen, Penelope, hoping to marry her and gain the throne. Penelope will not believe that Odysseus is dead. Telemachus receives the newcomer and invites 'him' into the palace, where he explains who the unwelcome suitors are and how they are impoverishing the kingdom with their slothful greed. Athene urges Telemachus to go and find news of his father – Nestor, King of Pylos and Menelaus, King of Sparta were his comrades and they may know something. And if Odysseus *is* dead, it would be better to know. Athene leaves, and Telemachus is resolved. For the first time he behaves as master in his house, to the surprise of his mother, Penelope, and the chagrin of the suitors; but to the joy of his devoted old nurse, Eurycleia.

BOOK II Telemachus calls an assembly of the people and reproaches the suitors for the intrusion – and for their greed. One of them, Antinous, points out that Penelope has never actually refused any suitor – she has simply pleaded for time to finish weaving a winding-sheet for

Odysseus' aged father, Laertes. She had started it four years ago – and then she had been discovered unravelling, each night, the work done on her loom each day. If she had returned to her father Icarius, a new husband would have been found and the matter settled: she has chosen not to, and now they will all wait for a decision, since the throne is vacant. Telemachus warns them that they may have to pay a terrible price for their behaviour; they have forced themselves on his mother; they devour huge stocks of food, and their conduct is gross and vulgar. Zeus chooses that moment to send two eagles to hover over the assembly. The eagles fight, and then fly away.

The seer, Haliserthes, warns the suitors that the signs are bad for them: furthermore, he had warned Odysseus, when he had set out for Troy, that it would be nineteen years before he returned – and when he did no one would know him. The suitors treat the old man rudely, and Telemachus too, trying to bluff him out of his resolve. Telemachus turns his back on them and tells Eurycleia to prepare food and clothing for his journeys to Pylos and Sparta. Athene, meanwhile, disguised as Telemachus, finds the best and most loyal men and a ship, and Telemachus sails with twenty companions, with further advice from Athene about behaving as a prince among kings.

BOOK III The ship arrives in Pylos, across the Ionian Sea. Athene is part of the company in the guise of Mentor, a trusted friend of Odysseus who was adviser to the young Telemachus. They are greeted warmly by Nestor's son, Peisistratus, and presented to Nestor, now a very old King but with all his wits unimpaired.

He recalls the long years at Troy, and praises Odysseus' good sense and courage in glowing terms. He relates what he knows of the fates of the other Achaeans – Agamemnon, Diomedes, Philoctetes, Menelaus – but of Odysseus he knows nothing. But no King who enjoyed the favour of Athene as Odysseus did would ever perish, he assures Telemachus. Athene reveals herself at that point, by flying back to the ship in the form of a sea-eagle. Nestor is joyful on behalf of Telemachus: promising that all will surely be well in the end. He sends for the companions of Telemachus, orders a sacrifice to Athene, and a feast in his palace for all. Telemachus shares a bed with Prince Peisistratus, who on the next day drives the chariot which will take Telemachus to Sparta.

BOOK IV In Sparta Menelaus is celebrating the coming marriages of his daughter Hermione to Neoptolemus and of his son Megapenthes to Alector's daughter. Telemachus and Peisistratus are impressed with the richness of the royal house. Menelaus tells them that he amassed his wealth on the travels he endured during the seven years it took him to complete the journey home from Troy. Helen, beautiful as ever, joins them and is startled by Telemachus' resemblance to his father. She tells him how she had recognised Odysseus in the streets of Troy, disguised as a beggar to spy on the Trojans: how she helped him, and how he escaped with much information after killing a number of Trojans.

Menelaus recalls how Odysseus had behaved in the Wooden Horse; how his discipline had stopped his friends from betraying themselves when Helen, from sheer wilfulness, had called out the names of all the Achaean leaders concealed inside.

Telemachus presses Menelaus for news of his father. Menelaus tells him how, becalmed in Egypt, he wrestled with the sea god, Proteus, to get from him the knowledge of how to raise a fair wind. Proteus told him many things: the fate of Ajax the Locrian, the murder of Agamemnon – and the whereabouts of Odysseus. Calypso is keeping him on her island and enjoying him: he cannot escape, having nothing to take him across the sea.

Telemachus is in haste to get back to Ithaca when he hears this. Menelaus gives him a parting present of a fine mixing bowl for wine, of chased silver with a golden rim – the work of Hephaestus himself.

At home in Ithaca the suitors prepare an ambush for Telemachus, intending to kill him when he returns. They are overheard by the herald, Medon, who hurries off to warn Penelope. The Queen, desperate, offers an agonised prayed to Athene, who promises Penelope that her son will make a safe return.

BOOK V At the bidding of his father, Zeus, Hermes has arrived on Ogygia. He tells Calypso that Odysseus must be allowed to leave her island and return to Ithaca. She is both tearful and angry: she saved Odysseus from death – she found him clinging to a spar, his strength nearly gone; and now that he loves him the Olympians want to spoil things for her. But she has to yield. (In Homer, Calypso is called a goddess by Odysseus. She is presumably goddess of the island.)

She gives Odysseus the means to construct a ship, and shows him where to find the best trees. After five days he is ready with his little craft, and she gives him plenty of food to take with him. He sails away lightheartedly, sure he is now on the way home. But his presence on the sea once more is spotted by Poseidon, who is determined to go on exacting payment for Odysseus's blinding of his son, Polyphemus.

Odysseus finds himself in a tempest, his little craft being smashed to pieces. The sea nymph, Leucothea, comes to his aid: she gives him her veil and tells him that while he wears it round his waist he can never drown. But he must wear no other clothes, and when he reaches land he must throw the veil back into the sea. The tempest increases in fury: Odysseus throws off his clothes and has just time to tie the veil round his waist before a mighty wave hurls him into the sea.

Battered and bruised, Odysseus is thrown up on a rocky shore and has to use his last reserves to save being pounded to pieces. He reaches land near the mouth of a small river, and falls into an exhausted sleep under an olive tree.

Book VI On the island of Scheria, the lovely Princess Nausicaa, daughter of King Alcinous of the seafaring Phaeacians, goes down to the sea with her maidens and a wagon piled high with linen from the palace. They take the linen to a small river with swirling pools, where they tread it clean, and then they spread it on the sea shore to dry in the sun. They enjoy their midday meal and then play a game of ball. The noise they make awakens Odysseus, who in his exhausted condition wonders if they are a group of nymphs. Whoever they are, he reflects, he'd better go and see, and, as he has nothing else, he holds a leafy branch in the appropriate place.

The maidens, startled by the appearance of a naked stranger, his hair and skin encrusted with salt, take to their heels. Nausicaa is startled too, but she is a King's daughter and stands her ground. Odysseus addresses her in fulsome terms, declaring he must be facing Artemis herself, and so on. Nausicaa pities him, anyway, and calls her maidens back. They give him food, find him clothes from the household linen, and give him oil and a comb. Odysseus retires to the river to bathe, and when he emerges, clean and in fresh clothing, he looks both handsome and presentable.

Nausicaa and the maidens load the clean linen into the wagon and prepare to return to the city. Nausicaa asks Odysseus to follow behind at a little distance – she is the King's only daughter and the townspeople will gossip about her if they are seen together. Odysseus is charmed by her modesty and flattered by her reference to him as a tall handsome stranger. He follows along the road to the palace of King Alcinous and his Queen, Arete.

BOOK VII Odysseus is treated with generous courtesy by his hosts, and awed by the richness and prosperity of the island. He tells Alcinous and Arete how he was kept a love captive by Calypso; how he got away from Ogygia and was wrecked by Poseidon's tempest; how he was saved from certain death by the veil of Leucothea, and how he was treated with such kindness by their lovely daughter, the Princess Nausicaa.

Alcinous promises the nameless wayfarer a ship to take him home – wherever that may be: the Phaeacians are the finest sailors in the world. Meanwhile the Queen orders a bedchamber to be prepared for him.

BOOK VIII A ship is prepared for Odysseus and a crew volunteers, inspired by Athene who, disguised as a herald, has been spreading the news far and wide that the King's new friend is as handsome and strong as to seem like a god amongst them.

In the hall that evening, while the bard Demodocus sings of Troy and the great deeds that were done there, Odysseus' emotions get the better of him. He tries to conceal his grief but Alcinous sees his guest's distress. He asks Odysseus to give them an account of his adventures.

BOOK IX Odysseus tells the Phaeacians who he is, and how he listened to Demodocus singing of events in which he played so large a part. His narrative opens with the departure of his twelve ships from Troy and their expedition to the land of the Cicones (in eastern Thrace) to find food to provision their ships for the journey home. They plundered the city of Ismarus and the townspeople fled to the hills. Odysseus urged his men to depart with their gains while the going was good but they were dazzled by the plenty which seemed to be theirs in an abandoned city. They stayed in the city feasting and drinking; meanwhile the Cicones rallied and a determined army swooped down on the Achaeans, who had to escape to their ships as best they could, losing seventy-two of their men.

They set their course for the south, intending to turn east at Cape Malea and then north to Ithaca. But a strong north wind carried them past the cape and the island of Cythera and they were at sea for another nine days. Their landfall was in Libya, at the land of the Lotus-eaters, where the people ate no meat, only the fruit of the lotus plant. Some of Odysseus' men ate the fruit – and immediately ceased to care about the past, their homes, their future: they were content to stay where they were forever, and browse on the lotus. Odysseus, alarmed, ordered the rest of his men to bring them back to the ship before further harm could be done to his depleted force. The men who had eaten the lotus were dragged back to the ship by force and put in irons: they were almost deranged with grief at being torn from their new-found content.

The ships reached a group of fertile islands, where there was plenty of water and wild goats to provide them with meat, but no people. Odysseus saw a larger island a little distance away and decided to investigate. He embarked with twelve men, and took a wine skin from Ismarus containing a very potent sweet wine. They reached the far island and found it very rich in pasture and flocks. In a cave there were shelves full of cheeses and beautifully ordered pens for the ewes. The men were nervous and wanted to take some cheese and leave: Odysseus was curious to see what sort of man the shepherd could be. They retired to a corner of the cave, made a meal of one of the sheep from a nearby fold and waited.

The shepherd proved to be a Cyclops, a one-eyed giant who drove his flock of fine sheep into the cave while carrying a huge bundle of pine logs on his shoulders. He closed the cave with a massive rock, and made a fire. The pine logs burned brightly and Odysseus and his men were revealed. To the Cyclops' questions Odysseus tried to answer wisely, sensing danger. He reminded the giant of the laws of hospitality, contriving also to invoke the protection of Zeus *Xenios*, the travellers' god. He said nothing of the rest of his fleet, and told how his own ship had been wrecked by Poseidon. The Cyclops listened to Odysseus and then told him he cared nothing for Zeus – then he seized two of the men, one in each hand. The rest watched in horror while he knocked their brains out on the wall of the cave, and then ate them, bones and all.

During the night Odysseus was tempted to kill the sleeping giant with his sword – but they would then have been trapped forever since they could never move the stone which closed the cave. In the morning the Cyclops ate two more men for breakfast, drove his sheep out to pasture, and sealed the cave behind him.

While he was away Odysseus made a desperate plan for their escape. In feverish haste they sharpened a staff of green olive wood, left in the cave by the Cyclops to season and be made into a staff. When the point was sharp enough they hardened it in the fire still smouldering from the day before. Then, when the Cyclops returned at sunset and devoured two more of the men, Odysseus approached him with a bowl of the wine of Ismarus, undiluted. The Cyclops tasted it, then drank it greedily and demanded more. He also asked who Odysseus was – he must reward him for this fine wine. Odysseus gave him another bowl of wine and told the Cyclops that his name was Noman. The Cyclops, his wits already clouded, said that he would reward Noman by eating him last. Then he fell over on his back, insensible.

Odysseus and his men heated the point of the staff and then thrust it into the giant's single eye. The Cyclops' scream of agony shook the cave: Odysseus and his men raced into the farthest corner where they waited, shaking, to see what the blinded monster would do. His screams disturbed his neighbours and the other Cyclops came to the cave, demanding to know why Polyphemus (this is the first time that Odysseus hears his name) was disturbing the peaceful night. Polyphemus' tormented voice told them that Noman was destroying him. The listeners replied that if no man was destroying him then it must be the gods – and they were powerless to help him. Then they all went away.

At dawn Polyphemus opened the cave to let his flocks out to pasture, and Odysseus and his men escaped by clinging to the thick wool of the sheep's bellies, so that the searching hands of Polyphemus, stationed at the door of the cave, could not detect them.

Safe on board their ship Odysseus called to the Cyclops and revealed his true name. Polyphemus hurled great stones at the sound of Odysseus' voice and nearly destroyed the ship. Then he warned Odysseus: the Cyclops were the sons of Poseidon – the god would listen to his plea. Odysseus would always have the sea as his enemy, and would find danger and disorder in Ithaca if he ever reached his home.

BOOK X Odysseus and his men mourned their dead comrades and resumed their voyage. They came to the floating island of Aeolus, god of the winds, and were helped by him in the best way possible – he imprisoned the boisterous winds in a huge leather bag, leaving only the west wind free to blow their ships on a steady course to the east and home. Odysseus stowed the bag away carefully and set sail for home, never resting through the watches of day and night. When, after ten days, his homeland was sighted, he fell into an exhausted sleep. But his men, meanwhile, had been wondering what the bag contained. As soon as someone voiced the suspicion that it contained a rich gift from Aeolus the men grew inquisitive, and while Odysseus slept they opened the bag to see for themselves.

Disaster followed – the winds erupted out of their prison to return to their master: the tempest carried the ships away from Ithaca and back across the sea to the island of Aeolus. And there the angry god turned Odysseus away, telling him he was plainly detested by the gods and undeserving of any help.

A subdued and unhappy fleet set sail again, and after six days happened on the island of the Laestrygonians. Eleven of the ships steered into the harbour but Odysseus, uneasy about this unknown island, made his ship fast to a rock outside. It was this that saved him and his crew: the island was inhabited by great cannibals and the other ships were trapped in the harbour. The Laestrygonians smashed them to pieces with carefully hurled rocks from the cliffs above: the men who floundered in the harbour were simply speared like fish and carried off to be roasted. Odysseus cut the hawser of his ship and his alone managed to escape.

With his utterly dejected and grieving shipmates he came eventually to the island of Aeaea, thickly wooded but with no sign of life until Odysseus climbed a high rock and saw a house in a clearing. Half the company was chosen to search for the house and to explore: Odysseus and the rest waited on board. The exploring party found the clearing and a palace in its centre – and strange beasts wandering about nearby. They were wild beasts, lions and wolves and boars, but when they saw the men they hurried up to them with every sign of pleasure, like dogs welcoming a master home. Inside the house a woman was singing, and soon she emerged, darkly beautiful, and invited them in. The woman was the witch goddess, Circe, daughter of Helios. All the men entered her house but one, the head of the party, Eurylochus, who was uneasy, having seen the strange behaviour of the beasts outside. He watched while Circe brought the men food and wine, and stared in horror as, before his eyes, they turned into pigs. Circe drove her new herd out of her house and into a sty, where she carelessly flung them a handful of acorns and beech mast.

Eurylochus raced back to the ship to tell Odysseus, who at once took his sword and, deaf to the pleas of his friends, set out for Circe's palace. On the way he met Hermes, and the young god warned him about Circe's powers. He gave Odysseus a herb to counteract the effect of anything Circe could put in wine or food and sent him on his way. Having eaten the herb Odysseus accepted the witch goddess's hospitality, and drank the wine she gave him. He even allowed her to touch him with her wand – and observed with satisfaction her amazement when nothing happened. He drew his sword and advanced on her, and she acknowledged that he had mastered her. She restored his men to their true shape and invited the rest of the crew to come to her palace and be feasted. Odysseus she took to her bed. The company stayed on the island of Aeaea for a whole year.

Odysseus, at the prompting of his restless crew, at last left Circe and her magic hospitality. He held her to her promise to show him how best to reach Ithaca, and the answer she gave him depressed him badly – he had first to visit the nether world and consult the shade of Tiresias. The long-dead seer would tell him what he must do.

So the lone ship and her unhappy crew sailed off again, with the loss of one man, Elpenor, who had slept on the palace roof and fallen to his death after a night of carousal. On board they carried a young ram and a black ewe from Circe's island, which they were to use to gain entry into Hades' kingdom. Circe conjured up a wind to take them to the edge of the world.

BOOK XI Odysseus followed Circe's instructions and was able to visit the nether world. Tiresias told him he might well reach home safely but warned him about further offences against the gods, particularly on the island of Thrinacie. He must sooner or later propitiate Poseidon – Tiresias told him how it was to be done – but until then the god was his enemy and he would have to reckon with that. He also told Odysseus that he would find trouble in his house, but that death would come to him, out of the sea, when he was well into a comfortable old age. The shade of Anticleia, Odysseus' mother, told him of the troubles besetting Penelope and Telemachus, and how she herself had died of grief for Odysseus.

The shades of many others came to speak with Odysseus. Elpenor, Agamemnon, Achilles; the shade of Ajax refused to speak to him. He saw the never-ending punishment of Tityus, Tantalus and Sisyphus. Then the nameless dead began to crowd in upon him and Odysseus fled in terror.

BOOK XII The ship returned to Circe's island, where Odysseus carried out his promise to give Elpenor's body decent burial. Circe, before they left again, warned Odysseus about the Sirens, about Scylla and Charibdys, and the island of the Sun. To cheat the Sirens, Odysseus plugged the ears of his men with beeswax: then they bound him to the mast and rowed on, unhearing of the Sirens' deadly and seductive songs and of Odysseus' plea for freedom to go to them. But at Scylla and Charibdys they lost six men to the monster who lay in wait for them before, with a mighty effort, they rowed themselves clear (see *Argonautica*, Book IV). The next land they saw was Thrinacie, the island of the Sun.

Odysseus, the words of both Circe and the dead Tiresias in his mind, warned his men that they must sail on – the island was too dangerous a place to land. But they were exhausted and depressed and he gave in to their pleas to at least take shelter there, even if they stayed by the ship. He made them promise to obey his orders, and to be content with the food Circe had given them. Odysseus, as tired as any of them, fell asleep as soon as he lay down on land. When he awoke, the first thing he was aware of was the smell of roasting meat. His men, led by Eurylochus, had broken their promise, and were feasting on the cattle of Hyperion, god of the Sun. Odysseus saw the hides of the divine cattle moving uncannily in the morning light, heard the roasting oxen lowing as the spits turned. A high wind was blowing and he couldn't put to sea. For six days his men feasted on Hyperion's herds. They did not know that their fate had been decided: Hyperion had already told Zeus of their sacrilege.

When the wind died Odysseus put to sea again, and the ship was far from land when Zeus destroyed her, smashing her to pieces in a squall of devastating force. Only Odysseus survived, clinging to a spar; he was eventually cast up on Calypso's island after nine days in the sea.

BOOK XIII King Alcinous and his court are completely silent – they have been spellbound by Odysseus' story. After a moment the King promises Odysseus that his ship will sail on the next day; the skilled Phaeacians are ready to take him back to Ithaca.

The next day Odysseus takes leave of the generous and hospitable Alcinous and his Queen and, loaded with gifts, embarks for Ithaca. The Phaeacians skim across the sea like swallows, and Odysseus sleeps peacefully content for the first time in nineteen years. The ship reaches Ithaca just before dawn, and the Phaeacians find a secluded cove to unload the gifts – and Odysseus, still in a deep dreamless sleep. They place him with care well away from the path, in the shade of an olive tree.

Poseidon, meanwhile, was furious that the Phaeacians had returned Odysseus to his homeland, and vented his spite on the generous people. He turned the ship to stone as it came back to Scheria, fixing it like a rock in the sea. Alcinous regretfully accepts the warning from Poseidon – in future the Phaeacians will have to stop giving help to voyagers in their open-hearted way. The sea god's designs may be upset, and he may take more drastic steps. The Phaeacians offer him a lavish sacrifice of twelve fine bulls.

Odysseus, meanwhile, has woken, and cannot understand where he is. Athene, as a young shepherd, explains that she has thrown a mist around them so that they can plan, unseen: but assures him he is safely home in Ithaca. She tells him of the situation in the palace, and disguises him as an old beggar so that no one will recognise him. She will go and fetch Telemachus home from Sparta: Odysseus must seek out Eumaeus, who is his swineherd and has remained faithful to him.

BOOK XIV Eumaeus hears his dogs barking furiously at a stranger and he rushes out to quieten them. Then he sees the travel-stained old man they were barking at and he invites him into his house for rest and food. Odysseus is moved by the goodness of the loyal old servant, to whom he represents himself as a Cretan, a soldier from the army that went to Troy with King Idomeneus. That night Odysseus sleeps with the farm workers, covered in a warm cloak lent him by Eumaeus while he goes out on his nightly watch of his herds.

BOOK XV Athene, meanwhile, has arrived in Sparta, where Telemachus and Peisistratus are asleep in Menelaus' palace. She urges Telemachus to return home without delay – the pressure from the suitors on his mother is growing. And the suitors are preparing an ambush for him. He takes his leave of Menelaus, his warm-hearted host, who accompanies the two young men to their chariot. As they walk they see an eagle carrying a white goose, snatched from a farmyard, swoop low over the chariot, then sheer away into the heights with his prize. Menelaus pronounces it a good omen: Odysseus will return to his kingdom and swoop down on the suitors. Before embarking at Pylos, Telemachus gives passage to one Theoclymenes, a fugitive from Argos.

In Eumaeus' hut, Odysseus declares his intention of walking into the town to try and find honest work. Eumaeus persuades him not to – he might fall foul of the suitors' servants, who will have no respect for his years. He must stay until Telemachus returns. While they prepare a breakfast, Eumaeus tells his guest of his origins, and how as a child he was sold as a slave. It was his good fortune to be bought by the kind King Laertes, the father of their lost King, Odysseus.

Telemachus avoids the suitors' ambush and lands in Ithaca. Theoclymenes, his passenger, is entrusted to the care of Peiraeus, one of the company. A hawk is observed, carrying a dove in its talons, the white feathers of prey fluttering down between the ship and Telemachus. Theoclymenes is delighted by this, because the omen is a good one for Telemachus. The hawk is Apollo's herald, and all will go well with Odysseus' son.

BOOK XVI At breakfast in Eumaeus' hut, Odysseus hears someone approaching. But no dogs bark, so it must be a friend. Eumaeus hurries out and finds his dogs joyfully welcoming Telemachus. The old swineherd is overjoyed to find him safe and hastens to tell him that all is well with his mother: he hurries him indoors, where Telemachus finds a stranger who rises and courteously offers him his seat. Eumaeus explains who the stranger is, and Telemachus confesses to feeling mortified that he cannot, with his house in disorder, make him his guest. But he will provide him with fresh clothes and food if Eumaeus will continue to house him.

Odysseus explains that he knows from his generous host that all is not well at the palace. Eumaeus persuades Telemachus to let him go to the palace and reassure Penelope and Laertes that he is safe and well, and Athene tells Odysseus that it is time to make himself known to his son. When Eumaeus leaves she restores Odysseus with a touch of her hand: the old man in his rags becomes Odysseus in fine linen, the chestnut hair replaces the grey. Telemachus regards him in amazement. Odysseus tells him that he is his father, and that the emotion he felt when he saw his fine brave son nearly overcame him. At last he is able to embrace him, and he breaks down completely.

They make their plans. The number of suitors has grown since it was first believed Odysseus was dead; now there are over a hundred, and their servants. Telemachus will go back to the palace now, and remove all the weapons from the hall, except for two swords, two spears and two shields which he will conceal. When the time comes, Odysseus assures him, Athene will give a sign. Odysseus himself will go to the palace disguised as a beggar, and Telemachus must ignore any rudeness shown to his father. And no one must know that Odysseus is back.

The suitors, meanwhile, are furious to learn that Telemachus is safely at home: the richest one, Antinous, declares that he must be killed. Amphinomous of Dulichium refuses this evil course, and the others agree with him. They are all suddenly confronted by Penelope herself, who makes it plain that she knows exactly what is in their minds; many of them owe their very lives to the King whose house they despoil and whose wife they would dishonour. She withdraws with her ladies, her words having produced a silence among them – but no hope of honourable behaviour.

Eumaeus reports back to Telemachus, and tells him that he saw a ship arrive in the harbour from which armed men disembarked. The old man does not know that it is the ship that brought Telemachus home, making formal arrival in the harbour after putting Telemachus down secretly in a safe spot. The men are the twenty chosen who sailed with Telemachus to Pylos.

BOOK XVII Athene, meanwhile, had changed Odysseus back to his beggar's guise, so Eumaeus had seen no difference in him. Next morning Telemachus hurries off to the city to see his mother and set the plans in motion. Odysseus and Eumaeus follow about noon. In the palace, Telemachus gathers about him the few friends there he can trust, Mentor, Haliserthes and Antiphus. They are joined by Peiraeus and Theoclymenes, whose qualities as a seer do much to reassure Penelope about the future.

Odysseus and Eumaeus arrive, and are insulted by a goatherd, Melanthius, they meet on the way. In the courtyard Odysseus is moved to see his old dog, Argus, lying on a dungheap. The faithful creature recognises him, and has strength for one last, hopeful wag of his tail before he dies.

At the palace Telemachus, who has been watching for their arrival, rises from the table and heaps a plate full of food to take to them. Then he gives Odysseus permission to ask alms of those seated in the hall. All the suitors give something, except Antinous, who insults him and strikes him a blow with a footstool. Odysseus does not flinch, and curses Antinous, promising him that he will die before his wedding day.

Penelope hears of the outrage to a guest, and tells Eumaeus to bring the stranger to her. Eumaeus advises caution: the suitors, and particularly the black-hearted Antinous, will be provoked to something dangerous if they hear that the Queen has received the strange beggar they all convince themselves they despise. Better wait until sunset when the suitors will not know. Eumaeus then returns to the farm to resume his care of his master's herds.

BOOK XVIII A newcomer enters the hall, a hefty bully named Arnaeus who runs errands for the suitors. These have nicknamed him Irus (messenger: the masculine form of the name Iris). They now give him a nod to remove Odysseus from his seat in the corner of the porch and the loud-mouthed bully orders him out – or else be thrown out, though Irus claims he would be ashamed to lay hands on an old man. Antinous thinks it all amusing; he and the other suitors crowd round to watch. Odysseus, to their surprise, agrees to fight Irus; Antinous offers a haunch of goat meat to the winner. Odysseus insists on no interference, and Telemachus guarantees it.

Odysseus gets on to his feet and throws off his rags – and Irus sees what a mistake he has made: the 'old man' has broad shoulders, strong arms and powerful legs and thighs – but it is too late to withdraw. Odysseus fells him with no trouble, drags him to the door, and orders him to sit there and keep the dogs and pigs away – that is his true level. Amphinomous, the suitor who rejected the idea of killing Telemachus, comes forward and offers Odysseus wine and bread from the table, and drinks to his health. This courtesy touches Odysseus and he tries to warn the young man of impending doom: but Amphinomous' fate has been decreed and, unwisely, he returns to his seat in the hall.

Penelope, meanwhile, decides on another challenge to the suitors. She comes down to the hall with her ladies, looking superbly beautiful and regal, and declares that no woman was ever wooed in this way – no matter what suitors thought they could get, they always brought gifts, surely? But these have brought nothing: how can she take them seriously?

Odysseus, sitting in his corner, is delighted with Penelope's wit and sees it work. The suitors vie with each other in presenting her with lavish and costly presents. At sunset the hall is lighted with great fires and some of the palace servant girls run about at the command of the suitors, attending them. Odysseus is enraged to see this and tells one of the girls, Melantho – to whom Penelope had been particularly kind, that she should be attending her mistress, not dancing attendance on her persecutors. But Melantho and the others have found lovers among the suitors, and she tells the old man to shut up, unless he wants a bloody nose from one of the men at table. Odysseus' true nature and authority overpower his disguise: his thunderous voice and threat of punishment terrify the girls, who run out of the hall. Eurymachus, one of the most offensive of the suitors, offers Odysseus work as a labourer: Odysseus returns that Eurymachus is a bully – when the King returns he will not find a doorway wide enough to escape through. Eurymachus hurls a stool at Odysseus, who dodges it, and uproar follows. Telemachus manages to quell it, and the suitors retire to their homes in various degrees of temper.

BOOK XIX Odysseus is alone in the hall. Penelope enters and takes her seat at the hearth. The servant girls come in to clear the long table, and Melantho is vulgarly rude to Odysseus again – earning a sharp rebuke from the Queen. Penelope has a comfortable seat placed near the fire and invites the stranger to sit with her and talk about his life. He is cautious still but gives a strong hint that Odysseus is alive – and will surely return. Penelope promises the stranger a rich reward if all comes true: she sends her ladies to prepare a bath and bedchamber for their guest. Odysseus declares that he is used to his present rough condition, though he is grateful for her kindness, and would shrink from the attentions of her comely and gently-bred attendants: is there, perhaps, some kind old woman of her household, of his own age? Penelope sends for Eurycleia, her son's devoted old nurse, who brings a bowl of hot water for his feet.

Odysseus, suddenly, knows that she will recognise him. But it is too late. He carries a scar on his thigh, sustained in a boar hunt, and Eurycleia sees it: she sits at his feet, joy and amazement in her face at the same time. Fortunately, Odysseus' back is to Penelope and he persuades Eurycleia to keep silent. Then, while Penelope turns to chat with her ladies, he secures her total co-operation to his plans.

Penelope tells him that, if she has to marry one of the suitors, it will be one who can equal her lost husband's strength and skill. Odysseus' bow is in the palace, the one he always used when he practised his skill, sending arrows through the gap made by twelve axes, standing in a row with the handles and blades forming an arc.

BOOK XX   That night Odysseus lies awake, and Athene visits him. She tells him to trust in the gods, and brings him sleep. But he awakes at dawn to hear Penelope weeping, and he prays to Zeus. He is rewarded with two signs: one poor servant girl, exhausted by the extra work the suitors make in the house, mutters a prayer to Zeus as she hurries about her endless labours, asking that this day will see an end of it; then a crack of thunder echoes across the sky. Odysseus, his hopes running high, prepares for the day.

Eumaeus comes to the palace with three fine hogs for the day's feasting. The goatherd, Melanthius, brings goats and again throws insults at the 'beggar'. Philoetius, a cowherd, brings a heifer – but he is both courteous and sympathetic, and declares that only his unquenchable hope that his master, Odysseus, may yet return keeps him in Ithaca, where things are unbearable for an honourable man. Odysseus' heart is warmed by the good man's loyalty: he promises him that all will be well.

The suitors, meanwhile, have reverted to the idea of killing Telemachus. But an omen frightens them: they see an eagle in the sky with a dove in its talons. The dove is still alive. They proceed to the palace and sit down at table in the hall. Odysseus is just within, near the threshold, and Telemachus makes it clear that his guest is not to be molested in any way. His tone is authoritative and the suitors are disagreeably surprised. But one of them, Ctesippus, insolently declares that the guest will have everyone's hospitality, and throws a cowheel at his head. Odysseus ducks the missile, which hits the wall: Telemachus, with murder in his heart, gives Ctesippus and all of them a last warning. While he speaks the light in the hall grows dim: Theoclymenes rises from his place next to Telemachus and addresses the suitors, telling them that darkness covers their faces, that the walls are splashed with blood – a catastrophe is upon them that they will not escape. But even as Theoclymenes leaves the hall the suitors simply jeer at the sort of friends Telemachus chooses, one an ageing beggar and another a mere vagabond who wants to be a seer.

BOOK XXI Penelope enters the hall, carrying the great bow and arrows of Odysseus, given him by Iphitus, son of the great archer Eurytus. Her ladies follow with the boxes containing the axes Odysseus used. The Queen challenges the suitors to string the bow, and they all try. Odysseus, meanwhile, makes himself known to Eumaeus and Philaetius, and tells them of his plans.

The bow defeats the suitors completely. To cover their embarrassment Antinous declares that this is no day for bows, being the feast of the divine archer, Apollo. Odysseus rises, and asks to be allowed to try, and the suitors don't like this at all. Telemachus turns to his mother and tells her she should retire from the hall: surprised, she does so while the suitors are voicing their resentment at a beggar's presumption. But Eumaeus, who has set up the axes, takes the bow to Odysseus, and then hurries out.

The dauntless old man goes to Eurycleia, and tells her to seal the doors from the hall to the women's quarters: she promptly locks them. Next Eumaeus gives a sign to Philaetius, who bars the door into the courtyard.

The suitors, meanwhile, are confounded: Odysseus has strung the great bow, and has fired an arrow with matchless accuracy through the row of axes. They have heard him tell Telemachus that the time is come, and seen Telemachus take his place at the stranger's side, armed with sword and spear. They have heard Zeus' thunder in the sky.

BOOK XXII Odysseus throws off his rags and fits another arrow to his bow. He fires straight at the black-hearted Antinous and hits him in the throat, killing him at once. The suitors spring to their feet and look desperately for the weapons – which Telemachus has hidden away. Odysseus, in a triumphant rage, tells them their doom is sealed –

they never expected to see the King return from Troy, did they? The suitors realise they must fight for their lives: the goatherd, Melanthius, finds the armoury left open by Telemachus from when he armed Eumaeus and Philoetius and he scurries into the hall with shields and helmets and spears for a dozen suitors. Odysseus and Telemachus are fighting with tremendous success – Odysseus is deadly with the great bow – so when Melanthius is seen hurrying to the armoury a second time Eumaeus and Philoetius follow and trap him there, trussing him up like a bundle and hanging him from the roof.

In the hall Odysseus is uneasy. His arrows are exhausted and now it will be four against a far greater number, fighting hand to hand –and the suitors left will still have their swords. Suddenly Mentor, Telemachus' old adviser, appears in the hall, to everyone's surprise. But it is Athene, in his guise. She has come to put fresh heart into Odysseus, and the four fight with renewed strength. Athene helps, diverting the spears of the suitors so that they strike into the beams and doors, and soon it is all over. Philoetius has the satisfaction of killing Ctesippus himself, while Eumaeus accounts for several suitors too. The only ones spared are the bard, Phemius, and the herald, Medon, neither of whom were guilty of the spoliation of Odysseus' house or of insults to himself.

Euryclea has heard the battle going on in the hall. Now Telemachus fetches his old nurse and takes her to his father, standing in the carnage of the hall with his two faithful servants. Euryclea almost gives a great cry of triumph at what she sees – but her master restrains her from exulting over the dead. He tells her to bring in the guilty servant girls: the three men will carry out the dead, and the servant girls will clean the hall. They arrive, twelve of them, and Odysseus tells them they will die. Telemachus, full of hatred for them for the way they dishonoured his mother and his father's house, hangs them. Melanthius, too, is given a brutal and shameful death. They cut off his ears, his nose, his genitals, and throw them to the dogs; then they cut off his hands and feet and leave him to bleed to death outside the gate.

His house restored, Odysseus is surrounded by the servants who were loyal to him: they flock into the hall, overjoyed to see him safe in his kingdom once more. Their unaffected joy moves Odysseus deeply: he stands among them weeping unashamedly.

Book XXIII Euryclea hurries to Penelope, hardly able to speak her joyful news. Penelope, not trusting her ears, goes down to the hall, now so empty after the noisy throng it lately held. She takes her place at the hearth and stares at Odysseus, struck dumb. In spite of Telemachus' urging, she sits there transfixed and disbelieving, her eyes taking in the beggar's clothes he still wears.

Odysseus, after a few moments, rises: he will bathe and put on fresh clothes. But even after he returns, looking like a king, she is unmoved, and Odysseus is driven to asking for a bed to be made ready for him somewhere, since his wife will not receive him. Penelope tells Euryclea to place the big bed, that Odysseus made, outside the bedroom for him. Odysseus, furious, tells her exactly how the bed was made – no one can move it, since the main post is a live olive tree around which the rest was constructed.

Penelope collapses in a flood of tears. Now she *knows* that her Odysseus has come back – no one else in the world knows how he built their bed.

BOOK XXIV Having restored his house, and been reunited with his wife, Odysseus has his little kingdom to put in order and his father Laertes to see. His aged father finds renewed life at the sight of his son, whom he also recognises by the scar that told Euryclea his identity. Then Odysseus and Telemachus, with Eumaeus and Philoetius, face the task of averting what bloodshed may occur after the killing of the suitors – their families may well seek vengeance. Indeed, there was an angry crowd assembled in the city at that very moment.

Antinous' father, Eupeithes, denounces Odysseus, who took away their finest sons to a useless war in Troy – now he returns, only to slaughter men of his own race. The crowd are responsive – many of them have lost fathers and sons. Medon and Halitherses arrive on the scene, and speak to the people of their own folly in allowing their sons to despoil Odysseus' house. But Eupeithes carries the day, and leads an armed crowd to Laertes' house, where Odysseus is known to be. Laertes and his stewards, with the King's party, are twelve in all. Laertes, furious at the way Eupeithes has turned the people against their King, hurls a spear at Eupeithes and strikes him dead. Odysseus leads a charge and Athene gives a great shout, which strikes terror into the people's hearts and scatters them in panic. There is a likelihood of terrible and useless slaughter – but Zeus intervenes. He casts a thunderbolt in front of his daughter, ordering her to make the fighting cease. Peace must be restored.

Athene calms all the lust for battle and the killing is averted. Then she resumes the shape of Mentor, and arranges peace in the kingdom of Ithaca.

Oedipus   The son of Laius, King of Thebes, and Jocasta, a daughter of one of the city's noble families. There are traces of conflicting traditions about the life and death of Oedipus in Hesiod and in Homer – where Jocasta is called Epicaste – but the most familiar myth is from the Theban cycle and this was the one used by the dramatists: Aeschylus, Sophocles and Euripides all wrote plays derived from the story of Oedipus. The one by Sophocles (see the next entry) has a fair claim to be called the greatest of the Greek tragedies – a flawlessly made play of extraordinary power.

Laius and Jocasta were told by the oracle at Delphi that any son born to them would kill his father – a punishment for Laius' abduction of Chrysippus, the son of Pelops at whose court Laius had once found refuge. Jocasta tricked her husband into sharing her bed and the child she bore was a son. Laius gave the child to one of his men and told him to abandon the baby on Mount Kithaeron. To make sure the baby could not even crawl to possible safety they nailed his feet together with an iron spike.

The servant, a kind man, could not bring himself to abandon the cruelly treated infant and gave him to a shepherd, a Corinthian, imploring him to take the baby to some safe place and rear it in secret. The Corinthian took it to his King, Polybus, who was childless. Polybus and Merope, his Queen, gladly made the child their own, and called him Oedipus from the cruelly maltreated feet (Oedipus – swollen foot).

Oedipus grew to manhood in Corinth, the contented son of the royal house, until one day at a feast a drunken guest told him that he was no true son of King Polybus. Oedipus, disturbed, went to Delphi to consult the oracle – and received the shocking prediction that he would kill his father and become husband to his own mother. He did the only thing he could think of: he turned his back on Corinth forever rather than bring grief on those he loved.

He travelled on the road east from Delphi, towards Thebes, and at the place where the road from Daulis joined the road from Thebes he met a chariot bearing a man of middle age, who ordered him out of his way. Oedipus, brought up as a king's son, would have none of this and a fight ensued, during which he killed the man and his charioteer. Another attendant fled for his life.

Oedipus continued on his way, and nearing Thebes encountered the Sphinx, a winged monster who was plaguing the city, devouring those who could not answer her riddles. Oedipus answered them, and destroyed the monster – and was welcomed by the Thebans as a hero and their deliverer. He found the Thebans without a king – he had been lately murdered – and was offered the throne by the Queen's brother, Creon, who was acting as regent, and the hand of the royal widow. He became King of Thebes, and for fifteen years he and his Queen, Jocasta, enjoyed a prosperous reign and became the parents of many sons and daughters.

Then, inexplicably, Thebes began to suffer misfortunes: the harvest failed, pestilence broke out, and the people went as suppliants to the King who had saved them once before. At this point in the story Sophocles begins his tragedy.

See also Laius.

Oedipus (Tyrannos) Sophocles' tragedy is often called Oedipus *Rex* but the Latin term is wrong, being merely a rough equivalent to the Greek description of an absolute ruler, not necessarily a king and often a usurper; not a 'tyrant' necessarily – the derivation most familiar to the modern world has acquired a different meaning from the original: the word 'King' is used for the sake of convenience. The play was first produced, as far as can be ascertained, about the year 425 BC. The scene is Thebes, before the palace of Oedipus. Altars to the gods are visible in the courtyard, which is crowded with suppliants.

The palace doors swing open and Oedipus comes out on to the steps. The suppliants crowd towards him and Oedipus asks a priest of Zeus, one of the crowd, what is required of him. The priest addresses him as the saviour of Thebes, to whom they turn once more in their affliction: they suffer from pestilence and lack of food. Oedipus answers that his people's need affects him deeply: he has spent sleepless nights trying to find ways to relieve their suffering but everything seems to be against Thebes and her people. His kinsman, Creon, has gone to Delphi to seek divine counsel: he has this very day returned to Thebes. The priest sees Creon approaching, and expresses the hope that he bears good news. Oedipus remarks that Creon looks pleased with his mission, as the crowd make way for him.

Creon, at the wish of Oedipus, addresses the people. He tells them of the oracle's answer: someone in Thebes is guilty of the murder of Laius, the late king; they must be discovered and driven out of the city. The leading Elder of Thebes suggests that Oedipus ask counsel of Tiresias, the blind seer. But Tiresias gives enigmatic answers and Oedipus hears him with mounting anger. The Elder tries to restore calm but Tiresias becomes angry too: he tells Oedipus that he himself is the unclean thing in the city, and living in shame with his next of kin. Oedipus wonders if there can be a plot in which Tiresias and Creon are involved. Tiresias repeats that the murderer of Laius is Theban born, and this day will see him exposed. Creon, who is Jocasta's brother, returns to the scene to find himself accused of treason. The Queen comes upon husband and brother quarrelling, and the Elder tells her what has transpired.

Jocasta scoffs at the oracle. She tells Oedipus that she had borne a son to Laius, and the oracle declared that he would kill his father. But Laius lived many years: they exposed the child on Mount Kithaeron with an iron spike through his feet, and Laius was killed by thieves at a place where three roads meet, on the way to Delphi. Oedipus is startled by her words; he had killed a man on the road from Delphi to Thebes, where the road from Daulis joins it. He orders a search for the messenger who brought the news of the late king's death back to the city. Then he tells Jocasta how, at Corinth, he was taunted with not being a true son of King Polybus; how he went to Delphi to find the truth; how the oracle told him he would kill his father and marry his own mother – even beget children on her; how he turned his face from Corinth forever after hearing this awful disclosure. On the road to Thebes he killed a haughty stranger who ordered him out of his way.

A visitor from Corinth arrives to tell of the death of King Polybus, and of the election of Oedipus as his successor. But Oedipus is depressed by the news; the oracle had said that he would bring tragedy to his mother, too. The Corinthian reassures him; he is not her son. He was a gift to that childless couple from the Corinthian himself. He goes on: he was a shepherd once, on Mount Kithaeron, and a fellow-shepherd had a baby, with a spike through its feet, which he had been ordered to leave to die. He could not bear to do it, and he gave the child to the Corinthian. Jocasta, shrinking with horror, runs from the scene.

The last to come to Thebes on this fateful day is an aged shepherd, one of Laius' men, brought to the palace on the King's orders. The Corinthian knows him, old though he is. He was the shepherd who gave him the baby, who became heir to Corinth, and is now King of Thebes. A terrible revelation is forced out of the poor old man: the child was the son of Laius and Jocasta; Laius had ordered that he be exposed on Mount Kithaeron – the oracle had foretold that he would kill his father. Oedipus – unwittingly guilty of parricide and incest with his mother, blinds himself. The wretched Jocasta had hanged herself when she realized the shocking import of the Corinthian's words. Creon takes the reins of government, and Oedipus leaves the city he defiled.

Oedipus at Colonus The subsequent fate of Oedipus was dealt with at length by the tragedians – see the entry for Antigone – but the most familiar version is found in this later play by Sophocles, produced in 401 BC after the poet's death.

Some years elapsed after the disclosure of the terrible truth which destroyed Jocasta and led to Oedipus' self-blinding. He had lived on in seclusion, comforted by the love of his daughters but made unhappy by the increasingly arrogant and selfish behaviour of his sons, Eteocles and Polynices. Then a cruel twist in the pattern spun by the Fates brought the long-deferred pronouncement from the oracle at Delphi: he was to be exiled from Thebes. Antigone went with her father, and Ismene stayed in the city to watch events in the fleeting hope that one day she could send news to her sister that all was well again and their father could come home.

After some wandering the ageing Oedipus and Antigone reached Colonus, near Athens. The people were hostile but Theseus, King of Athens, gave them his protection and promised Oedipus that his last years would be untroubled. Ismene joined her father and sister soon after their arrival. She had hurried from Thebes with disturbing news – Eteocles and Polynices, resentful of the regency of Creon, had rebelled against him. Each of them laid claim to the throne and Eteocles had the support of the Thebans as the elder son, but had agreed to a joint kingship with each brother ruling on alternative years. However, Eteocles, once secure on the throne, had repudiated the agreement and Polynices, who had spent the first year at the court of Adrastus, King of Argos, remained in exile. A new pronouncement from the oracle,

Ismene declared, brought the prospect of fresh harassment for her father: his presence near the city promised safety for Thebes, since his coming death was predicted and his wrathful spirit would bring destruction on anyone who dared approach the city in hostility. The oracle was known to both sons and to Creon, and Ismene had come to warn her father. Oedipus appealed again to Theseus, who confirmed his promise of sanctuary before returning to Athens.

Creon arrived first, accompanied by armed attendants. He found Oedipus deaf to his appeal to return with him to Thebes, so he seized Ismene and Antigone: he would hold them as hostages until Oedipus yielded. But the people, honouring their King's promise, surrounded Creon while Theseus and his men were summoned. Furious at the violating of Athenian sanctuary, Theseus ordered Creon to be held until the two girls were found and restored to their father. Then he turned him out of his kingdom, with a curse on his house delivered by Oedipus.

But all was not well – there was a new arrival at Colonus and Oedipus was confronted with his younger son, Polynices, arrived that day from Argos. He had married the daughter of Adrastus, and the Argive King had helped him raise an army to reinforce his claim to the throne. Success would be certain if Oedipus would give him support in the coming struggle.

It was too much for Oedipus. Blind, near to death, tried to the limit of endurance, he cursed his sons: they had treated him with callous indifference – even contempt – now they were squabbling like animals over possession of him. They would die at each other's hands. Antigone implored Polynices to disperse the army and call off the attack: his pride would not allow him to do so, and he would not dare tell his allies of his father's curse. He departed, and the stage was set for the next episode in the tragic history of the royal house (see The Seven Against Thebes).

Oedipus and his daughters, and the people of Colonus, watched the sky darken and heard the sound of distant thunder: Oedipus knew that his death was approaching. The people summoned Theseus, who was present to receive the blessing of Oedipus. The tormented man knew that he was soon to find peace: he blessed his daughters and then turned and made his way, unaided, into the grove of the Furies nearby. The people prayed for a peaceful death for him, and Oedipus walked away into the gathering darkness, to vanish forever from earth.

See also Adrastus, *Antigone* (Sophocles), Creon, Epigoni, Eteocles, The Seven Against Thebes.

Olympus, Mount The highest peak in Greece, Olympus is 9600 feet high and stands on the eastern extremity of the chain which forms the border of Greece with Macedonia. It overlooks the Vale of Tempe and was regarded as the home of the gods by the ancient Greeks.

Ops The goddess of the harvest in Roman religion, Ops was later identified with the Rhea of the Greeks. During her festival, on 25 August, the Pontifex Maximus and the Vestal Virgins presided over a ceremony which symbolised the storage of the state's crops by the king and his daughters. It dated from the time of the Roman kings and was held in a shrine in the ancient royal palace, the Regia.

Oresteia, The A trilogy of plays by Aeschylus, first produced in 458 BC, it is the finest of the tragedian's works (and the only trilogy of Greek tragedy) to have survived. Aeschylus took a cycle of myths familiar to the audiences of his time (the story of Agamemnon, Clytemnestra and their children), and fashioned a trio of plays which raise questions of eternal importance. What is true justice? Can man ever escape from his primitive instinct for revenge? Where does justice take precedence over a vicious circle of crime and retribution? What rights does a wife and mother really possess? How can man be forced to turn away from the ancient gods – and to what kind can he appeal when he seeks something better? But with all that as part of his great conception Aeschylus remained a tragedian and the *Oresteia* is also a magnificent play, a fine representation of the art and thought of Athens in its greatest days.

The first play, *Agamemnon*, deals with the return of that King to Argos after the conclusion of the Trojan War. His Queen, Clytemnestra, has never forgiven him for the murder of their daughter, Iphigenia, whom he gave as a sacrifice at Aulis when the armies were halted there, unable to sail because of the contrary winds. The sacrifice of Iphigenia brought the favourable wind and the armies embarked for Troy.

During the long years of the King's absence Clytemnestra found a lover, Agememnon's cousin, Aegisthus. The two men represent rival branches of the house of Atreus and Thyestes, and suffer from the curse pronounced on their grandfather, Pelops. Aegisthus thus enjoys the Queen's love and the satisfaction of cuckolding his enemy.

Agamemnon returns to Argos, and is welcomed by Clytemnestra. But he has brought a captive – the prophetess Cassandra of the royal house of Troy. Clytemnestra's speech of welcome is a remarkably subtle address – the effect, in spite of the fulsome words, is of reproach. She rounds it off by calling for a crimson cloth to be laid from the King's chariot to the palace doors – as befits a conqueror. Agamemnon is irritated but Clytemnestra persuades him. He enters the palace barefoot, walking on the crimson cloth. Clytemnestra and the palace retinue follow, and the enslaved Cassandra is left alone in the courtyard.

Cassandra, filled with dread, voices her fears. The people will see Agamemnon dead. Death is what awaits her, too, she knows and that she cannot avoid it. And worse will follow from this day's deeds. Cassandra tears off the emblems of Apollo, the prophet god, and hurls a reproach at him as her destroyer. Then she makes her way into the palace.

Soon after, the people hear a howl of agony from within, and a woman's scream. They cluster on the steps below the palace doors – which swing open to reveal the truth of Cassandra's vision: she lies dead; Agamemnon, his body enmeshed in crimson cloth, lies beside her. Clytemnestra stands over them, leaning on a sword; she has wiped her hand across her forehead, which is now red with blood.

Clytemnestra addresses the people with a speech of triumph, but there is a dreadful tiredness in her exultation. The horrified reproaches she faces are easily dealt with and out of her words emerges the truth of what she has endured as a woman and a mother – she is those too, as well as a Queen. A wife as well? Yes! But what of a husband's honour, and a father's?

The people, hopelessly confused, are silenced by the arrival of Aegisthus, whom they loathe. But Aegisthus also has a case to state – the people know very well what his house suffered at the hands of Agamemnon's: he has exacted a just price for that (see the entry for Pelops). Now he will rule.

The second play is *The Libation Bearers* (*Choephoroe*), and seven years have passed since the murder of Agamemnon. Argos has been firmly ruled by Aegisthus and Clytemnestra but the people have no love for them. Orestes, Agamemnon's heir, was taken out of the city by his sister, Electra: even before her father's murder she had been made fearful by her mother's behaviour; she took Orestes to safety with the King of Phocis and now she lives in longing for his return as a man. Of that event both Aegisthus and Clytemnestra live in fear; they have reduced the Princess Electra to a status almost as low as a slave's but she continues to defy them.

The play opens at Agamemnon's grave, where in the early morning Orestes is making an offering of locks of his hair. His friend, Pylades, stands watching, and he and Orestes step into the shadows when they hear some people approaching. Orestes recognises his sister Electra and some loyal servants: they are carrying libations of wine to the grave to offer for the spirit of the dead King.

The meeting precipitates the intention they both have to avenge the murder of Agamemnon – indeed Orestes has been commanded to the deed by Apollo, and while he knows the justice of what he must do he shrinks from becoming a matricide. But it is a god's command. Electra has no doubts, after the treatment she has received, and stiffens her brother's resolve. The servants are as uncompromising as their mistress, and join in the plot.

The play, from this point, follows the harsh tragedy also related by Sophocles and Euripides, with the Queen's warning to Orestes, not found in the other playwrights. He can kill his mother – but how will he deal with the Furies?

The servants and the people, crowding into the courtyard, are shown the bodies of Clytemnestra and Aegisthus. But even while their praises are sounding in his ears Orestes feels the first breath of terror. The Furies are near. He proclaims the justice of his deed – it was commanded by Apollo. The Furies are around him now: Orestes gives a howl of terror and runs from the scene.

The third play is called *The Eumenides* – The Kindly Ones, in fact the Furies themselves, in the euphemistic term used to both placate and describe them since they were universally feared.

The play opens in the shrine of Apollo at Delphi, whither Orestes has fled to escape the Furies: but they are there, too, and grouped around him while he lies exhausted. Apollo gives Orestes the protection of Hermes as an escort to Athens, where he will be tried before Athene. On the Areopagus, where the trial takes place, Apollo seems as much on trial as Orestes, and the court is formed by a tribunal of Athenian citizens. Athene herself presides. The cases both for and against Orestes are equally strong, but the leading citizen commands his fellows to judge by the promptings of their conscience, not from fear of the will of Zeus, whose command Apollo insists is what he delivered to Orestes.

The votes are equal. Athene resolves the case by giving her casting vote in favour of Orestes. There has to be an end, and reason must be brought to judgement as well as fear of ancient taboos.

See also Agamemnon, Calchas, Clytemnestra, Electra, Iphigenia, Orestes.

Orestes The son of Agamemnon and Clytemnestra, and brother of Iphigenia, Electra and (in Sophocles) Chrysothemis. He is perhaps best known as the avenger of his father, killing both his mother and Aegisthus when he was a grown man and able to undertake the deed. His story is given in some detail by the tragedians, and in fact rounded off by Euripides in his second play about Iphigenia. He is the subject of another play by the same tragedian, *Orestes*, which deals with his trial – the subject also of the third part of the *Oresteia*.

Orestes is mentioned by Homer in the *Odyssey*, where his vengeance on his mother is praised: she, by contrast, is inevitably hateful since she has killed his father. The older tradition dealt in absolutes in the case of Orestes, and it was left to the Athenian dramatic poets to make him interesting.

See also *Electra* (Sophocles), *Iphigenia in Tauris* (Euripides).

Orion In mythology Orion is generally a mighty hunter; that he is also a constellation of stars is acknowledged as early as Homer, though there is no apparent connection between the two facts, and the number of myths which bear his name suggest that the original story is irretrievably lost. The variants are impossible to connect, so there is no continuous thread which leads from his killing by Artemis to his translation to the heavens.

Most familiarly, Orion is the son of Poseidon and Euryale, one of the Gorgons. Poseidon gave him the power to walk on the sea. He wooed Merope, daughter of Oinopion, King of Chios, but consummated the union before the marriage could take place. The furious King thereupon made him drunk, and put out his eyes and left him abandoned on the seashore. Orion found a boy to guide him, and he travelled eastward on the sea with the boy on his shoulder, to find the rising sun. The sun's rays restored his sight; but when he returned to Chios looking for revenge Oinopion had disappeared, into an underground house built for him by Hephaestus. The myth seems to end there.

The story of his death has many variations but the usual one is that he presumed to challenge Artemis in hunting, for which presumption she killed him.

Orpheus Orpheus is one of the most celebrated figures of Greek mythology and one of the most difficult to identify. From the sixth century BC onwards he was celebrated by the poets, particularly Pindar; but whether he was an historical personage, or a legendary poet of the pre-Homeric period cannot be determined. One version of the myth makes him a Thracian and a follower of Dionysus, another the son of the Muse, Calliope. He was a musician of such power and sweetness that even the wild creatures would gather to listen to him. He took part in the expedition of the Argonauts, and when, on the return journey, the *Argo* had to pass by the Sirens, he saved his companions from their deadly lure by giving them sweeter music to listen to.

He is best known for his visit to Hades, when he tried to recover his dead wife from the shades. She was a dryad, Eurydice, who was loved by another man also. This was Aristaeus, one of Apollo's many sons. Eurydice did not return his love but Aristaeus persisted in his attentions, and one day Eurydice, trying to run away from them, trod on a snake from whose bite she died. Orpheus was able to enter the lower kingdom by charming Charon, the ferryman of the dead, with his music; he also used it to quieten Cerberus, the monstrous three-headed watchdog of Hades. His music, and his grief, so touched Persephone that she pleaded with her grim consort on his behalf, and Hades agreed to let Eurydice return to earth. But he made the condition that Orpheus must believe that Eurydice followed him – and not look back. But in his agony of uncertainty that Eurydice really was following him Orpheus did look back, and saw her slip away from him forever.

After that, according to a later tradition, Orpheus offended the followers of Dionysus by withdrawing his worship from the god. He was torn to pieces by the maenads, who threw his head into the river

Hebrus. The muses gathered up the rest of his remains and buried them at the foot of Olympus. The head floated down to the sea and came to rest at the island of Lesbos, where it was found and buried in a shrine of Apollo's.

The connection of Orpheus and Dionysus is a persistent one and a possible explanation is that Orpheus personifies the original sacrifice to that god, a sacrifice which recurs in *The Bacchae*, where Pentheus is also an opponent of Dionysus and eventually a sacrifice to him. The later tradition tells that Orpheus, after losing Eurydice, could not bear the promiscuity of the followers of Dionysus; it was this that aroused the fury of the maenads. But the common location of Thrace for the origins of both Orpheus and Dionysus, and the manner of Orpheus' death, suggest that a strand of the story has been lost.

See also *Argonautica*, Aristaeus, Dionysus, *The Bacchae* (Euripides).

Otus and Ephialtes The sons of Poseidon and Iphimedeia. They grew to giant stature by the time they were nine years old, and earned the wrath of the gods by trying to climb to the heavens. They stood Mount Ossa on Olympus, Mount Pelion on Ossa: but Apollo killed them before they made further headway. The story is in Homer (*Odyssey*, Book XI). The same writer tells the story of the indignity suffered by Ares at their hands (*Iliad*, Book V). They trussed him up and imprisoned him in a bronze jar, where he lay for thirteen months until Hermes found him and freed him.

Ovid The Latin poet who wrote the *Metamorphoses*. He was born in 43 BC, and enjoyed the privileges accorded to members of *equestrian* (knightly) families. He was widely travelled and three times married, and enjoyed a high reputation in fashionable Roman circles. He was fifty-one years old when he earned the displeasure of the Emperor Augustus, and some mystery surrounds the true reason. Ovid himself believed it was something he had written (in his *Ars Amatoria*); but it may have been his connection with the Emperor's daughter, Julia.

Whatever the reason, Ovid was banished to Tomis, the modern Constanza, on the western shore of the Black Sea, where he died after ten years. His third wife was loyal to him and shared his exile.

Ovid wrote to amuse, but his work was never lost and consequently had enormous influence before classical Greek became widely studied in the West. He was much read during the Middle Ages – Chaucer used several of his themes – and his influence can be found in Marlowe, Spenser and Shakespeare.

See also *Metamorphoses*.

P

Palamedes The son of Nauplius and a descendant of Poseidon, Palamedes was one of those who, like Cadmus, came to be credited with a part in the invention of written language. In mythology he is a clever man, more clever than Odysseus: but Odysseus harbours a grudge when Palamedes' wits ensure that he has to leave Ithaca to go and fight in the Trojan War.

Palamedes does not appear in Homer but other versions of the war story make him one of Agamemnon's commanders, and the Achaeans threaten to give their allegiance to Palamedes when Agamemnon recoils from the necessity to sacrifice his daughter, Iphigenia, at Aulis. Later, at Troy, Palamedes makes the mistake of compounding his offence against Odysseus, by finding corn for the Achaeans after Odysseus had failed in the same quest.

Odysseus' mean revenge was to bury a sackful of gold in the ground under Palamedes' tent; then he sent a message to Agamemnon that he had intercepted a letter from Priam to Palamedes, which said that the gold was a reward for betraying the Achaeans to their enemies. Palamedes' tent was searched and the gold was found, and Palamedes was stoned to death by the army.

Palamedes was also credited with the invention of dice; the first set ever made by him was dedicated to the goddess Tyce (fortune) in her temple at Argos.

Nauplius, when he heard of his son's fate, went to Troy and demanded satisfaction from the Achaean leaders. This was denied him, and he bided his time in gaining vengeance, which was to light false beacons on the coast of Euboea and wreck many of the ships returning from the war.

See also Iphigenia, Odysseus.

Palatine Hill The principal of the seven hills of Rome since it was there that the first settlements were made. In the *Aeneid* (Book VIII), the river god Tiberinus appears to Aeneas and tells him he will find an ally in Evander, whose city stands on the Palatine Hill. Evander shows him the cave of Lupercal there.

The name of the hill may have originated in *Pales,* the rustic spirits of place in Roman religion, or in *palus* (marsh), from the marshy ground between the Palatine and the Tiber. Our word 'palace' is derived from this source.

See also *Aeneid.*

Pales In Roman religion the rustic, ancient spirits of the earth, originally male but referred to as female by the time of Virgil and Ovid. The festival of *Parilia,* on 21 April, was one of ritual purification of flocks and a plea for increase in the coming season. The festival was very ancient, and was probably well established before Rome emerged as the chief power in Italy.

Pallas The name of several characters in classical mythology – but not one of them, with the exception of the son of Evander, took part in a myth of any importance. There was a giant called Pallas, who was killed by Athene in the battle between gods and giants (but see the following entry); a Titan of the same name, and an Attic hero who was defeated by Theseus.

See also *Aeneid,* Giants, Theseus.

Pallas Athene The exact meaning of 'Pallas' as part of the title of the goddess is not known, and some scholars believe that it was the name, originally, of another goddess who became identified with Athene. Some myths, such as the killing of a giant named Pallas by Athene during the war between gods and giants, simply attempt to explain the name in another way.

See also Athene.

Pan A god of the mountainous region of Arcadia in the heart of the Peloponnese, and a very ancient deity. In a region where cattle were rare the principal herds were of goats: Pan was a herdsman's god and inevitably came to be seen as part goat. He loved the wild country and the mountains, and was a notable musician with the syrinx or pan-pipes of seven reeds – an instrument which is still played by Arcadian shepherds.

Pan was a god acknowledged by all: what was remarkable about him in the context of Greek religion was his total detachment from any social or moral value. He *was*, he had always been, and perhaps more than any deity in Greek imagination personified instinct. His name, 'the pasturer' or 'feeder' of flocks, identifies him as a spirit as ancient as man himself.

It was inevitable that the formalising of Greek religion took account of the great god of Arcadia. He was called the son of Hermes (another Arcadian god) but no definite mother for him ever found her way into the myths. Pan himself will be encountered in a numer of them.

The most famous story connected with him relates to history rather than myth. On the eve of the Battle of Marathon, the Athenians sent the runner Philippides to Sparta to enlist the aid of that city against their common foe, the Persians. At Mount Parthenion, above Tegea, Philippides found that he had a companion – Pan had joined him. The god addressed him by name, and gave him a message for the Athenians. He was their friend: he had helped Athens before – and he would again; why then, did the Athenians not honour him? (Herodotus, Book VI).

After the victory, the Athenians instituted the worship of Pan in their city and gave him a shrine in a cave on the Acropolis. His cult spread beyond Arcadia from that time on.

Pan was believed to be the cause of sudden, unreasoning fear –panic – that could overcome people in desolate, lonely places. It afflicted animals, too, making them stampede for no apparent reason.

He was a lusty, playful god: sex was his principal diversion, as befitted a god who was worshipped in connection with fertility. The Olympians respected him, and one tradition declared that Apollo learned the art of prophecy from him.

See also Penelope.

Parentalia In Roman religion, the seven days of sacrifice in honour of the dead, from 13 to 21 February. During these days the temples were closed (the sacrifices were offered at the tombs) and no marriages took place. The *Parentalia* was concluded, on 22 February, with a ceremony of reunion and the worship of the Lares Familiares.

See also Lares.

Paris The son of Priam, King of Troy, and his Queen, Hecuba. The story of his famous Judgment is mentioned in the *Iliad* (Book XXIV) but not described: similarly his abduction of Helen, which is a part of the events which led to the Trojan war. For the part played by Paris in the struggle see the entry for the *Iliad*. A coherent account of his life and adventures is not to be found in Homer (nor any definite mention of his death) but inevitably the man who loved Helen would attract stories to him and something could be constructed from those.

When Hecuba carried him in her womb she had a dream that she bore a flaming torch from which serpents emerged. The soothsayers, when consulted, declared that the child must be destroyed as soon as it was born – the dream was plainly a prediction of disaster. Paris was born, and given to shepherds to expose: but they spared the child and he grew up among them on Mount Ida. He fell in love with the nymph, Oenone, but he deserted her when Aphrodite promised him the most beautiful woman in the world – Helen, the wife of Menelaus.

The most hansome of men, Paris was also a fine athlete, and he entered the games in Troy, beating the King's sons and winning three of the prizes. The princes' resentment of the stranger might have cost him his life, had not the shepherd disclosed his true identity to Priam, who was watching the games. The king was delighted to acknowledge his handsome and brillant son, in spite of the repeated warnings of the soothsayers.

Having regained his place as a prince, Paris was in a position to carry out the abduction of Helen – and the grim prophecies all came true. Because of Paris, Troy was destroyed.

Homer does imply *(Odyssey,* Book VIII) that Paris is already dead when the Achaeans break into Troy through the ruse of the Wooden Horse – it is to the house of Deiphobus, Paris' brother, that Menelaus goes in search of his wife. But there is no definite statement; it is in another version of the story that Paris· dies from the arrows of Philoctetes, and is the agent of Apollo in the death of Achilles – the god makes sure that Paris' arrow wounds Achilles fatally in his vulnerable heel.

See also Achilles, Deiphobus, Helen, The Judgement of Paris.

Pegasus The famous winged horse of Greek mythology, Pegasus was born from the body of the dying Medusa when Perseus cut off her head. He created the fountain of the Muses on Mount Helicon by stamping the earth with his hoof.

The idea of a winged horse probably reached Greece in very ancient times through Asia Minor, where Near Eastern ideas would have influenced the Greeks living there. Winged animals were to be found in Near Eastern mythology, and the name is not Greek in origin.

Pegasus is most closely associated with the adventures of Bellerophon, who was able to bridle him with the help of the goddess Athene.

See also Bellerophon, Gorgons.

Peleus The son of Aeacus and brother of Telamon. The brothers were intensely jealous of their younger half-brother, Phocus, Aeacus' favourite, and they feared that their father's island kingdom, Aegina, would be bequeathed to him. Encouraged by their mother, Peleus and Telamon killed their young brother.

When King Aeacus discovered the murder the brothers fled: Telamon to Salamis and Peleus to the court of Actor, King of Phthia, where the King's son, Eurytion, performed a ritual purification for him. But ill-luck seemed to dog Peleus, and he accidentally killed Eurytion in the Calydonian boar hunt. A fugitive once more, he made his way to Iolcos, where Acastus, too, performed a purification ritual for him. Unfortunately, Acastus' wife, Astydameia, fell in love with Peleus; he wanted none of her, and she was determined to make him pay for spurning her. Acastus was horrified to hear from his wife that his guest had attempted to molest her.

Acastus, unwilling to murder his guest, took him hunting on Mount Pelion. After a hectic day's sport Peleus fell asleep, whereupon Acastus stole his sword and hid it, and left Peleus to his fate – the centaurs roamed on Mount Pelion, and an unarmed man would be at their mercy.

Peleus awoke to find himself surrounded by hostile centaurs: but their wise and benevolent King, Chiron, forbade them to harm him. He also divined where the sword lay hidden, so Peleus was able to return safely to Iolcos, where he killed the treacherous Astydameia.

His last appearance in myth was as the husband chosen for Thetis by Zeus on the advice of Themis. Zeus loved Thetis; but the Fates prophesied that any son born to Thetis would be greater than his father, so Zeus could be overthrown if the son were his. Peleus and Thetis were married, and the gods attended their wedding. A son was born to them, and his name was Achilles.

See also Achilles, Aeacus, Telamon, Thetis.

Pelops The son of Tantalus, through whose wickedness Pelops makes his first appearance in mythology. Tantalus was a descendant of the gods and frequently their guest, and to test their omniscience he invited them to his table where he served them the flesh of his infant son Pelops mixed into a stew. All the Olympians (save Demeter, who was lately bereft of her daughter, Persephone) saw at once what they were being offered, and recoiled in horror: Tantalus had over-reached himself. He was duly punished, and the gods restored Pelops to life. For the part of him which Demeter had inadvertently eaten (the left shoulder blade) they substituted ivory.

Pelops grew up and began to look for a kingdom. Poseidon himself fell in love with him, and this love was to prove useful. The King of Pisa and Elis, Oenomaus, had a passion for horses and an incestuous love for his daughter, Hippodameia. He disposed of suitors by letting them take part in a racing contest: if the suitor's chariot could be overtaken by Oenomaus the King had the right to the suitor's life, and with his highly-trained horses he never lost. He had already killed thirteen suitors when Pelops came upon the scene.

The new suitor arrived well prepared: his lover, Poseidon, had given him a fine light chariot and a superb team of horses. But at the sight of the heads of the failed suitors, nailed in a row above the gates of the palace at Olympia, Pelops' heart sank, and he stooped to treachery to make doubly sure of winning.

Oenomaus' charioteer, Myrtilus, was a son of Hermes, and he lusted after Hippodameia. Pelops offered him the privilege of spending the bridal night with her if the race was won (Oenomaus drove his own team when the suitors competed). Myrtilus agreed, and that night he removed the linchpins from the King's chariot, filling the holes with wax. Pelops won: the King's chariot disintegrated during the race and Oenomaus was killed. Myrtilus was also killed, later in the day, since Pelops had no intention of honouring his shameful bargain.

Myrtilus cursed Pelops with his dying breath, and Hermes heard his son's wishes. Pelops became a rich and successful King but his line was never to know any peace, though he sought the favour of Zeus by the institution of the Olympic Games.

Pelops' sons, Atreus and Thyestes, were sought after by the people of Mycenae, who wanted a king and were advised by an oracle to choose one from the house of Pelops. The brothers, rivals since childhood, went to Mycenae and watched each other jealously while the people debated which to choose. At that point in the fortunes of the house of Pelops the curse of the dying Myrtilus began to work.

Hermes knew that Atreus had vowed to offer the finest of his flocks to Artemis. He and Thyestes had inherited Pelops' herds jointly, and Hermes added to them a golden-fleeced lamb – knowing that its presence would provoke a murderous quarrel since each brother would claim that it was his. Furthermore, Atreus would be reluctant to sacrifice the unique and beautiful creature in spite of his vow.

Atreus laid claim not only to the golden lamb but also to the throne of Mycenae, being the older brother. He used the appearance of the lamb as a sign that he was divinely ordained to be King. Thyestes, however, had not been idle. He had seduced Aerope, his brother's wife, and she was infatuated with him. Atreus sacrificed the golden lamb's flesh to Artemis – but kept the fleece as a proof of kingship. Thyestes persuaded Aerope to steal the fleece for him.

The day came when the Elders of Mycenae announced their choice. The holder of the Golden Fleece was plainly of great importance in their deliberations, and when Thyestes proved his possession of it he was awarded the throne. Atreus, aghast, implored the gods to help him and Zeus exposed the treachery – it was, inevitably, also revealed that Thyestes had dishonoured his brother's marriage bed. The throne was given to Atreus, after all, and Thyestes fled for his life, leaving his home and children behind.

Atreus, his throne secure, brooded about his brother's crimes and a way of making him pay. He killed Aerope and seized Thyestes' children and then sent a messenger to his brother proclaiming his forgiveness: Thyestes must return and share the throne with him. Thyestes gladly left his exile, and was received warmly by Atreus: a banquet was ordered to celebrate the occasion. Thyestes feasted, and asked for his children. Atreus brought him their heads – and told him that they had provided the meat for the banquet.

Thyestes, mad with grief, laid a curse on Atreus, compounding the dark shadow which already lay on Pelops' line: Atreus' children, Agamemnon and Menelaus, were to bear its weight. Thyestes then consulted the oracle at Delphi, and was advised to beget a son upon his surviving child, his daughter, Pelopia. So he journeyed to Sicyon, where the girl was a priestess of Athene and a ward of the King,

Thesprotus. One night he waited in a grove near the temple, wearing a mask to conceal his identity. Pelopia, waylaid by a masked stranger, managed to tear off his sword: but he succeeded in raping her. The empty scabbard he only noticed later, and he was afraid that the sword would identify him; he fled from the scene. Pelopia hid the sword in the sanctuary of Athene.

Atreus, meanwhile, haunted by guilt for the murder of Thyestes' children, went also to the oracle at Delphi, and was ordered to recall his brother from exile. But when he arrived in Sicyon Thyestes was gone, so he stayed for a while at Thesprotus' court where he became attracted to Pelopia, assuming her to be the King's daughter. The King, fond of Pelopia, did not undeceive him, and Atreus and Pelopia were married. But her first child was not the son of Atreus: he was the son of Thyestes, and he was named Aegisthus.

Ill-fortune descended on Mycenae: the harvests failed and the beasts died, and Atreus in desperation sent Agamemnon and Menelaus to find Thyestes. Against all expectations they did, in Delphi, and they took him back to Mycenae by force. Atreus, the oracle notwithstanding, was swept by the old hatred at the sight of his brother: he had him thrown into a dungeon and plotted his death.

One night Thyestes awoke in his dungeon to find a boy of seven standing over him with a drawn sword. It was Aegisthus, hoping to kill him and earn the approbation of his supposed father, Atreus. Thyestes easily disarmed the boy – and then he recognised the sword as his own. The time had come to turn the tables on Atreus – though Pelopia killed herself when she realised who the father of her son really was – and Aegisthus was persuaded to turn the sword on Atreus and acknowledge his real father.

There was peace for a time in Mycenae. Thyestes reigned as King and Aegisthus was the heir. But the curse lay over all the house of Pelops, and it was not long before Agamemnon, the eldest son of Atreus, rebelled against his uncle. He succeeded in driving Thyestes out of Mycenae, and dispossessing his cousin Aegisthus. Agamemnon married Clytemnestra, and became High King in Argos, and went to the Trojan war. But the curse on Pelops' line had not yet run its course, and Aegisthus waited for his day to come.

See also Aegisthus, Agamemnon, Clytemnestra, Electra, Menelaus, *Oresteia* (Aeschylus).

Penates In Roman religion, the guardians of the larder or store-cupboard, are regarded (with the Lares) as protectors of the household. In a different context there were state Penates, said to have been brought to Rome from Troy by Aeneas: those were the protectors of the Roman state, and it was to them that magistrates swore their oath.

See also Lares.

Penelope The name of Penelope is most familiar as the wife of Odysseus, plagued by suitors but faithful to her long-lost husband. Another Penelope, probably a nymph or a local goddess, is named by some mythographers as the mother of Pan: Hermes took the form of a ram when he lay with her.

See also *Odyssey*.

Penthesilea The Amazon Queen who fought on the Trojan side after the death of Hector. She does not appear in Homer, but in an eighth-century poem which makes her the daughter of the god Ares – who favoured the Trojans. She fought valiantly but was killed by Achilles, who thereupon grieved over her. This brought him insulting comments from Thersites: Achilles killed him in a rage and that led to a quarrel with Diomedes, who was Thersites' kinsman.

Penthesilea, in later versions of the story, accidentally killed Hippolyta, another Amazon Queen. She obtained ritual purification from King Priam, which was why she fought for the Trojans against the Achaeans.

Persephone The daughter of Demeter and Zeus, Persephone is inseparable from the mother goddess though she does appear in many myths in her own right, principally as the wife of Hades.

As the daughter of Demeter, Persephone is called Kore (maiden), probably representing the young corn still growing, while her mother is the ripe corn: the goddesses are plainly personifications of two aspects of fertility, and Persephone's annual sojourn in the nether world occurs during the months before the sowing and after the harvest. (See the entry for Demeter for the story of the abduction of Persephone by Hades.)

Persephone also appears in a religious myth of the movement called Orphism which first became popular in ancient Greece after the sixth century BC, and which emphasised the indestructibility of the soul –

which inhabited the corrupt body, from which it should strive to escape.

Persephone appears in Roman religion as Proserpine.

See also Demeter, Dionysus, Dionysus Zagreus, Hades.

Perseus The son of Danae and Zeus. Danae's father Acrisius, King of Argos, learned from an oracle that he would be killed by his daughter's son. His brother Proetus, with whom he was always quarrelling, had admitted to seducing Danae and Acrisius, fearful of his life, assumed that the son in question would necessarily be the child of Proetus. He shut his daughter away in a fortified chamber built of bronze: but the amorous Zeus found his way in there as a shower of golden rain.

Acrisius' worst fears seemed to be realised when his daughter proved to be pregnant. Not wishing to kill his daughter he waited until the child – a son she named Perseus – was born: then he placed mother and son in a wooden chest and cast it adrift in the sea. It floated in the island of Seriphos, where a fisherman named Dictys saved them from the sea and where the King, Polydectes, received them with kindness and gave them a place at court.

Perseus grew up, and his mother in the meantime had attracted the amorous intentions of the King. She had no wish to marry him but he persisted, and even grew threatening: only Perseus stood in his way as Danae's protector. Polydectes then declared he would seek another wife: Seriphos was only a small island and he asked his people to contribute to a gift which would be essential if he sought the hand of another princess. Perseus had nothing to give so he offered the King his services – he promised to do anything the King asked. Polydectes thereupon asked for the head of the Gorgon, Medusa, whose very glance turned men to stone.

Perseus, fortunately, had an ally of whom he was unaware. Athene was Medusa's enemy: the goddess had in fact given Medusa her frightening appearance as a punishment for defiling her temple. Athene warned Perseus never to look at Medusa directly, and gave him a highly-burnished shield to use as a mirror. Hermes gave him a sickle and a leather bag and by telling him where to find the Graiae, helped him borrow the cap of Hades (a *tarnhelm* which conferred invisibility) and a pair of winged sandals.

The whereabouts of Medusa were only known to the Graiae, the Gorgon's sisters who lived at the foot of Mount Atlas, and who had only one eye between them. They also knew how to reach the abode of the Stygian nymphs, who had the cap of Hades and the winged sandals in their care. Perseus crept up on the Graiae and snatched the eye as it was being passed from one sister to another. He refused to give it back until they told him what he wanted to know. Helpless, they had to comply.

Medusa dwelled away from mankind, shunned by every living thing. But Perseus, well-protected now, was able to kill her without looking at her, using Athene's burnished shield. He cut off her head with Hermes' sickle, and stowed it securely in the leather bag. He witnessed the birth of Poseidon's children – the winged horse, Pegasus, and the warrior, Chrysaor – from Medusa's body, then he began his homeward journey using the winged sandals.

On his return journey, Perseus saw a naked girl chained to a rock on the sea coast near Joppa. He flew down, and was just in time to prevent her from being devoured by a sea monster: he turned it to stone by uncovering the head of Medusa. The girl was the Princess Andromeda, daughter of King Cepheus of Ethiopia and his vain and stupid wife, Cassiopeia.

Cassiopeia had boasted of her beauty, declaring she was more beautiful even than the sea nymphs. This aroused the wrath of the sea-nymphs' protector, the god Poseidon, who sent the monster to ravage the country. Only the sacrifice of the King's daughter would put an end to the creature's depredations.

Andromeda was beautiful and Perseus, after releasing her and restoring her to her father, asked for her hand. This he secured only after defeating another suitor, Phineus, who brought an armed force to secure his claim: Perseus disposed of them by using the Gorgon's head to turn them into an army of statues.

Home in Seriphos, Perseus and Andromeda found that they were still not free of danger. Polydectes, believing that Perseus would never return, had tried to force his attentions on Danae. She had appealed to the fisherman, Dictys, who had saved her and Perseus from the sea. Now Danae and her only champion were in grave danger: they had fled to sanctuary in a temple but they were menaced by Polydectes and his armed attendants. Once more Perseus used the Gorgon's head: he presented himself at court and announced that he had brought the gift he promised. Neither the King nor his followers would believe Perseus, so no one tried to stop him from opening the leather bag. Perseus left them where they were, a petrified King and court, and brought his mother Danae and the valiant Dictys out of their refuge into a kingdom at last made safe. Dictys became the new King of Seriphos and Perseus, with his mother and his wife, returned to Argos.

News of the homecoming of Danae and her son reached the ageing King Acrisius, who hurried off to Larissa to avoid the grandson he dreaded. But Perseus, meanwhile, had been invited to Larissa himself: his deeds had made him famous and the new King of Larissa was honoured to have him at the funeral games for his father. So the fateful encounter which Acrisius had striven to avoid at last took place – though with no ill-will on the part of Danae or Perseus. However, the pattern of the Fates worked itself out inexorably: a discus thrown by Perseus at the games flew awry and struck Acrisius, who died from the blow.

Perseus was now King of Argos but he was reluctant to accept a throne so shadowed by tragedy. Some versions of the myth say he retired to Asia with Andromeda and his son Perses, who became the founder of Persia. But a more familiar (and in the context of the story more probable) version says that he exchanged the throne of Argos for that of Tiryns, where his uncle Proetus ruled. He also founded the city of Mycenae.

The cap of Hades, with the winged sandals, were returned to the Stygian nymphs, and the Gorgon's head was given to Athene, who fixed it on her shield.

See also Danae, Gorgons, Graiae.

Phaethon The son of Helios, the sun god, and the nymph, Clymene, Phaethon was the result of a brief love affair and grew up without knowledge of his father. One day, tired of being taunted in that respect, he demanded that his mother tell him his father's name.

When he learned that his father was the sun god, Phaethon set out in search of him, travelling to the east from where the sun always rises. He found his father's palace, and declared himself: Helios welcomed his new-found son and lavished affection on him, and offered him anything he wanted. Phaethon told him – he was dazzled by the splendour of his father's journey across the sky, and he wanted to drive the chariot of the sun for one day.

Helios tried to dissuade his son: but Phaethon wanted nothing else and the sun god was reluctant to refuse him the single thing he asked for. With some misgiving he allowed his son to take the the reins on the following dawn.

His worst fears were realised. Phaethon could not control the winged horses and they bolted with him – the chariot of the sun was out of control and soon began to scorch the world to which it was meant to bring warmth and light. Gaia (Mother Earth) appealed to Zeus who could only hurl a thunderbolt and kill Phaethon, who fell from the chariot. His father hastily took control, and righted the chariot, and the world was safe again.

The body of Phaethon hurtled earthwards and fell into the river Eridanus (Po), where his sisters wept for him on the banks and turned into trees. The trees continued to weep – the resin oozed from the bark and turned into amber. Another who mourned him was Cygnus, the ruler of Liguria, who loved him and who turned into a swan in his grief.

The story of Phaethon was known to the Greeks – Euripides wrote a play about Phaethon – but the most complete version we have is by Ovid, related in his *Metamorphoses*.

Philemon and Baucis The story of the hospitable old couple, like that of Phaethon, is best known from the version given in the *Metamorphoses*.

Zeus visted the earth accompanied by Hermes. The king of the gods wanted to observe mankind and see how they lived, so he and Hermes went disguised as travellers. They found little kindness: most people turned them away and refused them food or shelter.

The gods at last came to a poor hut in Phrygia with a roof of thatch and weeds, where lived an old couple, Philemon and Baucis. They had little, but they were content because it was enough, and they welcomed the travellers, their kindness making up for any lack of material things. They found a little honey to go with the simple meal, and pressed such wine as they had on their guests.

The modest dinner was a cheerful occasion – and then Philemon and Baucis noticed that the wine never seemed to diminish. They watched their guests and realised they were more than mortal men, and they felt suddenly ashamed that they had so little to offer them. They decided to kill the goose – their only one and the guardian of their little home. But the goose eluded them: they were old, and the goose regarded them comfortably from a safe spot.

Zeus and Hermes, touched by the goodness of the old couple, declared themselves: they related how harsh and unfeeling the people had been and how they would be punished. But their host and hostess deserved better, and they were asked to accompany the gods to the summit of a little hill. From there they were amazed to see all the land, except their humble home, drowned in an expanse of marsh. And while they watched their hut turned into a temple of marble columns and beautiful tiled floors.

Zeus asked Philemon and Baucis what he could do that would please them most. They asked to serve him and to guard his shrine: but most of all they asked that they might never be separated – in life or in death. So they were installed in the temple and lived out their days in contentment. And when their days were over they died together in perfect peace, Philemon becoming an oak and Baucis a lime tree: their boughs entwined and they remained together, even in death.

Philoctetes The great archer, who led a force and seven ships to the siege of Troy. On the way to Troy he put into Lemnos, where he was bitten by a poisonous snake. He was left there with his arms; the rest of the Achaeans abandoned him and proceeded to Troy. But the marooned Philoctetes was to be remembered by the Achaean leaders as the war dragged on interminably *(Iliad, Book II)*.

Philoctetes, Poeas' brilliant son, returned safely after the fall of Troy *(Odyssey, Book III)*.

The two statements given above are all that Homer has to say about Philoctetes. But he was a well-known hero to the Greeks and his story was given in greater detail – though with variations – by other writers, including Sophocles, whose play on the subject has come down to us.

When Heracles lay on his funeral pyre on Mount Oeta his friends could not bring themselves to kindle it. Philoctetes and his father – an Aetolian shepherd named Poeas – were on the mountain at the time and it was Philoctetes who kindled the fire. Heracles, in gratitude, gave the boy his bow and a quiver full of arrows.

Philoctetes became a king in Aetolia, and was one of the suitors for the beautiful Helen. This obliged him to join the Achaeans in the war against Troy, and led to the landing on Lemnos where he suffered the snake-bite in his foot that led to his being abandoned there. In some versions the island is Tenedos, and the snake-bite the work of Hera, who wanted to punish Philoctetes for having helped Heracles. The bite would not heal, and the wound became foul. The ships were close to Troy and Agamemnon ordered that he be abandoned: Odysseus took him to the lonely island of Lemnos and left him there, alone with his arms and his suppurating wound.

The siege of Troy dragged on for nine years until the death of Achilles and the growing despair of the Achaeans. Then Odysseus managed to capture Helenus, the Trojan prince who had the gift of prophecy: the seer, Calchas, had declared that Helenus could tell them what the Achaeans needed to bring the war to a successful conclusion. Helenus, in return for his life, told them that Troy would not fall without the arms of Heracles – which now belonged to Philoctetes. Odysseus and Neoptolemus (Achilles' son) were sent to Lemnos to get them.

Odysseus found the lame and ragged Philoctetes on the island and, when Philoctetes refused to go to Troy, shamelessly tricked him out of his arms – the only possession the unfortunate man had. But Neoptolemus was disgusted by Odysseus' treatment of a man already sorely tried, and was prepared to abandon the Achaean cause and see Philoctetes returned to his home in Aetolia. He was prevented by the appearance of Heracles, who related the will of Zeus. Philoctetes must go to Troy; he was the ordained destroyer of Paris, whose wickedness had caused the war. His wound would be cured, and the war brought to an end.

So Philoctetes went with Neoptolemus to Troy, and Machaon, son of Asclepius, cured the dreadful wound. He killed Paris with the arrows of Heracles, and the city of Troy eventually fell.

See also Heracles, Neoptolemus, Odysseus.

Philomela In Greek mythology the daughter of Pandion, King of Athens. Her sister Procne was married to Tereus, King of Thrace; but Tereus lusted after Philomela and could only possess her by a trick. He reported to Pandion that Procne was dead – and Pandion offered him Philomela as a new wife. Tereus escorted her from Athens to Daulis but even on the journey wanted his way. Philomela repulsed him, filled with distaste at his importunities: Tereus, obsessed with her, descended to rape. To conceal what he had done he hid Philomela away: to ensure her silence he cut out her tongue.

But Philomela managed to tell her story: she wove it into a piece of embroidery and sent it to Procne, who took a brutal revenge on the husband who had dishonoured her and mutilated her sister. She killed her son, Itys, and served his flesh to his father when she and Tereus next sat at table.

When he found a joint of child's flesh on his plate, Tereus realised the truth. The sisters fled from the palace, the maddened King pursuing them. But the gods intervened, and the tragedy was brought to an abrupt stop. They changed Procne into a nightingale, and Philomela into a swallow. Tereus became a hoopoe.

In late Roman mythology (the story is also told by Hyginus, second century AD) the roles of the sisters are reversed, and the later account has left us with Philomela as the traditional name for a nightingale. It has been suggested that Hyginus was ignorant of Greek, and therefore gave the story in a garbled form. Ovid makes no such mistakes; his account in the *Metamorphoses* follows the Greek pattern.

Phoebe A Titaness, according to Hesiod – one of the daughters of Uranus and Gaia. As the mother of Leto she has become associated with Artemis, her name ('the bright') contributing to this, especially in later mythographers who wrongly associated Artemis (through her identification with Diana) with the moon. The moon was sometimes given the name of Phoebe.

See also Artemis, Diana, Leto.

Picus A Roman god of agriculture, Picus was described in mythology as the son of Saturn, blessed with prophetic powers, who became the first King of Italy. Virgil makes him the father of Faunus and the grandfather of Latinus *(Aeneid,* Book VII).

The name, Picus, means woodpecker, and there are various myths in association with the bird. One story, told by Ovid, relates how he spurned the attentions of Circe – who spitefully turned him into a woodpecker. The woodpecker, however, was a creature of some importance to the Romans. It was sacred to Mars, was said to have taken food to the infants Romulus and Remus, and omens were drawn from both its appearance and the tone of its call.

Pindar The great lyric poet of ancient Greece was born near Thebes in 518 BC, a son of the distinguished Aegeidae clan. As a young man he went to Athens, which Pisistratus and his family had, by that time, turned into an important intellectual centre. He became acquainted with Aeschylus there, and visited the island of Aegina for which he developed a particular affection. Through his family he had a connection with Delphi, of which he also sings in his poetry.

Pindar was twenty years old when a noble Thessalian family commissioned him to write an ode in honour of one of their sons who had won the footrace in the Pythian Games (held at Delphi) and his reputation dates from then. His work brought him commissions from all over Greece to celebrate similar successes, but his work is far from being merely adulatory. A true poet, he used the opportunities to exercise his great lyric gifts to give expression to a profound and wide-ranging mind.

He attained, in his lifetime, a position of great fame, honoured by all, and was quoted as a classic as soon after his death as the time of Herodotus – hardly sixty years. He died at Argos in 438 BC, at the age of eighty. When Alexander the Great destroyed Thebes in 335 BC, he ordered that Pindar's house should be spared.

There is a fine modern translation of Pindar's work in English, by C. M. Bowra.

Pirithous The son of Zeus and Dia, the wife of Ixion (who was punished by Zeus for his wickedness), Pirithous was a Lapith and the friend of Theseus. Homer mentions him in both the *Iliad* and the *Odyssey*; in the *Iliad* Nestor numbers him among the bravest of men, and one of his sons fights on the Achaean side.

Pirithous married Hippodamia, daughter of Butes, and Theseus was among the guests. It was on that occasion that the great fight between Lapiths and Centaurs broke out: Pirithous invited his Centaur neighbours to the feast also, and they got very drunk and quarrelsome. Violence followed when the Centaurs molested Hippodamia: the Lapiths got the best of the fight and drove the Centaurs from their home on Mount Pelion.

Pirithous had other adventures which arose from his friendship with Theseus, and one of those – the attempted abduction of Persephone – brought about his death. Hades trapped both Theseus and Pirithous in deep chairs which clove to them and became part of their flesh. Heracles, in Hades' kingdom to steal Cerberus, managed to release Theseus; but Pirithous, the originator of the abduction scheme, he could not budge, and Pirithous was doomed to stay in the nether world for ever.

See also Centaurs, Ixion, Lapiths, Theseus.

Pleiades, The   The seven daughters of Atlas and Pleione. Both the Pleiades and their mother appear in a version of the myth of Orion, the mighty hunter, though a different tradition names one of them, Maia, as the mother of Hermes by Zeus.

Orion took a fancy to Pleione: his fancy was not encouraged – mother and daughters fled and Orion gave chase. But the gods intervened and now both pursued and pursuers appear in the heavens as stars.

The story has a particular interest in that the myth arises from the astronomy. The constellations of Orion and the Pleiades are quite close, in stellar terms.

The rising of the Pleiades at morning marks the beginning of summer: the setting of the constellation at morning the beginning of winter.

See also Orion.

Pluto   One of the names of the god Hades, meaning 'riches' – the riches of the earth in which Hades dwelt. It was by this name that the Romans adopted the Greek god of the nether world, often calling him by the Latin name, Dis.

See also Dis, Hades.

Plutus   According to Hesiod the son of Demeter and Iasion. Who Iasion was we are not told; one tradition makes him a 'hero' whom Demeter first met at the marriage of Cadmus and Harmonia. Demeter and Iasion made love in a ploughed field, and Zeus found out about it: he destroyed Iasion with a thunderbolt, according to Homer (*Odyssey*, Book V).

In Greek mythology Plutus was the personification of wealth, bestowed by Demeter and Kore (Persephone) on those they favoured.

Polyxena   A daughter of Priam and Hecuba in some versions of the myths about the siege of Troy. She is not mentioned in Homer.

After the fall of the city the ghost of Achilles claimed her as his share of the spoils, and his son Neoptolemus duly sacrificed, her on his father's tomb. Achilles' ghost had threatened the Achaeans with contrary winds: after the Trojan princess was slaughtered the favourable winds enabled them to sail.

Euripides, in his tragedy, *Hecuba*, places the story in Thrace, where the homeward bound Achaeans are becalmed. In the play Odysseus is once more the villain of the piece, insistent in his demand that Polyxena be sacrificed when Agamemnon might yield to Hecuba's entreaties and spare the girl.

See also *Hecuba* (Euripides).

Pomona The roman goddess of fruits and fruit-bearing trees. She had no festival, but a spot twelve miles outside the city, the *pomonal*, was sacred to her and she may, in origin, have been the goddess of a particular community. Her *flamen* was the lowest in rank of all the Roman priests.

Pomona had no mythology, though Ovid invented a story that she was wooed by an obscure Etruscan god, Vertumnus, who was honoured by those who engaged in trade. Vertumnus disguised himself as a harvester, and then as an old woman, to plead his own suit, and eventually won her love.

Pontifex Maximus In Roman religion, the Pontifices were the priests who assisted the kings in the performance of the duties of the state cults. They performed much the same service for state religion during the republic and the empire. They were the repositories of religious tradition, organised the observance of the state religion, and held the knowledge that gave order to the Roman calendar. The word itself – *pontifex* – means one skilled in the art of making or finding a way across a river. In tribal times he would no doubt have been a medicine man, which was not so far from being a priest.

The Pontifex Maximus was the chief of these, and as head of the priestly college appointed the Vestals, the *flamens,* and the *Rex Sacrorum* – the priest who took over the former kings' function in state religion and who was appointed for life.

The position of Pontifex Maximus was held by Julius Caesar, and thereafter by the reigning emperor until AD 375, when the Emperor Gratian declined it.

Portunus In Roman religion the god of Harbours – and probably also of city gates. He was an ancient deity and his exact function is not established, but he had an official feast day on 17 August and a *flamen* of his own.

Poseidon The son of Cronus and Rhea and the brother of Zeus and Hades. Poseidon, commonly thought of as a sea god, was a late holder of that office: he was in origin a god of people whose contact with the sea was minimal – he was an immigrant, so to speak, who found his way to Greece with the migrating peoples and kept forever his original epithets of 'earthshaker' and 'holder of the earth'. Those origins are implicit in his mythology, and the god who produced earth tremors could also, as the arriving Greeks came to see for themselves, cause the sea to recede before an earthquake happened. The holder of the earth would also be associated with its fertility, in his case with the waters – rain and rivers – that kept it alive. This aspect of Poseidon was the link with Demeter, the corn mother, which led to their apparently bizarre coupling as horse and mare. But that, too, stemmed directly from Poseidon's origins. As Poseidon *Hippios* (Lord of Horses), he brought with him his ancient association with fertility as the god of the herdsmen and horse keepers of a migrating race.

Like his brothers and sisters Poseidon was swallowed by their father, Cronus. Liberated by Zeus' successful rebellion, he was given the sea as his domain. The formal nature of that myth demonstrates that Poseidon effectively replaced the old god of the sea, Nereus, though the presence of both gods in Greek mythology can be very confusing.

It is as a sea god that Poseidon is best known: he plays a large part in both the *Iliad* and the *Odyssey* in that role. His consort was Amphitrite but he was as amorous as his brother Zeus, and his sexual adventures with both men and women are frequently an important element in familiar myths, such as those of Caenis, Pelops and Medusa. According to Homer *(Iliad, Book XV)* he is the younger brother of Zeus: Hesiod implies that Hades and Poseidon are the older.

Poseidon was widely worshipped in ancient Greece, both as a mariner's god and as the god of fresh water. He was propitiated as the god of earthquakes, and claimed by some as an ancestor god – particularly by noble families. The story of Theseus demonstrates how the idea could arise.

See also Amphitrite, Caenis, Demeter, *Iliad*, Medusa, *Odyssey*, Pelops, Theseus.

Priam King of Troy, Priam was the son of Laomedon and, according to Homer *(Iliad, Book XXIV)*, the father of fifty sons. Some of these were the children of Hecuba, his Queen; others were by various women – some of them concubines – and it is suggested by H. J. Rose that a vestige of Oriental character survives in his portrayal.

In the *Iliad* the gods seem favourably disposed to Priam: he is kind to everyone, even Helen, and he honours the gods. But the Fates are against him and he has deadly enemies in both Hera and Athene, as well as the inherited resentment of Poseidon, who was cheated by Laomedon.

Among Priam's children are Hector, Paris, Cassandra, Polyxena, Helenus, Polydorus and Troilus. The death of Hector is the cruellest blow suffered by the King in the *Iliad:* Achilles' despoliation of Hector's body leads to the memorable scene where Priam, alone, goes by night to the Achaean camp to ask Achilles to give him Hector's body for burial.

Priam's death in the fall of Troy is not part of the *Iliad* but is found in the fragments of an epic poem of a slightly later date. When the Achaeans stormed the city Priam and Hecuba took refuge with their daughters in the temple of Zeus. But Priam saw one of his younger sons, Polites, brought down and killed by Neoptolemus. The aged King seized a spear and attacked Neoptolemus, who thereupon dragged him from the temple and killed him. Priam's body was left to rot, without burial rites, on Achilles' grave.

See also Cassandra, Hector, Hecuba, Heracles, *Iliad,* Paris, Troy.

Priapus An ancient god of fertility, Priapus was a latecomer to the company of Greek gods: he was in origin a local deity of Lampsacus on the Hellespont. His symbol was the erect phallus, appropriately, though some representations show him as being the phallus itself – the other human attributes being incidental. His worship in Greece proper only dated from the time of Alexander the Great, about 330 BC, and some stories make him the son of Aphrodite and Dionysus.

The Greeks and the Romans rather liked their new god, and made him the guardian of their gardens, where his image – with explicit details – was frequently to be found.

Prometheus A Titan, the son of Iapetus and one of the daughters of Oceanus. Prometheus is a remarkable figure in Greek mythology – the first champion of man and, in some versions, his creator. His name means 'the foreseeing', and it is fascinating to speculate whether he was the product of reflective thinking, or in origin a culture-hero based on someone who actually existed. Probably the latter – he has parallels in other cultures – and lifted to a level of nobility by the literary genius of the Greeks: references to him are found in most of the classical poets, in Hesiod (both *Theogony* and *Works and Days),* and most memorably in Aeschylus' *Prometheus Bound.*

The tradition that Prometheus created man tells that he fashioned him out of clay at Panopea in Boeotia. He then persuaded Athene, at whose birth he had assisted, to breathe life into the images. But the more familiar myth has man already in existence, and Prometheus first acted on his behalf by ensuring that he should always have the better of any sacrifice to the gods. He made two bundles out of the carcass of an ox: for one bundle he wrapped the fat round the hide and bones, for the other he used the stomach, putting all the best meat inside. Zeus was asked to make his choice, and picked the succulent-looking one wrapped in fat – leaving man with the better part. The angry god, in retaliation, hid the knowledge of fire-making from mankind.

Prometheus championed man again. He stole fire from heaven and brought it back to earth hidden in a fennel stalk, where it smouldered long enough to be blown to life again. (In Aeschylus the fire is stolen from the forge of Hephaestus.) Then he began to teach man all the things that make him better than the beasts: how to build, how to use tools and metal, how to understand the positions of the stars, and how to use herbs for healing. Zeus watched all this from Olympus, his wrath growing. He sent for Hephaestus and ordered him to make a woman out of clay. Then he commanded Athene to breathe life into her, and called on the rest of the gods to make her irresistibly beautiful. She was called Pandora ('all-giving').

She was sent to earth, carrying with her a sealed jar. Zeus had planned her as the destroyer of mankind but he knew that Prometheus was far too astute to accept a gift from the gods. His brother Epimetheus ('afterthought') was more easily beguiled and, in spite of Prometheus' warnings, accepted her. Then, as Prometheus had feared, disaster came upon man – Pandora opened the jar. It contained every ill and failing that man is now heir to. One thing only was left inside: Hope, which gives man the will to go on while at the same time deceiving him.

Zeus' plan had almost succeeded. But in spite of its incomplete fulfilment there was something he could still do, and that was to punish his adversary, and make him submit to his will. Prometheus was seized by Kratos (strength) and Bia (force) and carried off to the mountains of the Caucasus. There Hephaestus chained him to a high rock on the orders of Zeus.

But Prometheus knew something that he refused to tell Zeus, and the king of the gods, full of vindictive fury, *knew* that he knew something. The secret was that Thetis, the Nereid, would bear a son destined to be greater than his father. Zeus and his brother Poseidon both had a fancy for Thetis – and a son of either born to Thetis could wreak havoc in the heavens. Zeus could be overthrown: he knew that he could be in danger from one of his sons but he needed to know the name of the mother. (Prometheus had been told the secret by Themis in some versions – but as 'the foreseeing' it was, in any case, something he would have known.)

Prometheus, exposed to the cruel mountain cold at night, was tormented by day by a vulture sent by Zeus. The bird tore at his liver, which healed by night. Prometheus was doomed to perpetual agony – unless he yielded up the secret. He refused; probably in the original myth he was doomed to remain chained to the rock for eternity, as the result of defying the gods. But the Greeks inevitably found a resolution – it was against their thinking that a champion of mankind should suffer eternally while the gods remained immovable. There had to be a reconciliation – even the gods had to learn to live with mankind. The resolution came in the shape of another champion – Heracles. Prometheus was released by him, and given immortality by the centaur, Chiron, who was in unceasing pain from the wound unwittingly inflicted on him by Heracles, his friend. Chiron accepted the mortality of Prometheus, and died in peace. Prometheus was reconciled to Zeus, and told him the secret upon which the maintenance of order depended.

Aeschylus' play, *Prometheus Bound,* is only one part of a trilogy dealing with the struggle with Zeus and, alas, the only part we have. It ends with Prometheus apparently doomed to the rock forever, and there is no way of knowing how the great tragedian resolved the struggle. The poet Shelley, in his *Prometheus Unbound,* makes the god the one who surrenders: but it is unlikely that his thought ran the same way as that of Aeschylus.

See also Chiron, Thetis, Zeus.

Proteus The ancient of the sea in Homer's *Odyssey* (Book IV). Proteus is a minor god who serves Poseidon and has the care of the sea creatures. He has the power to assume all manner of shapes when seized – but returns to his true one if steadfastly held. His knowledge is enormous and he is jealous of it: he changes his shape to escape the need to answer questions but will speak when his true shape returns.

Menelaus, becalmed off Egypt on his journey home from Troy, is advised by Eidothea, Proteus' daughter, on how to catch and question the sea god. Menelaus succeeds, and Proteus tells him that he is stranded because he was in too much of a hurry, and left Troy without proper honour to Zeus. After making the proper rites and sacrifices, Menelaus is able to sail home to Sparta.

Psyche The soul, and the name of the heroine in one of the best-known tales of Roman mythology. It appears in *The Golden Ass* of Lucius Apuleius (Books IV–VI).

The goddess Venus was jealous of the beauty of the Princess Psyche, and sent her son, Cupid, to make Psyche fall in love with some ugly or ungainly person. But Cupid fell in love with her himself. Psyche's father was told by an oracle that his beautiful daughter was to marry a winged serpent: the oracle must be obeyed, Psyche was to be conducted to the top of a hill and left there.

This was all done, but the frightened princess found herself carried off to a lovely valley and installed in a palace. Unseen hand-maidens prepared her for her wedding night, for which she was conducted to an unlighted room. There she heard the voice of her husband, though she did not see him, and from being frozen with terror she soon gave herself up to the embraces of a passionate lover. But he would not show himself: her nights were a delight but her days were lonely.

Her sisters visited her, and asked about her husband. Unable to tell them anything sensible, Psyche told them lies – and they saw through them. They suggested, spitefully, that he must be a monster indeed. This drove Psyche to disobey her unseen husband's wishes – she had to know what he looked like. That night, while he slept, she lit a lamp and saw him for the first time. He was none other than the god Cupid, who had been the author of the mysteries so that he could keep her for himself.

The god suddenly awoke, stung from sleep by a drop of burning oil which fell on his shoulder. He reproached her bitterly and left her, and went back to his mother. Venus, for her part, was determined that Psyche should suffer a great deal for the privilege of being loved by her divine son. The unhappy princess was roaming the earth, looking for her husband, and was evenutally found by Mercury and transported to the presence of the goddess of love, her rival in beauty. Psyche was pregnant, and Venus became even more spiteful when she saw it. The goddess confined her son, and made her daughter-in-law into a slave.

Psyche was beaten and starved, and given impossible tasks to perform. A huge heap of mixed grain had to be separated and sorted by nightfall: the ants took pity on the girl and did it for her. She was ordered to fetch some wool from some dangerous golden sheep: the pipes of Pan told her the sheep would be lulled to sleep in the heat of the afternoon, so the golden wool was easily obtained. Jupiter's eagle filled a jar for her when Venus ordered some icy water from the dragon-infested river that fed the Styx.

Venus tried again. She declared that her cares were wasting her beauty away: Psyche was given a box to take to the nether world, where she was to ask Proserpine to donate a little of her beauty to her sister goddess. Psyche wandered out on to the earth in despair, then she went to a high tower, determined to put an end to her impossibly unhappy life: but the tower itself spoke to her – she would soon be at the end of her trials and must not despair. She was told the way to the nether world.

Proserpine received her courteously, and took the box away to fill it, and soon Psyche was on her way back to the earth. But she was tempted to open the box and take a tiny pinch of beauty for herself, after all she had endured. She opened the box, and found no beauty there; instead a deep Stygian sleep swept over her and she collapsed on to the ground.

Cupid, meanwhile, had recovered from his burn, and escaped from his mother's watchful eyes. He found Psyche, and revived her, and she was able to deliver the box to Venus after all. Her lover, wasting no time, then went to Jupiter himself and begged him to intervene.

The king of the gods responded, well aware how often love had put him – Cupid's lord – into a difficult position. He decreed that the marriage of Cupid and Psyche should be celebrated lawfully, at once, and in heaven. Psyche was given a cup of nectar to drink, and so became an immortal, and this to some degree mollified the jealous Venus. She was less resentful of Psyche now that the girl was to be an immortal, instead of a mere human, and safely married.

Pyramus An ancient tale from Babylon, which is best known to us from the version given by Ovid in his *Metamorphoses*. It will be familiar to many from its use by Shakespeare in *A Midsummer Night's Dream*, as the subject of Bottom's entertainment.

Pyramus loved Thisbe, the girl who lived in the adjoining house. The lovers used to whisper endearments through a chink in the wall – their parents would not let them meet, having other marriage plans for them. But one day the lovers arranged a rendezvous by night, at the tomb of Ninus outside the city. There was a mulberry tree there, its white fruit overhanging a spring.

Thisbe arrived first – but while she sat and waited a lioness came, stealthily, still bloodied from the prey it had eaten. Thisbe fled into a cave nearby, leaving her cloak on the ground. The lioness drank, and, making its way back to the forest, came upon Thisbe's cloak, which it mauled with its bloodstained claws.

Pyramus, arriving on the scene, was alarmed to see the beast's footprints – and no sign of Thisbe. Then he found her cloak, with its red stains, torn to shreds. In that lonely spot at dead of night he believed her dead, and stabbed himself. His blood splashed the mulberies – they have all been dark red since that night – and he was dying when Thisbe found him. She joined him in death, and their sorrowing parents found the bodies lying together. They were buried together, their ashes placed in a single urn.

Q

Quirinus A Roman god who was probably, in origin, a war god of the Sabine people who lived in the area north-east of where Rome stands now, and who had a settlement on the Quirinal Hill. The Quirinal was later incorporated into the city of Rome, and its ancient deity into Roman religion. Quirinus was a state god, with Jupiter and Mars, but almost nothing of him or his worship is known though he has been named by some mythograpers as Romulus in his divine form. Quirinus had his own *flamen*, and his festival was celebrated on 17 February.

See also Romulus and Remus.

R

Rhadamanthus One of the sons born to Europa after her adventure with Zeus, and according to Homer (*Odyssey*, Book IV) the ruler of the Elysian Fields where favoured mortals went after departing this life.

Rhea The sister and, according to Hesiod, the unwilling consort of Cronus. She bore him Hestia, Demeter, Hera, Hades, Poseidon – and Zeus. Rhea saw her children swallowed by Cronus, who feared to be supplanted by one of them, and she gave him a stone to swallow in place of Zeus, the youngest, who eventually overthrew him.

Rhea had almost no cult of her own but she was identified with the Great Mother, the goddess of fertility who seemed to be a common focus of worship in the eastern Mediterranean and who had a number of names, and characteristics, which differed in detail from place to place. She was a goddess associated with Crete, and that led to the birth and infancy of Zeus being placed on that island.

See also Cronus, Zeus.

Robigus In Roman religion the *numen*, or spirit, of the red mildew or rust which attacks the growing corn. The pest was a very serious menace in an agricultural community, and propitiatory rites were performed on 25 April – when the ears were beginning to form – by the *flamen* of the god Quirinus. The festival was called the *Robigalia* and the rites included the sacrifice of a red, or rust coloured, dog and a sheep.

Romulus and Remus The twin brothers, who, according to legend, were the founders of Rome. The story is in fact a fairly late contrivance and cannot be traced, in most of its elements, farther back than the fourth century BC. The story which has come down to us is furthermore, H.J. Rose points out, very Greek in its form and ideas, and not

Latin – most of all in the idea of a god begetting mortal children, and one of those becoming a god.

The story begins in Alba Longa, a city founded by Ascanius, son of Aeneas. One of his descendants, King Numitor, was ousted from the throne by his younger brother, Amulius. The usurper, to bring an end to the lawful line of Numitor, seized his daughter, Rhea Silvia, and made her a Vestal so that she could never marry.

But the god Mars visited her – and Rhea Silvia bore twin sons. Amulius had her thrown into the Tiber, where she was received by the river god Tiberinus and made his consort: the twin babies were put into a box which was also thrown into the river. As it was, the Tiber was in flood, and the box drifted downstream, coming to rest near the foot of the Palatine Hill. The cries of the children attracted a she-wolf, which suckled them and saved their lives: a woodpecker also brought food to them in its bill (the wolf and the woodpecker were sacred to Mars).

Eventually a herdsman, Faustulus, found the twins and took them home to his wife, Acca Larentia, and they brought up the children as their own. The two boys grew up to be strong and stalwart young men – natural leaders, and one day were involved in a quarrel with some shepherds. This led to exploits more serious, and the shepherds managed to capture Remus, the younger twin, and take him to their employer for punishment. His foster-father, Faustulus, told Romulus what happened: more, he told him of his origins – Faustulus had to some extent guessed the truth. Now Remus was being brought before the landowner who was none other than the deposed King, Numitor, and Remus' grandfather.

Numitor was in fact very interested in the young man who stood before him – he had the wrong sort of bearing for a herdsman's son. Then another young man arrived, and Numitor sat looking from one to the other, the truth beginning to dawn. Romulus wasted no time in repeating what his foster-father had told him.

Grandfather and grandsons were soon allied, and Numitor was restored to his throne. Amulius was killed in the fighting and Alba Longa was at peace again. But the twins wanted a city of their own. They followed the Tiber upstream to where seven hills stood, one of them being the Palatine where they had been washed ashore. The new city would be built there but a question arose immediately concerning the choice of ruler – which twin should it be? One brother, Romulus, took up his station on the Palatine; Remus went to the Aventine, and both of them waited for a sign. When it came it was in favour of Romulus: six vultures flew over the Aventine, but twelve flew over the Palatine.

Romulus took formal possession of the Palatine by casting a lance from the Aventine – a distance of 250 yards; then he set to building the walls of the new city, which would be called after him, Roma. Remus, probably out of jealousy, was contemptuous of the new city being built by Romulus and his followers. He demonstrated that the walls were puny and useless by simply jumping over them – whereupon his brother in a rage killed him.

The city grew, and Romulus attracted new men to it by building a sanctuary on the Capitol hill for the outcast and the landless. Unfortunately they brought few women with them, and the people of neighbouring states refused to give their daughters in marriage, scorning the raw, upstart city on the Tiber.

The problem was solved by shameful means. The Sabine people were invited to the circus games to celebrate the new city, and the Romans promptly seized all the unmarried girls. The King of the Sabines, Titus Tatius, declared war.

Romulus was almost defeated, especially when the Capitol was lost through the treachery of Tarpeia, daughter of the commandant. An appeal to Jupiter Stator turned the tide, however, and the Sabines began to give way. A bloody and expensive battle was averted by the Sabine women themselves, when they rushed between the two armies and implored them to make peace.

The Sabines, after that, moved to Rome and the two peoples, with their two Kings, lived in harmony. Romulus lived for another forty years until one day, while he was reviewing his army, he disappeared in a sudden thunderstorm.

Romulus was eventually identified with Quirinus, the Sabine war god, and worshipped under that name.

See also Lupercalia, Mars, Quirinus.

Rumina A Roman goddess, the patron of nursing (suckling) mothers. Her shrine was at the foot of the Palatine hill, by the fig tree (*ficus ruminalis*) under which the she-wolf was believed to have suckled Romulus and Remus. Wine was never offered at her shrine, only milk.

S

Sarpedon King Priam's ally in the Trojan War, Sarpedon was the leader of the Lycian forces (*Iliad*, Book II).

He was the son of Zeus and Laodamia, daughter of Bellerophon, and was a staunch ally and brave warrior, taking a prominent part in the fighting (*Iliad*, Books VI and XII). His particular comrade is Glaucus, who mourns his death at the hands of Patroclus (Book XVI) and who fights desperately to stop the Achaeans from despoiling Sarpedon's body. His father Zeus, grieving for him too, has Apollo bear the body away from the battlefield so that it can be honourably buried in his homeland, Lycia.

Sarpedon was probably an ancient hero – there is strong evidence of a cult in Lycia in ancient times. A later tradition, which makes a connection with Crete by naming Sarpedon as one of the sons of Zeus and Europa, may point to the fame enjoyed by the original of Homer's valorous prince.

See also Glaucus, *Iliad*.

Saturn The god of agriculture ('the sower') in Roman religion, Saturn was probably a version of the Greek Cronus, reaching Rome by way of the Etruscans. His worship was different in detail from other Roman gods, notably in the manner of sacrifices to him which followed a Greek rather than a Roman pattern. His temple, at the foot of the Capitoline, housed the Roman treasury, the records of the law and the decrees of the Senate.

His festival was the *Saturnalia*, held from 17 to 19 December, and probably celebrated – though some scholars disagree – the autumn sowing. However that may have been it was a festival much looked forward to in Rome, a time of carefree merry-making when gifts were exchanged and slaves allowed temporary liberty, and with a Lord of Misrule (*Saturnalicius princeps*). The celebrations were transferred to the first day of the New Year some time in the fourth century AD and eventually became part of the traditional Christmas festivities after the pagan era came to an end.

Satyrs and Sileni The spirits of wild life in Greek religion, the satyrs were attendant on Dionysus. Often depicted with animal characteristics, they were sometimes lewd in their behaviour and bestial in their desires – but some myths make their older kindred, the Sileni, models of earthy wisdom, entrusted with the tutoring of Dionysus. Another tradition makes the god's companion a single character, Silenus.

Hesiod describes the satyrs as brothers of the Nymphs. Later tradition associated their frequently pictured characteristics – hoofs and sometimes horns – with Pan, and therefore with licence: they became identified as the symbol of male sexuality.

See also Dionysus, Midas.

Scylla The sea monster of Greek mythology who lived in a cave across the channel from the dangerous whirlpool of Charybdis. Homer merely says that she is immortal and can only be restrained by an appeal to her mother, Cratais or Hecate (*Odyssey*, Book XII), but does not disclose who was Scylla's other parent. She is described as a six-headed monster with twelve legs, who snatches seamen from their ships when they row too near her cave in an attempt to avoid Charybdis. She has a strange bark, like a yelping puppy.

Other traditions make her the daughter of Phorcys and Hecate, who was loved by Poseidon. The god's jealous wife, Amphitrite, poisoned the pool where Scylla used to bathe – and turned her into a monster, which is how she appears in both the *Odyssey* and the *Argonautica*.

The dangerous passage between Scylla and Charybdis has traditionally been placed in the Straits of Messina, for no better reason than that the location was a likely point in the passage of both Jason and Odysseus, and happened to be narrow. Scylla is often thought to be a magnification of the familiar Mediterranean octopus.

Sea Gods There is a confusion of sea gods in Greek mythology, but it will be found, by consulting the entries listed below, that time and tradition played a considerable part in the variation of their functions. Thus, while Poseidon is the most familiar and is found in the Heracles cycle, Nereus – an older god – appears there too. One sea god, Pontus, has no mythology whatever and can only be described as the sea personified.

See Glaucus, Nereus, Oceanus, Poseidon, Proteus, Triton.

Seasons, The In Greek mythology the Seasons (*Horae*) were, according to Hesiod, the three daughters of Zeus and Themis. They were attendant on the gods and, because of their ability to make things grow and flower, were always welcome as guests at Olympian festivals. They represented spring, summer and winter.

Selene The Moon in Greek mythology, Selene was the sister of Helios (the Sun) and Eos (the Dawn). According to Hesiod they were the children of the Titans Hyperion and Theia.

Selene drives a pair of horses on her journey through the night sky, and it was while following her course that she caught sight of the sleeping Endymion and fell in love with him. (The two-horse chariot is usually depicted but there are representations of her riding on horseback.)

The Endymion story is Selene's chief appearance in mythology: there is a fragment of a tale retold by Virgil of her seduction by Pan, who was said to have tempted her into the forest with a beautiful white fleece, and she was the goddess who afflicted Nemea with the lion which Heracles eventually killed. She had no cult of her own, but the Greeks held the moon in considerable awe nonetheless, believing that the time of the waxing moon was one of increase and prosperity and of growing physical passion. The waning moon was the negative phase, and Selene's return was anxiously awaited.

There was a confusion of Selene and Artemis in later classical times, probably because Apollo (Phoebus – 'the bright') was sometimes identified with the sun – his sister Artemis, therefore, was regarded as the moon. But the true sun and moon pair in Greek mythology are Helios and his sister Selene.

See also Diana, Endymion, Heracles, Labours of.

Seven Against Thebes, The One of the central episodes in the great Theban cycle of myths, and the subject of a tragedy by Aeschylus. The seven were the champions brought by Adrastus, King of Argos, to help Polynices, son of Oedipus, gain the throne of Thebes which was held by his brother Eteocles. The city of Thebes had seven gates: Eteocles set a champion to defend each one. Adrastus set a champion of his own to attack each one – and it was fated that ultimately the two brothers should be chief attacker and defender of the city.

The attackers were Adrastus, Eteocles, Tydeus of Calydon, Capaneus, Hippomedon, Parthenopaeus and Amphiaraus, the seer of Argos and the only one who knew that the venture was doomed. The defending Thebans were, at the Gate of Proetus, Melanippus; at the Electran Gate, Polyphontes; at the Neistan Gate, Megareus; at the Gate of Athene, Hyperbius; at the Borraean Gate, Actor; at the Homoloean Gate, Lasthenes. The Seventh Gate was defended by Eteocles himself when he heard that Polynices had marked it out as the point for his own attack.

The Electran Gate was attacked by Capaneus. He boasted that not even Zeus could stop him from taking the gate – whereupon the irritated god blasted him to ashes the moment he tried. This gave the Thebans the courage to counter-attack, and three gates, the Neistan, the Borraean and the Gate of Athene were made safe. At the Gate of Proetus, Tydeus was felled by Melanippus and lay half dead. Athene, his patroness, might have helped him – but in the meantime Amphiaraus had killed Melanippus. The seer threw his fallen enemy's head to Tydeus: it was a gesture of disgust, because Amphiaraus hated Tydeus. But the bloodthirsty Tydeus ate the brains from Melanippus' head, and Athene, revolted, let him die. Amphiaraus went on to his own point of attack, the Homoloean Gate.

Polynices, when he saw how badly the attackers fared, proposed to decide the issue in single combat with his brother Eteocles. Eteocles accepted the challenge – but it proved fatal to both of them: the curse of their father, Oedipus, was fulfilled. Everything now depended on the one Theban left of the royal house, Creon, the brother of the ill-fated Jocasta. He was equal to the occasion, and rallied the Thebans: the attackers were first thrown back, then routed. Adrastus fled from the field on the wonderful horse, Arion. Amphiaraus, fleeing in his chariot from the war he never wanted to fight, was in danger of death from the spear of a pursuing Theban: but Zeus recognised him as a just man and took him from the world by cleaving the ground by the river Ismenus with a thunderbolt. Amphiaraus went to reign among the dead, and the spot by the river became a famous oracular shrine.

But it was not the end of the troubles of the city of Thebes. Creon, victorious, was determined that the shade of Polynices should find no rest. He had dishonoured his own city, therefore his corpse would lie in the dust, a meal for carrion eaters. Antigone, the sister of Eteocles and Polynices, was determined that her brother should have the essential burial rites. The story is continued in the entry for *Antigone* (Sophocles).

See also Adrastus, Alcmaeon, Amphiaraus, Antigone, Epigoni, Oedipus.

Sibyl The name given to a female prophet. Though the exact origin and meaning of the name is lost, the earliest use of it is attributed to Heraclitus, a Greek philosopher of the sixth century BC. It was not used by the Greeks in the sense familiar to us, probably because their oracles, such as that of Delphi, were of great antiquity and the priestesses already had names.

There appears to have been more than one 'Sibyl' by the fourth century BC, and it is in Roman mythology (the *Aeneid*, Book VI, for instance) that they make the strongest impression. Ovid, in his *Metamorphoses*, makes the Cumaean Sibyl one of the loves of Apollo. Varro, a Roman writer of the second century BC, names no less than ten Sibyls – but it is plain from their names that some of them are really the priestesses of Greek oracles (Delphic, Samian, Hellespontic). The most famous one is the Sibyl of Cumae, immortalised by Virgil.

At Monte Cuma, near Naples, on the site of ancient Cumae, the chamber of the Sibyl was identified in 1932. It was reached by a corridor cut in the side of the mountain through a distance of 375 feet. The ceiling of the cutting is no less than 60 feet high.

For the strange intrusion of the Sibyl into Christianity, see the entry for Virgil.

See also *Aeneid*, Book VI.

Sibylline Books The utterances of the Sibyls were recorded, it is believed, but the ones that survive are of a late date – none is older than the second century BC – and are notable for their strong Judaeo-Christian tone. Legend says that the Cumaean Sibyl offered nine books of oracles to the Roman King, Tarquinius Superbus. But he regarded the price as too high, and refused, whereupon the Sibyl burned three of them. She offered him the remaining six; again he refused, and she burned three more. He bought the surviving three – and at the original price.

The Sibylline Books were entrusted to the care of two noblemen, this number of custodians being later increased to ten – five of whom were commoners. Finally, in the first century BC, the number was increased to fifteen, whose responsibility it was to consult the oracles at the direction of the Roman Senate, in the hope of avoiding the gods' displeasure in any undertaking. The books were kept in a vault under the temple of Jupiter on the Capitoline but were destroyed in the fire of 83 BC. A collection of oracles was then gathered afresh from shrines throughout the classical world, and used in the same way as the original Sibylline Books.

The new oracles were housed on the Palatine, in the temple of Apollo, by the Emperor Augustus, and there they stayed until the fifth century AD. Their fate is uncertain but they were possibly destroyed by Stilicho, the great Christian general of the reigns of Theodosius the Great and Honorius, when the former imposed orthodoxy throughout the empire.

Silvanus In Roman religion the god of uncultivated land. *Silvanus* is more an adjective than a name and the god referred to was feared in the way that unnamed deities tended to be in the ancient world – also the ground beyond the cultivated area of a primitive agricultural settlement could harbour many dangers, both real and imaginary. The extension of settled land involved the propitiation of Silvanus in a threefold ceremony: on behalf of the new boundary, the herdsmen, and the dwelling.

Silvanus was often identified with Pan and the Satyrs: his name also occurs as a title of Mars, who was originally a spirit of vegetation.

See also Mars.

Sirens, The In the *Odyssey* (Book XII), Circe warns Odysseus about the Sirens, past whose rock he will have to steer his ship. They live in a meadow filled with the bones of men who perished, drawn to the rock by the irresistible lure of the Siren's song. Circe refers to the *twin* Sirens' voices, and a celebrated vase painting shows two – one of them falling to her death because a mortal, Odysseus, has been able to resist her song. He is bound to the mast, while his men – their ears safely stopped with wax – row on to safety.

Homer never said that the Sirens were birds with the faces of beautiful women, but the idea – seen on vase paintings – was firmly rooted by the time of Apollonius Rhodius, who describes them thus, (without saying how many they were), and names them as the daughters of Terpsichore by the river god Achelous (*Argonautica*, Book IV). The

Argonauts are able to resist the Sirens because they have Orpheus on board – his song is sweeter than theirs. But one man, Butes, unable to resist them, leaps overboard and starts to swim to their rock: Aphrodite saves him by snatching him from the waves.

It is difficult to establish what the Sirens might have represented to the ancient Greeks. Modern psychology might see them as the personification of the death-wish but they probably form part of the manifold association of winged creatures with death that existed among primitive peoples. The soul itself was believed to leave the body, upon death, in the form of a bird.

Sisyphus The son of Aeolus and grandfather of Bellerophon, Sisyphus is described by Homer as being as cunning a rogue as ever man was (*Iliad*, Book VI). He turns up again in the *Odyssey* (Book XI): Odysseus relates how he encountered him in the nether world, condemned to push a great boulder to the top of a hill perpetually – when he got it to the summit the weight would send it crashing down, and Sisyphus would start again.

As so often happens in Homer, the reader is left with a gap in what he learns; in this case exactly what crime Sisyphus was being punished for – the detail has been lost in the passing of hundreds of years. He is a curious figure, considerable enough to have earned a shrine, the Sisypheion, on the Acrocorinth: this fact, together with his connection with Corinth (though in Homer he is an Argive), suggest that he was a popular folk hero and noted, among other things, for his wits. The most famous story tells how he got the better of Death (*Thanatos*).

When Zeus' lustful eye lighted on Aegina, her father Asopus was warned by Sisyphus. Zeus got his way, inevitably, but he nursed a spiteful feeling toward Sisyphus and sent Thanatos to fetch him. Thanatos produced manacles, but Sisyphus beguiled him into demonstrating how they were used – and locked up Thanatos. Zeus was obliged to send Ares from Olympus to unbind Death – no one on earth was dying in the meantime.

Sisyphus used the respite to extend his plans – he told his wife Merope to leave his body unburied. So when the angry Thanatos came for him a second time he surrendered in apparent resignation. As soon as he arrived in the nether world, however, he went straight to Hades (Persephone, in one version) and complained bitterly of his dishonoured corpse and his impious wife. Hades, the just god, allowed him to go back to earth to punish his wife, and arrange a decent burial . . . and Sisyphus was able to have a joyful reunion with his wife – he had no intention whatever of going back to the nether world, and lived to a comfortable old age.

See also Aegina, Hades.

Sophocles Of the life of Sophocles little is known, certainly no more than is known of the lives of the other two great tragic poets of ancient Greece. But his name, like theirs, stands at the summit of greatness in European literature and his difference from both Aeschylus and Euripides is one more testament to the richness of artistic life in Athens.

Sophocles was born at Colonus, near Athens, about 496 BC, the favoured son of a wealthy house. Such evidence as we have is unanimous in recording his gifts as a musician and a dancer, as well as testifying to his amiable nature and his remarkable good looks. He appeared in his own plays at first, but gave it up because he believed his voice was not strong enough for the demands of an actor's career. His first prize came at the age of twenty-eight – won from no less a competitor than Aeschylus himself.

As an Athenian citizen he took his duties seriously. He was twice a general, treasurer to the city, and an active colleague of Pericles during that statesman's lifetime. He was an officiating priest, and a devotee of Asclepius. He was in complete harmony with the religion of his time, and this acceptance is very marked in his plays, in contrast to the profound questioning of Aeschylus and the stormy criticism of Euripides. Sophocles' concern was with his craft, and the works of his which we possess demonstrate the fact that really great plays are not only marvellous theatre but rich in their observation of the human condition.

Of the 123 plays which he is believed to have written we possess only seven: *Ajax*, *Antigone*, *The Women of Trachis*, *Oedipus*, *Electra*, *Philoctetes* and *Oedipus at Colonus*, which was produced after his death. Sophocles introduced the third actor into his scenes – and drama took another great step forward – and made the part played by the Chorus a more integral part of the action. He lived to the age of ninety, his creative energy unimpaired. Classical Greece, as Professor Kitto points out, was favourable to long life and sustained energy.

See also Aeschylus, *Antigone*, *Electra*, Euripides, *Oedipus*, *Oedipus at Colonus*.

Sphinx Originating in Egypt, where it was probably a representation of royalty (the body of a lion with the head of a man), the idea of this mythological monster found its way to Greece from the near East – where it had in the meantime undergone the change that made Sphinxes into women. In Greece it was connected with death and was believed to be present at fatal combats; it also became a familiar motif for the decoration of tombs.

Hesiod makes the Sphinx the child of Echidna and Orthrus, the monstrous dog of Heracles' Tenth Labour, and makes her the specific curse of Thebes which was overthrown by Oedipus.

See also Echidna, Heracles, Labours of, Oedipus.

Styx The principal river of the nether world, Styx was a daughter of Oceanus and aided Zeus in his quarrel with the Titans. The real river Styx bore the honour connected with the mythological one, and was in fact the medium for oath-taking even in historical times. An oath by Styx was held to be inviolable.

In spite of its religious connection (the name means 'abhorrent') the real river is insignificant, a little tributary of the river Crathis which flows into the Gulf of Corinth.

T

Tages This strange figure is known to us from Latin writers but belongs to the older and more mysterious world of the Etruscans. He was a sort of divine child, the bearer of wisdom to mankind in the field of divination and augury. According to the myth, a farmer named Tarchon was ploughing in the fields near Tarquinia, when a child rose from a furrow. He proclaimed himself the grandson of Jupiter, and he taught the magic lore to the Etruscan people.

Talos The bronze giant of the *Argonautica,* Talos may have originally been a god – *Talaios* was a Cretan title of Zeus. In mythology he was the creation of the god Hephaestus, who constructed him for Minos to guard his island kingdom. He kept strangers away by using rocks as missiles: if any landed on the island Talos, who was invulnerable to fire, could make himself red hot and kill them simply by seizing them. His vital fluid was sealed by a membrane in his foot, and this was the means by which Medea defeated him in the *Argonautica* (Book IV). Another version relates how Medea promised him a draught of immortality, and gave him a drugged drink instead. While he lay in a stupor she prised out the bronze nail in his foot, and his life seeped away.

In the myth of Daedalus, Talos is the name of the nephew, his apprentice, whom Daedalus murdered out of jealousy.

See also *Argonautica, Daedalus.*

Tantalus The father of Pelops and Niobe, Tantalus was a fittingly evil ancestor for the Pelopid house. He was King of Sipylus in Lydia and, according to some versions, a son of Zeus. In most versions he enjoys the gods' favour, is frequently their guest, and his kingdom is immensely rich.

His part in Greek mythology is mostly concerned with offences against the gods. He stole the food of the gods and gave it to mortals, and he served his son's flesh in a banquet to which he had invited the gods. He was punished with the ruin of his kingdom and, since he had eaten the food of the gods and was immortal, was condemned to live in eternal punishment in Tartarus. Odysseus observes him there (*Odyssey,* Book XI), standing in a pool of water up to his chin – but mad with thirst because the water recedes whenever he bends his head to drink. He suffers eternal hunger, too: over his head are the boughs of trees, laden with fruit – but when he tries to grasp them the wind blows them out of reach.

See also *Pelops.*

Telephus The son of Heracles and the Tegean princess, Auge. The King made his daughter a priestess of Athene, an office that required her to remain chaste. But Heracles visited Tegea, and Auge found him irresistible.

The angry goddess Athene sent a pestilence to Tegea – Auge had not only dishonoured her office, she had done so in Athene's shrine – and the King went to the oracle at Delphi to discover the reason. Learning it, he stormed back to Tegea and ordered his daughter to be sold as a slave: if a child was born it was to be exposed. A child was born, and exposed on Mount Parthenion: Auge was bought by some merchants, who in turn sold her to King Teuthras of Mysia, a kingdom some distance south of Troy.

The baby boy was found by shepherds, being suckled by a hind. They gave him the name Telephus ('suckled by a hind'), and he was brought up at the court of their master, King Corythus. When he grew to manhood he began to search for his mother, and was advised by the oracle to visit King Teuthras. Auge, by then married to the King, recognised her son at once by his resemblance to his father, Heracles. The King, who had no son, welcomed Telephus to his court and gave him his daughter Argiope in marriage. Eventually, Telephus inherited the kingdom.

The peace of Telephus' kingdom was disturbed by the Achaeans, who crossed the sea to fight the Trojan War: they believed they had reached Troy and Telephus, defending his people, was wounded by Achilles. When they realised their mistake, the Achaeans returned to Aulis – but Telephus was left with a wound in the thigh that would not heal. At last he consulted an oracle, and learned that the healing must come from the instrument that gave the wound.

Telephus set out for the Achaeans' camp at Aulis and sought out Achilles, and the rust from his spear was applied to the wound. Eventually it healed, and in gratitude Telephus guided the Achaean fleet safely to Troy.

Tellus   A Roman earth goddess, Tellus had a festival of her own but no *flamen,* and is believed to have been a popular fertility deity dating back to long before the formalised religion of the Roman state. Her festival was the *Fordicidia* on 15 April, at which a pregnant cow was sacrificed to promote increase among the cattle and in the fields. The unborn calves were burnt; their ashes were kept for use in the *Parilia* festival – for the purification of shepherds and flocks – which followed six days later on 21 April.

Tethys   According to Hesiod the daughter of Uranus and Gaia, and the sister and wife of Oceanus. She was the mother of the Oceanids, and of Styx.

Teucer   The half-brother of great Ajax, and his companion in arms in the Trojan War. Teucer was a famous archer and plays an important part in the defence of the Achaean camp in the *Iliad* (Book VIII), bringing down numbers of Trojans until Hector manages to put him out of the fight with a carefully aimed stone that breaks Teucer's collar bone; but he returns to the field (Book XI) fighting alongside Ajax as always.

Teucer was absent from the Achaean camp during the madness of Ajax, and returned to find him dead by his own hand. Menelaus wanted Ajax's corpse left unburied, because of his deeds against his comrades during his madness. Teucer gave him short shrift and Ajax was honourably buried, but their father Telemon blamed Teucer for his brother's death declaring that Teucer should have been there to support Ajax's claim to the arms of Achilles.

After the fall of Troy Teucer returned home to Salamis, but the unforgiving Telemon refused to let him land. In exile, Teucer made his way to Cyprus and settled there. The city of Salamis on the island was founded by Teucer.

See also Ajax I, *Iliad*.

Thamyris A poet and musician who makes a brief appearance in the *Iliad* (Book II), where he is described as a Thracian. he had boasted that he could out-sing the Muses themselves, and they met him at Dorian in Messenia. The daughters of Zeus struck him blind for his presumption, and robbed him of his gifts as a musician.

Themis A daughter of Gaia, according to Hesiod, and the second consort of Zeus. She was the mother of the Seasons and the Fates, and in some versions of Prometheus. The meaning of her name ('steadfast') led to her being regarded more as an abstraction (order, justice, law) than as a goddess, and she was invoked as a guardian of oaths. But as an earth goddess, sometimes identified with Gaia (Earth) herself, Themis had various traditions associated with her. The most persistent was that the oracle at Delphi was hers before the birth of Apollo, and she was generally regarded as a prophetess.

See also Prometheus, Zeus.

Theogony Hesiod's history and genealogy of the gods. The poem, in 1022 lines, is the story of the world from Chaos to the establishment of Zeus as the king of the gods, and is a perpetually quoted source for mythographers. Hesiod is believed to have written his *Theogony* about

800 BC – the real date is impossible to ascertain – while some writers, including Herodotus, made him contemporary with Homer.

See also Hesiod.

Theseus The hero of Athens. The character of Theseus could be based on a real person; but the principal accounts of him as written are fairly late and there are echoes of the myths of Heracles in the Theseus stories. Classical scholars generally agree that parts of an earlier epic cycle have been used to serve a second hero, and that Theseus (a mythological hero of ancient, pre-Trojan War times) was subjected by the Athenians to an elaborate 'treatment' to make him a fitting ancestor hero for their city. And it must be said that the Athenians succeeded – Theseus has as secure a place in heroic myth as Heracles and Odysseus. (Odysseus encounters Theseus, briefly, in Hades. *Odyssey, Book XI.*)

For the story of his begetting, see the entry for Aegeus.

When her son was sixteen the Princess Aethra of Troezen took him a short way out of the city to a rock that stood by the road. She asked him to lift it, if he could. The boy, Theseus, did so without trouble, and found beneath it a sword and a pair of sandals. His mother explained that the tokens had been placed there by Aegeus, King of Athens. Theseus was his son and his heir: now that he had recovered the tokens he had only to take them to Aegeus and claim his birthright.

Theseus could have made his way to Athens by a short and comfortable sea voyage but, conscious now of his destiny, he decided to travel by land over the dangerous Isthmus road that joined the Peloponnese to Attica. It would give him his first chance of adventure; he was confident of his strength and skill as a wrestler, and aware of the strange rumours at the court of his grandfather, King Pittheus, which spoke of another sire, the god Poseidon.

His first test came before he had travelled very far, at Epidaurus. There he got the better of the evil cripple Periphetes, who waylaid travellers and killed them with a huge brass club. Theseus' dexterity helped him dodge the attack, and he killed Periphetes, with his own club. But he was no sooner on the Isthmus road when he had to fight another killer, Sinis, who was strong enough to bend pine trees down to the ground. Theseus killed him, too, and the brigand Sciron, who kicked the bodies of his victims into the sea. Theseus kicked him into the sea. At Crommyon, he found the people in dread of a savage and monstrous sow that ravaged their fields and had killed some of them.

Theseus killed the sow, called Phaea after the old woman who had unwittingly bred it, and earned the gratitude of the people. He was now in Attica, the country of which Athens was the chief city.

Continuing on his way, he came to Eleusis, where he was challenged to a wrestling match by the King, Kerkyon, who had never been defeated and who always killed his opponents. Theseus proved his match, and Eleusis had no king from that day on, coming under the leadership of Athens. The wrestling ground of Kerkyon was a famous site in Eleusis.

Athens was in view by now, the road continuing there from Eleusis, but Theseus had one more peril to overcome. A son of the evil Sinis kept a lodging house by the Athens road and Theseus rested there, not knowing that his host, Procrustes, was a madman who tried to fit his guests to his bed. If they were too long he hacked off their feet, or their head; if they were too short he stretched them on a rack. Once more Theseus' skill as a wrestler saved his life, enabling him to over-power the madman, and kill him. Theseus had cleansed the road of its dangers and he travelled on to Athens.

During the years which had passed since the birth of Theseus, Aegeus had given refuge to Medea, the royal sorceress of Colchis who had to flee from Corinth after killing the King of that city, and his daughter, in a jealous rage. Aegeus had fallen victim to Medea's charms and had married her; they had a son, a boy called Medus. Medea knew who Theseus was, but she kept the truth from Aegeus. She persuaded him that the stranger was an adventurer, looking for a throne, and that he must be removed.

She first thought to destroy him by telling Aegeus to send him against the great Cretan bull which was terrorising the people of Marathon. Heracles had brought it to Hellas as one of his Labours and set it free in Argos: it had found its way across the Isthmus and was now roaming loose. Theseus accepted the challenge, and at Marathon was shown kindness by an old woman, Hecale, before he began his fight with the great beast. He won the fight and returned to the old woman's house for refreshment: but the kind old creature was dead, and Theseus honoured her memory in Athens with the Hecalesian Rites.

Aegeus then allowed Medea to plan the stranger's death by poison, and invited him to the palace so that the deed could be carried out. Medea wanted the throne for her own son and when Theseus arrived at the palace she had a goblet of poisoned wine ready to offer him.

But the plan misfired. Aegeus recognised the sword of Cecrops which the young man wore at his side – and dashed the poisoned wine from his hand. Medea had to flee from Athens with her son, and Theseus was at last in his kingdom.

It was then that Aegeus told him of the dread which hung over the city. Years before, Androgeus, the son of Minos, King of Crete, had been murdered in Athens, suspected of a plot. Minos exacted a heavy penalty for the death of his son: each year seven youths and seven maidens were taken from Athens to die in the Minotaur's lair in the Labyrinth. A ship with black sails carried them away from their homes.

In spite of his father's anguished pleas, Theseus determined to take his place as one of the seven youths on the next tribute ship. The Minotaur must be killed, somehow, and the dreadful traffic brought to an end. He promised Aegeus that he would return safely, and his father would know all was well by the sight of the ship returning with white sails.

Minos was at the harbour to see the ship arrive in Crete, and his overbearing manner provoked an exchange with Theseus, who warned him not to presume on his power even with his victims; he declared that Poseidon was his protector, and would have to be reckoned with. Minos regarded him with scorn for a moment; then he drew a gold ring from his finger and threw it into the sea. He turned to Theseus and told him to retrieve it – that should be easy enough, for a son of Poseidon? Theseus leapt into the sea at once, and swam down to the depths. Poseidon's consort, Amphitrite, had sent the Nereids skimming around the sea bed and they had brought the ring to her. She handed it to Theseus, who shot to the surface and confounded King Minos by restoring it to him.

One of the bystanders during the scene at the harbour was Minos' eldest daughter, Ariadne. She fell in love with the handsome Athenian, and that night she sought him out. She explained that the most fearful thing he faced was the Labyrinth – no one ever escaped from its maze of crossing and twisting corridors: the Minotaur devoured them at his leisure since they were too starved and exhausted to put up a fight. Theseus had to defeat the Labyrinth before he could defeat the Mino-taur. Ariadne gave him a ball of stout thread she had concealed in her dress, then she took him to the entrance of the Labyrinth, where she had concealed a sword. She fixed one end of the thread to the lintel and gave the ball to Theseus: then she waited while he made his way into the gloom, unrolling the thread as he went.

Theseus killed the Minotaur, and released the other tribute youths and maidens. The tribute ship, at his request, had been standing off-shore, and was ready to embark the fugitives when they raced down to the harbour, Ariadne with them.

On the way home the ship put in at Naxos where, unaccountably, Theseus abandoned Ariadne. (A detail of the myth is missing – but see the entry for Ariadne.) Another call was made at Delos, where the returning Athenians performed a ritual dance to celebrate their deliverance: the people of Delos continued the ritual annually, thus commemorating the adventure.

They headed for home, where King Aegeus, tormented with anxiety, stood on a cliff top, day after day, hoping for his son's safe return. Then the tribute ship returned, with black sails, and the King in his grief threw himself to his death in the sea. The horrified Theseus remembered, too late, his promise to return with white sails.

The sea got its name from Aegeus, King of Athens, and has been called the Aegean ever since. Theseus became king in his father's place, and strengthened the position of Athens by bringing under his dominion the other towns of Attica, Megara and Eleusis. He invited people with useful skills to come to Athens and become citizens; he instituted the Isthmian Games, and put them under the patronage of Poseidon.

As King of Athens his adventures continued. He defeated an invasion by the Amazons, and made their Queen, Hippolyta, his wife. She bore him a son, Hippolytus. The Lapith King, Pirithous, invaded Marathon: but he and Theseus took a liking to each other and became firm friends. Theseus and Pirithous shared the adventure of the Calydonian boar hunt, the abducting of the beautiful Helen, and the subsequent adventure in Hades when Pirithous tried to steal Persephone – the adventure was fatal to Pirithous, and Theseus would have shared his fate if Heracles had not saved him (the encounter in the *Odyssey* suggests that Theseus *did* share his friend's fate). In the meantime the Dioscuri had invaded Athens and rescued their sister Helen.

During his reign Theseus' power came to be widely acknowledged in Hellas, and he used it to good account. He forced Creon, King of

Thebes, to give honourable burial to the fallen enemy after the attack by Polynices (the Seven Against Thebes); he guaranteed the sanctuary of King Oedipus in the last hours of his life, and cared for Heracles after the attack of madness when he killed his wife and children.

After the death of his wife, Hippolyta, Theseus sent his son to King Pittheus of Troezen, who made him his heir, and then married the Princess Phaedra of Crete, who was Ariadne's younger sister. That princess became the victim of Aphrodite – the goddess was jealous of the devotion shown to Artemis by Hippolytus, and made Phaedra fall in love with him. The subsequent tragedy (see the entry for *Hippolytus*) deprived Theseus of both wife and son, and was the beginning of the end of his heroic life. In Athens, a descendant of the ancient line of Erectheus, Menesthius, had returned during the invasion by the Dioscuri when they rescued Helen, and he succeeded in raising a rebellion against Theseus. The rebellion was successful, and the Athenians banished their King.

Theseus set sail for Crete, now ruled by Phaedra's brother, Deucalion, who had promised him refuge. The ship was blown off course and took shelter on the island of Scyros, where long ago Theseus had inherited a small estate. King Lycomedes of Scyros made him welcome but he had no intention of harbouring an ageing and broken King who could lay claim to land in his kingdom. He persuaded Theseus to walk with him on a fine day, ostensibly to show him his estate from a high rock. He threw Theseus from the height, and put it abroad that his guest, no longer sure-footed, had fallen to his death.

In historical times some bones of great size were discovered on the island of Scyros, and the statesman Cimon declared them to be the remains of Theseus. He had them brought to Athens, and a hero's shrine built to house them (about 474 BC). It was strange that Cimon could have persuaded the Athenians – or himself, for that matter – that there was any truth in the idea. Theseus was frequently shown in Greek art as a trim, athletic man, not as a giant at all, and nowhere do the myths suggest that he was of enormous size.

Theseus was a favourite character of the tragedians – Athenians themselves – and makes a number of appearances in the plays.

See also Aegeus, Ariadne, *Heracles* and *Hippolytus* (Euripides), Minos, *Oedipus at Colonus* (Sophocles), Pirithous.

Thetis One of the Nereids, the sea-nymph daughters of Nereus. Thetis was fated to bear a son who would be greater than his father. The knowledge of this was gained by Themis, who disclosed it to her son, Prometheus, who in turn only disclosed it as the price of his freedom. Both Zeus and Poseidon were hopeful of the love of Thetis, and Prometheus could see that the consummation of that love, if it resulted in a son, would bring disaster to Olympus.

Once the knowledge was revealed to Zeus, he determined that Thetis should marry a mortal. The husband chosen was Peleus, the son of Aeacus, and the son born to them was Achilles. Like her son, Thetis plays a large part in Homer's *Iliad*, where she has the status of a goddess.

See also Achilles, *Iliad,* Peleus, Prometheus.

Tiberinus The river god of the Tiber, and much honoured by the Romans who knew perfectly well the importance of the river Tiber in their lives. His shrine was on an island in the river, and his festival was held on 27 August when he was called Volturnus ('rolling river'). The festival was called the *Volturnalia*.

Tiresias The blind seer of Thebes, and an arresting figure in Greek mythology. Tiresias was known to both Homer and Hesiod. He was part of the Theban epic cycle and Sophocles uses him to striking effect in *Oedipus,* where his unshakable authority as both prophet and seer creates the first breaches in the King's certainty. He also appears in two plays by Euripides, *The Bacchae* and *The Phoenician Women.* The character drawn by the two tragedians is very much the one to be expected from his appearance in Homer: in the *Odyssey* (Book X) Circe tells Odysseus that he must consult the shade of Tiresias – the great man's wisdom is unimpaired by death. In Book XI, in the nether world, the encounter takes place.

Tiresias was a descendant of the Spartoi, the sown men of Cadmus: his parents were Eueres and the nymph, Chariclo. According to Hesiod he lived for seven generations, and was once walking on Mount Cyllene when he came upon two snakes coupling. They attacked him and he killed the female – and was turned into a woman. He remained one long enough to acquire knowledge unique in the experience of man, until he passed the same spot on Mount Cyllene years later. Two snakes were again coupling, and again they attacked him. This time he killed the male – and became a man once more.

He was asked to mediate in a quarrel between Zeus and Hera, who were both declaring that the other's sex got the more pleasure out of physical love. Only Tiresias could know the answer, and he said at once that women got the most pleasure out of love – whereupon Hera struck him blind. His gifts as a seer, and his long life, were bestowed on him by Zeus in compensation.

Tiresias died when the Thebans retreated from the city during the attack of the Epigoni. On the journey he died of a chill, probably caught through drinking the icy waters of the Tilphussa spring.

The figure of Tiresias is probably a mythological realisation of the particular quality of a man who is out of the ordinary. Just as a lame man could become essential to a community if he had skill with metals (and become a god – see the entry for Hephaestus), so the blind man with his highly developed touch and hearing would acquire a definite respect from those around him.

See also *The Bacchae* (Euripides), Epigoni, *Odyssey, Oedipus* (Sophocles).

Titans   The children of Uranus and Gaia, and generally the race of gods – though there is no tradition of their being worshipped – who held sway before the ascendancy of Zeus and the Olympians. Hesiod gives their names as Oceanus, Coeus, Crius, Hyperion, Iapetos, Theia, Themis, Mnemosyne, Phoebe, Tethys, Cronus and Rhea: the last named were the parents of Zeus.

See also Cronus, Gaia, Rhea, Uranus, Zeus.

Tithonus   The son of Laomedon, King of Troy, and brother of Priam. He was loved by the goddess Eos (dawn), who was captivated by his looks and who bore him a son, Memnon, one of the heroes of the Trojan war. Eventually Eos carried Tithonus off to Olympus and begged Zeus to make him immortal. Zeus did so – but Eos had forgotten to ask Zeus to make him ageless as well.

Tithonus degenerated physically but did not die, eventually subsiding into a shrivelled thing which was little more than a disembodied voice.

See also Eos, Memnon.

Tityus   The son of Gaia and a giant, Tityus attempted to assault Leto, the mother of Apollo and Artemis, when she went to Delphi. Apollo, or both Apollo and Artemis, or in yet another version, Zeus, killed him. Odysseus sees him bound in Hades (*Odyssey,* Book XI), covering nine acres of ground, Vultures feed on his liver eternally.

Triton The son of Poseidon and Amphitrite, and one of the minor sea gods of Greek mythology. He was often portrayed as a sort of merman, human above the waist and fish below. He is best known for his assistance to Jason and the Argonauts.

See *Argonautica* (Book IV).

Troilus One of the sons of Priam and Hecuba. This Trojan prince is only mentioned by Homer once – *Iliad* (Book XXIV) – where his father tells of his death. Another story from a later myth relates that he was killed by Achilles quite early in the fighting.

The story of Troilus and Cressida (Chryseis) which appears in the work of Chaucer and Shakespeare comes from the medieval romance *Le Roman de Troie,* which was itself based on a late Latin version of the events of the Trojan War.

Trojan Women, The A tragedy by Euripides, first produced in 415 BC. Athens and Sparta had been at war for sixteen years, and feeling both against and in favour of the war ran very high in Athens. In the year before the production of this play Athens had been guilty of an appalling crime in the destruction of the people of Melos. The island, traditionally friendly to Sparta, had refused Athens' demand for a contribution to her war effort, not acknowledging the city's hegemony. The Athenians attacked and captured Melos, slaughtered every man on the island, and sold the women and children as slaves. There is little doubt that Euripides was portraying to his fellow Athenians, through the setting of the fallen Troy, the consequences of what they had done. (It should be remembered that the Trojans were of the same race as their destroyers, just as the people of Melos were as much Greeks as the Athenians.)

The play opens with the god Poseidon watching the plundered city he once helped to build, and reflecting on how the resolution of Hera and Athene has helped bring about its destruction after ten years of siege. But Athene comes to him and now asks his help in destroying the victors themselves – they have dishonoured her sanctuary and now she wants Poseidon's help to make them pay. He promises her that the Achaeans will suffer a stormy voyage in their homebound ships, and that few will survive.

The gods leave the scene, which is occupied now by Hecuba, the Queen of defeated Troy and Priam's widow, who is trying hard to face the worst. The fate of a slave is all that she can expect, if she is allowed to live. She mourns her sons, and rages against Helen, the cause of the war. But she has a new agony to face – what will happen to her daughters? The women of Troy, bereft of homes, husbands and children, all share the same future and they gather round their Queen.

The play then divides into a series of episodes, with only Hecuba and the chorus of Trojan women present throughout, the Achaean herald Talthybius appearing at intervals to bring news of how their lives will be disposed. His first announcement concerns Hecuba's daughter, Cassandra.

Agamemnon wants her. She is a consecrated priestess – but that is nothing to him. A princess of the defeated house will be his concubine. Andromache, Hector's widow, will go to Achilles' son, Neoptolemus – he has acquitted himself nobly in the war and Andromache is a great prize. What of her other daughter, Polyxena? Hecuba demands. Talthybius mutters something about her attending Achilles' tomb, and then evades further questions. And Hecuba? She will go to Odysseus as a slave.

Cassandra treats the herald's news with contempt. She knows the future and she knows that she will be there when the blow falls that extinguishes the pretensions of Agamemnon forever.

Andromache carries Hector's son, Astyanax, in her lap and it is she who tells Hecuba the truth about Polyxena. The Achaeans have killed her on Achilles' tomb, as a sacrifice. Hecuba, after the first shock of the news, does her best to console Andromache. Perhaps she could be a good wife to Neoptolemus and earn his love? Andromache is wrestling with the thought when Talthybius returns.

The child she carries is Hector's son, and the Achaeans will not suffer him to live. The royal line of Troy must be extinguished. The child is taken from her: Talthybius promises the shattered Andromache that he will do his best to bring the body back to her for burial.

The one Achaean leader in the play is the next on the scene. Menelaus, longing to revenge himself on Helen, looks for his erring wife among the broken and defeated women of Troy. But Helen does not look like one of them in the least: when the soldiers find her and bring her to the scene she is composed, mistress of herself, and her beauty is undimmed. Menelaus orders her to board the ship, and promises Hecuba that justice will be done. But the feeling is already present that Helen will win.

Talthybius returns to the scene. He carries the poor broken body of the child Astyanax on Hector's shield. The Achaeans threw him from the walls of Troy. Talthybius has kept his promise, and even paused on the way to wash the body before returning it. The Trojan women give their last possessions so that the body of the last Trojan prince may be suitably wrapped; then, in their rags, they bury him on Hector's shield in Trojan earth.

The last appearance of Talthybius also heralds the end of the play. He arrives with a detachment of soldiers as the burial is completed, and while fire begins to leap up the towers and palaces of the city. The Achaeans have burned it, and the flames grow brighter as Hecuba and the other women are escorted to the ships which will take them to slavery.

See also Andromache, Cassandra, Hector, Hecuba, Odysseus.

Troy   The historical Troy was first excavated by the great German scholar, Heinrich Schliemann, in 1870. During the third year of the work, 1873, he came upon a treasure of gold which he believed to have been that of Homer's King Priam. But Schliemann had in fact found the remains of no less than nine cities on the same site, and the treasure came from an earlier period than the Homeric city. The Troy of the *Iliad* was the sixth city up, so to speak.

Schliemann, a self-made man, confounded the theorists of his day by basing his work on the Greek classics – quite simply, he went to look for Troy where Homer's work suggested it would be, and found it, at Hissarlik in modern Turkey. Priam's city proved to be quite small, about 200 yards across (see the *Iliad*, Book XXII), and more a great citadel, rising in terraces of houses with the palace on the central height, and three gates, than a city as the name is understood today. According to the archaeologists it fell to the invading Achaeans about 1240 BC.

In mythology Troy was founded by Dardanus, son of Zeus, and destroyed by the Achaeans after a ten-year siege. The King of Sparta, Menelaus, lost his wife to Paris, a prince of Troy. Her name was Helen and she was the most beautiful woman on earth. In response to Menelaus' appeal his brother, Agamemnon, the High King of Argos, invoked an oath of loyalty from the other Achaean princes to support him in a war – and led an army to Troy to get Helen back. Homer's *Iliad* begins with the besieging army in a quarrelsome, half-defeated mood: it ends with the funeral rites of the Trojan prince, Hector. The fall of the Troy is not related by Homer, but the story was an oft-told one and is found in considerable detail in the work of other Greek writers.

See also Dardanus, Helen, *Iliad*, Laomedon, Paris, Priam.

Tyche The ancient Greek conception of fortune, or chance. As the beliefs in the old gods weakened the belief in chance increased; Tyche attained the status of a goddess in Hellenistic times (after the death of Alexander the Great) and was identified with the Roman goddess, Fortuna, a deity of great antiquity. Tyche has no mythology, and there is almost no record of a cult.

Tydeus The father of Diomedes and one of the Seven Against Thebes. Tydeus was the son of Oeneus, King of Calydon, and was exiled when he was suspected of murdering his brother, Melanippus. (The name of the brother indicates a confusion of traditions. The same name was given to one of the defenders of the Theban gates.) He made his way to Argos, and at the court of King Adrastus met – and quarrelled with – Polynices, the Theban prince who was also in exile. This encounter led to the famous expedition whereby Polynices hoped to gain the throne of Thebes.

As the father of one of the heroes of the *Iliad* Tydeus is twice mentioned by Homer. Agamemnon describes (Book IV) how he was chosen as herald to the Thebans by the Seven; as a guest he took part in the games, and won all the prizes, and this incurred the spite of some Thebans who waylaid him. He succeeded in killing them all. Athene tells the same story (Book V) when she encourages Diomedes to return to the fight: she also tells him that his father was a small, but powerful man.

Athene favoured Tydeus – but she allowed him to die when she saw him eating the brains of his fallen enemy, Melanippus, during the attack on Thebes.

See also Adrastus, Diomedes, *Iliad,* The Seven Against Thebes.

Typhon A monster, borne by Gaia after coupling with Tartarus, put forward as a challenge to the newly-assumed power of Zeus and the

Olympians. Gaia was resentful of the way her defeated children, the Titans, were treated.

Typhon is described by Hesiod as having a thunderous voice and a hundred heads, and in that version is successfully defeated by Zeus, using thunderbolts, and thrown into Tartarus. Another version, of an oriental flavour that accords more with the sort of monster described, makes the struggle of Zeus against him less easy. Typhon fled eastward at first, but turned to fight on the borders of Syria. He wrested the sword from Zeus (or the sickle – there is an echo of the castration of Uranus), and cut the sinews from his hands and feet. Then he thrust the helpless Zeus into a cave in the mountains of Cilicia.

He was eventually found by Hermes and Pan, who managed to steal his sinews back and to restore him to Olympus. The struggle was renewed: Typhon was now on Mount Nysa, and the Fates deceived him with succulent fruits which they promised would maintain his strength. But it was the food of mortals, and weakened him. He made his last stand on Mount Haemus ('blood mountain') in Thrace, where Zeus injured him so severely that his blood ran in streams on the mountain. He fled to Sicily, but Zeus was the victor now and disposed of him finally by crushing him under Mount Etna, which still heaves and smokes with his convulsions.

A simpler form of Typhon is represented in Greek art, where he is a winged monster, man from the waist up. From the waist down he is a double serpent.

Tyro According to Homer, the mother of Neleus and Pelias by the god Poseidon. Ill-treated by her stepmother, Sidero, Tyro fell in love with the river god of Elis, Enipeus. He gave her no encouragement, and Poseidon, who wanted her, disguised himself as Enipeus (*Odyssey*, Book XI).

Tyro, afraid of Sidero, bore twin sons in secret and exposed them on a mountain side, where they were found and cared for a horse herder. When the boys grew up and found out who they were, they were determined to make Sidero pay for her cruelty to their mother. Sidero fled to the temple of Hera but Pelias killed her at the goddess's altar, an offence which he was to regret.

Tyro, free at last from oppression, married Cretheus, the founder of Iolcos, and became the mother of Aeson: his son was Jason, the enemy of Pelias and the hero of the *Argo's* voyage.

The story is plainly a variant of the theme of twins so frequent in classical mythology.

See also Amphion and Zethus, the Dioscuri, Idas and Lynceus, Neleus, Pelias, Romulus and Remus.

U

Uranus The personification of Heaven, and the son born to Gaia (Earth) when she emerged from Chaos. The account of Hesiod (*Theogony*) is the one which mythographers generally used, as a convenient and well-ordered statement of the beginning of things.

Uranus became the husband of Gaia: his rain made her fertile and earth became fruitful; Gaia bore the Titans, the Cyclops and the Hecatoncheires. But Uranus grew jealous of his children, and confined them in the earth, and Gaia found the burden so intolerable that she conspired with her bravest son, Cronus, to overthrow his father. Cronus castrated him with a sickle of adamant (flint, or possibly iron). But cronus was also destined to be overthrown by his son.

See also Cronus, Gaia, Titans, Zeus.

V

Vaticanus In Roman religion the *numen* (spirit) which opens the mouth of a new-born child and enables it to give its first cry.

Venus The Roman goddess who became identified with Aphrodite was originally the *numen* of gardens – gardens where food and herbs were grown as well as flowers. She was not otherwise connected with fertility of any kind. Her cult grew in importance when she was identified with Aphrodite, who was the mother of Homer's Aeneas in the *Iliad*; thus she was the ancestress of the Roman people.

The identification is believed to have begun with the cult of Aphrodite at Eryx in north-west Sicily, who became Venus *Erycina* to the Romans. They dedicated their first temple to the goddess in 295 BC. As the ancestress of the Roman people – Venus *Genetrix* – a temple was dedicated to her by Julius Caesar in 48 BC after the Battle of Pharsalus.

Ver Sacrum   In Roman religion the sacrifice of the complete produce of the coming spring. The *ver sacrum* (sacred spring) was usually made during times of distress or danger, and included the creatures born in the spring – children in very ancient times as well as beasts. One of these sacrifices recorded in historical times was to Jupiter during the Second Punic War in 217 BC; but by then the immolation of children had ceased. They were dedicated, nevertheless, but the more humane practice was to send them out of the city at the age of twenty, to go where they would and found new settlements.

Vesta   The Roman state goddess of the hearth, Vesta was also worshipped in every household. The sacred fire of the state burned in Vesta's temple on the Via Sacra, just below the Forum; it was renewed on 1 March, the first day of the Roman year – otherwise it burned perpetually. She was etymologically connected with her Greek counterpart, Hestia, and fulfilled the same functions to a remarkable degree.

Her festival, the *Vestalia*, was held on 9 June and on that day her beast, the ass, was given a holiday from labour and decorated with garlands of violets and strings of small loaves. The storehouse of the temple of Vesta was opened from 7 to 15 June, to enable the Roman matrons to bring offerings to the goddess. During this period all public business ceased.

See also Hestia.

Vestal Virgins   The temple of Vesta in Rome represented the house and hearth of the ancient kings, and just as the *Rex Sacrorum* was a priest who represented the King, the Vestals represented the King's daughters. They were originally four in number, later six – but always high-born girls from patrician families. They had a number of duties but they were principally the guardians of the fire of the state hearth in the Temple of Vesta. The office was a very ancient one, older than Rome itself.

The Vestals were vowed to absolute chastity but they could return to private life after thirty years' service. If, during that time, one was found guilty of breaking her vow, she was buried alive, in an underground chamber near the Colline Gate, conveyed there bound hand and foot in a covered litter. She was made to descend a long wooden stair, which was then drawn up. The entrance was then sealed with earth.

Virgil The great Latin poet (properly Publius Vergilius Maro) was born in 70 BC near present-day Mantua in what was Cisalpine Gaul. His father may have been a farmer but this is not certain; certainly he owned land and he was able to give his son an education that took him to Cremona and Mediolanum (Milan) as well as to Rome itself. Virgil's first compositions, the *Eclogues* (short pastoral poems) were written when he returned to his father's land.

His family were dispossessed in the troubles following the assassination of Julius Caesar and the defeat of the conspirators at Philippi, but his petition found favour with Octavian and the family's lands were restored. He was later to enjoy the patronage of Octavian when he became the Emperor Augustus. Virgil was then about forty years old, and had published his *Eclogues*, and his *Georgics* – poems about the rural life which are to many readers his finest work.

His great epic poem, the *Aeneid*, occupied the remaining eleven years of his life – he died at the age of fifty-one in 19 BC. Virgil was a dark, rugged-looking man but in fact his health was not good and he kept away from Rome.

Among classical writers Virgil enjoys the unique distinction of having always been accepted by the Christian church. The *Aeneid* became a school textbook almost from the time of its appearance and maintained that position into the Christian era. Virgil's natural piety was valid in any creed; furthermore, the Early Christian Fathers managed to find a Messianic utterance in his Fourth *Eclogue*, where a child is foretold who will usher in a golden age. (The poem was addressed to a friend, Asinius Pollio, but no one knows if Virgil was referring to a friend's child, expected, or indeed to that of the Emperor Augustus who, as it happened, proved to be a girl.) More striking, perhaps, are the closing lines of the Sixth Book of the *Aeneid*, which were really interpreted as foretelling the destiny of Rome as the dispenser of a new humanity. And whatever effect the lines may have had on the Early Christian Fathers they do reflect the quality of Virgil, the man.

A strange inheritance from the pagan world, through Virgil and the Sixth Book of the *Aeneid* in which she plays a large part is the figure of the Sibyl, who enjoyed, in early Christian literature, a position similar to that accorded the Prophets of the Old Testament.

See also *Aeneid*, Sibyls.

Vulcan The ancient god of fire, Vulcan was worshipped by the Romans throughout their history. He was originally associated with volcanic fire – which could be seen to exist, without having to be made – and there was an ancient shrine at Puteoli (modern Pozzuoli) in the shadow of Vesuvius. His temples were always situated outside the city, since volcanic fire was destructive and it is probable that in early times he was worshipped in propitiary terms – to avert fires and danger from them.

His festival was the *Volcanalia*, held on 23 August. Vulcan had his own *flamen*, and his festival was the scene of a peculiar sacrifice – live fish from the Tiber were flung into the fire. This may have been a calculated offering to maintain his goodwill, since fishes were obviously creatures rarely in danger from fire.

Vulcan was later identified with Hephaestus but the identification was mistaken: Hephaestus was the divine artificer, while Vulcan was only a fire god.

See also Hephaestus.

W

Works and Days The poet Hesiod will probably always be better known for his *Theogony* but most scholars regard his later *Works and Days* as a finer work. In essence it is a poem about the ordinary life of the man whose living is gained from the land: what he can expect and how he can make the best of it; how he can most profitably order his working life throughout the farmer's year. The poem is full of information about the times in which Hesiod lived and is the earliest work of its kind in Greek literature that we possess.

The early lines contain a certain amount of mythology, notably the story of Pandora, and the Five Ages of Man – the Golden Age had gone, and the world had degenerated, the poet felt, through the Silver, the Bronze and the Heroic down to the present Iron Age; so a toilsome time (his own) was man's unhappy lot.

See also Hesiod, *Theogony*.

Z

Zephyrus The west wind in Greek mythology. According to Hesiod Zephyrus was the son of Eos (dawn) and Astraeus (the stars). He had little mythology; he is perhaps best known as Apollo's rival for the love of Hyacinthus.

See also Aeolus, Hyacinthus.

Zeus The son of Cronus and Rhea (the eldest, according to Homer, and the third according to Hesiod). Zeus was born in Crete and kept hidden from his father in a cave on Mount Dicte: or he was born in Arcadia and taken to Crete and hidden in a cave on Mount Ida; the latter version is the later one. He was nourished by the goat, Amalthea, and guarded by the Curetes, who made sure that his infant cries would not be heard. When he reached manhood he overthrew his father Cronus, with the help of his mother, Rhea.

The outline of the childhood of Zeus has a number of strands in it which point to a myth of Cretan origin; the ritual of the Curetes comes from that island, and his mother Rhea is identified with the mother goddess of Crete. The connection seems dubious, and probably reflects the inevitable process of reconciliation, which took place over centuries, between the ancient deities and the later ones.

Having won the universe from Cronus, Zeus divided it with his brothers according to lots: Hades drew the nether world, Poseidon the sea and the waters, and Zeus the heavens. Olympus and the earth became the concern of all three.

Zeus' first consort, according to Hesiod, was Metis (counsel), who conceived a child by him. Uranus and Gaia warned Zeus that if the child was a son it could overthrow him. He promptly swallowed Metis; but a child was born of the union nevertheless – the goddess Athene.

After Metis came Themis, and she bore the Fates and the Seasons. She was followed by Eurynome, the mother of the Graces, and the next consort after her was his sister Demeter, the corn goddess who gave birth to Persephone. Mnemosyne (memory) followed Demeter, and gave birth to the Muses; next Leto, the mother of Apollo and Artemis, and then came his sister Hera.

The sequence given above is according to Hesiod but Homer makes Hera the first wife of Zeus, and says they were lovers even before the fall of Cronus (*Iliad*, Book XIV). Homer also speaks of another consort, Dione, who became the mother of Aphrodite, and another tradition gives us Maia, daughter of Atlas, the mother of Hermes. The children of Zeus and Hera were Ares, Hebe and Eileithyia.

Zeus is an inescapable presence in Greek mythology and the reader will be led to the principle stories by consulting the names listed at the end of this entry. He was the father god, all powerful, and it is fascinating to realise that he can be identified in the same form among the different peoples of the Indo-European migrations. He was Jupiter to the Romans, Dyaus Pitar to the Aryans who moved down into India; the German god Tiu, and the Deipatyros of the Illyrians, were also forms of Zeus.

Most interesting of all, perhaps, is the fact that Zeus was not a creator god – the 'father' should be seen in terms of a *pater familias*, the protector and ruler of the family of man. He was a sky and weather god of the migrating people and became, in Ancient Greece, the consort of the powerful native goddesses – Hera, the great goddess of Argos, being the best example – because order in religion was essential and Greek society was based on the family.

Zeus was the maintainer of customary laws, and this conception probably took on firm outlines during the Mycenaean age of which Homer writes: thus he often appears as a king with unruly vassals to control. And while kings faded from the Greek mind the idea of Zeus did not, he remained as the personification of order through power. He was perhaps the perfect example of a god who, if he had not existed, would have been invented. The Greeks evolved him over the centuries and for the most part he suited them very well.

Zeus was invoked under a number of names. As the father and saviour of man, *Soter*; as the protector of the house, *Herkeios*; of the rules of hospitality, *Xenios*; as the guardian of property, *Ktesios*; as the god of marriage, *Gamelios*. As Zeus *Chthonios* he was the god of the earth and fertility and, allied to that, he was *Meilichios*, the serpent form of Zeus to whom offerings of honey were made. He was also the guardian of liberty, Zeus *Eleutherios*; as the highest civic god he was Zeus *Poleius*.

But in spite of all these epithets Homer brings us back again and again to the origins of Zeus as a sky and weather god. In the *Iliad* he calls him, always, *nephelegeretes* – 'cloud-gatherer'.

See also Cronus, Curetes, Demeter, Giants, Hera, Leto, Maia, Metis, Muses, Prometheus, Rhea, Themis.

FURTHER READING LIST

Aeschylus: *The Oresteian Trilogy*. 1956
  Prometheus Bound, The Suppliants, Seven Against Thebes, and *The Persians*. 1961
    Translated by Philip Vellacott. Penguin Books
Apollonius Rhodius: *The Voyage of Argo* (Argonautica). Translated by E. V. Rieu. Penguin Books. 1959
Apuleius, Lucius: *The Golden Ass*. Translated by Robert Graves. Penguin Books. 1950
The Archaeology of Greece and the Aegean. Stewart Perowne. The Hamlyn Publishing Group Limited. 1974
Aristophanes: *Plays*. Translated by Patric Dickinson. Oxford Paperbacks. 1970
The Dawn of the Gods. Jacquetta Hawkes. Chatto & Windus. 1968
The Dramatic Festivals of Athens. A Pickard-Cambridge. Oxford University Press. 1968
Euripides: *Alcestis, Hipplytus*, and *Iphigenia in Tauris*. 1953
  The Bacchae, Ion, The Trojan Women, and *Helen*. 1954
  Medea, Hecuba, Electra, and *Heracles*. 1963
  Orestes, The Children of Heracles, Andromache, The Suppliant Women, The Phoenician Women, and *Iphigenia in Aulis*. 1972
    Translated by Philip Vellacott. Penguin Books.
The Geographic Background of Greek and Roman History. Max Cary. Oxford University Press. 1949
The Gods of the Greeks. C. Kerenyi. Thames & Hudson. 1951
The Golden Bough. Sir James Frazer. 1 Vol. Edition, Macmillan. 1922
Greek Hero Cults and Ideas of Immortality. L. R. Farnell. Oxford University Press. 1970
Greek Mythology. John Pinsent. The Hamlyn Publishing Group Limited. 1969
The Greek Myths. Robert Graves. 2 Vols. Penguin Books. 1948
The Greeks. H. D. F. Kitto. Penguin Books. 1951
Greek Tragedy. H. D. F. Kitto. Methuen & Co. Ltd. University Paperbacks. 1966
A Handbook of Greek Mythology. H. J. Rose. Methuen & Co. Ltd. University Paperbacks. 1964
The Heroes of the Greeks. C. Kerenyi. Thames & Hudson. 1959
Heroic Song and Heroic Legend. Jan de Vries, translated by B. J. Trimmer. Oxford Paperbacks. 1963
Herodotus: *The Histories*. Translated by Harry Carter. O.U.P. The World's Classics. 1962
Hesiod: *Theogony, Works and Days*, and Theognis: *Elegies*
    Translated by Dorothea Wender. Penguin Books. 1973
A History of Greece to 322 BC. N. G. L. Hammond. Oxford University Press. 1959
History of Greek Religion. M. P. Nilsson, translated by F. J. Fielden. Oxford University Press. 1949

Homer: *The Iliad*. Translated by E. V. Rieu. Penguin Books. 1950

The Odyssey. Translated by E. V. Rieu. Penguin Books. 1946

Men of Athens. Rex Warner. The Bodley Head. 1972

Men and Gods. Rex Warner. Penguin Books. 1952

Myths of the Greeks and Romans. Michael Grant. Weidenfeld & Nicolson. 1962

The Nature of Greek Myths. G. S. Kirk. Penguin Books. 1974

Oxford Classical Dictionary. N. G. L. Hammond & H. H. Scullard. 2nd Edition. Oxford University Press. 1970

The Oxford Companion to Classical Literature. Sir Paul Harvey. Oxford University Press. 1937

Ovid: *Metamorphoses*. Translated by Mary M. Innes. Penguin Books. 1955

Pindar: *The Odes*. Translated by C. M. Bowra. Penguin Books. 1969

Plutarch's Lives. Dryden's Edition, revised by Arthur Hugh Clough. 3 Vols. J. M. Dent & Sons Ltd. Everyman's Library. 1942

The Rise of the Greek Epic. Gilbert Murray. Oxford Paperbacks. 1960

Roman Mythology. Stewart Perowne. The Hamlyn Publishing Group Limited. 1969

The Roman World. Michael Grant. Weidenfeld & Nicolson. 1960

Sophocles: *The Theban Plays (Oedipus, Oedipus at Colonus, and Antigone)*. 1947

Electra, Ajax, The Women of Trachis, and *Philoctetes*. 1953

Translated by E. F. Watling. Penguin Books

Virgil: *The Aeneid, The Georgics*, and *The Eclogues*. Translated by James Rhoades. O.U.P. The World's Classics. 1921

The White Goddess. Robert Graves, Faber & Faber. 1948

★

INDEX OF MINOR CHARACTERS AND PLACE NAMES

★